REVIEWS FOR
THE NEW NATURAL DEATH HANDBOOK

'Gives excellent advice'
Cosmopolitan

'Excellent book'
*The British Holistic Medical
Association Newsletter*

'What could be more healthy than bringing society's last taboo
out of the closet?'
The Observer

'Demonstrates to people dissatisfied with conveyor-belt
funerals that there are kinder alternatives'
The Times

'Investigating Natural Death is a cheering experience and I
would recommend it to anyone facing bereavement'
Midweek

'Inspiring'
Church Times

'Strongly recommended for its scope, interest and practicality'
Network

'Full of amazing advice and information'
Sunday Independent

'I'd advise anyone interested to get hold of a copy of *The
Natural Death Handbook*, altogether a very good thing'
Green magazine

The Natural Death Centre is especially grateful to John Bradfield and the A. B. Wildlife Trust Fund – the Natural Death Centre largely relies on the Trust for sound information on law and ecology (although the Trust is not responsible for any errors or shortcomings within the text).

Thanks are also due to solicitor Desmond Banks for advice on wills and probate; Joseph Elliot and Gil Elliot for the first draft editions which they prepared of chapters two, three and eight; Lindesay Irvine for his assistant editorial work on the second edition; Richard Ross-Langley, Lindesay Irvine and Stephen Evans for their proofreading; Richard Doust for his design for the book's layout; Christine Mills for researching the first edition's funerals chapter and for help with other chapters; Yvonne Ackroyd, Mary Bradbury, Roger Knights and Marion Schmidt for their research help; Marcelle Papworth for her translations; Diana Senior, Josefine Speyer, Yvonne Malik, Mary McHugh, John Wilkey, Maureen Taylor and Milena Petrova for their help; and all those who suggested improvements to the first edition, including Heather Albery, Sheila Barratt, Denise Brady, Joanna Gilpin, Christianne Heal, John Horbury, Avril Jackson, Margaret Hayworth, Elizabeth Lawlor, Julian Litten, David Lorimer, Dr Mary Neal, Renée O'Sullivan, Derek Roberts-Morgan, Caroline Sherwood, Jane Spottiswoode, Solveig Taylor, Sheila Thompson and Pam Williams.

THE NEW
NATURAL
DEATH
HANDBOOK

Edited by Nicholas Albery, Gil Elliot and Joseph Elliot
of The Natural Death Centre

RIDER

LONDON · SYDNEY · AUCKLAND · JOHANNESBURG

3 5 7 9 10 8 6 4 2

The Natural Death Centre
20 Heber Road
London NW2 6AA
(tel 0181 208 2853; fax 0181 452 6434)

All royalties from this book are going to The Natural Death Centre, an educational charity, towards its work in supporting those dying at home. The Centre is grateful to all the many people and publishers who freely contributed items and is apologetic to any whom it failed to trace or acknowledge.

First published by The Natural Death Centre in 1993

This revised edition published in 1997 by Rider, an imprint of Ebury Press, Random House, 20 Vauxhall Bridge Road, London SW1V 2SA

Random House Australia (Pty) Limited, 20 Alfred Street, Milsons Point, Sydney, New South Wales 2061, Australia

Random House New Zealand Limited, 18 Poland Road, Glenfield, Auckland 10, New Zealand

Random House South Africa (Pty) Limited, Endulini, 5A Jubilee Road, Parktown 2193, South Africa

Random House UK Limited Reg. No. 954009

Papers used by Rider Books are natural, recyclable products made from wood grown in sustainable forests

Printed and bound by Mackays of Chatham PLC, Chatham, Kent

A CIP record for this book is available from the British Library.

ISBN 0-7126-7111-0

Formal disclaimer: Neither the publisher nor The Natural Death Handbook can accept responsibility for any action taken as a result of reading this book; the reader would be wise to get a second opinion or to consult professional advisers. Please send all corrections, updates and suggested additions to the Centre at the above address.

CONTENTS

Chapter 1

THE NATURAL DEATH MOVEMENT

The idea that launched the Natural Death Centre

The Natural Death Centre is an educational charity, founded in 1991 by three psychotherapists – Christianne Heal, myself and my wife Josefine Speyer. For Josefine and me, the idea for the Centre grew from our experience of the birth of our son. Back in 1975, Josefine was pregnant and I'd taken a long spell off work to help her to fulfil a cherished fantasy of travelling by horse and cart. With our horse Patience (on £2 a week rent from the Heavy Horse Preservation Society) and our converted manure tip cart, we meandered our way through the wilder parts of Wales, looking for a cottage for the winter and the birth. Josefine was adamant that she wanted to be at home for the birth. As she put it: 'I'm not ill, why should I go into hospital?' At last we found a place by the river Teifi and a doctor who was willing to come to the farm cottage – 'I don't mind if you give birth on a haystack, I'll come wherever you want,' he told Josefine.

In the event we were very lucky. It was a short, almost painfree and ecstatic labour for Josefine, and all the preparation helped – the Raspberry Leaf tea, the natural birth books and classes, the visualisations and breathing exercises – and the doctor and midwife were like guests in our home for this Leboyer-style birth of low lights and quiet.

In 1988, my father died at home and his death triggered in me a realisation of the need for a natural death movement to parallel the natural childbirth movement, and to spread the tenets of good hospice care to home care for those dying of all causes, not just cancer. It wouldn't suit everybody, but why shouldn't those families who wanted it be fully supported by the NHS in looking after the dying person at home, with adequate financial and other help for carers? Wouldn't more people, if it were possible, prefer to die at home amongst friends rather than in the anonymity of a big and noisy hospital? As with birth, could preparation, exercises and rituals help reduce the anxieties that people feel about dying? Could dying at least for a lucky few become as easy and as ecstatic a process as our experience of birth? Granted that no one can be certain what happens after death, could it be that preparation matters, as the Tibetans argue, to enable the soul at the point of death to merge fearlessly with that bright light reported by many who have recovered from Near-Death Experiences? I remembered how a friend's mother insisted on being given her travelling rug to die with; could the process of dying be the labour pains of the soul, with sometimes the same feeling of expectation and transition as at birth?

Just as many people want to experience birth as consciously as possible, so some people want to face death with minds as unclouded as their circumstances permit. It is here that the analogy between birth and death breaks down somewhat, for drugs are more likely to be necessary to relieve pain for the dying, if only because dying can be a much more long drawn-out labour than giving birth – but nevertheless further research is needed into drugs that are strong enough to relieve terminal pain whilst enhancing alertness.

As related later in this book, Aldous Huxley sat by his wife Maria at her death, urging her with hypnotic repetition to 'go towards the light'. Perhaps many people would like an Aldous Huxley-type figure sitting by them as they go. Perhaps there could be a new profession of 'Midwives for the Dying', people skilled in holistic care of the dying patient's practical, emotional and spiritual needs (and the needs of the family), and more intent on creating a calm and supportive atmosphere than on high tech medical interventions to prolong life to the utmost. There is a need for such skills in modern life, for as Aldous Huxley wrote: 'The living can do a great deal to make the passage easier for the dying, to raise the most purely physiological act of human existence to the level of awareness and perhaps even of spirituality.'

Introduction by Nicholas Albery, co-editor of
The Natural Death Handbook.

As the sixties-generation Green movement people get older, so the natural death movement will inevitably become a force in health politics, bringing about a redirection of NHS and other resources towards home care and proper provision for carers. The Natural Death Centre aims to be in the vanguard of such changes. It acts as a kind of Society for Home Deaths, and works to implement its long-term plans for Midwives for the Dying, with volunteers to back up the midwife; and does whatever it can to help improve the quality of living and dying. It has founded the Befriending Network, co-ordinated by Diana Senior and based in Oxford and London. The Befriending Network trains volunteers who visit the home where someone is critically ill, sit with the person who is dying, assist the carer and maintain contact with the carer after the death. Christianne Heal offers Living With Dying workshops for the general public on preparing for dying. Josefine Speyer, who helped develop the training programme for the Befriending Network volunteers, provides individual counselling for those who are anxious or bereaved. She offers workshops for nurses, doctors and others concerned with looking after people who are dying, and workshops for the public on the theme of 'Accepting Death and Living Fully'.

At present, dying mostly happens 'off stage', as it were, in old people's homes and hospitals, and many people are superstitious enough to believe that the less they think about the subject the longer they will live. Two thirds of the UK adult population have not even taken the first step of writing a will, thus potentially leaving additional problems for their survivors. The Centre wants to make death and dying an unexceptional topic for daily meditation and conversation, and to that end has hosted a series of tea 'salons' and large dinner discussions with candlelit tables and gourmet food and wine on subjects ranging from Near-Death Experiences to care for those who are dying. It also organises an English Day of the Dead celebration for the third Sunday in April each year, inspired by the Mexican Day of the Dead festivities – a day for remembering our friends and relatives who have died and a day to contemplate our own mortality.

Once a family has looked after someone dying at home, they are more likely to want to take care of the dead body themselves too. But whatever the reason, the Centre has found itself submerged in mail from families wanting ecologically sound, inexpensive funerals, without using funeral directors. A great deal of research later, the material for the funeral chapters in this book was assembled. Chapters Four to Six cover not only on how to run a funeral without using a funeral director, at a fraction of the normal cost, but also detail who are the best professionals to approach, should you want help.

The Centre now acts as a consumers' association, available by phone or letter, giving for the first time an in depth consumer's perspective on the whole funeral trade. It also perforce has had to campaign on behalf of the public with the National Association of Funeral Directors, the Office of Fair Trading and the Department of Trade and Industry, to try to ensure, for instance, that itemised price breakdowns on funerals are available to the public and that cardboard or regular coffins are sold to those people who want to organise a funeral themselves. The kind of changes in policy that seem necessary are outlined in the chapter 'The Politics of Dying' which also includes a Declaration of Rights for the person dying at home.

'The Natural Death Handbook' gives awards to the funeral industry – see Chapter Five for the list of Award winners.

The Natural Death Centre in 1994 launched an Association of Nature Reserve Burial Grounds, in an attempt to ensure that every locality should have its own woodland burial ground, where a tree is planted instead of having a headstone. Already, almost 50 such grounds are open.

The Centre is financed on a shoestring – half its income comes from the sale of publications and from members of the public becoming Friends of the Natural Death Centre (£20 per annum) and the other half comes from foundations such as the Gulbenkian Foundation and the Nuffield Foundation. This Handbook too requires your assistance if it is to become ever more useful in future editions – if you have a recommendation, update, correction, tip or experience you are willing to share with others, please send it in.

The purpose of this book is not only to collect together all the information that the Centre has gathered to date, but also to introduce readers to the great pioneers of the natural death movement and to the ideas in their writings. The very best books on the subject are marked ❍❍❍ in the Resources chapter; some of these have been published in the United States but deserve a wider readership in the

UK. Information for ordering them is at the back of this book and, if not available through your local bookshop, most can be obtained from the publishers. The Centre's own books can be obtained by mail order or credit card from the Centre itself.

An information pack updating this book – particularly its listings of woodland burial grounds – is available from the Centre for six first class stamps (or a £1-56 cheque). These updates and most of the Centre's books are accessible free on the Internet via the death and dying section of the Global Ideas Bank (<http://www.newciv.org/GIB/>).

What have these other writers had to say about the need for a natural death movement? Douglas Harding has emphasised our resistance to thinking about our own mortality:

The cult of youth-at-all-costs

Our current resistance to such an investigation, to any candour or realism concerning our own mortality, can scarcely be exaggerated. Witness the popular cult of youth-at-all-costs in the worlds of advertising and fashion. Witness those communities of old folk dedicated to being 'as young as you feel' and to avoiding all reminders of old age, sickness, and death. Witness the newspeak and double-talk of 'seventy years young' in place of 'seventy years old' and 'elderly person' or 'senior citizen' in place of 'old man', 'old woman'. Witness the funerary nonsense so tellingly described in Evelyn Waugh's 'The Loved One'. Witness cryonics – the freezing of the newly dead for revival when technology is further developed, thus giving effect to the view that 'death is an imposition on the human race, and no longer acceptable'. Witness the cultists who seriously maintain that death is unnecessary and unnatural, and we can choose to live as long as we wish. How unlike the veneration of old age and the preoccupation with death and the hereafter which are such marked features of some great cultures! And again, what a contrast with the *memento mori* (remember you must die) of earlier centuries of our own civilisation – its human skulls carved on tombstones and displayed on mantelpieces, its countless engravings and paintings confronting the living with the grim spectacle of Death the Reaper and the imagined sequel!

Reproduced by permission of Penguin Books Ltd from 'The Little Book of Life and Death' by D. E. Harding.
For fuller details of all main book references see the booklist in the Resources chapter.

Ivan Illich in 1975 wrote about the torments inflicted on the dying in some hospitals:

The medicalisation of society

Today, the man best protected against setting the stage for his own dying is the sick person in critical condition. Society, acting through the medical system, decides when and after what indignities and mutilations he shall die. The medicalisation of society has brought the epoch of natural death to an end.

From 'Medical Nemesis: The Expropriation of Health'
by Ivan Illich, Calder and Boyars Ltd, '75.

The isolation of the dying and the bereaved in a centralised society that has lost almost all sense of neighbourhood has been highlighted by Tony Walter:

Neighbours no longer share the loss

Because the elderly person who has died may well not have been widely known by the friends of those left behind, the grief of the bereaved is not shared. When someone dies in Ambridge, or in an African village, or in a police unit, an entire community feels the loss: everyone knew the person and everyone to some degree mourns the loss. But when most old people in Britain die today, only a few close relatives are still in touch to feel the loss.

Nor is this true only when the deceased is elderly. In a relatively isolated nuclear family in which outsiders have played little if any role in child care, the death of a child may be a uniquely isolating experience. Contrast this account by Miller after the destruction of the primary school in Aberfan: 'One bereaved mother told me that when she lost her child the company she sought was not that of other bereaved mothers but of her neighbours. They might not have lost a child themselves, but she realised they had lost her child. It was the neighbours who had helped to bring him up, who had minded him when she went out, had watched him grow and had taken pride in his achievements. In a very real sense they shared her grief.' Usually though, friends and neighbours may be sympathetic, but they do not know the child well enough truly to share the loss. Friends in their thirties or younger may never have experienced any close bereavement.

So the bereaved today often are isolated, and may well report being treated as lepers.

From 'Modern Death: Taboo or Not Taboo?' by Tony Walter,
Sociology, Vol. 25, No. 2.

Tony Walters shares the Natural Death Centre's perception that the Green movement and the natural childbirth movement will tend to lead to the acceptance of death and dying as natural processes to be shared with our family and friends:

Natural childbirth leads to natural death

The Green movement surely must lead to a more realistic acceptance of the fact that human beings are natural creatures who must die. This movement has prompted all of us to question our technological hubris; we all know now that we are part of a delicate natural system; we are less able to split a heroic, rational soul from an inconvenient body.

This new attitude surely underlies the natural childbirth movement. Giving birth may be painful, but it is part of the natural human experience, and many women would not wish it anaesthetised away. Nor do they want to be socially isolated; they want to share this miracle of nature with their partners and their other children.

Death is also a natural part of being human, and therefore I do not wish to be drugged into oblivion: I want the pain to be controlled, but I would like to be conscious and in control as far as is possible. And I would like to share this unrepeatable and important event with my partner and my children.

From 'Funerals and How to Improve Them' by Tony Walter.

Tony Walter pointed out in a letter to the Natural Death Centre that 'natural' does not necessarily mean adopting the practices of pre-technological societies:

The diversity of non-Western, pre-modern death practices is astonishing – many segregate the dying, the Hopi have as many taboos as we do, and the ceremonies of most hunter gatherer societies are as 'thin' as are our own. Not many traditional societies see death as 'natural'.

The historian Roy Porter has shown convincingly that it was doctors in the late 18th century who introduced the idea that death is a natural event, which then eased out older notions of death as ordained by God and as a spiritual passage.

I'm inclined to agree with Arney and Bergen in 'Medicine and the Management of Living' (Chicago, UP, 1984) that it's doctors, not a consumer revolt, that first pushed the demedicalisation, ie naturalisation, of death. Would it all have happened without medics such as Kübler Ross, Saunders, Parkes and Jolly?

There are, moreover, many kinds of natural death. It is just as much a part of nature to die abruptly or in agony, through accidents or violence or illness, as it is to die with ease and dignity. But even in such circumstances, to feel prepared for any eventuality may help. Gandhi was assassinated, but his almost automatic reaction to the bullets was to chant the name of God. He was prepared, in his own way.

As Jung appreciated:

Death as a goal in old age

Willy-nilly, the ageing person prepares himself for death. Thoughts of death pile up to an astonishing degree as the years increase. That is why I think that nature herself is always preparing for the end. Objectively it is a matter of indifference what the individual consciousness may think about it. But subjectively it makes an enormous difference whether consciousness keeps in step with the psyche or whether it clings to opinions of which the heart knows nothing. It is just as neurotic in old age not to focus upon the goal of death as it is in youth to repress fantasies which have to do with the future.

From 'The Soul and Death' by C. G. Jung in 'The Collected Works, series XX, vol. viii, translated by R. F. C. Hull, Princeton University Press, 1969.

Many people ask: Is it not morbid to think about death and dying earlier in life? No, it is necessary, for preparing for dying is half a lifetime's work. The main preparation is that which the Dalai Lama advises: 'For most of us ordinary people who lead busy lives, what is important is to develop a kind, generous heart to others. If we can do that and live accordingly, we will be able to die peacefully.' And for those who have the opportunity and the necessary circumstances, he adds, there are higher spiritual preparations available through religious and yogic practices. But above all, an awareness of death can sweeten every remaining living moment. Yeats is not the only poet to warn:

'Begin the preparation for your death'

Get all the gold and silver that you can,
Satisfy ambition, animate
The trivial days and ram them with the sun ...

But then:

No longer in Lethean foliage caught
Begin the preparation for your death
And from the fortieth winter by that thought
Test every work of intellect or faith,
And everything that your own hands have wrought,
And call those works extravagance of breath
That are not suited for such men as come
Proud, open eyed and laughing to the tomb.
From 'Vacillation' by W. B. Yeats.

Ageing to Yeats was a growing of the soul:

An aged man is but a paltry thing,
A tattered coat upon a stick, unless
Soul clap its hands and sing, and louder sing
For every tatter in its mortal dress.
From 'Sailing to Byzantium'.

Stephen Levine sees death as the graduation ceremony for this cocoon-abandoning soul:

Death as graduation

Death is another transformation through which we move, an adventure to surpass all adventures, an opening, an incredible moment of growth, a graduation.
From 'Who Dies?' by Stephen Levine.

To adopt this new outlook, we have first to rid ourselves of a great deal of cultural conditioning. Paula Hendrick has surveyed the natural death movement from an American perspective and concludes that our technological mastery of nature and our focus on personal autonomy and self-development have made it very hard for us to accept the inevitability of death:

Natural dying – an American perspective

In the world of nature, death provides a service because it makes room in an ecological niche for a young one. People are part of nature, too, and when people die, they make room for more people. In a time of population explosion, it would be useful to be able to die without making too much of a fuss about it. But we humans, particularly in the affluent cultures of the first world, face the final journey of life with a load of weighty baggage. We avoid talk of death, and we dread the realities of the aging process.

We as individuals don't necessarily create and lug around this excess baggage on our own. Something pervasive in our society moulds our collective choices. Michael Ignatieff, writing in 'The New Republic', offers this explanation: 'Cultures that live by the values of self-realisation and self-mastery are not especially good at dying, at submitting to those experiences where freedom ends and biological fate begins. Why should they be? Their strong side is Promethean ambition: the defiance and transcendence of fate, the material and social limit. Their weak side is submitting to the inevitable.'

We have become victims of the health care system that our cultural values have created. The dying process has been transformed into a series of wrenching choices. A woman, getting along pretty well after a stroke at age eighty – some confusion, but lots of independence and zest for life – develops increasing heart problems. She has no family support, just a few friends who do the best they can. The doctor recommends a pacemaker. She says no but he persuades her. There are complications during surgery. Now she's totally disorientated and can barely walk even with assistance. Her pacemaker keeps her going.

Out of the apparently needless suffering of countless people has grown a strong movement towards patients' rights and natural death – that is, death with a minimum of medical intervention. Advances are continually – albeit slowly – being made in legislation and public education. The Patient Self-Determination Act, which went into effect in the USA in December 1991, requires health care facilities to inform patients of their rights to refuse treatment and to formulate advance directives such as a living will or health care proxy. Difficult moral dilemmas are also being debated on the topic of 'aid-in-dying', or physician-assisted suicide. The goals of the broader 'natural death movement' are to guarantee choice for individuals and to bring about a large-scale cultural shift. An article in The Economist of London describes such a large scale shift this way: 'To civilise death, to bring it home and make it no longer a source of dread, is one of the great challenges of the age ... Gradually, dying may come to hold again the place it used to occupy in the midst of life: not a terror but a mystery so deep that man would no more wish to cheat himself of it than to cheat himself of life.'

Excerpted from In Context magazine No. 31 (subs. from PO Box 11470, Bainbridge Island, WA98110, USA, tel 0101 206 842 0216).

Fasting to death

The Natural Death Centre gathers research on the theme of death by fasting. The Hindus who go to die in Benaras in India, for instance, consider ceasing to eat as a natural part of preparing to die – not as a form of passive euthanasia or as a way of accelerating death.

There are examples of pioneering Westerners following a similar path. 'We rarely if ever,' writes Scott Nearing's wife, 'used doctors, pills or hospitals. Yet Scott lived to a hale and hearty 100 and died when he decided to – by fasting for a month and a half at the very end.'

Scott's dying, as Helen describes it, was like nature itself:

Scott Nearing – 'death like a leaf falling from a tree'

He did more than his share of mental and physical work up to his last years. At ninety-eight he said 'Well at least I can still split and carry in the wood.' And when he was close to the end, lying in our living room, his one regret at leaving this Earth plane was on watching me lug in the wood for our kitchen stove, 'I wish I could help with that,' he said. He was a help unto the end.

A month or two before he died he was sitting at table with us at a meal. Watching us eat he said, 'I think I won't eat anymore.' 'Alright,' said I. 'I understand. I think I would do that too. Animals know when to stop. They go off in a corner and leave off food.'

So I put Scott on juices: carrot juice, apple juice, banana juice, pineapple, grape – any kind. I kept him full of liquids as often as he was thirsty. He got weaker, of course, and he was as gaunt and thin as Gandhi. Came a day he said, 'I think I'll go on water. Nothing more.' From then on, for about ten days, he only had water. He was bed-ridden and had little strength but spoke with me daily. In the morning of August 24th, 1983, two weeks before his hundredth birthday, when it seems he was slipping away, I sat beside him on his bed.

We were quiet together; no interruptions, no doctors or hospitals. I said, 'It's alright, Scott. Go right along. You've lived a good life and are finished with things here. Go on and up – up into the light. We love you and let you go. It's alright.'

In a soft voice, with no quiver or pain or disturbance he said 'All...right,' and breathed slower and slower and slower till there was no movement anymore and he was gone out of his body as easily as a leaf drops from the tree in autumn, slowly twisting and falling to the ground.

Excerpted from In Context magazine No. 26 (subs. from PO Box 11470, Bainbridge Island, WA98110, USA, tel 001 206 842 0216).

Caroline Walker, a nutritionist dying of cancer, also decided to stop eating for the weeks before she died:

Caroline Walker – a gentle death by fasting

Caroline was exasperated rather than fascinated by her illness. We did learn a lot, though; enough to make another book. For example, when a doctor says you have cancer he (it's usually a he) will no doubt go on to say what will become of you. Our advice is take note, say thank you, shop around, and take your own decisions. After all, if a builder says you have dry rot, you do not immediately take his word for it, sign his estimate without looking at the small print, shut your eyes and resign yourself to the pickaxes. (No disrespect intended, to doctors or builders.)

There again, just as there are societies to encourage home births, there should be societies for home deaths. Being looked after at home is more trouble, of course, just as home cooking takes more time. But dying in hospital as most people do now, stuck full of tubes in white rooms, surrounded by sufferers and strangers, with those you love kept at the end of a telephone, is a sad and bad ending. Caroline thought being sent to hospital to die is like being put in a skip. (Again, no disrespect to builders or doctors.)

At home in August, Caroline finished planting our garden, with seeds and bulbs identified with little flags, so I would know what to expect the next spring and summer. She gave two interviews: one at the beginning of the month, for the Guardian, on her sense of death, as we ate lunch; the other from her bed, at the end of the month, for 'The Food Programme', on the meaning of her work.

Our home filled with family and friends and flowers. Pain was the only uncertainty. The surgeons had warned me that obstruction caused by the cancer would eventually be horribly painful. Not so; Dr Anne Naysmith, consultant at our local community hospital, a woman about Caroline's age, disagreed; and with a careful cocktail of drugs, Caroline rested at home, and took responsibility for her death, simply by stopping eating, two weeks before she died. Around midnight as her last day began, she foresaw her death. How was it – what did the thought feel like? 'Oh, lovely,' she said; and we laughed. And it was lovely to be with her when she died.

From 'The Good Fight' by Geoffrey Cannon.

That was how Caroline's husband Geoffrey Cannon saw her death. Her friend Judy Sadgrove was the Guardian interviewer:

She was resting after a long conversation in which she described what it was like to die. As she spoke, I could forget her gaunt and fleshless body. I'd known her as the campaigning nutritionist, attacking the food industry and the Government.

The ultimate irony was that Caroline was dying from cancer of the colon. Despite her emaciation, her spirit was still strong. Her campaign now was to urge us to come to terms with death in general. We are all so afraid of death, she said.

There was a phase when every time she shut her eyes, she'd see her own face, pallid, yellowish, grey, empty – already dead. She had visions a religious person might construe as significant. Towering crucifixes reared above her. But to Caroline the crosses were simply the archetypal symbol of death. 'After all, when I was young I went to church every week and gazed at crucifixes. Death in Christian society is mentioned only in association with Jesus. Were I a Muslim I would probably dream up quite another symbol.'

She derived most comfort from the regular presence of a healer, Julian Leech. 'I love seeing him. Not because I think he's going to come up with a miracle cure but because he's so relaxing to talk to. He's used to being with people who are dying and he has tremendous respect for the process, with no rejection or fear.'

'I have to live with it. Why can't other people? I know they find it difficult and disgusting, but whoever said that life was easy? Or that dying was a piece of cake? What do they want? Tinsel and gift-wrapping?' These are the people who said 'Poor you' and bought their way out with flowers. Caroline didn't feel poor. She was consumed by pain, which made her sometimes tense and fractious, but she was not poor. She did not want an Enid Blyton attitude to death. Indeed, she felt she had to be viciously blunt in imposing her death on the world. 'Dying is an alien state. You have to make the effort to communicate otherwise you are totally cut off. And you have to help others come to terms. Although I wasted much precious energy trying to prop up other people, I slowly learned who was important and who wasn't.'

Caroline has shone some light on the mystifying business of dying. She has been brave enough to expose her fear and other people's. We cling to life, avoiding thoughts of death until the very end. Surely that's too late?
From The Guardian (Sept. 7th 1988).

These stories reinforce the accumulating medical evidence that fasting and even dehydration are not necessarily such terrible ways to die. The debate on euthanasia, in Chapter Nine, brings in the wider implications of death by fasting.

Near-Death Experiences

Near-Death Experiences (NDEs) are another theme on which the Natural Death Centre gathers research, believing that such experiences can often help people reconcile themselves to their mortality.

While many people who have had NDEs are totally convinced about what has happened to them and the transformations that have occurred in their lives, many sceptics are convinced that the whole phenomenon has nothing to do with life after death, or God, or infinity, but is explicable in simple mechanistic, that is, neurological terms.

Thus Dr Robert Buckman views the sense of peace and tranquillity in an NDE as being caused by substances produced in the brain called endorphins, which are somewhat like painkillers. The nineteenth century explorer, David Livingstone, felt calm, peaceful and painless whilst being crushed across the chest in a lion's jaws. It led him to believe that 'death agonies' may appear so to the onlooker, but may be experienced differently by the patient, protected by a bodily defence mechanism switched on at the approach of death.

Dr Susan Blackmore, a Bristol University psychologist, explains the common NDE vision of a long tunnel with a bright light at the end, as the retina at the back of the eye becoming starved of oxygen, with nerve cells beginning to fire at random. There are more nerve cells in the most sensitive part, the fovea, so a bright spot that looks like the end of a tunnel is seen.

Her explanation is linked to the most common physiological explanation for NDEs, which is that the brain is in receipt of insufficient oxygen (cerebral anoxia). Or that NDEs are the result of temporal lobe seizure. This can produce similar effects to those of some NDEs, without necessarily accounting for the complete range of near-death phenomena. Whereas temporal lobe seizure causes distorted perceptions of the immediate environment, this is not always the case with NDEs.

Whatever the truth of the matter, to know that nature has evolved a way of allowing dying humans to feel blissful can only be reassuring, even for the sceptic who dismisses the visions and feelings as delusionary. It is also reassuring to know that the term 'Near-Death Experience' is in some cases a misnomer – the same, or a seemingly almost identical, experience is accessed by people during 'peak' experiences, by mystics and by others who have not as yet suffered physical harm - such as those falling from a mountain or bridge, who have their NDE before even hitting the ground, when they have been no more damaged than a free-fall parachutist. The difference between the person falling from the mountain and the parachutist is one of expectation of harm and thus degree of shock; and this seems the essence of many experiences of heightened consciousness. The trigger is any severe jolt to our normal consciousness, whether or not physically damaging, which brings about a complete change of perspective and releases us into a world of rich and strange magic.

In the end it comes down to a choice. Do you see consciousness as being contained and confined to the brain? For William James, Ferdinand Schiller and Henri Bergson, for instance, the brain was merely the transmitter of consciousness, necessary for our personal experiencing of consciousness but not its source, just as a radio set is necessary for the reception of programmes but is not their origin:

The brain a transmitter of consciousness not its source

James asked his audience what type of function the brain performed. Does it produce thought, or transmit it? Most, if not all, the major organs of the body are transmitters. The lung takes in air and transmits its nutrients to the rest of the body. There is, therefore, nothing unusual about organs that absorb and transmit; the difficulty would rather be to find an organ which, in any perfect sense, produces. The body neither manufactures the air it breathes nor the food it eats. If we do not manufacture what we eat or what we breathe, why assume that we manufacture, rather than regulate, what we think?

This transmission theory of the brain has the advantage that it solves problems, rather than creating them. The problem of the inrushes experienced in some mental illness, the problem of psychic phenomena and the problem of pure randomness in neo-Darwinism are real difficulties for the scientific world view.

This theory proposes a natural force of intelligence, which is perhaps received and transmitted by the brain, and also influences evolution in the direction of survival. That would restore purpose to nature, but it would also make possible, as James argued, the concept of human survival after death.

From an article by William Rees-Mogg
in The Independent (July 29th 1991).

An NDE account that seems to transcend a simply and solely neurological explanation is Professor Wren-Lewis's story of eating a poisoned sweet in Thailand. Among the more unusual elements in his NDE are that it is still continuing – he can switch back into it by mentally re-focusing on it at any time; that he used a dream-remembering technique – one that seems to help in recapturing the fullness of the NDE on first regaining consciousness; and lastly, that he experienced not the usual white light but rather a black darkness, albeit a radiant one. Here is his eloquent testimony:

The reluctant mystic – an NDE that didn't go away

I had spiritual consciousness thrust upon me in my sixtieth year without working for it, desiring it or even believing in it. The crucial event was a shattering, out-of-the-blue mystical experience in 1983 which, to the astonishment of everyone who knew me, and most of all myself, left me with a permanently changed consciousness, describable only in the kind of spiritual terms I had hitherto vehemently discounted as neurotic fantasy-language.

What happened in 1983 would nowadays be called a 'Near Death Experience', or NDE, though it differed in several notable ways from most of those I'd read about in the rapidly-growing literature on this topic (which I had, incidentally, dismissed as yet another manifestation of the mind's capacity for fantasy). In the first place, I had none of the dramatic visions which have hit the headlines in popular journalism and occupy a prominent place even in serious scholarly studies. As I lay in the hospital bed in Thailand after eating a poisoned sweet given me by a would-be thief, I had no 'out-of-body' awareness of the doctors wondering if I was beyond saving, no review of my life, no passage down a dark tunnel to emerge into a heavenly light or landscape, and no encounter with angelic beings or deceased relatives telling me to go back because my work on earth wasn't yet finished.

I simply entered – or, rather, was – a timeless, spaceless void which in some indescribable way was total aliveness – an almost palpable blackness that was yet somehow radiant. Trying to find words for it afterwards, I recalled the mysterious line of Henry Vaughan's poem 'The Night':

'There is in God (some say) a deep but dazzling darkness.'

An even more marked difference from the general run of NDEs, however, was that I had absolutely no sense of regret or loss at the return into physical life. I lay on the bed, relaxed, and began to take myself back in imagination, in a series of steps, right to the point of coming round. 'Here I am, lying on this bed, with someone asking if I want supper; here I am, just before that, becoming aware of someone shaking my arm; here I am, before that again, with my eyes closed, and ...' Often this process brings back the dream one has forgotten, but what came back this time was nothing like a remembered dream. What came flooding back was an experience that in some extraordinary way *had been with me ever since I came around without my realising it*. It was if I'd come out of the deepest darkness I had ever known, *which was somehow still right there behind my eyes*.

What manifested was simply not the same 'me-experiencing-the-world' that I'd known before: it was 'Everything-that-is, experiencing itself through the bodymind called John lying in a hospital bed'. And the experience was indescribably wonderful. I now know exactly why the Book of Genesis says that God looked upon *all* that He had made – not just beautiful sunsets, but dreary hospital rooms and traumatised sixty-year-old bodies - and saw that it was very good.

What I am trying to describe is no vague feeling of 'good to be alive'. On the contrary, I no longer cared if John lived or ceased to be altogether, and the change of consciousness was so palpable that to begin with I repeatedly put my hand up to the back of my head, feeling exactly as if the doctors had removed the skull and exposed my brain somehow to the infinite blackness of space. Occasionally I still do so, for *the new consciousness has remained with me ever since* – which is the third and most significant difference from what happens in the general run of NDEs, and also from the 'altered states' experienced with psychedelics.

There is in no sense a high from which I can come down. The sense of awe-ful wonder has at the same time a feeling of utter obviousness and ordinariness, as if the marvel of 'everything-coming-into-being-continuously-from-the-Great-Dark' were no more and no less than 'just the way things are'. From this perspective, the term *altered* state of consciousness would be a complete misnomer, for the state is one of simple normality. It seems, rather, as if my earlier state, so-called 'ordinary' human consciousness, represents the real alteration – a deviation from the plain norm, a kind of artificially blinkered or clouded condition wherein the bodymind has the absurd illusion that it is somehow a separate individual entity over against everything else.

In fact I now understand why mystics of all religions have likened the enlightenment-process to waking up from a dream.

As I was walking in the hot sun to the police station to report the poisoned sweet crime I was struck by the sense of loss that the Dark was missing, and my first thought then was: 'Ah, well, you've had the Vision – I suppose now you'll have to join the ranks of all those Seekers who spend their lives trying to attain Higher Consciousness.' And then, to my amazement, I suddenly saw *it was all still there, just waiting, as it were, to be noticed* – the Dark behind my eyes and behind everything else, bringing again the perception that *of course* everything exists by emerging fresh-minted from the Dark now! and now! and now!, with a shout of joy yet also in absolute calm.

The NDE had evidently jerked me out of the so-called normal human state of chronic illusion-of-separateness, into a basic 'wakefulness', interrupted by spells of 'dozing off' – simply forgetting the Dark until the sense of something missing from life brings about instant reawakening with no effort at all.

The key feature of God-consciousness as I know it from my own first-hand experience, is its quintessential ordinariness and obviousness – a feature actually emphasized by many mystics. I know from my own first-hand experience that God-consciousness doesn't abolish human appetites. When I'm in it I don't lose my taste for meat or wine or good company or humour or detective fiction – I actually enjoy them more than ever before. I don't cease to enjoy sexual feelings, nor do I see anything inherently dirty about money.

What the consciousness does bring is the cheerful equanimity of knowing that satisfaction doesn't depend on any of these special preferences of John's bodymind being met; it is inherent simply in being, in the Great Dark which is (in G.K. Chesterton's marvellous phrase) 'joy without a cause'.

> *Prof. John Wren-Lewis, 1/22 Cliffbrook Parade, Clovelly, NSW 2031, Australia. He is preparing a book for publication on this theme, entitled 'The 9.15 to Nirvana'.*

Pagan return to nature

A final thread running through this book is an almost pagan wish to return to the world of nature. This is sometimes expressed by those who are dying as a preference for being outdoors or to be surrounded by plants and flowers. In the following instance, it concerns a 15 year old girl's dying wish to swim with dolphins.

Lee – 'dolphin therapy' for a dying 15 year old

'It's not easy to die when you are 15, but Lee had already accepted her fate,' said Robert. As he spoke, his eyes were full of tears and he could barely keep his voice steady. 'She knew she had an illness that would not spare her. She knew that in spite of their finest efforts the doctors couldn't save her. She suffered a lot but never complained. This particular evening she seemed tranquil and composed but suddenly she said, "Mama, daddy – I think I'm going to die soon and I'm afraid. I know I'm going to a better world than this one and I'm longing for some peace at last but it's hard to accept the idea that I'm going to die at only fifteen."

'We could have lied, telling her of course she wasn't going to die, but we didn't have the heart. Somehow her courage was worth more than our pretence. We just cuddled her and cried together. Then she said, "I always dreamed of falling in love, getting married, having kids ... but above all I would have liked to work in a big marine park with dolphins. I've loved them and wanted to know more about them since I was little. I still dream of swimming with them free and happy in the open sea." She'd never asked for anything, but now she said with all the strength she could muster, "Daddy, I want to swim in the open sea among the dolphins just once. Maybe then I wouldn't be so scared of dying."

'My wife and I talked it over and decided to do everything we could. We had heard of a research centre in the Florida Keys and we phoned them. "Come at once," they said. But that was easier said than done. Lee's illness had used up all our savings and we had no idea how we would be able to afford air tickets to Florida. Then our six year old, Emily, mentioned that she'd seen something on television about a foundation that grants the wishes of very sick children. So I phoned the number and three days later we were all on our way.

'When we arrived at Grass Key, Lee was pale and terribly thin. The chemotherapy she'd been having had made all her hair fall out and she looked ghastly, but she didn't want to rest for a minute and begged us to take her straight away to the dolphins. It was an unforgettable scene. When she got into the water, Lee was already so weak she hardly had the strength to move. We had all put her in a wet suit so she wouldn't get cold, with a life preserver to keep her afloat.

'I towed her out toward the two dolphins, Nat and Tursi, who were frolicking around about thirty feet away from us. At first they seemed distracted and uninterested but when Lee called them softly by name they responded without hesitation. Nat came over first, raised his head and gave her a kiss on the end of her nose. Then Tursi came over and greeted her with a flurry of little high-pitched squeaks of joy. A second later they picked her up with their mighty fins and carried her out to sea with them.

"It feels like flying!" cried Lee, laughing with delight. I hadn't heard her laugh like that since before she became ill. I could hardly believe it was true, but there she was gripping Nat's fin and challenging the wind and the immensity of the ocean. The dolphins stayed with Lee for more than an hour, always tender, always attentive, never using any unnecessary force, always responsive to her wishes.

'There are no words to describe the effect that swim had on her. When she got out of the water it was as if she had been reborn.

'The next day she was too weak to get out of bed. She didn't even want to talk, but when I took her hand she squeezed it and whispered, "Daddy, don't be sad for me. I'll never be afraid again. The dolphins have made me understand that I have nothing to fear." Then she said, "I know I'm going to die tonight. Promise me that you'll cremate my body and scatter my ashes in the sea where the dolphins swim. They have left me with a great feeling of peace in my heart and I know they will be with me on the long journey that lies ahead." Just before dawn she woke and said, "Hold me, daddy, I'm so cold." And she died like that in my arms a few minutes later – passing from sleep to death without a ripple. I only realised her suffering was over because her body became colder and heavier.

'We cremated her as she wanted and went out the next day to scatter her ashes in the ocean amongst the dolphins. We were all crying, I'm not ashamed to say; not just my wife and I and our three other children, but even the sailors on the boat that had taken us out into the bay. Suddenly, through our tears, we saw the great arching silver shapes of Nat and Tursi leaping out of the water ahead of us. They had come to take our daughter home.'

From 'Acquainted with the Night' by Allegra Taylor.
Note: In the UK, the Starlight Foundation (see the Resources chapter) attempts to grant the wishes of critically ill children.

May this present Handbook on improving the quality of all aspects of dying prove a useful contribution to the contemplation of this magnificent and awe-inspiring subject. Above all, may it allow people to 'die in character' as Elisabeth Kübler-Ross puts it. Dr Buckman in his book on how to support a dying person is rightly adamant on this point:

It should be your objective as friend and supporter – as it is my objective when I'm looking after dying patients – to help your friend let go of life *in his own way*. It may not be your way, and it may not be the way you read about in a book or magazine, but it's his way and consistent with the way he's lived his life. You can and should help your friend achieve that.

From 'I Don't Know What To Say – How to Help and Support Someone who is Dying' by Dr Robert Buckman.

Chapter 2

PREPARING FOR DYING

I am quite terrified of death. Not of dying, but of death itself.

I am a fit pensioner, in my seventies, and for about the last four years I have tried to get people to talk about the subject, with little success. It is very much a taboo subject.

I have spoken to many clergy and they seem uncomfortable about the subject, or else trot out the accepted teaching about the Resurrection. I am familiar with that as I have been a churchgoer all my life. My head accepts the doctrine but my heart is frightened.

There is much bereavement counselling but nothing to prepare one for death.

I am quite terrified and this fear spoils and destroys the quality of my life.

From a letter to The Natural Death Centre.

How can we ever be prepared, either for our own death or the deaths of those around us? How can we 'prepare'?

At first the idea may seem futile, or morbid. Yet most of us find ourselves responsible, at some stage in our lives, for meeting the needs of a dying friend, spouse or relative, and having to learn our way through the difficult process of helping someone who is dying. A wealth of revelations accompany this process, but, more often than not, time, practical considerations and our inability to come to terms with what is happening conspire to leave many things unfinished or unsaid. The same goes for our own death.

How do we want to be cared for? What will be our legacy to our loved ones? Will we have time to find out what needs to be done and then do it? And to what extent are our attitudes towards death and our anxiety about death affecting the quality of our lives now?

As a society we are not geared towards handling death as humanely as we could. The letter above expresses the fundamental problem: we don't want to deal with it until it is inevitable or has already happened. Talking about death, even thinking about it, does not come naturally to many of us. Our fear of death seems to prevent us from coping with it. Indeed, as another letter received by the Natural Death Centre points out:

Fear of living

What has struck me about the majority of people's attitudes towards death is not so much the fear of dying, as an all-consuming fear of actually living.

It seems to me that people are not only afraid of life but also have tremendous difficulty accepting the concept of free choice. Why else would we struggle year after year to maintain dead relationships and unfulfilling jobs?

I was trained as a nurse twenty years ago and my initiation into the dying process at the age of eighteen with little to no experience of death was being told that I was never to mention the subject even if the patient asked, nor was I to speak about it to any relative no matter what the situation. I witnessed some appalling deaths. We were allowed to lay their bodies out, but we were not allowed to talk about it.

From a letter to The Natural Death Centre.

It is important to break the silence: we need to find ways to communicate and share thoughts, feelings and experience. Becoming more aware of the process of dying, and of the demands it makes on us and others, is a practical and valuable undertaking.

This chapter looks at ways of 'training' for dying. We begin with ways of acknowledging and exploring the reality of death, and overcoming our fears; and move on to practical considerations of making a will and making our wishes known.

Courses and workshops

A growing number of resources exists nowadays for taking care of the practical as well as the philosophical aspects of dying. In the UK two university courses have been launched, one run by the Open University, and one by St. David's University College, Lampeter. They differ greatly in approach:

The Open University – Death and Dying

In 1990, the Minister of Health announced a grant of £484,000 to make an Open University course on Death and Dying. Very few of the more than one million care workers in Britain, or the many family carers and volunteers, receive any serious education or training for working with dying or bereaved people. Existing courses, however good, reach only a handful of carers each year. At the same time, there is a rising awareness that the process of dying could be made more humane if lessons learned in recent years were shared with carers in hospital and community settings.

The studentship is drawn from those who have regular, extensive contact with dying and bereaved people. Some carers and dying people themselves study the course.

Key themes:

• The dying person's needs and strengths.

• Open communication and decision-making.

• Keeping everyone in the picture. Respecting confidentiality.

• The range of cultural and religious expectations and rituals concerning death and dying.

• The need for support for all those involved in terminal care.

From Open University preliminary course information.

While the OU concentrates upon practical considerations for carers, the one-year M. A. in 'Death and Immortality' at St. David's is philosophical in content:

Death and Immortality Course

The course focuses much of its attention on the paranormal so-called 'Near-Death Experience' and its possible implications for proving the existence of a life hereafter. All the students at Lampeter take a core course examining the philosophical arguments for and against a future life.

In the future it may well be that going on a course about preparations for dying will become as normal as learning first aid. The Natural Death Centre, for instance, offers workshops for the general public entitled 'Living with Dying' run by Christianne Heal, and workshops for nurses and others entitled 'Accepting Death and Living Fully' run by Josefine Speyer (for details, please send an SAE to The Natural Death Centre.) On the whole death is not an easy or welcome subject for general, informal conversation, and so a setting in which death is discussed and explored is a welcome opportunity, as Christianne Heal explains:

Living with Dying

Death is a crisis, but some view it as a crisis with a point to it. We complete exercises in the workshops that enable people to work out at what stage in the process towards death they are, and how they can feel more comfortable about it. It is the airing of the subject that is important to a lot of people: just being able to talk about it. Participants get a great deal out of it. Some simply want the opportunity to discuss their fears, worries and concerns without someone cutting them off because it is a difficult subject. Some people come because they are dying, others because they have been or are nursing someone who is dying and they don't know how to handle the issue, and others because they are old and near their own death experience. I even had a boy of thirteen come whose father had died before he was born. He needed to talk about this and we gave him the opportunity. I was surprised at just how positive the workshop was for him.

Christianne Heal, interviewed in Counselling News (Sept. 1991).

Linda and Martin, who attended Christianne's workshops, each describe the experience:

Christianne Heal created a safe atmosphere with her sensitive and grounded approach. We first examined our childhood beliefs and experiences of death, and then we sat in pairs, with eyes shut and we took it in turns to be each other's death. 'Hello Ruth, I am your death. I am like the dark side of the moon; you can't see me but you know I'm there. I have known you all your life and now it is time for you to know me, do not be scared, I am nothing to fear.' To hear my death speak was uncanny and this effect is heightened because in the silence you hear all the other deaths in the room quietly talking to their partners. I was amazed how the universality of death drew us closer as a group; we listened, and supported each other.

Linda.

Christianne asked us to draw a 'map' and to mark around us all the people who are important to us, living or dead. Then we worked in pairs, one partner listened, while the other had half an hour to say goodbye to all the people he or she had placed on the map. I found this very painful, I think everyone did. It is also beautiful to listen to your partner talking to their friends and family in such a loving and powerful way, expressing the very core of their feelings. Where else would we get the space to say these things to our loved ones, especially those who have died? Funerals only serve this function up to a point, and not at all when it comes to expressing the anger which often accompanies bereavement.

We danced a 'dance of death' to beautiful music with our eyes shut, improvising, imagining death, gently moving amongst each other. We painted death, fascinated by how different all the pictures were – some people started by drawing only black, but then realised that there had to be colour and light there too.

There was an exercise on 'what you would do if you only had six months to live'. Try it some time, take it seriously and you may be surprised at what you reveal to yourself.

We had the opportunity to write our own obituary and were given the freedom to fantasise about the life for which we would like to be remembered.

The difference in people's aspirations was quite lovely: from one person who had built his own chicken shed to another whose assassination at a political rally precipitated world revolution.

At the end one person said: 'I've never laughed so much in a weekend.'

Martin.

The Fruits of Life Project

The Fruits of Life Project is an initiative based on prizewinning work conducted by Jozef van der Put, of PRISMA (see the Resources chapter), a Dutch organisation that trains groups of volunteers who then work with individuals. The project targets people who are experiencing difficulty in accepting and coming to terms with old age and dying. The project's approach is to use personal biography and life history to review the major life events of each individual. The aim is to resolve conflicts or other unfinished business and to gather in 'a harvest of the fruits of each life'.

Where appropriate, a volunteer helps the individual to compile a life story which can be shared with those relatives and friends left behind. For instance, the volunteer may ask the person to write a brief description of a dozen important 'stepping stones' in his or her life, events or decisions that significantly influenced the way the person's life developed; and then to discuss these.

Anxiety about dying

Anxiety about dying can be experienced by people at any age. The Natural Death Centre has designed the scale below to help you to find out how likely you are to be anxious about death and dying when the time comes, if you were to remain as you are at present, and to help you to identify those specific high-scoring, high-anxiety areas that could suggest a focus for 'personal development' or other changes in your approach or lifestyle. There is no need to fake your scoring. There is no one to fool but yourself.

Death-Related Anxiety Scale

Give marks out of 4 to each of the following statements:
Not true at all = 0 / Mainly not true = 1 / Not sure = 2 /
Somewhat true = 3 / Very true = 4

☐ I tend not to be very brave in crisis situations

☐ I am an unusually anxious person

☐ I am something of a hypochondriac and am perhaps obsessively worried about infections

☐ I have never had a semi-mystical, spiritual, out-of-the-body, near-death or peak experience

☐ I tend to be unusually frightened in planes at take off and landing

☐ I do not have a particular religion or philosophy that helps me to face dying

☐ I do not believe in any form of survival of the soul after death

☐ Personally I would give a lot to be immortal in this body

☐ I am very much a city person and not really close to nature

☐ Anxiety about death spoils the quality of my life

☐ I am superstitious that preparing for dying might hasten my death

☐ I don't like the way some of my relatives died and fear that my death could be like theirs

☐ My actual experience of friends dying has been undilutedly negative

☐ I would feel easier being with a dying relative if they were not told they were dying

☐ I have fears of dying alone without friends around me

☐ I have fears of dying slowly

☐ I have fears of dying suddenly

☐ I have fears of dying before my time or whilst my children are still young

☐ I have fears of dying before fulfilling my potential and fully using my talents

☐ I have fears of dying without adequately having expressed my love to those I am close to

☐ I have fears of dying before having really experienced much 'joie de vivre'

☐ I have fears of what may or may not happen after death

☐ I have fears of what could happen to my family after my death

☐ I have fears of dying in hospital or an institution

☐ I have fears of those caring for me feeling overwhelmed by the strain of it

☐ I have fears of not getting help with euthanasia when the time comes

☐ I have fears of being given unofficial and unwanted euthanasia

☐ I have fears of getting insufficient pain control whilst dying

☐ I have fears of being over-medicalised and unconscious whilst dying

☐ I have fears of being declared dead when not really dead or being buried alive

☐ I have fears of getting confused near death or not being able to follow my spiritual practices

☐ I have fears of what may happen to my body after death

☐ I have fears of mental degeneration near death

☐ Overall I would say that I am unusually anxious about death and dying

☐ **TOTAL**

The extremely anxious (scoring over 65 or so) might consider the need for counselling or therapy; the unusually anxious (scoring over 40) might want to find a method of meditation, self-hypnotic autogenic training, chant, dance, co-counselling relationship, therapy workshop, philosophy, spiritual practice or similar that could help them to experience, explore and accept their feelings; the averagely anxious (scoring under 40) don't have to be too smug – in certain respects anxiety can correlate with intelligence; and once the shaman's advice to 'make friends with one's fear' has been absorbed, anxiety is free to transform into energy and ecstasy – perhaps there is a Zen Art of Being Anxious, just as there seems to be a Zen Art of everything else, from archery to flower arranging.

For the record, Nicholas Albery, one of the co-editors of this book, scored an anxiety rating of 45 – 'no doubt a need to face my anxiety on the subject is what attracted me to it in the first place,' he says.

The scale is perhaps more interesting for the questions it poses than for the number it produces. Most of us will recognise that it is possible to be 'overanxious' about death, to the extent that it lessens our enjoyment of life; and indeed the possibility that we are so anxious about death that we deny any anxiety at all. It is to be hoped that people who do take the test do not become anxious about their anxiety rating!

Some people find that their anxiety about death becomes manageable in unexpected ways, as in these examples:

Da Free John

A contemporary American spiritual teacher Da Free John, reports in his autobiography, 'The Knee of Listening', how he overcame the fear of death by 'dying'. When his fear of death became almost overwhelming, he discovered the ancient wisdom of giving in (which is quite different from giving up) and cooperating with the process, flowing with the pressure, letting 'death' take its full and natural course. Here's what happened:

'I was lying home alone in the afternoon. It was as if all my life had constantly prevented this experience from going to its end. All my life I had been preventing my death.

'I lay on the floor, totally disarmed, unable to make a gesture that could prevent the rising fear. And thus it grew in me, but, for the first time, I allowed it to happen. I could not prevent it. The fear and the death rose and became my overwhelming experience. And I witnessed the crisis of that fear in a moment of conscious, voluntary death. I allowed the death to happen, and I saw it happen.

'When the moment of crisis passed I felt a marvellous relief. The death had occurred, but I had observed it! I remained untouched by it. The body and the mind and the personality had died, but I remained as an essential and unqualified consciousness ... There was just an infinite bliss of being.'

Da Free John quoted in 'Practical Guide
to Death and Dying' by John White.

Birth, love, courage and death

It was getting pregnant with my first child ten years ago that started a process within me that revolted against the 'normal', expected, over-medicalised hospital birth. So I set about finding an alternative and by following my instinct (with some determination) I was able to have my first child at home. The experiences of that birth, and the following ones, brought me closer to death than I have ever been – and were comforting for that. I felt I was part of a process that was greater than me and that although it was terrifying in its unknown expectations, it responded to love and courage! I was acutely aware that I would have been unable to function had I not been given the quality of emotional support that I was given. And I thought that if I could die in the same way, I could accept it without too much fear.

I have been afraid of death since I was a very young child and I think the two things that have helped me are giving birth and being in therapy. I hope one day I will be able to welcome death without fear and I fiercely believe that people should die at home if they can and that we should all be able to talk about it.

From a letter by Jehane Markham to The Natural Death Centre.

Death without fear or pain

In our family there has been a strong taboo, or kind of a 'hush' on death as a subject even for mention, and we have had no education or experience. Deaths have occurred but somehow I have always been protected or just not there (when young) and now as an adult I'm all at sea about it.

When our son was on the way, I learned about 'birthing' (the theory) and went to relaxation classes. When he was born I had no fear, hardly any pain (merely discomfort) and he came along almost in record time. I wonder: if we could feel the same way about our deaths, mightn't it help the person involved and everyone else concerned? Perhaps the baby born to an unafraid and relaxed mother might feel better about being born than if the mother is all tense and hurting. Things may go a bit wrong afterwards, but at least she or he has had a fair start. The same could apply to dying.

From a letter to The Natural Death Centre.

The parallels between dying and giving birth are very strong. As Anya Foos-Graber in her book 'Deathing' urges us: 'Look at death's counterpart – fertilization, pregnancy and birth! Not knowing about the 'birds and the bees' doesn't ward off pregnancy! Knowing the process, whether of birth or death, means you can positively utilise it.'

Death Weeks

It seems probable that more anxiety is caused by ignorance and apprehension than by facing up to the fact of dying. A series of 'Death Weeks' were conducted by Peter Prunkl and Rebecca Berry, in which groups of young students were asked to simulate 'dying', to really imagine it intensely, over a period of seven or eight days. The organisers maintain that a remarkable degree of realism is obtained with a well-constructed simulation, and it is clear from the various participants' journals (excerpted below) that they were able to engage themselves fully in their roles as dying people. It is also apparent that the experience ultimately had a profoundly positive effect for them:

• To begin, let me share what I have learned from my experience of Death Week. I learned about myself. In fact, it was the first time in a great while that I took a very close look at what I am really like. I discovered that I am strong and persevering and that strength comes from a very deep faith in God. I learned about life, not because I had 'only seven days to live' and wanted to cram every experience into that time that I could, but because, as I was 'dying', I became more aware of the events happening around me. The very minute and trivial things of life seemed to become peak experiences for me, so much so that at times my senses were bombarded by stimuli which overwhelmed my mind to the point of great excitement, followed by confusion, and finally ending in total exhaustion. It was during these low points, these times of loneliness and depression, that I would come to an understanding of life. The understanding was not profound or shockingly new, but was remarkably simple. The simplicity gave me such a feeling of comfort and joy that as the week progressed, I became excited about my death. I was finally going home and that made me very happy.

• Yes, I no longer take life for granted. I have become aware of how precious every day is.

• It has made me more content about myself.

• The most significant effect is that I no longer fear the inevitable reality of death.

• The experience made me decide to tell my family how I wanted to be dealt with after death. I wanted to tell them what I wanted done. It is my last opportunity to take care of things for me. After all, it is my life and my death. I have talked to each of my children and husband about cremation and this is what I want done. Before Death Week, I just figured after I am dead what does it matter, but it does.

It seems to me that during that period after Death Week I became more comfortable with myself and expressed how I really felt to my friends and family. I gradually became less dependent on people for my own happiness and my relationships became more open, honest and mutual in their give-and-take aspects.

From 'Death Week' by Peter Prunkl and Rebecca Berry, Hemisphere (1101 Vermont Ave, NW # 200, Washington DC 20005. 1989, ISBN 0 89116 112 0, $14).

Rehearsal for death

'Philosophy is a rehearsal for death,' says Plato. There is no reason why our everyday activities should not include such rehearsals. Alexander the Great's father, Philip of Macedonia, one of the most powerful men of his time, gave to one of his retinue a single, simple duty: regardless of how much the King protested, raged or grew violent, the man's only task was to approach him every day and say: 'Philip of Macedonia, thou too shall die.' This was a highly dangerous job, as the king often did rage and grow violent; yet he continued to keep the man in his employ. Fortunately for us there are less expensive (and safer) ways of rehearsing.

One stimulating way is to write your own obituary – use a formal newspaper style if you wish, or imagine that you know you are to die within days and complete as many of the following sentences as you find suitably provocative:

D-i-y obituary

• Outside observers would probably say that my main achievements have been ...
• For myself, what I am most pleased with and proud of in my life, are ...
• One of the most important lessons that I have learnt in my lifetime is that ...
• During my life I have used my ... [list three positive personal character-istics, for example: imagination, sense of humour and intelligence] through my ... [list three activities, for example: writing, running groups and parenting] with the underlying vision, I now realise, of helping work towards a world in which, one day, ... [describe your long-term Utopia, for example: 'people are kind and sensitive to each other, nature is at ease and magic is alive'].
• The people I have felt closest to in my life have been ...
• One generalisation I could make about the quality of my relationships with others is that ...
• If I regret anything, it is that ...
• If I had known how short a time I had left to live, I would probably have ...

The purpose of this obituary, besides that of evaluating your achievements and failures, is to flush out whether a more acute awareness of your own mortality would lead you to want to make changes in your life, in case you might wish to make them now, rather than being filled with regrets on your deathbed.

Another way of preparing for death is just to imagine dying, which many of us must have done in our own way. Here is one version:

Meditating on dying

You close your eyes and imagine that you are on your deathbed.

You feel yourself drifting. You don't have any more energy to do anything. Your desk is piled high with unanswered letters, bills to be paid, unfinished projects. Either someone else will pick them up for you or they will remain undone. It doesn't matter much. No one will know that the idea you meant to work out never came to expression. No one will feel the poorer for it. Then there are the people in your life. If you loved them well, they will miss you and grieve for you. Over time the poignancy of your absence will fade and only a warm remembrance will be left. There will be those for whom you did not care enough, those you rejected, those with whom there is still some unfinished business. It doesn't matter now. There is nothing you can do about it.

There is only one thing you can do, and that is to let go. Let the tasks of the world slip away. Let your loved ones mourn a little while for you and then go on their way. Let go of everything, your home, your possessions, your feelings and your thoughts. Allow yourself to float. You begin to feel lighter. You have shed the heavy load you have been carrying. What was the heavy load? It was your sense of self-importance. It was your belief that everything you did had intrinsic importance, therefore you had to do it fully and perfectly no matter what the cost. Or, conversely, it was your belief that your work was so important that you couldn't possibly do it well enough, so the burden you carried was the unfulfilled responsibility. But, either way, don't you see how temporal it is, when you are facing your own death? This practice can help you to learn to do a little less, do it a bit more slowly, do it with care, and do it with love.

From 'Seeing Through the Visible World: Jung, Gnosis and Chaos'
by June Singer, Mandala/Harper Collins, 1990.

Many meditations on dying are to be found in Tibetan traditions, some charming ones as in the first passage below by Stephen Levine, inspired by 'The Tibetan Book of the Dead', and some at least superficially rather gruesome ones, as in the second extract below:

Shining true being

Imagine that your body no longer has the strength, the energy, to maintain its connection with the life-force, with the body of awareness within. And imagine now that you are beginning to experience the process of dissolving out of that body. Sensations from the body no longer so distinct, melting away, leaving just a spaciousness. Dissolving out of the body. Leaving that heavier form behind. Dissolving into consciousness itself.

My friend, listen now, for that which is called death has arrived. So let go gently, gently, of all that holds you back. Of all that pulls you away from this most precious moment. Know that now you have arrived at the transition called death. Open to it. Let go into it.

Recognise the changing experience of the mind as it separates from the body, dissolving.

Dissolving now into the realms of pure light. Your true nature shining everywhere before you.

My friend, maintain an open-heartedness, a spaciousness of being that does not grasp. Let things be as they are without the least attempt to interfere. Grasping at nothing.

Enter the essential nature of your own being shining there before you, a great luminosity. Rest in being. Knowing it for what it is. This light shining, luminous. Your true self.

Let go, gently, gently, without the least force. Before you shines your true being. It is without birth, without death.

Let go of all which distracts or confuses the mind, all that created density in life.

Go gently into it. Do not be frightened or bewildered. Do not pull back in fear from the immensity of your true being. Now is a moment for liberation.

Know that you are well guided by your compassion and love. You are the essence of all things. You are the light.

From 'Who Dies?' by Stephen Levine.

Visualising death

There are both external and internal ways of practice. An external technique is to dwell in a charnel ground and observe the stages of decomposition of the corpses in it, while keeping the mind fixed on the thought that these corpses represent the final destiny of one's own body.

An internal means is to visualise oneself as lying on one's deathbed awaiting the approach of death. Visualise that your parents, relatives and friends surround you, lamenting and upset. The radiance of your countenance has faded and your nostrils have sunk back. Your lips dry, slime begins to form on your teeth and all grace leaves your body. Bodily temperature drops, breathing becomes heavy, and you begin to exhale more deeply than you inhale. All the negative karmas [actions] generated during your life arise within your mind and you become filled with regret. You look to all sides for help, but help does not come.

From 'Tibetan Traditions of Death Meditation'
by Ge-she Nga-wang Dar-gye.

Allegra Taylor describes the way her wishes became clear and focused through participation in a group exercise:

The death bed imagined

... An impromptu drama in which we took it in turns to play the different characters in a deathbed scene: the distraught relative; the voluntary worker; the withdrawn child; the dying person.

As I lay there, my eyes closed, trying to visualise everything I love receding from me, I knew without a shadow of a doubt that what I most wanted was to be treated as I always had been, as me. I felt a need to finish relationships and say my goodbyes calmly. I saw myself as weak and frail but with a last great longing to pass on something of value. I wanted someone to put a baby in my arms for me to hold. A last connection with life – a symbol of love and renewal.

From my family I wanted only closeness, an easy honesty and assurances that they would be all right. From visitors I wanted to know that they would provide a support network for the family after my death. I did not want anyone to take heroic measures to save me or to save my soul. Anyone who spoke to me of spiritual things needed to be supportive of my own beliefs and not a representative of alien ones.

I did rather feel that it was my show, and that the most loving last thing people could do for me would be to set aside their own needs and help me have the kind of death I wanted.

From 'Acquainted with the Night' by Allegra Taylor.

It is through these rehearsals, these meditations, that we begin to develop our own understanding of death, beyond our received ideas. Our anxieties about social status and material possessions seem no longer as important, perhaps we even find death taking on new meanings for us. Relating realistically to impermanence is the essence of both the spiritual life and of living fully. The key point about death is that time runs out – there are no more chances to get it right. As Caroline Sherwood puts it: 'If I live my life "finishing business" by keeping myself up to date and clear in my relationships, living from the deepest truth of myself, working to dissolve the barriers to love in my life – how much more easy my death might be.'

Life is precious for the already-dead

Once someone asked a well-known Thai meditation master: 'In this world where everything changes, where nothing remains the same, where loss and grief are inherent in our very coming into existence, how can there be any happiness?' The teacher, looking compassionately at this fellow, held up a drinking glass which had been given to him earlier in the morning and said, 'You see this goblet? For me, the glass is already broken. I enjoy it, I drink out of it. It holds my water admirably, sometimes even reflecting the sun in beautiful patterns. If I should tap it, it has a lovely ring to it. But when I put this glass on a shelf, and the wind knocks it over or my elbow brushes it off the table and it falls to the ground and shatters, I say, "Of course." But when I understand that this glass is already broken, every moment with it is precious. Every moment is just as it is and nothing need be otherwise.'

When we recognise that, just as that glass, our body is already broken, that indeed we are already dead, then life becomes precious and we open to it just as it is, in the moment it is occurring. When we understand that all our loved ones are already dead – our children, our mates, our friends – how precious they become. How little fear can interpose, how little doubt can estrange us. When you live your life as though you're already dead, life takes on a new meaning. Each moment becomes a whole lifetime, a universe unto itself.

From 'Who Dies?' by Stephen Levine.

Death in Mexico

Most of us Westerners are to an extent estranged from death. By contrast, the Nobel prizewinning writer Octavio Paz explains the Mexican attitude towards death:

Death as a favourite plaything

To the Modern Mexican death doesn't have any meaning. It has ceased to
be the transition, the access to the other life which is more authentic than this
one. But the unimportance of death has not taken it away from us and
eliminated it from our daily lives. To the inhabitant of New York, Paris or
London, death is a word that is never uttered because it burns the lips. The
Mexican, on the other hand, frequents it, mocks it, caresses it, sleeps with
it, entertains it; it is one of his favourite playthings and his most enduring
love. It is true that in his attitude there is perhaps the same fear that others
also have, but at least he does not hide this fear nor does he hide death; he
contemplates her face-to-face with impatience, with contempt, with irony:
'If they're going to kill me tomorrow, let them kill me for once and for all.'
  From 'The Labyrinth of Solitude' by Octavio Paz, Penguin, 1985.

Many of the exercises we have seen have been concerned with individual
introspection. In the Natural Death Centre's workshops and group exercises
there is an added dimension of shared experience. Taking this one step further,
the London-based City Dying Group organises candlelit vigils in cemeteries.
Each of the participants brings a candle, which they light one by one, saying
goodbye to somebody (or something). This relaxed ritual has been going since
1985; the group also organises picnics in cemeteries. Strange as this may seem,
it is not unlike the Mexican festival called 'El Dia de los Muertes' (The Day of
the Dead) when Mexicans celebrate the memory of lost loved ones with
cemetery vigils, dancing and riotous parades, in the (loosely-held) belief that
their loved ones return in spirit to join in. Mexico is like most of the world, in that
infant mortality and adult illness are much more common than they are here.
Death is more a part of life, and perhaps because of this, Mexicans treat it with
a healthy mixture of respect and irreverence.

The Mexican Day of the Dead

That a festival to do with the dead should be a joyous occasion perhaps
strikes those of us from other cultures with our different perceptions as
something hard to come to terms with. The Day of the Dead is just that: a
festival of welcome for the souls of the dead which the living prepare and
delight in. The souls return each year to enjoy for a few brief hours the
pleasures they once knew in life.

  In the urban setting of Mexico City and other large towns the celebration
is seen at its most exuberant, with figures of skulls and skeletons everywhere. These mimic the living and disport themselves in a mocking modern
dance of death. It is not surprising that so colourful an event should have
become a tourist event.

  Not far away from the tourist routes there is, however, another Mexico.
In the rural areas, in every village or small town, the Day of the Dead is
celebrated beyond the glare of flashbulbs. Each household prepares its
offering of food and drink for the dead to be set out on a table among flowers

and candles. The blue smoke of burning copal incense sanctifies the ceremony, just as it has done for centuries. Outside the peace is shattered by the explosions of the rockets set off to mark the fulfilment of an obligation deeply felt. The whole company of the living and the dead share in the flowering and fruiting of the land which both have cultivated.

The Day of the Dead is essentially a private or family feast. It has a public aspect at community level, but the core of the celebration takes place within the family home. It is a time of family reunion not only for the living but also the dead, who, for a few brief hours each year, return to be with their relatives in this world.

> *From 'The Skeleton At The Feast' by Elizabeth Carmichael and Chloë*
> *Sayer, British Museum Press (46 Bloomsbury St, London WC1B 3QQ),*
> *1991, ISBN 0 7141 2503 2, £12-95.*

The Day of the Dead is celebrated on October 31st, the eve of All Saints' Day, on which day the same custom of visiting the dead in their last resting places used to be common throughout Christendom, and is still widely observed, in France for example. These practices enable us to commemorate and celebrate our loved ones, and keep our own sense of death in perspective, by giving death and the dead a time as well as a place.

The Natural Death Centre has inaugurated a smaller-scale English Day of the Dead, for the third Sunday in April of each year. Make contact with the Centre for the details, or if you have a suitable event to suggest. Each year has different themes and events, which have included: a festival and exhibition; death-related poetry, music and art; a coffin-making workshop; a lunchtime debate on euthanasia; an evening dinner discussion on Near-Death Experiences; an open day at woodland burial grounds around the country; and video workshops where people could prepare their own video messages for their descendants.

Making your will

For those in good health there is one obvious and sensible preparation for death. Make a will! Some of us avoid doing this because it is an admission that we are going to die. For that reason alone it is a valuable spiritual exercise, as well as a highly practical and normalising procedure. Maybe we are not entirely comfortable with our death, maybe we have not fully joined the human race, until we have got hold of that document, filled it in, signed it and have got it witnessed.

In fact, as the Law Society has been campaigning to remind us, only about one in three adults in Britain has a will. This may not matter so much for single people without children, but it can lead to unnecessary financial hardship for many families. If you die without a will ('intestate'), the intestacy rules dictate who receives your estate (the total of your house and its contents, car, various insurance policies and savings accounts may well come to more than you realise). The rules will also decide who should manage the affairs of your estate. It is important to realise that unmarried partners may have no claim on the estate (unless dependant, but this could be expensive to establish). Even a legal wife or husband may have to sell the home to pay the other automatic beneficiaries.

Of particular importance in the case of divorced or separated parents, the rules will determine who the legal guardians of your children will be; with a will you can name the person you would like to act as your children's guardian.

The standard way to get a will drawn up is to consult a solicitor (this would be likely to cost from about £50). It is worth familiarising yourself with the procedure before you visit a solicitor as this could save you time, money and possible confusion. There are six simple steps to take before you make a will:

(1) Before you see your solicitor, list all the items you have to leave – house and contents, car, savings accounts, etc, and their rough value.

(2) Consider who you would like to provide for and in what way. (Write down the full names, including middle names, and the addresses and dates of birth, of all children to be named in the will.)

(3) Consider whether you would like to leave money or property 'in trust' for children or grandchildren until they are grown up and at what age you think they should inherit your gift.

(4) Decide who you would like to receive your sentimental belongings. These may be of little financial value but you can pass them on to someone you know will appreciate them.

(5) Consider whether you would like to leave some money to charity (bequests to charities are not liable to inheritance tax).

(6) Choose one or more executors to 'wind up your affairs'. The executors can be spouses or members of the family or friends, although it is as well to get their agreement in advance. If, in the event, they find the task too onerous, as they well may, they can always ask a solicitor to take over.

Adapted from 'The Granada Action Factsheet,
Death: A Practical Guide'.

As a postscript to the above, if you must appoint a professional executor, choose a (cheap and specialist) solicitor rather than a bank, as the latter tends to charge far more. Find a solicitor prepared to forego the standard hourly 'charging clause' in the will – replace this with a statement as to the maximum amount of money chargeable to the beneficiaries for the administration of the estate. Bear in mind that the solicitor will not be under any obligation to take on the task of being the executor when the time comes.

Here is an example of a will for a married man with two children who is concerned to minimise long-term liability to inheritance tax, and with several other unusual features (check their reliability with your legal adviser!):

Will for a married man with two children

WILL of Donald Roland Winterton of 26 Oxford Gardens, London W10, made this fourteenth day of April one thousand nine hundred and ninety seven.

1. I revoke all previous Wills and Codicils made by me. I appoint as my executors my brother Arthur Winterton of 48 Book Lane, London N8 (tel 0181 286 2194) and my sister Alice Maples of 12 Montrose Road, London

N4 (tel 0181 937 4582) – or if either or both of them is unable or unwilling to act my friend Alan Beam of 12 Corry Close, London WC2 (tel 0171 208 9432) is to be an executor.

2. My funeral wishes are that I be buried in a nature reserve burial ground with a tree planted by the grave instead of having a headstone and I would like my executors to contact an information source such as The Natural Death Centre (tel 0181 208 2853) or A. B. Wildlife Trust Fund (tel 01423 530900) to find out the nearest or most suitable such ground after my death.

3. If my wife Rosemary dies before me or does not survive me for thirty days I appoint my sister Alice Maples and her husband Michael Maples as the guardians to the age of eighteen of my son Arthur my daughter Mary and any other children I may have.

4. I give the following bequests free from all taxes and duties payable on or by reference to my death. These bequests and legacies are to lapse automatically if the recipient dies before me or if a total of six letters or telephone calls in any particular case fails to trace him or her within six months of the first attempt to do so. No advertisement or any other means need be used.

(a) my painting by Emily Young to my friend Amelia Hart of 88 Forge Terrace, Thornhill, Derby (tel 01437 3333)

(b) such motorbike as I may own at my death to my nephew Joseph Lawlor of 33 Warren Street, Church Stretton, Shropshire (tel 01331 3227).

5. I give the following further legacies free from all taxes and duties payable on or by reference to my death:

(a) £500 to each of my executors who proves my will

(b) £1000 to my secretary Janet Simmonds of 51 Victoria Road, Chesterfield, Derbyshire (tel 01437 34282)

(c) £1000 to the Fourth World Educational and Research Association Trust, 20 Heber Road, London NW2 (tel 0181 208 2853) Registered Charity Number 283040 for the benefit of their project The Natural Death Centre. I declare that the receipt of the charity's treasurer or other person professing to be the duly authorised officer shall be a full and sufficient discharge to my executors.

6. I give free from all taxes and duties payable on or by reference to my death all my interest in the property at 41 Baldwin Lane, Caversham, Reading to my executors as trustees. They are to sell everything not in the form of cash but they may postpone the sale of anything as long as they like. They are to invest or apply what is left in any type of property just as if it were their own money. They may borrow money from institutions in advance of probate if the money is needed to pay the Inland Revenue with the loan to be repaid in due course as my assets become available.

7. After the executors have paid my debts any taxes and duties payable on my death and the expenses of my funeral and of administering my estate I give to my wife the whole of the rest of my estate except for my interest

in the property at 41 Baldwin Lane, Caversham, Reading but including its contents and furniture.

8. My trustees may give to the guardians of my children any part of what is left to enable them to acquire property as needed for my children or to apply for my children's benefit.

9. My trustees are to divide whatever is left from this trust for sale (including any income from it) between such of my children as reach the age of eighteen – if more than one then in shares as near to equal as is reasonably practicable. My children are my son Arthur (born 3/1/86) my daughter Mary (born 28/7/78) and any other children I may have in future. The trustees may apply the actual assets rather than cash if they think fit without requiring the consent of any other person. Each of these children is to have a contingent rather than vested interest in my estate until he or she has attained the age of 18.

10. If any child of mine dies before me or dies under the age of eighteen leaving children who do reach that age then my trustees are to divide as equally as is reasonably practicable between these grandchildren the share of my estate which their parent would have received if that parent had lived long enough.

11. If my trustees think it proper they may at any time apply for the maintenance education or benefit of any beneficiary under the provisions of the two previous paragraphs any part of the capital of the property to which he or she would have become entitled on reaching eighteen.

12. The receipt of the guardian or any person professing to be the proper officer of any school college or other education establishment which any of the children are attending at that time shall be a full and sufficient discharge to my trustees in respect of that beneficiary.

13. Any person contesting this will or attempting to set aside any part of it before any court is to be denied any benefit from my estate.

Signed by Donald Roland Winterton
in our presence and then by us in his:
Signature

First witness:	Second witness:
Signature	Signature
Name	Name
Address	Address
Occupation	Occupation

Some points about this will:

• On the whole a will can be written in plain English. Avoid any possible ambiguities of meaning.

• In the passages above where it descends into legal gobbledegook it is for a reason, so beware if you make significant changes in such wordings. Beware generally, and seek legal approval of your will if in any doubt. A very useful guide, used in designing the above will, is the 'Which?' book, 'Wills and

Probate' edited by the Consumers' Association (for details see under Books in the Resources chapter).

• Always revoke previous wills even if you have never made any.

• Note the absence of commas in the text, except in the addresses, an absence which lawyers think helps guard against fraudulent alteration of a will and against the need for judicial interpretation of the comma's meaning. If the will goes over one side of paper, continue on the back of the paper. If further pages are needed, these should be numbered and you and the witnesses should sign at the bottom of each sheet.

• Those appointed as guardians for children can also be executors of the will, unless you think there could be a conflict of interest – for instance the possibility of the trustees enriching themselves; or, on the contrary, of the trustees not taking enough, through being too diffident to recoup expenses.

• New woodland burial grounds are opening all the time and some may be closer or more appropriate than any currently available, so this document allows for future developments by asking the executors to contact information sources such as the Natural Death Centre after the person's death.

• Inheritance tax was described by Roy Jenkins as 'a voluntary tax, paid only by those who distrust their heirs more than they dislike the Inland Revenue' – which nevertheless is forecast to raise £1.55 billion in 1997-8. There is no inheritance tax payable when the spouse inherits, but when the spouse in turn dies, then the tax is payable on net assets over £215,000 (the current figure, which alters regularly). To avoid this in advance, the will (above) gives a house to the children, and the contents, furniture, cash, etc, to the wife. This would obviously only be appropriate in a case where the children are to be trusted not to evict or harass the wife and where the house is not worth more than the inheritance tax limit.

• Phone numbers and dates of birth are not normally put in a will, with all such details on separate sheets put with the will. But, as long as the details are correct, what harm can it do? Do not, however, fasten information sheets or anything else to the will itself, whether by pins, staples or paperclips.

• The reference to bequests lapsing if the beneficiaries are not readily traceable is to prevent the executors having to go to enormous lengths, including placing ads in the London Gazette, to find beneficiaries – as sometimes happens, especially when a person has lived to a grand old age and lost contact with those remembered in the will.

• A will such as this containing several vital technicalities and creating a 'trust for sale' for the children (which avoids various legal pitfalls and needs careful wording) should at the very least be checked by a solicitor. One way we have done this for free in the past is through one of the house insurance free advice schemes – in this case Frizzell, tel 01202 292333. Frizzell offer 24 hour free medical, domestic and legal advice service to their clients. Faxing two prototype wills to them provoked a marvellous six page letter of comment from their solicitor in reply.

• The children have a 'contingent' interest – ie contingent in this case upon the each reaching the age of eighteen. If the child dies earlier, then that gift will lapse (unless there are children of that child), and the gift will go to the other children. A vested interest on the other hand would have formed part of the child's estate.

• Denying any part of the estate to those contesting your will may not stand up in court, but it could put them off trying – or it could make lawyers rich interpreting the clause! Another way to reduce the risk of dependants from previous relationships contesting the will is to insert a clause that says: 'I have reviewed my obligations to [...] and consider that I have already made adequate and proper provision.'

• Neither the witnesses nor their spouses should benefit from your will, or they will forfeit any provision made for them. Ideally, witnesses should be traceable after your death, in case there is a dispute as to the will's validity. Desmond Banks, a solicitor in Notting Hill and one of the Natural Death Centre's honorary consultants, recommends that the testator and witnesses should all use the same pen if possible, to help demonstrate that the testator signed the will in the presence of both witnesses and that they then signed in the presence of the testator.

The following points are worth noting about wills in general:

A will could be left in a safe place in the house, along with your other main papers. This would be simpler and quicker than leaving it with a solicitor or depositing it at the bank. Tell your executors, your spouse and your children where you have left it and consider giving them copies (note on the copies who has the original and where; and write at the bottom of the copies: 'We certify that this is a true copy of the original', with signatures from the testator and the witnesses).

If your circumstances are such that the will is not certain to be found, you may like to phone the deposit of wills section at the Probate Registry on 0171 936 6000. They will send you an envelope and a form. You then send them the will and a fee of £1. They hold hundreds of thousands of wills on deposit.

If is it known that there is a will and it cannot be found, those handling your affairs may be required to write to every solicitor in the region, and the bill for this can mount up.

A will is automatically negated by marriage (unless made in anticipation of marriage), so make another one at this time. It is as well to make another one too if you divorce.

Tax can sometimes be saved within two years after death by the beneficiaries of the will entering into a deed to vary its terms.

To repeat: be careful in your use of words in your will. Do not write for instance 'I give all my money to ...' if what you really mean is 'I give everything I own to ...'.

Avoid inadvertently giving your spouse a mere 'life interest' in your property (where the person is only able to get income from the house and no capital). You could make this mistake by specifying what is to happen to the property after the spouse's death. Such considerations should be left for the spouse's own will to deal with.

In Scotland, your spouse and children have rights to one third or more of your estate (other than lands or buildings) whatever your will may say to the contrary.

If a person has property abroad, a will should also be made in that country.

Many more such interesting points are raised in the 'Which?' book mentioned above.

Altering a will by codicil

Typing errors in a will are best avoided. If retained, they must be signed with your signature and that of your witnesses in the margin. To make small changes in a will, one way is to add a codicil, with two new witnesses signing at the end, using the same legal formula as in the main will ('signed by ... in our presence and then ...'). Part of a sample codicil might read:

> This is the first codicil to the will made the fourteenth day of April nineteen ninety seven of me Donald Roland Winterton of 26 Oxford Gardens, London W10.
>
> (1) I revoke the bequest of £1,000 to Janet Simmonds.
>
> (2) In all other respects I confirm my will.

But normally it is safer to make an entire new will rather than to attempt to draft your own codicil.

If you want to find a solicitor or will-writing company to draw up your will, you could phone around in the Yellow Pages for the cheapest and best, or you could ask friends for personal recommendations. Beware that making a solicitor your executor can be like writing a blank cheque.

S. V. Wadsworth & Co, Solicitors, Freepost BM6255, 240 Stratford Road, Shirley, Solihull, West Midlands B90 3BR (tel 0121 745 8550) charges £29 for a will.

Christopher Hill Associates, C & J Willwriting Services, 49A and B London Road, Cowplain PO8 8UJ (tel 0800 454605) charges £25 for a will ('over 50 years professional experience; full insurance indemnity').

Willmaker, 65 Newman Street, London W1P 3PG (tel 0171 436 8445) is a 'specialist will-writing company'. It charges £25 for a single will (£40 for a couple) and £17-95 for its Enduring Power of Attorney pack.

The Will Consultancy, Old Bank Chambers, Market Square, Pontypridd, Mid-Glamorgan CF37 2SY, Wales CF32 2SY (tel 01443 485147) offers a legally-supervised will service for £49 (£74 for a couple). These prices were quoted for London – its consultants can visit you at home.

The charity, Age Concern (see under Organisations in the Resources chapter), offers a will-making service, again based on a questionnaire, for £50.

You may be able to get a will drafted at subsidised cost by a solicitor under the Legal Aid Green Form scheme if you are not only over 70 years (or blind or partially blind or deaf or hard of hearing or handicapped by illness or injury) but also of modest means with low savings.

Inheritance tax information is available from the Inland Revenue's Capital Taxes Office: Ferrers House, PO Box 38, Nottingham NG2 1BB (tel 0115 974 2400). For general information, ask for booklets IR 45 and IHT1. Or you can obtain a helpful and detailed free guide 'Planning for Inheritance Tax' from the financial advisers Chamberlain de Broe (tel 0171 434 4222).

A reminder: if your total estate after debts is likely to be worth over the inheritance tax limit (currently £215,000) then it may be worth taking measures to reduce this figure, such as leaving the first £215,000 of your estate directly to your children – so that your children will not be hit by the tax when your spouse dies. There are ways to set up trusts and to take out life insurance so as to reduce inheritance tax liability. One of the cleverest for a couple seems to be a life assurance investment bond, owned by one partner, who leaves it in trust for the children. It stays in force as long as one of the couple remains alive. The owner may draw income from the bond whilst alive, and the trustees can lend money to the partner after the owner's death (from an article by financial planner Colin McLachland of BDO Binder Hamlyn in Edinburgh, tel 0131 225 6366 – an accountancy firm which may refund to the client some of the high initial commission charges for such products).

A final warning from the 'Which?' book:

Pitfalls of d-i-y wills

The one thing worse than not making a will at all is making a mess of making a will. Many lawyers would say that they can make more money out of poor home-made wills than they do out of drawing up wills for clients. There is probably some truth in this. There are many ways in which people who prepare and sign their own will can go wrong. This can, later, lead to long and expensive court cases to resolve the matter, with enormous legal costs for the lawyers. This can reduce by staggering amounts the size of the estate to which the beneficiaries are entitled.

A will is a technical legal document; it is not surprising that some laymen go astray when they try to make a will unaided. If you have any doubts, you should seek a solicitor's advice.

From 'Wills and Probate' edited by the Consumers' Association.

Enduring Power of Attorney

At the same time as making a will, it is a good idea to fill in a form entitled 'Enduring Power of Attorney' (available from Oyez Stationery Ltd, 144 Fetter Lane, London EC4A 1BT, tel 0171 405 2847). This enables you to nominate one or more people to represent you at some future stage should you become mentally incapable of handling your affairs. Your form would only be officially registered with the Court of Protection if and when required. Filling in such a form in advance could save your relatives up to £1,000 a year or more, as otherwise a receiver would have to be appointed by the court. It could also place a friend between you and any local authority trying to extract money from your account to pay for the cost of your care in a residential home.

A pre-death information dossier

In the same envelope as your will it is worth including a dossier of information that will be helpful for your survivors, including perhaps this book and the Benefits Agency guide 'What to do after a death' (D49) and these details:

Registering a death – details needed

Address and phone number of the local register office (under 'R' in the phone book); your full name (exactly as on birth or marriage certificate); maiden name if a married woman; date and place of birth; home address; (last) occupation; full name and occupation of the husband (and in Scotland, the names and occupations of the spouse, male or female, and of all previous spouses and of the deceased's father; and whether the parents are alive); your NHS number; date of birth of your spouse; information about state or war pensions and allowances. Your birth and marriage certificates and NHS medical card (or at least its number) should also if possible be in this dossier, for taking along to the register office in due course.

Other helpful information you could leave for your relatives after your death could include some of the following:

Addresses, telephone numbers, account numbers, etc for: your bank; landlord; building society; credit cards; mortgage; house insurance; council rent department; local Benefits Agency office; local gas, electricity, water and telephone offices; life insurance; hire purchase agreements; debts or loans; car details; passport office; share certificate details (or the originals of these certificates); premium bonds; pension details; your doctor; your solicitor; your accountant; your stockbroker; your local inspector of taxes and your tax district and tax district reference number; your employers and professional associations; your main clients; your local priest or rabbi or British Humanist officiant or similar, depending on your religion or lack of it; those friends and relatives you would like invited to your funeral; which newspaper, if any, you would like your death announced in; what kind of funeral you would like; your preferred undertaker, if any; your burial rights if pre-bought.

Protecting your assets from community care charges

A local authority will give you a means test if it should prove necessary to assess your need for community care, irrespective of whether this care will be provided through a residential home or within your own home. Unless your total assets (which may include the value of your house) are less than £10,000, it can then charge you for these services (percentages of these charges apply to assets totalling less than £16,000). Your home may be at risk – the local authority can place a 'charge' on your home; it can bring bankruptcy proceedings against you. If you disburse your assets to avoid these risks, then *if* the local authority can show that you did so with avoidance as your main aim, it can force you to pay, however long ago you gave it all away.

You may want to pay your full contribution, in which case no preparation is required, but be aware that the average cost of nursing home care is about £18,000 per year at current prices.

If you do want to shelter your assets, you should get specialist advice, from organisations such as the Carers National Association or the Citizens Advice Bureau (see the Resources chapter) or from solicitors specialising in issues concerning old age, such as Jonathan Wilkey of Gwyn James & Co (Commercial St, Cinderford, Glos GL14 2RR, tel 01594 822277) – the latter is writing a book on this topic, provisionally entitled 'Preparing for Death' (ask your library or bookshop to look for it under the author's name). Ironically, however, once you start taking active measures, it would be more sensible to instruct a non-specialist solicitor, as this person's actions are less likely to be construed by the local authority as avoidance tactics than the use of schemes that have been marketed with this in mind. Other small tips include:

• Have a good and legitimate reason for giving away your assets.

• Do so as far ahead as possible.

• Spouses need to consider opening separate bank accounts, so that less remains in the account for assessment once you have begun paying charges.

• Joint owners of houses will be better protected if they sever any Joint Tenancy and create a Tenancy in Common.

• Consider adding the names of those family members living with you to the title deeds of the house, so reducing your part's value for assessment purposes.

• The value of your house may anyway be disregarded if the house is also lived in by your spouse, your partner or a relative who is incapacitated or over 60.

• Your children or heirs may prefer to club together to pay your care fees, rather than lose the house.

• Insurance policies are best written in trust, so that the proceeds will not be regarded as your capital.

• Your pension may be used to fund care fees, leaving your dependants in hardship. Options available include taking the maximum lump sum you can, so you can use this money to ensure your spouse's financial security, having the benefits transferred to another person, or going for a deferred annuity or phased retirement, so leaving funds in place for the future.

• Beware that if you give your house away to a relative, this person may die without making provision for you, or may go bankrupt or go through an expensive divorce – or he or she may lose their own entitlement to state benefits. It should also be someone you trust absolutely.

For further information, see the guide 'Care in the Community' available for £1-95 from Mature Tymes (Customer Interface Ltd, Bradley Pavilions, Bradley Stoke North, Bristol BS12 OBQ, tel 01454 620 070).

Simplifying your affairs before death

Anyone who has looked into the complexities of probate (the administration of your estate after death) will know that you can greatly simplify matters, before death and especially if death is imminent, by dividing your assets among the relevant beneficiaries. It should be more enjoyable too, making these gifts whilst still alive. Assets given to the spouse are not liable to inheritance tax (although they may be when the spouse comes to die); nor are small gifts of up to £250 per recipient; nor are gifts up to £3,000 in total per year (you may also be allowed a further £3,000 if your previous year's allowance was not used; and a marriage gift can be up to £5,000 to your own child); nor are assets liable that are given away more than seven years before death (such assets attract a proportion of the tax between three and seven years). If the family home is given to the children, however, the donor may either have to vacate the house or take a lease and pay rent, so as not to be benefiting from the gift (although a recent High Court judgement, against which the Inland Revenue is appealing, decided that a woman remaining rent-free in the house she had given her children did not attract inheritance tax). Note too that children who are given a house which is not their principal residence may pay out more as capital gains tax when they sell the house than they would have if they had simply paid inheritance tax instead.

If no precautions are taken, a spouse can be left with access to very little money, as death freezes (non-joint) bank accounts: so, if death is near, it is as well either to take money out of the bank or to open joint bank or building society accounts. Probate on stocks and shares – sending forms to lots of firms and all the minute accounting involved – is excessively complicated: again, if death is imminent, it might be as well to cash them in, or to transfer them into the name of one's spouse (more complicated this – 'Con40' stock transfer forms are obtainable from Oyez Stationery Ltd). In fact your executors may be able to avoid the whole problem of probate altogether if you leave behind you only cash and 'personal effects' (car, furniture, etc), having previously disposed of house, shares, bank accounts, pension arrears, etc. If you must maintain a personal store of money in your own name until your death, consider National Savings accounts at the post office, as these do not require a 'grant of probate or letters of administration'. Up to £5,000 in any of these can be handed over to the appropriate relative after death simply by that person filling in form DNS 904 from the post office and sending this in with a death certificate copy and, if relevant, a photocopy of the marriage certificate. Trustee Savings Bank investments may also be paid out if there is less than £5,000 in any one account.

If you can keep the total net worth of your estate (including any jointly owned property) at your death below £180,000 (the current figure, not to be confused with the £215,000 inheritance tax figure), your executors can avoid the Inland Revenue rules demanding a full account of the estate.

If you are taking out life insurance, make sure that it is 'written in trust', so that your beneficiaries can get the money out without waiting for probate.

Living Wills

Jackie Onassis drew up a 'Living Will', setting out that she wished to be allowed to die at home. Her Living Will was respected, and she died peacefully in her own bed, surrounded by friends and family. The Independent newspaper reported the background to such cases:

Among the most enduring of all horrors is the prospect of a slow, painful death. Those who witness the protracted terminal illness of a friend or relative often view the eventual death more as a relief than a tragedy.

An Advance Directive or Living Will sets out the kind of medical treatment a person wishes to receive, or not receive, should he or she ever be in a condition that prevents them expressing those wishes. Such documents, much in vogue in the USA and some Commonwealth countries, are becoming increasingly popular in Britain.

A clear distinction must be drawn between actions requested by an Advance Directive, and active euthanasia, or 'mercy killing'. A doctor who takes a positive step – such as giving a lethal injection – to help a patient die would, as the law stands, be guilty of murder.

An Advance Directive, however, requests only passive euthanasia: the withholding of medical treatment aimed solely at sustaining the life of a patient who is terminally ill or a 'vegetable'.

Thousands of people in the UK have lodged Advance Directives with their GPs.

Douglas Harding, a retired headmaster, is 63 and physically fit and active. He has completed an Advance Directive out of the desire to avoid a drawn-out, painful death like that suffered by his wife, who contracted cancer during pregnancy.

'It was clear from the beginning that she was going to die. But she had an appalling and very protracted death. By the time she died, she had only one breast, she had a lump on her head the size of an ostrich egg, she was blind, and her spine was twisted. I never want to suffer the same way,' he says.

Equally important to Douglas Harding is to maintain some control over the time and manner of his death. 'I'd like doctors always to treat me as a sensible being.'

Nuala Scarisbrick, a member of the Committee Against Euthanasia, believes Advance Directives are unnecessary – there is an increasing number of hospices providing the means for people to die with dignity – and are vulnerable to abuse. 'Advance directives are really about killing people. They are open to the danger of relatives colluding with an unethical doctor. It all comes down to money,' she says.

The enforceability of the Advance Directive stems from the notion, long accepted in English law, that a person who is both old enough to make an informed decision and *compos mentis* is entitled to refuse any medical treatment offered by a doctor, even if that refusal leads to the person's death. A doctor who forces treatment on a patient against his or her wishes is, therefore, guilty of an assault. Case law exists in the USA and several Commonwealth countries that extends this right of autonomy over one's life to patients who write an Advance Directive refusing treatment and subsequently lose their reason.

From an article by Simon Denison in The Independent.

The legal position of Living Wills

In 1994, the House of Lords Report of the Select Committee on Medical Ethics confirmed that Advance Directives were legally binding in the UK, despite the lack of specific legislation. These are extracts from the report:

182. There is at present no legislation governing Advance Directives, and their legal status has not been specifically tested in the United Kingdom. However the courts have pronounced on the subject from time to time, in particular in the case of *Re T (Adult: Refusal of Treatment)*, which was discussed in the evidence of the Centre of Medical Law and Ethics (pp 57, 58). In that case the judges in the Court of Appeal made it clear that they considered an anticipatory refusal of treatment to be binding, provided it fulfilled certain conditions. They were that the person concerned was competent, had contemplated the situation which later arose, appreciated the consequences of refusing treatment, and was not unduly influenced by another. More recently, in the case of *Bland v Airedale NHS Trust*, Lord Goff of Chieveley said 'it has been held that a patient of sound mind may, if properly informed, require that life support should be discontinued ... the same principle applies where the patient's refusal to give his consent has been expressed at an earlier date, before he became unconscious or otherwise incapable of communicating it'.

183. The Crown Prosecution Service said that if an incompetent patient had previously made an Advance Directive, 'doctors must abide by the terms of that previous expression of intention or wish, though special care may be necessary to ensure that any prior refusal of consent to medical treatment is still properly to be regarded as applicable in the circumstances which have subsequently occurred' (p 81). The Centre of Medical Law and Ethics said that 'when applicable, their [Advance Directives'] legal validity and binding force is now beyond question' (p 58). The Law Commission also regarded Advance Directives as 'recognised at common law, which does not permit treatment to be provided which the patient has previously refused', provided the conditions set out by *Re T* have been met (p 144).

184. In October 1993 the High Court ruling in *Re C* was greeted by some press reports as confirming the status of Advance Directives. C, a schizophrenic patient at Broadmoor Hospital, had a gangrenous leg for which his doctors proposed amputation. C refused consent to the operation. Since the hospital trust where he was being treated refused to undertake not to operate in future should C become incompetent, an injunction was sought forbidding the amputation now or in the future. The Court held that C was competent to make a decision about the proposed treatment and that his decision should continue to be binding even should he become incompetent, and issued an injunction. While the law is obviously in a state of rapid development, the case shows a move towards judicial recognition that the choice of a patient may have prospective as well as immediate effect.

The British Medical Association's view

In its 1995 booklet, 'Advance Statements About Medical Treatment', the British Medical Association warns doctors that they are legally obliged to obey a patient's advance refusal of medical treatment. Here are extracts from some of the main points and suggestions made:

13.4 If a health professional is involved in the management of a case and cannot for reasons of conscience accede to a patient's request for limitation of treatment, management of that patient must be passed to a colleague.

2.2 Competent, informed adults have an established legal right to refuse medical procedures in advance. An unambiguous and informed advance refusal is as valid as a contemporaneous decision.

6.5 Patients should be reminded about the desirability of reviewing their statements on a regular basis (eds: at least every five years), although a statement made long in advance is not automatically invalidated.

6.6 Patients should be advised to avoid rushing into specifying future treatments when they have only recently received a prognosis or when they may be unduly influenced by others or depressed.

7.4 Women of child bearing age should be advised to consider the possibility of their advance statement or directive being invoked at a time when they are pregnant. A waiver covering pregnancy might be written into the statement.

The BMA suggests that patients who have drafted an Advance Directive carry a card (eds: see the sample card in this chapter) indicating that fact as well as lodging a copy with their doctor.

Religious considerations

Deborah Duda's examination of the religious considerations for the United States is equally relevant to the UK:

If you are Catholic, you may already be aware that the June 1980 Declaration on Euthanasia concluded: 'When inevitable death is imminent, it is permitted in conscience to take the decision to refuse forms of treatment that would only secure a precarious and burdensome prolongation of life.' The United Methodist Church says, 'We assert the right of every person to die in dignity without efforts to prolong terminal illnesses merely because the technology is available to do so.' The Central Conference of American Rabbis said, 'The conclusion from the spirit of Jewish Law is that while you may not do anything to hasten death, you may, under special circumstances of suffering and helplessness, allow death to come.'

She also reports a study carried out by an American educational council into the effect a Living Will might have on a life insurance policy:

They reported that signing a Living Will would not invalidate any life insurance policy and would not be construed as an intent to commit suicide.

Insurance companies stand to save lots of money if people are not kept alive artificially for months or years in hospitals or nursing homes.

Reprinted with permission from 'Coming Home: A Guide to Dying at Home with Dignity', © 1987 Deborah Duda, Aurora Press, PO Box 573, Santa Fe, NM 87504, USA.

The following Living Will has been adapted by the Natural Death Centre from those put out by the Voluntary Euthanasia Society, the Terrence Higgins Trust and others. The Life Values Statement section is the copyright of Chris Docker, who works at the Voluntary Euthanasia Society of Scotland (VESS), and is an acknowledged expert on Advance Directives around the world.

You would be well advised to discuss your Living Will with your GP and to give or send your GP a copy; you may want to change doctor, if yours is particularly hostile to the Living Will concept. You should also leave a copy with your will and with your closest relative or friend. If you go into hospital for any serious reason, you can show it to your doctor or ward sister there and have a copy put in your notes. You may want to update the form every so often, especially if you have a progressive illness – even if just to sign (and to get witnessed) the statement (at the end) to the effect that it still represents your wishes. Strike out any words or phrases which you do not wish to apply to your case, add anything you wish – or write your own version entirely.

The Life Values Statement (Part Two) may help doctors to decide what you would have wanted in circumstances that are not covered by your Living Will.

If you appoint representatives (see below) these should be people whom you trust absolutely, especially if they would benefit financially from your death.

Living Will & Life Values Statement

TO MY FAMILY, MY DOCTOR, MY HEALTH CARE TEAM, MY SOLICITOR AND ALL OTHER PERSONS CONCERNED. This Living Will and Life Values Statement are made by me at a time when I am of sound mind and after careful consideration. In the event of a clash of interpretations, I wish my Living Will (Part One) to take precedence over my Life Values Statement (Part Two)..

Part One: Living Will

I wish to be fully informed about any illness I may have, about treatment alternatives and likely outcomes.

I DECLARE that if at any time the following circumstances exist, namely:

(1) I suffer from one or more of the conditions mentioned in the schedule below; and

(2) I have become unable to participate effectively in decisions about my medical care; and

(3) two independent physicians (at least one a consultant) are of the expert, considered opinion, after a full examination of my case, that I am

unlikely to make a substantial recovery from illness or impairment which involve severe distress or incapacity for rational existence,

THEN AND IN THOSE CIRCUMSTANCES my directions are as follows:

(1) that I am not to be subjected to any medical intervention or treatment aimed at prolonging or sustaining my life – such as life support systems; artificial ventilation; antibiotics; surgery; using a kidney machine; or blood transfusion.

(2) that any distressing symptoms (including any caused by lack of food) are to be fully controlled by appropriate analgesic or other treatment, even though that treatment may shorten my life.

(3) that I am not to be tube fed into the stomach or vein; nor artificially hydrated (although I wish my mouth to be kept moistened).

(4) that I wish to be allowed to spend my last days at home if at all possible.

I consent to anything proposed to be done or omitted in compliance with the directions expressed above and absolve my medical attendants from any form of litigation arising out of such acts or omissions.

I wish to be as conscious as my circumstances permit (allowing for adequate pain control) as death approaches. I ask my medical attendants to bear this statement in mind when considering what my intentions would be in any uncertain situation.

I RESERVE the right to revoke this DIRECTIVE at any time, but unless I do so it should be taken to represent my continuing directions.

SCHEDULE

A Advanced disseminated malignant disease (eg a cancer that has spread considerably).

B Severe immune deficiency (eg AIDS).

C Advanced degenerative disease of the nervous system (eg advanced Parkinson's Disease).

D Severe and lasting brain damage due to injury, stroke, disease or other cause.

E Senile or pre-senile dementia, whether Alzheimer's, multi-infarct or other.

F Any other condition of comparable gravity.

My additional instructions (if any, such as pregnancy waiver) are:

....

....

Part Two: Life Values Statement

This Life Values Statement gives indications of the personal value I attach to my life under various circumstances. I ask my health care team to bear these in mind when making decisions about my treatment or non-treatment, especially in situations not covered by Part One above. Where I have indicated that life under such circumstances would be 'much worse than death', this means that I would find the situation totally unbearable and unacceptable, and that I would prefer all life-sustaining treatment to be stopped or withdrawn rather than to exist for the rest of my life in such a state.

[*Instructions. Please give a number to the circumstances below as follows:*

1 = 'Much worse than death: I would definitely not want life-sustaining treatment.'

2 = 'Somewhat worse than death: I would probably not want life-sustaining treatment.'

3 = 'Neither better nor worse than death: I am not sure whether I would want life-sustaining treatment.'

4 = 'Somewhat better than death: I would probably want life-sustaining treatment.'

5 = 'Much better than death: I would definitely want life-sustaining treatment.']

(a) Permanently paralysed. You are unable to walk but can move around in a wheelchair. You can talk and interact with other people.

My number for this is ....

(b) Permanently unable to speak meaningfully. You are unable to speak to others. You can walk on your own, feed yourself and take care of daily needs such as bathing and dressing yourself.

My number for this is ....

(c) Permanently unable to care for yourself. You are bedridden, unable to wash, feed, or dress yourself. You are totally cared for by others.

My number for this is ....

(d) Permanently in pain. You are in severe bodily pain that cannot be totally controlled or completely eliminated by medications.

My number for this is ....

(e) Permanently mildly demented. You often cannot remember things, such as where you are, nor reason clearly. You are capable of speaking, but not capable of remembering the conversations; you are capable of washing, feeding and dressing yourself and are in no pain.

My number for this is ....

(f) Being in a short term coma. You have suffered brain damage and are not conscious and are not aware of your environment in any way. You cannot feel pain. You are cared for by others. These mental impairments may be reversed in about one week leaving mild forgetfulness and loss of memory as a consequence.

My number for this is ....

I have lodged a copy of this declaration with the following doctor, who is/is not my GP, with whom I have/have not discussed its contents :

Name
Address

Tel No

Should I become unable to communicate my wishes as stated above and should amplification be required, I appoint the following person to represent these wishes on my behalf and I want this person to be consulted by those caring for me and for this person's representation of my views to be respected:

Name
Address

Tel No

If this person named above is unable to act in my behalf, I authorise the following person to do so:

Name
Address

Tel No

MY SIGNATURE   Date
My name
My address

WE TESTIFY that the above-named signed this document in our presence, and made it clear to us that he/she understood what it meant. We do not know of any pressure being brought on him/her to make such a declaration and we believe it was made by his/her own wish. We are over 18, we are not relatives of the above-named, nor do we stand to gain from his/her death.

Witnessed by: [two witnesses]

Signature:	Signature:
Name:	Name
Address	Address:

FOR RENEWING DOCUMENT IN LATER YEARS:
I reaffirm the contents of all my statements above.

MY SIGNATURE   Date

Witnessed by: [two witnesses]

Signature:	Signature:
Name:	Name:
Address:	Address:

If you fill in the part appointing a person to represent your wishes on your behalf, it should be someone whom you trust absolutely, especially if they stand to inherit under your will.

If you would like to see the 'Advance Medical Directive' from which the Living Will is adapted, contact the Voluntary Euthanasia Society (VES), 13

Prince of Wales Terrace, London W8 5PG (tel 0171 937 7770) or the Voluntary Euthanasia Society of Scotland (VESS), 17 Hart Street, Edinburgh EH1 3RN (tel 0131 556 4404). They have further interesting information on this topic on their Internet site at the location <http://www.netlink.co.uk/users/vess/vh.html>. (In Scotland a 'tutor dative', a legally enforceable proxy, can be appointed by the court; and witnesses are not needed, it is sufficient to sign, writing above your signature the words 'adopted as holograph'.) The Life Values Statement is © Chris Docker (BM718, London WC1N 3XX, UK) – although the layout in the version above has been altered. The Terrence Higgins Trust Living Will is available from 52-54 Gray's Inn Road, London WC1X 8JU (tel 0171 831 0330). For a copy of the set of forms that includes the above Living Will, please send four first class stamps to cover expenses to: The Natural Death Centre, 20 Heber Road, London NW2 6AA (tel 0181 208 2853; fax 0181 452 6434).

Living Will
summary
to carry
around
with your
credit
cards

> **LIVING WILL:** I have made a Living Will stating, inter alia, that, if terminally ill, I do not wish to have my life prolonged by medical interventions. This Living Will is lodged with Dr...
> Tel.. and with my
> proxy ....
> Tel...

Alongside or instead of the legally-worded version above, you may like to write your own informal Natural Death Instructions. Here, for instance, is a wonderfully idiosyncratic version written by Scott Nearing (and honoured in the event by his wife – see the chapter on 'Brave and Conscious Deaths').

Natural Death Instructions

This memorandum is written in order to place on record the following requests:

1. When it comes to my last illness I wish the death process to follow its natural course; consequently:

a. I wish to be at home not in a hospital.

b. I prefer that no doctor should officiate. The medics seem to know little about life, and next to nothing about death.

c. If at all possible, I wish to be outside near the end; in the open, not under a roof.

d. I wish to die fasting; therefore, as death approaches I would prefer to abstain from food.

2. I wish to be keenly aware of the death process; therefore, no sedatives, painkillers, or anaesthetics.

3. I wish to go quickly, and as quietly as possible. Therefore:

a. No injections, heart stimulants, forced feeding, no oxygen, and especially no blood transfusions.

b. No expressions of regret or sorrow, but rather, in the hearts and actions of those who may be present, calmness, dignity, understanding, joy, and peaceful sharing of the death experience.

c. Manifestation is a vast field of experience. As I have lived eagerly and fully, to the extent of my powers, so I pass on gladly and hopefully. Death is either a transition or an awakening. In either case it is to be welcomed, like every other aspect of the life process.

4. The funeral and other incidental details:

a. Unless the law requires, I direct that no undertaker, mortician, or other professional manipulator of corpses be consulted, be called in, or participate in any way in the disposal of my body.

b. I direct that as soon as convenient after my death my friends place my body in a plain wooden box made of spruce or pine boards; the body to be dressed in working clothes, and to be laid on my sleeping bag. There is to be no ornament or decoration of any kind in or on the box.

c. The body so dressed and laid out to be taken to the Auburn, Maine crematorium of which I am a paid member, and there cremated privately.

d. No funeral services are to be held. Under no circumstances is any preacher, priest, or other professional religionist to officiate at any time or in any way between death and the disposal of the ashes.

e. As soon as convenient after cremation, I request my wife, Helen K. Nearing, or if she predecease me or not be able to, some other friend to take the ashes and scatter them under some tree on our property facing Spirit Cove.

5. I make all these requests in full consciousness and the hope that they will be respected by those nearest to me who may survive me.

Excerpted from 'Loving and Leaving the Good Life', © 1992 by Helen Nearing, with the permission of Chelsea Green Publishing Company, Post Mills, VT 05058, USA.

Choosing the attitude

Most people die at the end of a period of illness. Someone who is going to die has the right, so far as possible, to choose the circumstances, particularly where it will take place. But even when we can no longer control the circumstances of our living and dying, we can still decide on our attitude, as Deborah Duda writes:

Choice of attitude – the ultimate freedom

When we can no longer control the circumstances of our lives, we can still control our attitude about them. We can choose our attitude about dying. We can choose to see it as a tragedy, teacher, adventure, or simply as an experience to be lived. Our attitude will determine the nature of our experience.

When we choose to surrender to life, we are free; and when we are free, we are in control. This paradox lies at the heart of our human existence.

To surrender and to be free we have to accept life as it is instead of holding on to how we think it should be. We can't change something we don't first accept. Surrender and acceptance are not to be confused with resignation and succumbing. Resignation and succumbing are passive – something just overpowered or overcame us and we had no choice but to give up. Resignation is self-pity and believing the illusion that we're powerless. Acceptance and surrender, on the other hand, are positive acts. 'I choose to let go, to give up control and accept life as it is. And there will be things I can change and things I can't.'

If we deny dying and death, we're prisoners to them. When we accept them, we're free and regain the power lost in resisting them. We let go of our resistance by letting go. It's easy to do and can be hard to get ready to do. The choice to let go must be made in the heart. A choice made only in the head, unsupported by the body, feelings and soul, is unlikely to be carried out.

If we remember that choice of attitude, the ultimate freedom, is always available, we make a spacious place in which to experience dying. We can be free whether we are dying ourselves or sharing in the dying of someone we love. We can be free whether we die at home or in a hospital. Choosing our attitude is easier at home than in an atmosphere that unconsciously says dying should be isolated from life and is, therefore, not OK.

Reprinted with permission from 'Coming Home: A Guide to Dying at Home with Dignity', © 1987 Deborah Duda, Aurora Press, PO Box 573, Santa Fe, NM 87504, USA.

More specifically, you can discuss with your family and friends how you would like to die. Henry Tennant, an Aids patient, made up a list of simple demands for how he wanted to die. Some of these he was able to arrange himself, for some he needed his friends and helpers to be aware of his wishes. Allegra Taylor reports his reflections:

'I want to die chanting'

As I become iller, AIDS becomes my life. I long to take a holiday from it – from waking every morning feeling so lousy. But you have to accept the reality of your life and then create maximum value out of what you've got. I'm so much helped by my Buddhism because it gives me a strong and vibrant focal point which is not AIDS.

I want to die in a state of true happiness. I want to die chanting. I want to be in control of my death and have people with me who know what kind of spiritual atmosphere I would like around me.

It's a pity that society's current taboo about death, particularly untimely death, is denying us all an invaluable source of learning and personal development. We need death to savour life. Do what you can in the time you have. You can't expect to be 'normal' again once you're diagnosed with AIDS, but accept the fact that you can be changed by it.

From 'Acquainted with the Night' by Allegra Taylor.

Your wishes may take more specific, personal or light-hearted forms. How would you like to spend your last few weeks? Would you go on one final holiday? Would you take up smoking right at the end? Would you write rude letters to your bank manager? Would you want a bench in your memory? What would you want to say to your family and friends? Is some of it worth saying now? What would your loved ones have to remember you by? A tape of your voice, a home movie? If it enabled you to be utterly decadent for just one month or one week or one day, what would you want to do? Eat at an expensive restaurant? Swim with dolphins? Meet your hero(-ine)?

This is where the death plan comes in – it is similar to a birth plan and indicates what a person would ideally like in terms of atmosphere and environment as he or she lie dying. Of course no one can be sure how they will die or whether such a plan in the event will be of any relevance, and they may change their minds when the time comes; but nevertheless, a death plan may help friends and relatives to know one's orientation and wishes.

In the hope of encouraging readers to improve on the following list, or to send in their sample filled-in versions of this list, or to write a list of their own, here is a first attempt at a Death Plan. [An A4 copy of this form is part of the Natural Death Centre's set of forms mentioned at the end of the Living Will. Separate sheets can be used for longer responses, using the numbers below to refer your responses back to. Underline or tick or cross out or amplify as relevant. This form can be photocopied for personal use.]

Death Plan

(1) If my condition is terminal I would like to be told the full details / plus implications of treatment and non-treatment / a summary / not to be told at all / other [specify].

(2) If possible, I would / would not like the doctor to tell me a guess as to how much time I might have left, the best and worst cases, and the average.

(3) I imagine I would / would not like every effort to be made to find alternative medicine and approaches / latest medical breakthroughs that might give me a miraculous last-minute remission.

(4) I have / have not made a Living Will, specifying how much high tech medical intervention I wish for when dying and whether or not I wish to be force fed [if yes, the location of this Living Will].

(5) I imagine that I will / will not choose to fast as death approaches.

(6) If possible, when I am dying I would like to be cared for at
.... [location, whether hospital, hospice, at home, indoors, outdoors, etc].

(7) I would like to be surrounded by .... [flowers,
nature, photos, mementoes, etc].

(8) My next of kin is [name, address, phone number].

(9) If I go into hospital / when I die, what I would like to happen to my
pets is ....

(10) I would / would not like for close relatives / friends / everyone to be
told that I am terminally ill.

(11) Those friends or relatives who I would most like to be involved in
my nursing care are ....

(12) I would like .... to be able to sleep in the same
room / bed as me.

(13) I may change my mind, but I imagine I would / would not like
visitors when near the end. The ones I would particularly like to visit me
include .... [give addresses and phone numbers if
necessary].

(14) I would / would not like to be left as alone as possible when dying.

(15) I imagine that I would / would not like to discuss the fact that I am
dying with these visitors, and would / would not like to make explicit the
possibility that these are final goodbyes.

(16) My religion / spiritual practice / philosophy is mainly
.... and therefore for my dying I would like
....

(17) Depending on my medical condition and feelings at the time, the
kind of ministrations I might appreciate when dying include:

(18) Music. My favourite pieces would be ....
[state specific music or broad range].

(19) Live singing, chanting, hymns, psalms, particular prayers or
texts, etc [as specific as desired].

(20) Physical contact [eg hand held].

(21) Massage.

(22) Aromatherapy [or other such approaches].

(23) The person(s) I would most like to be there at the moment of my
death is / are ....

(24) I would like to be as conscious / unconscious as possible as I die, and
would like pain control prescribed accordingly. The drugs I imagine I might
appreciate include .... [specific or class of drugs].

(25) For the moment of my death I would / would not like all life support
machinery and monitors disconnected from my body.

Signed by:
Name
Signature
Date

This signing is witnessed by the two undersigned, neither of whom stand to benefit from the signatory's Will:

Name of first witness
Signature
Witness's occupation and address
Name of second witness
Signature
Witness's occupation and address

Dying wishes

It is worth remembering that 'dying wishes' or messages can assume extreme importance for those you leave behind. It gives them a way of giving to you when you are no longer there. It may be a focus for meaningful or constructive activity when everything is falling to pieces. It can be a creative and humorous act of warmth which proves long-enduring. Death has an uncanny way of freezing certain memories and moments; if they are happy and loving they will prove repeated comfort for the people who mourn you. A difficult request ('I want to be buried in Bolivia') or prohibition ('Don't marry that ghastly man') will stick too!

Your family will have to make certain decisions as to your funeral arrangements: should you be buried or cremated or buried at sea? What sort of casket should they use? What sort of service? What should be the tone of the wake, if there is one? If your spouse, partner or family is aware of your wishes, at least in general, it could save them considerable distress about 'getting it right'.

In her workshops Christianne Heal encourages people to consider the art of funeral preparation.

Imaginative sendoffs

Everyone knew it wasn't the done thing to plan your own funeral, but, said Christianne, most of us put plenty of effort into organising weddings and christening parties, so why did funeral parties have to be such thrown-together, dismal affairs?

Thus prompted, ideas for imaginative sendoffs flowed thick and fast. Bridget wanted a pub crawl for all her friends, followed by a short service at a harbour during which her body would be thrown into the sea. Peter wanted a funeral *al fresco,* preferably on a hillside, with a ragtime band playing his favourite melodies. Monica said she would like a 'green' funeral, with her body buried in a biodegradable bag rather than a tree-wasting coffin. Christianne suggested that anyone with ideas of how they'd want their funeral to be conducted ought to write them down and leave them with a close family member. 'Families have enough to think about after a death without spending hours trying to imagine what the dead person would or wouldn't have wanted at their funeral.'

From an article by Joanna Moorhead,
Weekend Guardian (Aug. 25th 1990).

Liz has gone further, and has taped her own funeral service in advance:

Taping my own funeral

A little of myself: I am a nurse (well-qualified) of 33 years standing and have personally experienced the death of countless people in the last few years while working full-time with terminally ill patients in their own homes and in nursing homes. This has made a lasting impression on me and always raised the question within myself of how I would cope with all the eventualities that certain death, at whatever age, would entail.

It wasn't until I found myself comparatively recently in the throes of emphysema and kidney failure (it chokes me to write the words) with a considerably shortened life expectancy that I had to look at my exit from this world and what I wanted for friends and loved ones.

It has been, and still is, a painful and saddening thought, but there is so much I have, and can still do. I have my will organised, my personal wealth (that's a laugh!) and treasured belongings all listed and named for the beneficiaries. As regards the funeral service I have chosen what means the most to me and I am sure in many ways my friends and those regular worshippers on a Sunday will no doubt raise an eyebrow. The easiest part was my choice of music: a recording of Lloyd-Webber's 'Pie Jesu' because the beauty of clarity and pureness exudes from this work and provides vital uplifting of the soul. Second, a hymn sung by the congregation 'Crimond – The Lord's My Shepherd'(hopefully with descant). As a finale, a recording of 'Now is the Hour' sung by the Maoris of New Zealand. I would like to share how these pieces in particular, and music in general, have often enabled me to transcend severe physical pain. Having made a positive decision on this and the readings I want I sat back – it was something else marked off the agenda.

Some time later whilst listening to music and in pain, I reflected again on those that I would leave behind. It eased the pain, my belief that this life is only a stage, a platform, and that each step takes us into a different realm, and from each of these, lessons are learnt in betterment of the soul and spirit. At this point it became of vital importance that I left messages of love and hope and thanks to those who had greatly influenced my life. For this, the obvious way was by incorporating into the service my own voice on tape, for however good, nobody can convey the uniqueness of the human voice, the intonation and inflection and the vocal mannerisms that we associate with a particular person. It was also important to me that my voice be known not clouded by analgesics – the clarity should be unmistakable, so that at my farewell my friends will experience the love and sincerity I feel for them. It will be a service of joy not sadness: after all, I will be hovering above and overseeing all! God help them!

To end this letter, I recognise how painful saying goodbye will be, and many will find it hard – I can hear it now: 'Don't talk about it,' 'Some cure may be found,' or 'I don't want to hear.' I understand, I've used those words myself. My way, of speaking to everybody and to some personally, in my final farewell, and offering my favourite music, will perhaps ease the heartbreak and the tears and help my friends, who have known me in this life, to begin to see me as – I hope – a celestial being! Still Liz, saying, 'Talk to me – say goodbye now. I love you always. I'll be waiting to meet you again later on, and God bless you all.'

My tears have flowed in the writing of this as they have flowed in making the arrangements for my funeral and death.

From a letter to The Natural Death Centre.

A simple note left with your will may be all you wish to leave to express your funeral wishes, or even to state that funeral arrangements are not important to you, that there is no 'right way'.

Advance Funeral Wishes

The following may stimulate you to think of the kind of funeral you might or might not like; and will help to make sure that those who may be responsible in the event will know your wishes. Where sample prices are given below, these are 1996 prices. Suggested improvements to this form are welcomed. See also The Natural Death Centre's Death Plan form for requirements whilst dying, and the Centre's Living Will form. [Separate sheets can be used for longer responses, using the numbers below to refer your responses back to. Underline or tick or cross out or rewrite or amplify, as relevant. This form can be photocopied for personal use.]

(1) I have / have not written a Will [location....................... ....] which expresses / does not express my funeral wishes. [If there is such a Will] Please treat this present document as expanding on the wishes expressed in that Will, with the Will taking legal precedence if relevant.

(2) My next of kin is [name, address, phone number].

(3) With this Will / this present document is also added all potentially needed information such as NHS card, birth and marriage certificates, bank account details, credit cards, hire purchase agreements, mortgage and home insurance details, council rent department, local gas, electricity, water and telephone offices, life insurance, car details, share certificate details, premium bonds, pension details, details of doctor, solicitor, accountant, stockbroker, employer, main clients. Also my home address, my last occupation, full name and occupation of spouse and my maiden name [if a married woman]. Plus any deeds to a grave.

(4) I have / do not have any preferences about what happens to my body. [If no preferences] I leave it all entirely in the discretion of
....

(5) I do / do not wish to donate my body / my organs [specify which and to whom, if relevant; those to contact include the NHS Organ Donor Register, PO Box 14, Patchway, Bristol BS12 6BR (tel 0117 975 7575); and the HM Inspector of Anatomy, tel 0171 972 4342, re body donation].

(6) If possible, I wish my body left undisturbed after my death for .... hours / days.

(7) Nurses attending the death normally lay out the body, but I would like it very much if .... could also assist / do this instead.

(8) If a postmortem after my death requires the consent of my next of kin, I would like them to give it / not to give it.

(9) I would / would not like my body to be brought back to my home after death / to remain at home until the funeral if I die at home / to remain in the hospital or other establishment's mortuary if possible / to go to a funeral director offering a refrigeration service.

(10) I do / do not wish for my body to be embalmed [incidentally, sea burial is not permitted for embalmed bodies].

(11) I have / do not have a prepaid funeral plan / funeral insurance scheme [if so, please give details and make sure your next of kin are aware of the existence of this plan. Some of what follows may then not be relevant in your case].

(12) The friend(s) or relative(s) I wish to be mainly responsible for arranging my funeral is / are ....

(13) I would / would not prefer for the above-named to arrange it without using a funeral director [if using a funeral director some of what follows may then not be relevant in your case].

(14) If a funeral director is used, I would like it to be .... / I would like someone to phone around the yellow pages for the cheapest / most suitable funeral director's quote / I would like someone to phone The Natural Death Centre (tel 0181 208 2853) to see if they have a recommendation for a helpful funeral director locally.

(15) In general terms, I would like the expenditure on my funeral to be about average [£1,000 in 1996] / below average / well below average / above average / well above average.

(16) I would like to be cremated / buried [for burial options see (26) below] / deposited in a vault / catacomb / mausoleum.

(17) I would like the cheapest chipboard with veneer coffin [from about £100 incl. delivery] / painted coffin [from about £300] / coffin made of recycled wood [about £500] / cardboard coffin [if allowed by the funeral establishment concerned; from about £55] / body bag on plank and covered in drape [if allowed by the establishment concerned; from about £15] / coffin, if possible made by friend or relative or local carpenter [specify any details] / my coffin is already in store waiting [location] / burial shroud / burial sheet / willow coffin [about £250, advance commission advisable] / other.

(18) I would like my body to be transported to the relevant place in our / a friend's large estate car / van [give details where relevant] / I would like a large estate car / small van to be hired for the occasion / I would like a funeral director to be asked to supply a hearse with / without following cars / I would like a horse-drawn hearse [normally from about £600] / other transport [specify].

(19) I would ideally like .... as the bearers of my coffin.

(20) I would / would not like flowers brought to my funeral / one flower per person / no flowers / donation instead to ....

(21) I would / would not like my death and funeral announced in the following publications ....

(22) I would / would not like a funeral service.

If to be cremated:

(23) I would like my funeral service [if having one] to take place at a church / other venue [specify] before my body is delivered to the crematorium [if a double service in this way, state what if anything is to happen at the crematorium and who is to attend there] / I would like the funeral service to take place at the crematorium.

(24) After cremation, what I would ideally like done with my ashes is ....

(25) [If an urn to be used] The kind of urn I would most like is .... home-made by .... / standard crematorium container / wooden / marble / china [advance commission advisable] / other.

If to be buried:

(26) I do / do not have a burial place reserved / in mind [details if so]. I would like to be buried in a churchyard / cemetery / green burial ground where a tree is planted instead of having a headstone / friendly farmer's land / own garden or land / at sea [please give added details where relevant.] [Note that sea burial is difficult to arrange as the Ministry of Agriculture and Fisheries goes out of its way to discourage it; done through a funeral director it is also very expensive. Contact The Natural Death Centre on 0181 208 2853 for details.]

(27) If own garden or land, although not legally obliged to, I have / have not cleared this with those who will inherit my estate, also / but not with other next of kin / neighbours etc.

(28) If green burial ground, I would / would not like those in charge of my funeral to phone an information source such as The Natural Death Centre (tel 0181 208 2853) or the AB Wildlife Trust Fund in Harrogate (tel 01423 530900) to find out the nearest or most suitable site at the time of my death [given that so many new ones are opening all the time]. I would prefer such a site to be run by a local authority / farmer / wildlife trust / doesn't matter.

(29) If allowed, I would / would not like .... [names] to help dig my grave / fill my grave.

If having a funeral service:

(30) Amongst those I would most like invited who might otherwise be neglected are .... [names and addresses and phone numbers].

(31) The kind of numbers I would like at my funeral service are

.... I see it as ideally a very small family affair / family and friends / all comers.

(32) I would like a funeral service to take account of the fact that my religion / spiritual belief / philosophy is ....

(33) I would like the service led by .... [relative / friend / named or duty priest / minister / rabbi / British Humanist Association officiant / other].

(34) The form of service I would like is ....

(35) The kind of music, hymns, psalms, songs etc I would like include .... [be as specific as you like] played by / sung by ....

(36) The kind of texts / poems I would like include .... read by ....

(37) If possible I would like a main address about my life given by .... or by ....

(38) At this service / at some later occasion [specify] I would / would not like my friends to have a chance to speak up about me.

(39) I would / would not like an open coffin [assuming body is relatively presentable].

(40) Other rituals I would like to see at this time include .... [eg single flowers placed in coffin / grave lined with hay, flowers / football scarf or other identifying symbol placed on or in coffin].

(41) I have / have not left a last message / audiotape / video or other text for my family or friends [if yes, location], and wish for this to be played at the funeral service / some other occasion [specify].

Party or gathering after funeral

(42) I would / would not like a party / gathering after the funeral.

(43) [Assuming one is wanted] In general terms, I would like as much money spent on a gathering after the funeral as on the funeral itself / less money / much less money / more money / much more money.

(44) The form I would like this gathering to take is .... [indoors / outdoors / location / food / drinks / etc].

(45) The rituals I would most like it to include are ....

Memorial service

(46) I would / would not like a memorial gathering some .... months after the funeral.

(47) The form I would like this memorial gathering to take is ....

(48) The rituals I would most like it to include are ....

(49) Those who may not have come to the funeral that I would like invited to the memorial service include ....

(50) I would like the memorial service announced in the following media ....

Commemoration

(51) I would / would not like a tree / flowers [specify kind of tree or flowers] planted on / near grave / other location, in memory of me.

(52) Memorial objects or ways of commemoration I would ideally like include: entry in memorial book of funeral establishment / plaque / headstone [suggest wording of epitaph] / garden bench / window / book / entry in one of the Internet's online Gardens of Remembrance / endowment [details].

(53) I would / would not like there if possible to be a ritual or remembrance on the anniversaries of my death. Ideally the form this could take would be ....

(54) Amongst things left unsaid to particular people that I would like to say now are: ....

(55) I shall find out for sure in due course, but as a matter of interest, I do / do not believe in an afterlife, which I visualise as ....

Signed by:
Name
Signature
Date
Witnessed by the two undersigned who do not stand to benefit from the signatory's Will:
Names
Signatures
Witnesses' occupations
and addresses

For a copy of a similar set of forms to those in this chapter, please send four first class stamps to cover expenses to: The Natural Death Centre, 20 Heber Road, London NW2 6AA (tel 0181 208 2853).

Widow's budget

Some people choose to leave informal instructions which go beyond funeral arrangements. When Stan Chisman learned that he had cancer, writes his wife Margaret:

> His first thought was to draw up a 'Widow's Budget' to see if I would have to sell this house, but with economy and no really bad inflation we found it would be possible for me to continue to live here.
>
> *From 'Interim' by Margaret Chisman.*

A will covers the legal allocation of your property and the legal guardianship of your children. A Living Will covers your wishes in case of debilitating, intractable illness. There is a wealth of other matters in which you might like a say, or to leave guidance for your family and friends:

Do you have an organ donor card? Does anybody know? (See the Good

Funeral Guide chapter on how to offer your body after death.) By contrast, is the idea against your wishes?

Do you want to leave a message for your spouse, family or friends? Letting go of their loss will be a slow and painful process. Is there a simple way of telling them that it's OK to let go?

Are there any obvious conflicts which could be avoided? You will not be able to tell someone how much you love them, to forgive them, or let them know that in fact you weren't as angry with them as you made out. Are you willing to relax some of the views for which you are known after your death? Carrying on with life after losing someone is hard enough, without having to try not to step on their toes!

Can you make it easier for your partner or spouse eventually to move on to a new phase in their life, perhaps changing their job, interests, home or town? Do they know that you don't mind their eventually finding someone else, if that's the case? Compassion exercised from beyond the grave could be a last loving act which spares your circle of loved ones a great deal of distress.

Christianne Heal includes in her workshops exercises to help people focus on what they would want to say.

Rehearsing last goodbyes

Alison, a student in her early twenties, was trying to voice the words she knew she should speak to her mother. They had never been close, she explained. Her mother always seemed distant, more interested in her younger brother than in her. 'I don't know how to begin – we've just never had that kind of conversation,' she said haltingly. Her partner nodded sagely. 'Do it,' she said. 'However hard it is, try to talk to her. My mother and I didn't get on very well, but now she's dead there's so much I wish I'd ...' 'That's it,' said Christianne triumphantly. 'The end of the exercise. Please stop talking straight away. Death, when it comes, won't allow you to finish your sentence.'

From an article by Joanna Moorhead,
Weekend Guardian (Aug. 25th 1990).

I didn't know what to say . . .

So far we have looked at ways of 'preparing' ourselves for death, our own training for dying. What do you say when someone tells you that a loved one of theirs is dying – or that they themselves are dying? Many of us find ourselves caught between the feeling that there's nothing we can really do to help and the fear of upsetting the person by touching their pain, so instead we just gloss over the subject. In the chapter on 'Improving Grieving', we quote Jean Baker explaining how other people's reactions to her husband's death were often to 'cross the road if they saw me coming'. Her advice on how to relate to the recently-bereaved is equally relevant for supporting the dying person and the family: 'The most helpful thing people can do is listen, just let you talk and be compassionate. People think it will hurt you to talk. Or they fear they will be reminding you – as if you had forgotten.'

If you are not someone's close friend or relative, there is a tendency to think that the dying or bereaved person is best looked after by that close network of support, and that it is best not to interfere. There is also perhaps even the fear of being 'landed' with someone else's grief. However, people in such circumstances can experience this as being ostracised. At the time when most they need to be connected to their community, they are hermetically sealed within a bubble of pain, along with the few friends who have the courage to step inside it with them. They may, of course, have chosen to isolate themselves. Either way, the gentle reassurance that you are still there, that you can tolerate their talking about their grief, even that you are not afraid of them, made through words or a gesture, will make a difference and gives them a choice. If you are stuck for words, would a hug not do?

Our wider community

Preparing for dying is not just about ourselves. We have still a long way to go as a society. It is not hard to see that we accord many of the same prejudices, fears and apprehensions to the issues of illness in general, and ageing, that we do to dying. Why is it that so many people assume the role of the 'elderly' when their minds and bodies are fit enough to allow them to expect so much more from life? Why do people hide the terrible suffering of long illness? Why, as a society, do we contract our caring for, and management of, illness and dying out to other people, and then refuse to become involved ourselves? Why is it that some of us deal with the problems of hundreds of dying people, and the rest of us barely see death?

Chapter 3
PRACTICAL CARE
AT HOME

Facts and figures

In a recent study, 54% of deaths occurred in hospital, 13% in nursing or residential homes, 4% in hospices and 23% at home. The percentage dying in hospital has gone up over the years – in 1960 it was less than 50%.

Pam Williams discussed this trend in her nurse's dissertation:

As a result of changes in family structure – smaller families, more mobile society, women working, unemployment and poverty – it is harder for families to cope with caring for the dying at home, even though it is generally accepted that most people wish to die in a familiar surrounding, and that the home environment (even with limitations) is the 'ideal' place to die.

The same study cites the aim of the World Health Organisation's 'Global Strategy of Health for All by the Year 2000', that

Everyone should be afforded dignity and comfort at the time of death. By the year 2000, all those dying who are in contact with health and social services should be able to choose where they spend their last days, and, wherever that is, they should be able to expect optimal pain relief, physical comfort and psychological support from professionals.

It needs pointing out, to put these matters in perspective, that 50% of deaths in Britain are sudden. Here we are concerned with slow deaths, the dying process. Studies show that hospital nurses have more difficulty managing slow than quick dying.

The hospice movement offers great expertise in the care of the terminally ill, 'both inside their walls, and through staff such as Macmillan nurses going out into the community to give support to patients and relatives at home. But since the modern hospice owes its being and related service development to major cancer charities, the emphasis is on support for patients dying of cancer. Yet 75% of people who die do not have cancer\'.

That home for many is the preferred place to die is confirmed by a study of home care services as an alternative to hospices:

Information provided by the carers three months after the patient's death indicated that patients who died at home preferred this, while half the patients who died in a hospice or hospital would have preferred to have been at home.

> *From 'Home Care Services – an Alternative to Hospices?' by*
> *Audrey W. M. Ward, in Community Medicine Vol. 9 No. 1.*

A 1993 Gallup Poll in America found that nine out of ten respondents, if faced with a terminal illness, would prefer to die at home.

Hospital attitudes

It is generally accepted that 'in the past many nurses and doctors viewed death as a failure of their skills, and rejected the dying person as a reminder of the limitations of their ability to sustain life' (Pam Williams). Much has been done to improve hospital care of the dying in recent years – for instance with the introduction of hospital palliative care teams and hospital-based Macmillan nurses – and attitudes have dramatically improved; but institutional change can take a long time to show its benefits in practice:

> In 1961, 90% of doctors indicated a preference for not telling patients they had cancer, but in 1979 this was reversed, with 97% indicating a preference for passing on the diagnosis. Yet even today, many nurses are frequently being put on the spot by patients who have been told something ambiguous by the doctor and want more information.
>
> *Pam Williams.*

Doctors and nurses have testified to the difficulty of coming close to the dying patient in hospital surroundings (although the small community cottage hospitals have a better reputation). Here are three such accounts, the first by Dr Sean Spence:

Television in hospital

One night in cubicle number one there was a child dying of a rare tumour. She was three years old with her hair short, as if shaven, as a result of chemotherapy. In the corner of the room the television eavesdropped. It played shadows of blue, white and red across the room, silhouetting the bars at the end of the bed, the forms of the parents waiting, its light enough to reflect them in the window opposite me. I could see their tears in that window. It became a mirror in the night. The emotions playing across the room did so without me, carried on around me. My presence was superfluous. No medical intervention would save her now. Curing is easy, but not curing is so hard, an impotence in the soul.

The gathered relatives, extended family, filled the rest of the room. Middle-aged men in suits crouched, sitting on plastic chairs, with tabloid newspapers open before them. They appeared to read the inane headlines by the glow of the artificial light, so that other agencies' realities flooded theirs. Their own state of reality must have been so great – a grandchild about to die – yet they chose to ruminate on external symbols, signs, secrets, intrigues, consumer durables which would not sustain them. When our own internal, subjective world becomes too real, when our own consciousness is too connected, do we then retreat into the external, the objective, the unreal?

From 'Television and the Retreat from Consciousness', by Dr Sean Spence, in Beshara magazine.

A dying nurse

I am a student nurse. I am dying. I write this to you who are, and will become, nurses in the hope that by sharing my feelings with you, you may someday be better able to help those who share my experience.

We're taught not to be overly cheery now, to omit the 'everything's fine' routine, and we have done pretty well. But now one is left in a lonely silent void. With the protective 'fine, fine' gone, the staff is left with only their vulnerability and fear. The dying patient is not yet seen as a person and thus cannot be communicated with as such.

I know you feel insecure, don't know what to say, don't know what to do. But please believe me, if you care, you can't go wrong. Just admit that you care.

Anon, American Journal of Nursing, 1970.

Doctors withdrawing from the dying

I have recently completed a dissertation, related to how much information terminal patients are offered regarding their diagnosis and prognosis. The results of the study have convinced me that death and dying are over-medicalised, the disease process assuming primacy over the person. Patients within the study firmly located the fear of cancer and dying within their doctors; rather than within themselves. They reported having to 'fight for their diagnosis and prognosis' with very little, if any, information offered voluntarily.

The most disturbing (for me) feature of the study was the reporting by patients that doctors and nurses 'withdrew' from the patient once the patient knew their prognosis. This was despite patients feeling that this was the time they most needed emotional support from their doctors and nurses.

Keith Ward, c/o Wakefield and Pontefract College of Health Studies, Pontefract General Infirmary, West Yorkshire.

In spite of these testimonies, modern hospitals are not soulless machines; doctors and nurses are not ogres.

Their fears and withdrawals cannot be wholly blamed on the hospital environment; they are part of the wider 'alienation from death in our age':

Orderly death

The kind of death one would hope for today - that is, to die in one's sleep, ignorant of the event, was, in the Middle Ages and the Renaissance, only wished upon one's enemies.

An orderly kind of death was part of an orderly life, and a number of ceremonies were an intrinsic part of dying. A will was written, psalms were chosen, and the speeches to be held were well prepared: these tasks were well in order long before death actually occurred.

If one fearfully retreats from the new and unknown in life, one will also attempt to flee from death. The need constantly to seek out continuity (non-change) is, in itself, an expression of fear of death.

From 'The Anxiety of the Unknown' by Jorn Beckmann and Henrik Olesen, Odense University Hospital, Denmark, 1988.

Nurses are human too (like the rest of us!) as testified in the next letter from a nurse to The Natural Death Centre, which is followed by an account by a priest of visiting an old friend dying in hospital.

Nurses too busy

I do understand the need for a dying patient to be holding someone's hand and for nurses to communicate with them, but most of the time we cannot spare the nurses. Also, some people die quickly and others live for a long time - for one of our patients it was three weeks before he passed on. Many a time I just wanted to sit with patients who are dying for all of my shift, and give them tender loving care - to talk to them, hold their hand and give them the knowledge that someone cares.

From a letter to The Natural Death Centre.

Dedication despite distractions

There was a pulsating machine behind the bed with a digital reading of 30, and which progressively crept up to 35 over the period of my visits. I supposed this to be an oxygen regulator to the pair of tubes which had been inserted into her nostrils. There was another tube emerging from under the bedclothes which was draining off some body fluid and on her wrist a plastic valve had been fitted to enable her to be given subcutaneous injections of antibiotics. On my last visit the nostril tubes had been replaced by a transparent plastic oxygen face mask. There was a perpetual background noise of radio from one of the adjoining beds, so pervasive as to make it difficult to locate its precise origin, and so persistent as to madden one with its inescapably inconsequential form of distraction.

However one might interpret its labours there was no mistaking the sheer dedication of the nursing staff to the wellbeing of the patients. One evening the old black lady was visited by a young, fresh-faced nurse. She chatted with the patient for a few moments and then said, 'Well, good night Amy, I am going off duty now.' And proceeded to plant a firm kiss on the old lady's withered cheek. 'Now give me a kiss,' she continued, 'and have a good night's sleep. Oh no, that's not a proper kiss; now give me a real one. Come on now.' She bent lower over the bed and duly received her benefit.

'That was lovely,' she said, holding the patient's hand, 'Goodnight now, see you in the morning.'

Revd. John Papworth, Editor, Fourth World Review, 24 Abercorn Place, London NW8 9XP (tel 0171 286 4366).

Hospice facilities

Like every institutional movement, the hospice system is shaped by its source of funding and forms of administration. In the United States the first main hospice was founded by Elisabeth Kübler-Ross. Since then, all hospice funding in the States has been done through the medical hospital system, with a few independent exceptions. The UK hospice movement has been going since the mid-nineteenth century, and there are approximately 210 hospices currently operating. As noted previously, the source of funding is mainly cancer charities and the emphasis is on patients dying of cancer. However, much current energy and thought is devoted to extending the hospice philosophy to hospitals and people's homes and to providing community facilities, as described in this extract from a letter to The Natural Death Centre from a hospice volunteers' co-ordinator:

> Cancer Relief Macmillan Fund have moved away from the idea of raising money to build bedded hospices because of the vast running costs. They now feel it is more economic to encourage the building of day centres where people can be given both specialised care – eg assisted baths, physiotherapy, aromatherapy, massage – and social activities that keep them in the community and also give their carers a break from looking after them. In this way, people can stay at home longer, taking pressure off scarce hospital and hospice beds. The provision of twenty-four hour care at home is still out of reach in most places, but some people do see that as the ideal. Marie Curie nurses are available in some areas to stay with patients all night. Or there may be Iain Rennie Hospice At Home services who will provide twenty-four hour nursing care if necessary.
>
> *From a letter to The Natural Death Centre*
> *by Christine Mills.*

The Hospice Information Service, at St Christopher's Hospice, puts out a regular newsletter giving the latest developments on the domestic and international scene, and information about local hospices, etc (see under Organisations in the Resources chapter).

Dying at home – the legal situation

A resource worth acquiring by any family contemplating looking after a dying person at home is Deborah Duda's previously mentioned book 'Coming Home'. This present chapter is very much imbued with her advice and approach, adapted to the UK situation as necessary. For instance, Duda advises that it is our basic legal right to leave a hospital or hospice and to return home whenever we please, with or without a doctor's approval. An important consequence of this is that if a person is unable to make or express their own decisions (in legal terms 'incompetent'), their family (or next of kin) has the legal right to make decisions for them. This includes the decision to remove the person from hospital to go either to a hospice or back home. You may have to sign a form which states that the patient has been checked out against medical advice. Even if this is the case, it is worthwhile discussing your decision in detail with the relevant doctors and staff. They will be able to advise you about the future or backup role which the hospital will play in the care of your relative, and can put you in touch with relevant local support services.

This is the basic enabling right that helps us to bring a dying person home. There are other important legal rights, and in each case the issue is one that requires deep thought and consideration. The Voluntary Euthanasia Society of Scotland has published 'guidelines for the relatives of patients nearing eighty or more who are faced with a major operation, setting out medical factors to be considered before consenting on the patient's behalf'. It needs to be stressed that all such patients who are mentally competent should make such decisions for themselves and that the factor of chronological age is an irrelevance, it is more a question of biological age and mental and physical frailty. But the Society does make an important point:

Very elderly patients facing major operations

No operation is undertaken without the expectation of the patient's survival and the policy of treatment is therefore one of 'maximum recovery', even if it involves resuscitation, the use of artificial breathing apparatus, etc.

In general, before consenting on a very elderly patient's behalf, be sure that he or she has a genuine zest for life and will be content to suffer the stresses and struggles of 'maximum recovery'.

For a Declaration of Rights that a person dying at home should have, see our chapter nine, The Politics of Dying.

Making the decision

It has been said many times that 'we die alone', but there are degrees of loneliness, and the feeling of being unwanted at the end of life may be the most poignant of all human emotions:

Mother Teresa on being wanted

I have come more and more to realize that it is being unwanted that is the worst disease that any human being can ever experience. For all kinds of diseases there are medicines and cures. But for being unwanted, unless there are willing hands to serve and a loving heart to love, I don't think this terrible disease can ever be cured.

Mother Teresa, quoted in 'Coming Home' by Deborah Duda.

Deborah Duda summarises some of the arguments for 'coming home', both for the dying person and for the carer:

Easier to adjust at home

Bringing dying people home reassures them they're wanted and won't be deserted. Dying people fear losing control over their lives. In the hospital, the staff take over and largely dictate what the patient can and cannot do, when you can see them, etc. You and the dying person don't have time to adjust gradually to loss of control. At home, on the other hand, you can take a few steps at a time toward giving up control, which makes dying easier.

The feeling of being totally wrenched by an unnatural catastrophe, common in sudden deaths and many hospital deaths, is less likely to occur at home. You know you're doing all you can do. If the thought comes up afterward, 'Maybe I could have done more,' you're likely to let go of it much more quickly than if you'd been isolated from a loved one in a hospital. After caring for someone who dies at home most people report feeling peace as well as loss - a feeling of appropriateness and completion and a greater openness to the new life ahead.

Reprinted with permission from 'Coming Home: A Guide to Dying at Home with Dignity', © 1987 Deborah Duda, Aurora Press, PO Box 573, Santa Fe, NM 87504, USA.

The patient who is unconscious may already have expressed a desire to be home. It may still be possible to elicit a response through signals where the level of consciousness is uncertain: 'Do you want to go home? Squeeze my hand for Yes - blink for No.'

Determining the best interests of a person who cannot express his or her own wishes, or who wishes to go home against the advice of the doctor, may be difficult. It is worth being clear as to who in the family has to make the decision, and how each person might be affected by it. A family discussion to decide, or to talk about the decision once made, may be appropriate. You may want to work out how you might share some of the tasks, and to make others aware of the sort of changes that will be happening. As Deborah Duda points out, 'Once you've made the decision for home, keep in mind that your focus shifts from curing to making comfortable.'

There will be circumstances where dying at home would not be appropriate – for instance if the person wanted to donate organs after death; or if it would involve the carers in overmuch difficulty, anxiety and pure physical exhaustion (especially if there were young children also needing care). Almost everyone asked blandly 'Do you want to go home?' would say Yes, but all the factors need to be carefully considered, and it is important that those carers who decide that they cannot cope at home for whatever reason should not be made to feel guilty. There may be an insufficiency of family and neighbours to help look after the patient. That the person is entirely alone in the world, however, need not always be an insuperable bar, as Dr Elizabeth Lee described in a letter to The Natural Death Centre:

Discharging from hospital against medical advice

I recently talked to my community nurses about the death of one of their patients at home. She was an elderly widow, very strong minded and cantankerous, so much so in fact that neither her family or neighbours offered any practical support for her at home. She took her own discharge from hospital against medical advice and came home to die alone. In spite of her isolation she was able to achieve the death she wanted. She received a tremendous amount of support from her home help, community nurses, GP and night nurses. She was cared for very well at home and had one-to-one attention for many hours a day. She died peacefully one morning when the community nurse was with her. Although I have not added up the hours that she was alone, I am sure it was considerably less than the patients in hospital. Perhaps she knew that by going home to die she would be less isolated and alone than those who die surrounded by professionals in hospital.

The decision to bring or to keep the dying person at home may sometimes be made in circumstances that place an initial burden on the person making the decision. Here is a moving account of such a case, where a woman in Scotland found there was more support for her decision than she had imagined, in spite of official unhelpfulness.

Sharing the bed at home

My husband had had a pain below his chest for several weeks and finally went to see his GP. At first the doctor thought that he had pulled a muscle, but on a second visit took a blood test. The doctor then decided that my husband should go to a specialist at our local hospital and he was subsequently taken in for a biopsy.

The specialist then told my husband that he had liver cancer and nothing could be done for him. He died ten weeks later. I regret that the specialist told my husband without first telling me or asking me to be present and that he was so blunt about it. I also felt it negative to give no treatment of any kind as I feel there are many alternative treatments that could have been tried and that might have given hope. Soon after my husband told me the result of his biopsy, a friend advised me to get in touch with Macmillan nurses. I went and asked my GP how to contact them and he told me they would not be needed yet and did not seem to know where they were based. I then rang a cancer charity in Edinburgh who told me that they were in the same hospital where the specialist was based and had a part-time cancer doctor working with them.

I got in touch and from that time their support was invaluable. They are in fact not just nurses but specialists in the treatment of cancer and also counsellors. The nurse who called at the house regularly soon realised that my husband was in far more pain than he would admit to the doctor and arranged for him to have increased painkillers. When later he was given drugs to combat sickness, constipation, etc, she was able to tell me whether the way he reacted to them was normal. She gave me her telephone number and I was able to ring her at home any time I needed advice. I find it sad to think that the specialist does not send his patients along the passage to see the Macmillan nurses as soon as he has had to tell them that they have terminal cancer. The doctors appear not to want to recognise that these nurses can help the patients and families more than they can.

We had the choice whether to keep my husband at home or whether he should go to hospital. He was always very attached to his house and family and although we never talked to him about it, I was sure he would wish to stay at home, as we were able to carry on as if he had an illness from which he might recover. I was able to sleep in the same bed with him right until the day he died.

I was lucky enough to have a friend, who had been a nursing nun, with me during the last days, as well as my daughter. It was particularly nice to have somebody whom we all knew and who was a Catholic as we were. However I could have had a Marie Curie nurse daily or nightly if she had not been there. My husband did not need much nursing until the last week. Although he might have been a little more comfortable with a special bed, bed pans, etc, in a hospital and also have had more confidence in a nurse giving him the pills regularly, I am sure the fact that we could be with him most of the time in a normal way, and not as a hospital visit, made up for that.

While my husband was dying we were all able to pray together and I tried to see death as Christianity teaches us. I do feel however that the Church still tends to regard death as a tragedy and not as God's plan. The world makes us feel that dying is unacceptable. Those who live to a great age are congratulated so that conversely those who do not are almost regarded as failures. I have a great belief in another life and also that those who have died are still around in spirit. Both my daughter, who is not a practising Catholic, and I feel that my husband is still looking after us. He was a particularly caring person and, as she said, he has more power to help others now. The book that has helped me more than any Catholic book is 'Who Dies?' by Stephen Levine. I came across it accidentally about a year after my husband died, and it made a great difference to me. I understand that it is not even on the reading list for those training as CRUSE counsellors and I feel that it should be more widely known.

From a letter to The Natural Death Centre.

Elizabeth Lawlor in Cheshire has written to the Natural Death Centre. She has no regrets about her decision to bring her husband home to die, despite the lack of support from outside agencies:

Dying amidst familiar chaos

My husband Peter died on New Year's Eve 1991. He had been diagnosed with lung cancer in February 1990 – and I think surprised everyone by living so long. He had pneumonia and was admitted to hospital in November. The consultant was not able to face what we realised - that Peter was dying. So at the beginning of December, when our local hospice opened beds for the first time, it was thought to be a good idea for Peter to go there. The doctors were still talking about curing the pneumonia!

Probably because the unit was so new, our experience of the hospice was *not* good and after ten days I 'kidnapped' Peter - they would not organise transport, so I managed to get him into the car somehow. And home into his own bed, with intrusive cats, kid's music reverberating and cobwebs that threaten to garotte the unwary!

The day before he died, the drains blocked and Dyno-Rod spent an unbelievably noisy afternoon. I think that Peter was unconscious, but if there was even a flicker, he would have loved the chaos.

District nurses did their best but were rather limited. The Macmillan nurse never showed up - she was on holiday over Christmas and New Year. We had a Marie Curie nurse for one night – ie 11.30pm to 5am – which was disastrous. But I did have my wonderful doctor friend, who bullied GPs and made sure that Peter had enough heroin at the end.

She and I were with Peter when he died. Brain death had been at about 7.30 in the morning, I think. I was in bed with him – as I had been throughout – and I got a sense that his soul (or whatever one calls it) had detached itself. And at 11am, he quietly stopped breathing.

Mary and I washed him and laid him out, to the disapproval of the funeral director. It was very real, very loving, and I was able to keep literally in touch with Peter. Then I kept him at home, in our bed, until ten minutes before the funeral. We live near the church and the local Coastal Forces veterans' association put the coffin onto the bier (usually used for transport from the church to the grave) and wheeled him round to the church - no hearse.

Now I am again being perhaps a bit difficult and organising the headstone I want and think Peter would have wanted, with the help of Harriet Frazer's Memorials by Artists [see the Good Funeral Guide chapter]. Mottled black marble wasn't Peter's 'thing'! And it is taking time, and I am working through the grieving process in my own time, my own way, with the erecting of the headstone after a year or more as a symbol of letting go.

Elizabeth Lawlor, Furnival Cottage, Acton,
Nantwich, Cheshire CW5 8LD.

Getting an Assessment for Care in the Community

Diana Senior of the Befriending Network describes some of the pitfalls of the UK's 'Care in the Community' programme.

Caring for someone at home should be easier since the introduction of Care in the Community, but this is not always the case. Provision under Care in the Community differs wildly from area to area. Even within the same area, how it works can depend on how clued in, efficient or sympathetic your social worker or GP is, or at what point in the financial year you happen to need it. Jaqueline Worswick, who founded Helen House Hospice, and who has recently had to agree a Care Plan for her now adult daughter says: 'Only two words in that phrase "Care in the Community" bear any resemblance to reality: "in" and "the".'

Theoretically, anybody who needs care at home can ask for an assessment from their local social services department. (Eds: Beware, however, that you will be means tested. Your very home could be at risk – see the section entitled 'Protecting assets from community care charges' in the Preparing for Dying chapter.) A social worker or 'care manager' will come to assess your needs and work out a basic Care Plan with you and your carer. This should take account of your personal needs (help with dressing, washing, food preparation, etc.); your physical needs (physiotherapy, or aids like wheelchair, ramps, toilet seat, etc). It should also take some account of other needs, including things like recreation or day care. The care manager can also liaise with the GP or district nurse if he or she feels regular visits from them are important to your care. If you have a carer, he or she should get an assessment of their needs as well: time off while you have some respite care; or an unbroken night's sleep courtesy of a night sitter.

If you are on a low income, and have capital assets of under £10,000 (Eds: See the Preparing for Dying chapter), the care agreed on your Care Plan will be arranged for you, free, by social services, although you may be expected to contribute some of your Disability Living or Attendance Allowance towards paying for personal care and housework. As your income and assets go up, so does the contribution you are expected to make towards the cost of your care.

Even if you are in the position of having to pay for the full cost of your care, it could be worth asking for a Care in the Community Assessment, so that you are fully linked in with local resources; and a good care manager, like a good GP, is an invaluable ally. However, if time is limited, do not wait for an assessment. The advice given in 'The Natural Death Handbook' should help you to devise your own Care Plan.

A drawback with Care Plan assessments is that very often you are required to state your needs before you are fully aware of what they will be. Because Care Plans are supposed to be 'needs led' rather than 'resources led', you can often be unaware of what is available if only you'd asked for it. The advice from a carer is: 'Remember, if it has not been offered to you, it does not mean it does not exist.' This principle also applies to getting help from your GP.

If you have or are a carer, a very useful place to get help and advice is your local Carers Centre. Like everything else these vary from area to area. Consult the Carers National Association (see the Resources chapter) for the address of the nearest centre: They should provide up-to-date information on local resources; help with reviewing your Care Plan, and advocacy if things go wrong; a chance to share your feelings with a caring professional or other carers; and much more. The Carers Centre should also be able to provide you with access to charities and grant-giving bodies who will give financial help towards items not covered in your Care Plan.

Anne looked after her husband, Richard (the names have been changed) over five years until his eventual death from multiple sclerosis. Diana Senior describes the Care Plan that was set up for Richard on his discharge from a hospital stay:

A Care Plan in action

The district nurse came every Wednesday, did any nursing tasks, checked on Richard's general health and would call the doctor if anything needed further investigation.

A carer from Crossroads (who have a service agreement with the local social services to care for people with high physical dependency) came every morning, except for Wednesdays, to assist with getting him up.

A night nurse came two evenings per week, and a carer from Crossroads came on the remaining five evenings to help him get to bed. They were able to do this quite late, 10 or 11pm, as this was what Richard preferred.

Meanwhile he also had an assessment from the Occupational Therapist, to work out the sort of chair, bed and other practical aids he needed. The district nurse assessed and provided aids that were necessary for nursing care, for example a hoist and supplies for incontinence.

There is a team of night nurses who will come in and turn the ill person in the night, several times if this is necessary. But Anne avoided the need for turning by getting an air mattress, one that was continually pumped with air, and, once they got used to the noise of the pump, this was wonderful. They hired one, called a KC1 One Step Mattress, from a medical supply company, Huntley Nesbit Evans (HNE) in Abingdon (tel 01235 533090). They later bought it from them, at a total cost of about £1,000 (or you can hire them through the Red Cross or borrow one through your GP; advice can be sought from a local orthopaedic centre or from the Disabled Living Foundation).

Anne found that Macmillan and Marie Curie nurses were much better than social workers or the GP about making suggestions for life-improving things, both practical aids, and ways of using carers. Unfortunately, their expertise is mainly available only to people with cancer.

Other problems included the lack of reliability of the carers, and lack of reviews of the Care Plan to cope with Richard's increasing needs. Particularly, he should have had regular wheelchair assessments. He finally had a new chair made especially for his needs, and this really made the last weeks much easier, but it was a pity it didn't come earlier.

Luckily they were able to supplement the Care Plan. The two most useful things were: physiotherapy, from a private agency – there was a long waiting list for NHS community physiotherapy; and live-in carers during the last months. This enabled Anne to have regular breaks away.

The first live-in carer was a New Zealander whom they met through Crossroads. They were so satisfied with this young Antipodean that when she went off on her travels, they advertised for her successor through the expatriate magazine TNT (tel 0171 373 3377). It was hard to define the special quality of these carers: perhaps it was the oomph and curiosity which had led them to go travelling in the first place. All three who lived with Richard and Anne were positive, gentle and worked hard. They were happy to fit in and rough it a bit, and had lives of their own.

Anne's main tips for other carers would be:

• You must look after yourself, even if this goes against the grain, even if it seems selfish. If you don't look after yourself, you aren't going to be any use as a carer.

• Admit to yourself that you can't do everything. Do not see this as failure.

• It is very important not to become isolated as a carer, and you must accept the help that is offered, or, if you can afford it, buy it in (Eds: see, for instance, under 'Nursing Agencies' in your Yellow Pages.) This seems obvious, but it takes time and effort to organise outside care to fit in with the pattern that suits you and the ill person best, and sometimes this seems too much trouble, it appears easier just to do it yourself. For instance, agency carers (normally offered through the Care Plan) differ enormously, ranging from brilliant to less than useless; they can also be very unreliable, arriving early or late or not at all. A live-in carer or night sitter can invade the little space you have to yourself. But resist the temptation to cancel carers; both you and the ill person will benefit from regular visits from people outside.

• If you have a period of feeling helpless and not being able to do anything, remember just being there helps. And simple physical contact is tremendously important. The odd hug can do more than any amount of medication.

• Acknowledge that you are going to feel angry and trapped quite a lot of the time, and so is the person you are looking after. (Value the good bits, the sharing and the laughs.)

• Recognise the need to let the person go.

Anne said that the instinct to cure and revive was so strong, that she found it hard when her husband became difficult to rouse. She was grateful for the reminder 'You've got to let him go'. At the same time she valued being told that people in a coma often retain their hearing and a sense of their surroundings, so there is no exact point when you stop talking to them, or stop keeping things peaceful and right in the room.

Financial help

Where cost of medication is an important factor, the patient may be entitled to assistance on the grounds of age. Otherwise the patient should apply for exemption from payment because of a 'continuing physical disability'. Free prescription forms (FP91) are available from post offices or doctors' surgeries.

A maze of regulations governs the benefits available to carers and those cared for (again, be sure to read the Preparing for Dying chapter and its warning on means testing) and you might like to consult your local Citizens Advice Bureau or Carers Centre for the latest situation. An up-to-date book on the subject is 'Teach Yourself Caring for Someone at Home' (see the Resources chapter) which warns that the most underclaimed benefits available are:

• The Disability Living Allowance – a benefit that is tax free, is not means tested and does not require you to have paid National Insurance contributions. It is for those under 65 and has special rules so that those who are likely to die within six months can get their benefit quickly.

• The Attendance Allowance is a similar benefit, but for those over 65.

• The Constant Attendance Allowance is similar again, but is for those who also receive either an Industrial Injuries Benefit or a War Pension.

Available in addition are:

• Incapacity Benefit. Those who are terminally ill, are of working age and who have paid National Insurance contributions should receive a low rate of (taxable) Incapacity Benefit for the first 28 weeks and thereafter the highest rate.

• A similar benefit, that does not depend on having worked or on National Insurance contributions, is called the Severe Disablement Allowance.

Claimable for the carer rather than the cared-for is:

• Invalid Care Allowance, a grand £36-60 per week. This is for those of working age; and who are not earning more than £50, after expenses and National Insurance (one expense you can deduct is the cost of paying someone to do the caring whilst you are at work). You must be responsible for looking after someone with a severe disability for at least 35 hours a week (and be receiving one of the three benefits above).

These benefits are all claimed from the Benefits Agency (the new name for the Department of Social Security – see the Resources chapter).

Support structures

Dr Elizabeth Lee, in her very useful book 'A Good Death – A guide for patients and carers facing terminal illness at home', suggests ways to orchestrate the support structures that may be available. Here is our summary of some of her best tips:

• Explain to the professionals caring for you that you would like your own favourite professional to be your 'key worker' – whether GP, district nurse, social worker or home care specialist nurse.

• 'How long have I got [till I die]?' This is the question that everyone asks and no one answers. The unwritten code of practice among doctors is to reply, 'I would love to give you an answer but the truth is that no one knows'. If you need an answer to this question, you should encourage them to throw caution to the wind and make a best guess. Those who stubbornly refuse can often be pinned down by your asking 'If it was *your* mother who was ill like this, how long would you guess?'

• If you don't get on with your doctor and find her unsympathetic, try not to say that you find her difficult, rather say something like 'Although I appreciate all you are doing, I find that I am very comfortable with Doctor X, and hoped he might be able to visit me more often'.

• You may have a long list of questions for your GP. It may help to write them down before you see her.

NHS services vary in different regions and are sometimes provided in conjunction with voluntary bodies. These include domestic help, delivery of meals at home and special laundry services for bed-linen. In some areas, as already mentioned, night nurses or night attendants may be available.

It is worth exploring the help available from local societies and local voluntary agencies which are experienced in this form of care and may offer technical help and services as well as emotional support.

Individual circumstances vary, and the most crucial area of support in a particular case may range from the official to the highly informal. Here is a useful checklist:

Checklist of possible assistance locally

- NHS provisions
- Social Services
- Macmillan Nurse
- Marie Curie Nurse
- Crossroads or Leonard Cheshire Foundation Care At Home
- Home Help
- Occupational therapists (for walking sticks, frames, etc and for some equipment loan – or try Red Cross)
- Physiotherapists
- District nurse
- Meals on Wheels
- Laundry Service
- Night Sitters
- Local support groups and societies
- General Practitioner
- Hospital specialist
- Local Carers Centre (via Carers National Association)
- Befriending Network volunteer or similar befriending service
- Priest/Vicar/Minister and church groups
- Friends, relatives and neighbours

If you do not know how to contact any of the services on the list, ask those you can contact. See also the list of Organisations in our Resources chapter. It is worth writing down a list of your needs, so that you can ask each source for more information (as well as being a good way of getting them in perspective for yourself). The Marie Curie nurse is perhaps the key figure in the natural death movement at the present time. She (or a team of such nurses) can be available to give support for up to seven nights a week. This is an enormous factor in preventing unnecessary hospital admissions. Otherwise relatives can reach the end of their tether and allow the patient to be admitted to hospital because they know no alternative. Most advisers stress that the carer should not become isolated in the task of looking someone at home. One recommends that 'there be at least two people at home to take turns supporting the dying person'. This may not always be feasible. If necessary, ask the local priest or doctor to mobilise potentially helpful neighbours on your behalf. Care of the dying can be shared with friends and relatives, and with neighbours too. This is good, not just for the health and wellbeing of the caring person, but, as Ruth I. Johns points out, for the health of society as a whole:

We need the dying in our neighbourhoods and lives

At best, death is very peaceful, quick; at worst, long, protracted and accompanied by illness, pain and suffering. But it is happening to a person and that person matters. The neighbourhood needs – for its own health – to help its members in death and not pass them on to impersonal 'helpers'. In this kind of discussion, some people are always quick to say that they know someone whose life 'was ruined' because of 'having to' care for an elderly person for whom they did not feel any particular affection. To have to appear to care for someone purely out of a sense of duty is never easy and can even be injurious to all concerned: yet this is exactly the way our social systems are designed. Perhaps we have never bothered sufficiently to recognise the immense difference between pseudo-personal care and affectionate personal care? Maybe it is the people who have been 'saddled' with 'caring' for those they did not really care for who have precipitated the increase of the same blight within the formal social helping systems? The people who quietly get on with their affectionate personal care accept it, and, hard work though it may be, feel enhanced by it.

I would venture the suggestion that some of the young people who play with violence are only seeking a substitute for a suppressed and unrealised natural need to be involved in the whole process of life. We protect them (and ourselves) from real death, which is, thereby, devastatingly lonely for the dying.

Perhaps we actually need the inclusion of dying in our lives to use up energies which otherwise can pop up as actual or fantasised aggression?

Being part of the dying of a loved relative or friend makes life more livable and death a reality. The more we push it into the back of our minds, the more it will bounce back to haunt us with substitute fantasies and impersonal aggression.

It is only by becoming deeply personally involved with family, friends and neighbours that we can demonstrate that they mean something to us: thereby we become more at home in ourselves. If we feel whole we can more easily see ourselves as having a niche in the continuing affections of others: beyond our own death. Life certainly becomes more tenable once we accept some personal responsibility for death.

> *From 'Life Goes On - Self-help philosophy and practice based on ten years' pioneering work with Family First Trust, Nottingham' by Ruth I. Johns, 1982 (£6 from 'Unknown Publisher', PO Box 66, Warwick CV34 4XE, 1982).*

Of all the people around you, some will want to help 'somehow'. Others will be overwhelmed by the thought of having to deal with it all. Take the statement, 'if there's anything I can do to help, let me know,' at face value, and give them a concrete practical task: walking the dog, making a meal or participating in a round of bridge. These would be manageable favours for them, and it allows them to visit with a specific purpose, rather than just mouth the empty question 'How are you feeling?'

Within the family, how is the responsibility shared? Often it is concentrated in one person, even when the decision has been made to share it. The family's help can be organised along similar lines as the ones above. Responsibility can be split into three components: tasks; time spent in the role of chief carer (shifts); and the feeling of responsibility. The latter is automatically shared if the first two are shared successfully.

The needs of children may have to be taken into account:

Guilt feelings in children

Guilt feelings can be particularly strong in children. They may believe that by some misdemeanour they caused the death of the loved one. Some children will then misbehave more in order to earn the punishment they believe they deserve. It is vital that such feelings are discovered, in order that the child does not go through life burdened and emotionally crippled by such beliefs.

> *From 'Dying at Home' by Harriet Copperman.*

Generally it is believed that it is healthier for children to be involved. Most authorities advise that throughout any terminal illness and following the death, the children should remain an integral part of the family. Children will regard death as abnormal if they are kept away from the scene, and prevented from contact with their relative either just before or just after death. How to tell a child of an approaching death in the family may be discussed with whatever support persons are available. It may be useful to consider how much worse a sudden unexpected death would be for the children than one for which they had been prepared. There are many good books available for children too – some are on the booklist in the Resources chapter or contact The Compassionate Friends (also in the Resources chapter) for their specialist children's book list (they have a postal lending library too).

Support may be forthcoming from unexpected quarters. It may come from people who step out of their formal roles as vicar or GP or neighbour and become especially supportive individuals. Help for the dying is an emotional business. Not everyone can handle it but some leap into it with enthusiasm, like the four-legged friend in the following example!

Comfort for the dying from a dog

A four-legged therapist named Inky works every day giving the most precious love of all. She comforts the dying. In her own small way the ten-pound Chihuahua-mix dog is as much a hero as the valiant animals who save victims from blazing buildings or raging rivers.

'Some of the most impressive emotional healing I've seen is brought about by Inky,' says Rose Griffith, nursing director at the Hospice of Saint John in Lakewood, Colorado. 'Inky brings back life and humour to the terminally ill - whose existence has been dulled by pain, fear and loneliness.'

And Pam Currier, former hospice director, says: 'In many cases Inky is more effective than any two-legged therapist.'

Says hospice spokesman Peter Wellish: 'One of the greatest tragedies is how many patients die without loved ones by their side. For these patients, Inky's presence is a true blessing. Dying patients don't seem to demand much. All the riches and money in the world are no longer important. Quality time is what matters most.

'For those patients who really need her, Inky will spend the entire night. If there are two who need her, Inky will intuitively divide her time between them.'

Getting and training a canine therapist to help the dying was the idea of volunteer Sister Helen Reynolds of the Sisters of Loreto. She found Inky in a humane society shelter. 'I wanted a dog who wouldn't hesitate to jump into people's laps, to spread love instinctively and impartially,' she explains. 'When Inky first leaped into a patient's arms, she jumped into the hearts of all!'

From the National Examiner (USA) October 8th 1991.
In the UK contact P.A.T. Dog (see under Organisations
in the Resources chapter).

Befriending services

The Buddhist Hospice Trust have volunteers in their Ananda Network who are prepared to sit with and befriend those who are terminally ill, whether the latter are Buddhists or not (see the Resources chapter).

The Terrence Higgins Trust (see the Resources chapter) can provide Buddy volunteers to visit those with AIDS in the London region and may be able to refer you to other similar schemes elsewhere in the UK.

The Befriending Network (see the Resources chapter), started by The Natural

Death Centre, trains volunteers who visit the homes of those who are critically ill or dying from whatever cause, normally for visits of two to three hours each week. The volunteer is there for the person, and will do whatever they can within their particular competence to assist either the patient or the carer, from running errands, to chatting, acting as a counsellor or giving simple massage.

Of all the experts visiting the home whilst the person is dying, the befriender tends to be the only one who is not being paid to be there, who does not have numerous other clients to rush off to and who can spend a substantial time each week with that person, even acting as their intermediary on occasion with the other services.

The Befriending Network's aim is also to fill the gaps left by the other disease-specific support groups; and it is often summoned for those who have few members of the family, neighbours or friends to support them.

The Befriending Network at present has bases only in Oxford and London, but it seeks to assist others trying to set up similar schemes elsewhere – a 'How To Do It' manual is in preparation.

Those wanting a befriender can make contact direct, they do not need to be referred by professionals. But the Befriending Network does need more volunteers prepared to make the commitment of time required. Each volunteer takes part in over 50 hours of initial training, and then, besides the two to three hours of visiting each week, there are continuing support groups and supervision sessions.

Carer's needs

The best advice to carers is to remember that 'we also serve by respecting our own needs'. It is sensible to be aware in advance of the burden that supporting a seriously ill person places on the care-giver, and to anticipate some of the difficult feelings such as resentment and hostility that may arise. This needs to be said more than once:

Carer's resentment...

Your lifestyle may be affected as much as (or even more than) the patient's. You may be spending your time doing things you don't really want to do. You resent that the burden of the relationship may have fallen on your shoulders.

You cannot but help feel resentment. But you can help (both yourself and the patient) by recognising that you do feel some resentment and by not pretending that it does not exist. If you understand that you are feeling this way, you can respond to the patient by saying something like, 'This is really tough and I'm getting very bad tempered' (which is a way of describing your feelings) rather than 'You never do anything except lie there and grumble' (which is a way of exhibiting your feelings, and quite likely to lead to an argument).

From 'I Don't Know What To Say' by Dr Robert Buckman.

...and anger

The most usual and, for many people, the most frightening feeling is anger. If you have very high expectations of being patient and loving every second of the day, it can be upsetting to feel angry and frustrated. But feeling guilty about it will not help – that simply turns the anger on yourself and sooner or later you will start to feel depressed.

Carers have every reason to feel angry and resentful if they are left to cope alone. You may feel tied and trapped by caring, and angry at the opportunities you have missed.

Anger may also be a reaction to loss – witnessing the suffering of someone you are close to can make you feel angry at the injustice of it all. Or it may be a reaction to the anger expressed by the person you look after: carers often bear the brunt of that anger and frustration.

> *From 'Help at Hand – the Home Carer's Survival Guide'*
> *by Jane Brotchie.*

Jane Brotchie's book, 'Help at Hand – the Home Carer's Survival Guide' is recommended (see the Resources chapter). It is a useful and sensitive book which helps carers through the practical and emotional difficulties with clarity, and is in itself a source of moral support.

The emotional ups and downs of the situation can cause conflict. The dying person and their family may be going through necessary stages of denial, or experiencing a lot of anger and confusion. Dying does not give one an obvious target for one's anger, and so it is easy to lash out at those nearest to you instead. It can also feel safer to express overwhelming anger in terms of mundane things: a cup of tea which is too hot, or someone else's forgetfulness.

If you can, as Deborah Duda advises, stop before entering the room, and arrest your own 'down' feelings, just for a moment. Relax, breathe in deeply and centre yourself. Touch a place of receptive stillness within that allows the process to unfold as it must. Focus on that aspect of being that is larger than the sick body and the distressing symptoms.

Perhaps a smile is all that is needed to make the difference: the negative side of things is there already, and doesn't need reinforcing. Balancing sadness with cheerfulness and humour can be tricky – if your words are taken the wrong way, stand by what you know you meant. If you feel that the other person is playing emotional games, sidestep them rather than joining in. The oldest technique of them all, and one to use when really riled, is to breathe deeply and count to ten.

Stress can result from many side issues, apart from the obvious, especially if you do not allow yourself selfish feelings. If you can recognise the causes of stress, you are more able to deal with its effects. Jane Brotchie provides the following list of common causes:

My source of stress is...

• not knowing for how long I am going to be giving home care.
• having had the decision of caring forced on me rather than having freely chosen it.

• being of advanced age or having ill-health myself.
• not having the training or information I need to provide care.
• lack of free time for myself.
• loss of freedom.
• changes in family life.
• family conflicts.
• competing demands between my role as a carer and other roles in my life.
• loss of social contacts and social life.
• feelings of guilt.
• financial losses or difficulties.
• having to carry out tasks I find unpleasant or embarrassing.
• changes in the personality of the person I care for.
• lack of sleep.
• needing a complete break from caring.

From 'Help at Hand - the Home Carer's Survival Guide'
by Jane Brotchie.

Most importantly, try not to become too locked into the roles of carer and patient. Remember that you also exist for each other outside those roles, and that sometimes you can reverse the roles: the carer may need looking after, and the patient may be able to offer support. Coping is not the care-giver's sole responsibility, and an active role for the patient is recommended where possible. It may be worth gently reminding each other of this from time to time: 'Can I speak to John my husband, not John the patient? Just for a minute.'

At times the care-giver will need to escape. Whether this means sharing a worry-free activity with the ill person or getting out of the house to go to the cinema, don't feel guilty about it. Don't feel surprised if at times you resent the other person, just ensure that you get some space and time to yourself.

Enjoy yourself

Do what *you* want and what you think the person you are looking after would want. Then you feel as if you are still in control of your own life, and the person dying is in control of theirs. Everyone is different, so every death is different. There are no 'right' or 'wrong' ways of doing anything within the process.

Ask for what you want or need. You may not get it but there is quite a lot of help around. Conversely, don't accept well-meaning help that makes you feel in any way uncomfortable.

Make sure you (as carer) continue to be as normal as possible. Eat/drink/ laugh/ take the dog for a walk.

Tell people how you feel if it helps you - 'I'm fine' is probably not true!

For me, Peter's dying was very intense emotionally. You can't ever do it again, so *go for it*!

From a letter by Elizabeth Lawlor
to The Natural Death Centre.

The carer may feel extremely lonely, isolated both from the non-care-giving world and from the relative or partner as they knew them. A support group can go some of the way towards filling that gap – who better to talk to than people in your own position? If you need someone to help you find a way through complex problems, you may benefit from seeing a trained counsellor. In the wake of public disasters in recent years, counselling is gradually becoming widely recognised as an important way of coping with life crises. Counselling is completely confidential, and counsellors are trained to help you to clarify and resolve tangled emotions and problems. Contact the British Association for Counselling (see under Organisations in the Resources chapter), or ask your GP or friends who may be able to recommend particular counsellors.

Most carers begin their roles with little experience and inadequate information. Even if we do eventually become near-perfect carers, it is only reasonable to assume that on the way we will have made many mistakes. Over the whole period of time, we will have been only half-perfect! What now follows is a practical guide to looking after someone who is dying at home. If you are reading it in advance of any need to apply it you may get a clearer idea of what dying at home involves and whether you can provide for it. If you are caring for someone it will serve as a primer and resource for the whole process, to be supplemented by local nursing help and expertise. If you are in a rushed situation you may find in places that some advice needs to be discarded as impractical for a short period, and you may find that other advice makes all the difference.

Preparation and equipment

Physical comfort is regarded as the number one priority for the dying patient. Certain needs clearly have to be met before worrying about emotional requirements. If the bed is wet, the sheets must be changed. If the patient is in an awkward position, he or she should be helped to move. If the sheets are tangled, they need rearranging. If the patient is unwashed, he or she may be uncomfortable. Pain and toilet requirements must be dealt with immediately. Here common sense prevails. Physical comfort is basic to a person's dignity and clarity of thought, and is the mainstay of the care which must be provided. Paying close attention to the patient's physical environment and needs is itself a form of emotional care.

A bed downstairs?

Location of the bed may require considerable thought and analysis of the available conditions. Elizabeth Lawlor's sensitive advice is again based upon her own experience of looking after her husband Peter:

> Keep everything as normal as possible. If the cat/dog usually sleeps on the bed, let it. And if the bed can stay in its usual place, all the better. It is a way of maintaining a feeling of reality which is comforting when someone is drifting in and out of consciousness. The bed should be accessible on both

sides to facilitate moving and turning the patient and the making of the bed, as well as bed-bathing, etc. If possible, a chair by the bed that is easy to transfer into is initially good for morale – the patient can spend the periodic half-hour sitting – which is also useful for the bedmaker. Later on the chair is good for visiting family, etc, and is an accepted piece of furniture in that location.

Other important considerations can be taken into account. If the bedroom is upstairs, the staircase may become an increasingly awkward and frustrating barrier to the rest of the house as the patient becomes less mobile. The experience of negotiating a flight of stairs with little or no strength of one's own is for some an unbearable reminder of their condition, and so the stairs can become a symbol for feelings of isolation and impotence, both for the patient and the carer.

If the patient is moved downstairs then calling for the carer may be less hit-and-miss, and just popping one's head around the door to check may be less tiring. In some cases the same energy expended on coping with stairs could instead be used to get some fresh air outside. This must be balanced with the feasibility of nursing the patient downstairs. Ideally there will be room for a bed and for creating a space which the patient feels is suitably self-contained and private. If this is the living room, the patient may feel invaded by visiting relatives unless there is another room in which they can be greeted and entertained. Are the sleeping arrangements suitable for both partners? Temporary compromises, such as a sofa for the patient, can be quite practical, as long as change will not upset everyone's routine or sense of place. Washing and toilet requirements are also very important.

Ultimately some form of compromise will have to be made. It is important for the carer not to feel guilty that arrangements are not perfect (few people choose a home with all this in mind), just as it is important to make sure that the carer's needs are taken into account. It is easier to be selfless when you have had a few hours' sleep.

Often the sense of what feels right is most important. The care-giver may find unbearable the idea of eventually having to sleep alone in the bed in which their partner spent their last few weeks. Alternatively they may feel that any other way is wrong. The patient may have strong opinions or an obvious need one way or the other: whether to keep everything as normal as possible, or deliberately to create a special environment in which the patient is 'spoiled rotten'. As conditions change a new setup may be required.

Having said all this, what will very probably happen is that events take over and these decisions are made by circumstance! Wherever the bed is, a bedside table is useful for bottles, tissues, flowers and a constant supply of water and juices.

Other practical equipment needed might include the following, which is an extended list based upon suggestions from 'Who Dies?' by Stephen Levine:

Practical equipment list

A rope and a bell by the bed so the patient feels in contact and can summon help; a stand-up bed tray if appropriate; two hot water bottles, one for the feet and one for easing the pain; an ice bucket; a thermos; possibly a hot plate in the room.

A bedpan, slipper bedpan or urinal bottle may be essential, as well as incontinence pads and plastic sheets. Plastic bedpans are less cold to the touch than metal. A plastic washing-up bowl for bed baths may also be useful.

TV, video recorder, radio, walkman according to requirements. With telephone arrangements, bear in mind the needs of both patient and carer for privacy.

Extra nightgowns or pyjamas that are easy to put on and take off, socks and non-skid slippers.

Paper towels and tissues, cotton towels, drinking straws that bend, favourite pictures and photos, a potted plant or bunches of flowers! Bring nature indoors as much as possible.

Consult with your nurse, doctor, or your local physiotherapist to find out about the provision of walking sticks, walking frames and wheelchairs. These can sometimes be borrowed from the Red Cross (see the Resources chapter). Some local councils can provide handrails for toilets, bathrooms and stairs, as well as access ramps for wheelchairs - contact the Benefits Agency department. A shower seat and nonslip bath mats help with bathing. A step-up stool is useful for relatively mobile people.

Bed and bedding

A hospital bed may be preferred (and may be better for the carers if lifting is involved – low divans can wreck lifters' backs) although some patients may be upset at having to give up their own bed. Again, Stephen Levine makes a useful comment:

A hospital bed

A hospital bed with side rails is often quite useful for comfort, because it can be adjusted in so many ways. And the side rails can act as protection during the night so that one does not restlessly or absent-mindedly fall from the bed. Though a hospital bed is very useful, many prefer to die in their own bed and would rather use a foam wedge for support and a few extra pillows than have the up-and-down movement of a strange bed.

From 'Who Dies?' by Stephen Levine.

Special bedding can give extra comfort and prevent bedsores. Sheepskins and pillows are helpful in this respect.

Bedding and comfort

A Spenco mattress helps with preventing sores, as does a fleece. The district nurse should provide that. There should also be a fleece under the heels which should be washed, dried and rubbed regularly to prevent sores.

A wedge of foam under the head of the mattress gives a firmer base than pillows for a half-upright position. The triangular, orthopaedic pillows are also good.

From a letter by Elizabeth Lawlor to The Natural Death Centre.

Special mattresses are available depending on patient requirements (see also above for Diana Senior's information on air mattresses – in 'Care Plan in action'). A large-cell ripple mattress offers protection to pressure areas in cases of severe need. However, this is a highly specialised piece of equipment requiring advice and consultation. A bed cradle, V-shaped pillow, sponge or air rings for sitting on, sheepskin squares for sitting or lying on, and sheepskin pads or booties for the feet provide additional comfort. Fresh clean sheets are important, perhaps helped by a rubberised flannel undersheet with a duvet as a comfortable underblanket. You should consult with your nurses or local hospital as to which combination of equipment is best, as well as for details of how to get hold of them (they may themselves be able to provide you with some items). Hospital suppliers are listed in Yellow Pages, although they normally want large orders. There are specialist chemists, such as John Bell & Croyden (see the Resources chapter). Their sheepskin rug, for instance, costs £35. And the Red Cross, as mentioned, can lend equipment (again see the Resources chapter).

A supply of soft pillows and towels is useful for extra comfort - between or under the knees, behind the back, underneath the patient's book, or at the foot of the bed to lift the top sheet - all according to need. Experts emphasise the need for prevention in dealing with bedsores (see below).

Moving

An EC Directive on 'manual handling of loads' came into force in 1993, whereby employees such as nurses would not normally be expected to lift a patient weighing eight stone or more without a 'mechanical handling device' such as a hoist. Why should carers at home be less well equipped? Introduce a 'no lifting' policy in your home, in imitation of the most progressive hospitals, and insist that your house be fitted with hoists, slings, bath aids, monkey poles, rope ladders, turntables, stair lifts or whatever equipment you may need to protect your back from damage. Take note that one in four qualified nurses has had to take time off for back trouble. And, in an ideal world, there need to be at least two carers at any one time, able to share the strain of moving the patient.

Nevertheless, if it is well within your capabilities to help the adult or child to move in bed or out of bed, advice and perhaps demonstrations of certain standard moves can be given by your district nurse. Several of these are demonstrated in a now unavailable and somewhat out-of-date video, 'Caring for your relative at home', produced by Marie Curie Cancer Care. The instructions which follow are based on the video, although a revised booklet on this topic, 'Partners in Caring', should soon be available without charge through your local Marie Curie nurse. Practise these complicated instructions on a friend who is well first, until you feel proficient, rather than on a patient in pain.

So, in case you will one day find yourself on your own, here are a few basic general guidelines. You are advised to ask a nurse to guide you with these:
• Make sure that the person understands what you are doing;
• Allow the person as much independent movement as possible;
• Make sure that you have a firm footing, and remove any bedclothes that will get in the way;
• Keep the person warm; cover her or him with a towel or dressing gown if necessary;
• Take the manoeuvre one step at a time, agreeing or explaining each step before you carry it out together;
• Take tricky steps, where you have to co-ordinate moving together, on a count of three;
• If you find that you are lugging the person, or that she or he is experiencing discomfort, you may need to break the move down into simpler steps;
• If you are lifting the person, make sure that your back is straight and that your knees are bent;
• Don't overdo it! You may just have to wait until you can find someone to help you.

Turning in bed

Frequent changes of position are important for comfort, to avoid bedsores, and to facilitate washing. These steps are used to turn someone onto their side from their back. The basic idea is that you turn first the legs, then the arms and shoulders, and then the back:
• Stand at the side of the bed towards which the person wants to turn;
• Remove covers and excess pillows;
• Take hold of the person's far leg (at the knee and ankle), and cross it over the other leg towards you;
• Take hold of the person's far arm (at the elbow and wrist), and cross it over their chest towards you;
• Place one hand on the person's hips and the other on their uppermost shoulder, and gently pull their torso towards you.

Moving to a chair or commode

These steps are used to help someone move to a chair from lying down in bed. The basic idea is that you help the person to sit on the edge of the bed, to get up and to shuffle round to a chair behind you.
• Position the chair or commode a few feet from the side of the bed;
• Remove the covers and stand by the bed in front of the chair;
• Help the person to turn towards you (see 'Turning in bed', above);
• Put one arm under the person's lower knee, and the other under the lower ankle. Lift the person's legs and gently pull them towards you, over the side of the bed;
• Put one arm under the person's shoulders, and the other hand on their hips;
• Ask the person to push up with their lower arm, at the same time as you use

a rocking motion to bring them up by pulling their shoulders and pressing lightly down on the hips. Have a breather.
- Facing the person, place your feet firmly beside theirs so that you sandwich their feet;
- Bend your knees and keep your back straight;
- Ask the person to put their arms around your shoulders, as you put your arms around their waist;
- Transfer the person to their feet by straightening your knees;
- Stay holding each other and shuffle round slowly to the chair;
- Support the person as they sit down. If using a commode, you may have to help the person lift their nightdress/nightshirt or lower their pyjamas as they sit.

Changing sheets with the person in bed

The basic idea here is that you unmake and make half of the bed at a time:
- Remove the covers. Leave one pillow;
- Help the person to roll onto one side, facing away from the centre of the bed (see 'Turning in bed' above);
- Untuck the free side of the sheet, and roll it up as far as you can towards the person;
- Tuck in the fresh sheet on the same side, and fold up the rest close to the dirty sheet;
- Gently help the person roll over the rolled sheet and the folded part of the fresh sheet onto the clean side of the bed;
- Remove the dirty sheet; tuck in the rest of the clean sheet;
- Change the pillowcases and help the person roll back to the middle of the bed;
- Put on a fresh top sheet and replace the covers.

If many changes of sheets are required, a single sheet lengthwise on a double bed can be changed more easily than a double sheet.

Accidents

If the person falls to the floor, check for obvious signs of injury. If he or she can't move fingers or toes, if tentative movement produces sharp pain, or if you are unsure, assume that there are injuries. Call a doctor or ambulance. Make sure that the person moves as little as possible before examination. Make the person comfortable with pillows and blankets. Give reassurance that the situation is being dealt with as well as possible.

Eating

Peter stopped wanting to eat or drink when he had pneumonia. The hospice tried to bully him into eating which upset him. Once he was home, I would ensure that something that he could manage was always available, but didn't make an issue of eating or drinking. Hence, I think that the actual cause of death was kidney failure. But it meant he didn't need to pass urine very often, and he could have a bit if he wanted. On Christmas Day he managed two sips of whisky!

From a letter by Elizabeth Lawlor to The Natural Death Centre.

It will probably be necessary to find alternatives to 'three meals a day'. The person is likely to find their appetite waning, and may be too weak to eat more than a small amount at a time anyway. It is important to consult your nurse or doctor about nutrition, but the basic idea is this: offer small and more frequent helpings, and try to make food available to fit the person's sporadic hunger. Liquid food is easier and less tiring to take in: try soups, milk shakes (with a beaten egg for extra nourishment), yoghourt, and so on. Available from chemists, or with a prescription, are a range of nourishing drinks (some very sickly and sweet!), such as Complan, Build Up, Fortison and Ensure (they do a savoury version of this), which are acceptable if the person is only able to take in small amounts of food, although some are constipating if no bran-type roughage is added. Your doctor can prescribe food supplements, which are taste-free powders that can be sprinkled on food.

Help the person to sit up as much as possible before they eat and immediately after, if possible in a chair. Not being completely flat can help prevent nausea. If they feel dizzy or weak from the movement, they may need a calm moment to recover before eating. If the person feels nauseous, try smaller snacks, a boiled sweet, mineral water or a fizzy soft drink, or dry toast in the morning, or try waiting to give liquids for an hour or two after meals and avoid fried or fatty foods. If nausea is preventing eating, contact your GP for advice.

IVs and dehydration

Intravenous drips (IVs) are used when a person is too weak to take in enough food or liquids to stay alive. Your doctor will be able to explain the medical implications of using an IV, although in the vast majority of cases the effect is simply to prolong life artificially. Palliative care experts at a recent conference voted 89% in favour of the proposition that 'artificial rehydration is inappropriate in those who are imminently dying'.

Wherever possible, the patient's decision should be respected: many people find IVs cumbersome, uncomfortable and alienating, and some people react angrily to their use. On the other hand, if a dying person needs to feel that everything possible is being done to keep them alive, this may include intravenous feeding.

If the decision is made to use an IV, the doctor or nurse will be able to explain how it works and what to check for. It is worth clearing with them any worries you may have about the operation of the IV. A nurse will either stay with the patient, or come to check the equipment at least several times a day. IVs are not themselves dangerous, but the needle can be painful and can cause inflammation.

The alternative is to accept that death is imminent, and to concentrate upon making the dying person's remaining time more comfortable and dignified, rather than longer. Someone who does not take in enough liquid becomes dehydrated. The effect of dehydration is often somewhat anaesthetic, with a sense of mild euphoria. In a 1989 study by Andrews and Levine quoted by Chris Docker in 'The Art and Science of Fasting – Abstinence from food and drink as a means of accelerating death':

> Of the hospice nurses surveyed, 71% agreed that dehydration reduces the incidence of vomiting, 73% agreed that dehydrated patients rarely complain of thirst, 51% reported that there is relief from choking and drowning sensations when fluids are discontinued ... and 82% of the nurses disagreed with the statement that dehydration is painful.

Feelings of thirst and a dry mouth can be alleviated by applying a wet cloth to the lips, filling a drinking straw with water to drip into the mouth, or giving the person crushed ice. Ice can be made with juices or cordials and crushed; or the patient may suck chewing gum or boiled sweets or tinned or fresh pineapple chunks (this last contains an enzyme that makes it a wonderful mouth freshener); or a chemist can prepare artificial saliva concentrate (Luborant or Glandosane in various flavours), which can be diluted and taken in small and frequent doses. Swallowing is easier in general with a slightly raised head.

Washing and hygiene

Bathing

Regular washing is best not skimped, as not washing soon leads to discomfort, sores and infection. It is well worth establishing a routine: ideally a full wash once a day, with either another full wash in the day, or a hands-and-face wash when needed. Where possible, help the person with a bath or shower (a shower seat makes this easier). Be sensitive as to whether they would enjoy being pampered, or whether it is best to allow them to wash themselves as much as possible. The best way to cope with getting a frail person out of the bath is to get in yourself, stand at her head, put your arms under hers, ask her to bend her knees and then lift her up and forward.

If mobility makes going to the bathroom difficult, then help the person with a bed-bath. Wash all areas of the body in turn: help the person move into the most appropriate position each time, and keep the rest of the body warmly covered. Pay special attention to hidden areas: the back, underarms, buttocks, groin and between the legs, feet, under the breasts and/or folds of skin. As you wash, check for signs of redness or sores. Change the water in the bowl several times during the wash. Make sure that the soap is rinsed off thoroughly and, especially important, that the skin is dried completely. If the skin is too dry in patches, apply an effective moisturising cream such as Atrixo.

Mouth care

It is very important to maintain a regimen of oral hygiene, as this can be a source of considerable discomfort. If normal teeth brushing, twice a day, is difficult, then a soft toothbrush or cotton wool buds can be used. Failing that, a mouth rinse from the chemist can be used. After eating, a pinch of bicarbonate of soda in a glass of water used as a mouth rinse keeps the mouth clean and fresh. False teeth should be soaked daily in denture-cleansing solution, and brushed with a soft toothbrush. There may come a point when false teeth no longer fit - in which case they should not be used, as they may cause ulcers.

It is important to examine the mouth periodically for ulcers and to watch for the symptoms of thrush. Thrush is a very common fungal infection which shows up as very sore white patches on the tongue, gum and inside the cheek. You should report thrush to your GP.

Hair care

It is possible to wash hair in bed. You can buy Dry Shampoo powder (Aero) and liquid No-rinse Shampoo (La Professionelle) from your chemist and use it in the same way as normal shampoo, but without water: apply sparingly and then towel off. For wet washing, your district nurse may be able to supply you with a special bowl with splash attachment. You can use an ordinary plastic bowl: support the person's neck with a rolled towel, and lay plastic sheets or plastic sheeting (a bin liner will do) underneath. Or have the person hang her head over the foot of the bed.

Trim finger and toe nails regularly. Men may of course need help with shaving.

Bedsores and skincare

Prevention of bedsores may be achieved by a regime of turning the person in bed regularly:

> This takes the form of strict attention to regular turning at four-hourly intervals, or two-hourly if necessary and possible. A certain amount of hectoring the patient about changing his position is justified because it can prevent so many future problems. Following an explanation, these problems will usually be appreciated by the patient.
>
> *From 'Dying at Home' by Harriet Copperman.*

Careful positioning and avoiding pressure also help. Where two parts of the body touch, such as the thighs or the knees, prolonged pressure leads to impaired circulation which leads to skin breakdown which leads to bedsores. It is important to protect the bones, particularly if the person is very thin. See the 'Beds and bedding' section above. This can also be done with thick cushions, towels and pillows, when seated. The most common pressure points – areas prone to sores – are: the back of the head, shoulder blades, elbows, spine and coccyx (tailbone), hips and heels. These should be checked for signs of redness daily. An obvious time to do this is during washing.

Special dressings are available to prevent bedsores and skin-toughening substances can be used. If the skin does redden and break down, a doctor or nurse should be consulted for suggestions. Massage may be used as a regular method of keeping the blood circulating in sensitive areas, as well as to enhance the patient's wellbeing generally (see below).

Infected wounds can be very smelly. CancerLink, in their booklet 'Caring for the Very Sick Person At Home', say that the doctor may be able to prescribe special tablets to reduce the smell and they advise that 'concentrated lemon spirit, from the chemists, mixed with a little water' will mask most other smells. Or use joss sticks, scented candles or spray deodorisers; and give the patient a handkerchief dabbed with their favourite scent.

Bowel management

Aspects of bowel management such as constipation or diarrhoea may arise. Some of these may be managed by comforting and attention to diet. Others may involve help and advice from a nurse or doctor.

Constipation

A blockage in the bowels can cause discomfort and pain and eventually may be life threatening. Constipation is generally caused by inactivity, insufficient fibre in the diet or as a side-effect with certain pain-relieving drugs. It can usually be eased with a combination of the following dietary measures: bran and other fibre foods, fresh vegetables, prunes and fruit in general, live yoghourt, coffee, herbal tea and plenty of fluid. Cut out white bread and rice, cheese and meat if possible. Enquire at health food shops for natural and homeopathic remedies.

Incontinence

The occasional soiling of bedclothes may be inevitable, is unpleasant, and can be alarming for the patient. It is obviously important to change the sheets and help the person wash immediately; it is also important to be sensitive to what reassurance and affection she or he may need. Ask your district nurse about obtaining disposable incontinence pads from the Incontinence Laundry Service in your area; or the nurse may recommend a catheter (a hollow, flexible tube that drains urine from the bladder into a bag; and that works best if the patient remains unconstipated and drinks plenty of fluids).

Insomnia

The cares and concerns of a dying person may cause sleeplessness. If your patient has difficulty sleeping, see if you can help without sleeping pills and barbiturates.

Addiction is not a real concern with the dying, but why interfere more with delicate body balances? Some possibilities are to take, before bedtime: calcium tablets (two grams), camomile tea, valerian with B-vitamin complex, a warm glass of milk, or tryptophan. Tryptophan is an amino acid in meat, milk and cheese. Turkey is high in tryptophan. Try a warm bath, hot foot bath, a back rub or foot massage, or a guided meditation.

Stroke the hair and scalp and encourage the person to let all thoughts float away and to let the head feel spacious and empty, clouds drifting in and out. When I can't sleep I use the Bach Flower Remedy, Sweet Chestnut. Avoid coffee, black tea and all dark coloured colas before bedtime. They contain eye-opening caffeine. It's also OK not to go to sleep even when someone else thinks it's time. Encourage the person to read, write, watch TV, listen to soothing music or think for a while. If not sleeping continues to trouble the patient, ask a doctor about sleeping medications.

Reprinted with permission from 'Coming Home: A Guide to Dying at Home with Dignity', © 1987 Deborah Duda, Aurora Press, PO Box 573, Santa Fe, NM 87504, USA.

Depression/anxiety

Anxiety will probably be experienced to a greater or lesser degree by most patients.

Some may become mildly anxious on reaching such a significant point in their lives. Others have always been so anxious with any new event or change of circumstance, however minor, that the advance of debilitating illness and the approach of death, fills them with a terror which is sad to behold. The main treatment is listening, and honest discussion with the patient of the many causes of his anxiety.

Depression, like anxiety, usually involves taking the time to listen to the patient or encouraging him to talk. He may understandably be depressed for many reasons, but if this is the result of boredom or inactivity it should be possible to find a remedy.

From 'Dying at Home' by Harriet Copperman.

Consult your doctor, of course, if you feel medication for anxiety or depression may be called for.

Relaxation

A cassette recorder may be particularly useful:

The person may listen to the wide variety of music and guided meditation tapes available that might encourage investigation and letting go [see under Tapes in the Resources chapter]. Speaking of the process of letting go at two in the afternoon when the patient feels relatively well and is not particularly open to investigating dying may not seem appropriate or even be well received. But a tape about working with pain or preparing for the moment of death, left at the bedside, may be appreciatively absorbed when the patient feels it is the right moment. Perhaps at four in the morning when sleep has become impossible and the pain in the body has intensified, that individual may then feel prepared, open to hearing what earlier in the day may have seemed beside the point or frightening.

From 'Who Dies?' by Stephen Levine.

Richard Boerstler advocates a meditative Tibetan-inspired breathing technique. The carer copies the patient's breathing pattern, making the sound 'Ah' on the outbreath, strung out as 'Aaaaaaaaaaaahhhhhhhh'. The patient may like to make the same sound at least for the first ten breaths or so, or may prefer just to listen. This simplest of exercises can greatly enhance the patient's sense of physical comfort and wellbeing. (See under Videos in the Resources chapter – also for Joanna Gilpin's details; she runs seminars in the UK on Boerstler's method.)

Massage

If you have Lymphoedema, swellings caused by damage to the body's lymphatic drainage system, there is a form of gentle lymph drainage massage you can give yourself on a daily basis. Ask your nurse for the excellent book 'Living with Lymphoedema – Your Guide to Treatment', published by Marie Curie (see the Resources chapter).

Massage in its various forms is useful in decreasing tension and anxiety whilst deepening personal contact. Simple touching, aromatherapy or foot massage can all be relaxing and encouraging. (Be careful about massaging or applying lotions to skin damaged by radiotherapy.) A personal account of giving scalp massage shows that it can offer many benefits to the dying patient:

Scalp massage

Last year a friend of mine died of cancer. She found it very difficult to open up or to ask for much. I offered to give her scalp massage. She loved it. She said it made her feel wonderful and I did it for her for many of her last days. It made her feel relaxed and cared for and sometimes she talked easily and personally - although I never pushed her to. It was wonderful for me to have something to offer which she really wanted.

This massage offers an easy way to loving physical contact. It gives the patient a relaxing time and I suspect that many will find it a good time to talk: relaxed, loved, but not always looked at. (Some people, as a parallel example, will talk on a car journey where they have company but are not looked at.) It is easy to do once explained: you use your finger tips to move the scalp over the skull. Ask the person you massage to tell you what they like and don't like, and if you are doing it too hard or soft. They should sit or lie comfortably and not 'help' by holding their head in a 'good' position – they should just relax. You move their head gently if necessary. (Try also gentle face massage, as well as neck and shoulders, all places where tension accumulates.) Feedback is the key to getting it right.

I have seen people sitting next to a dying person having run out of things to do, say or offer. I felt that this idea might mean a lot to many people.

From a letter by Margaret Ryder to The Natural Death Centre.

Contact

Simpler than massage is a hug. A spontaneous hug, or ritual 'good morning' hug, may seem out of place for whatever reason. If there is something in the way, you can either offer a hug, which gives the other person the chance to say No, or just surprise them!

Having people going about ordinary activities in the same room is another way of keeping close. While you read a book, eat dinner or watch television, you can just be with your relative. Make sure that everyone in the family is aware of when it would be a good idea to leave the person in privacy.

Making contact can involve simple but valuable actions:

Even when someone is apparently unconscious, do keep talking to them. On a very deep level it is reassuring, and apparently hearing is the last sense to go. Touch and smell are also important.

When my husband was in hospital I started putting a notepad by his bed. Every time I visited, before I left I would write down when I would be back, where I was going, etc – and that I *had* been. Once home, I kept it up so he had a memory prompt. And when he died, I had a record of the last weeks.
From a letter by Elizabeth Lawlor to The Natural Death Centre.

Small gestures mean a lot.

Pain management

Natural pain relief may be useful in addition to any medication the patient is taking.

Breathing and visualisation techniques can be very useful in working with pain. If there's delay in getting a pain reliever, you might try them. In some cases, they may preclude your needing drugs at all. Breathing can be as useful for dying as it is for birthing. When we feel pain, we tense up and tend to stop breathing fully. Our cells don't get the oxygen they need to clean out toxins and keep the nerve signals straight, and the pain gets worse.

One of the first things to do for pain is to keep breathing. Unless someone has had previous experience with breathing consciously, he or she may focus on the pain and fear and forget to breathe. As the helper, encourage the person to breathe deeply, to breathe into the area that hurts, and then down into the toes. Ask the person to relax, to 'soften' around the area that hurts, and open him or herself to the sensation of pain. As the person surrenders, gives up resistance, more oxygen enters the area and the pain may lessen. The body senses that its message is received and relaxes. Keep repeating, 'soften, relax, open'.

Paying attention to pain helps relieve it if we don't judge it as bad! It just is.

I find it helpful to combine breathing techniques with hot water bottles and foot massages. While the person is breathing into the area that hurts, partially fill two hot water bottles with hot, not boiling, water. Cover the bottles with a towel so you don't burn the person's skin and place them under the feet and on the area that hurts. If you don't have hot water bottles, put the person's feet into a bucket of medium-hot tap water. Put a hot washcloth on the forehead. Together these seem to keep energy moving through the body so pain is lessened or eliminated. Some people prefer ice packs and cold water. Either is OK. (If the pain is severe and you're unprepared, call a doctor.) If it feels right to you, add a foot massage to further relax the person and to stimulate increased circulation.

Breathing and foot massage are useful techniques for calming anyone in a stressful situation. You might want to take time for them yourself.

I sometimes hear talk in New Age circles that taking drugs for pain is somehow not spiritual. That's baloney. Again, physical pain is a message that something's not working right in the body. The dying get the message loud and clear only this time there's nothing they can do about it. The body can't be fixed. Taking drugs is useful to free us to experience dying on other levels and not to fixate on one level – the body. If we're in pain, the body has our undivided attention. And if dying teaches us anything, it teaches us that we're more than just a body.

If, as many New Age people believe, our essential identity is God, why torture God's body – or anyone else's – by not taking pain medication? That's cruelty. If we truly believe that everything is equally sacred, morphine is just as sacred as the herb from which it's derived.

Reprinted with permission from 'Coming Home: A Guide to Dying at Home with Dignity', © 1987 Deborah Duda, Aurora Press, PO Box 573, Santa Fe, NM 87504, USA.

It is advisable to keep your GP informed about the person's changing pain relief needs. The Beecham Manual of Family Practice advises doctors that many patients 'are given too little analgesia too late'. Strong opioids (such as morphine – or its recent alternatives, with fewer side-effects, such as the new Zydol SR, an opiate analog; and Durogesic fentanyl, applied through a three-day skin patch) are required for most patients with cancer pain – so recommended the 1994 Working Party on Clinical Guidelines in Palliative Care. Other types of pain may require anti-convulsants or antidepressants, local radiotherapy, nerve blocks, ultrasound, heat or transcutaneous nerve stimulators. If necessary, ask to be referred to the Pain Relief Clinic at your local hospital – they will advise not only on the best medication, but also on additional methods of pain control, such as meditation. Patients dying at home can often have better pain relief than in hospitals, where doctors are loth to use drugs, especially the opiates, appropriately – mainly through ignorance, or fear of legal consequences. In her letter to The Natural Death Centre Elizabeth Lawlor says that she kept a chart of the medication which her husband received, 'partly to see if there was a pattern of when it was most needed, and partly for the doctor to see what was going on'. In this way it may be possible both to pre-empt pain and to establish clear communication about the person's needs. Pain is made worse by fear, loneliness and anticipation of pain to come.

Here is a pain meditation, for the patient to read or that can be read aloud very slowly by a friend. You could record it on a tape - leave up to ten second gaps between each direction, the reason being that the body responds at a much slower rate than the mind. This is a considerably reduced version – see Stephen Levine's book for the text in full and for other equally helpful meditations. (See also under Videos and Tapes in the final chapter.)

Guided pain meditation:

Sit or lie down in a position you find comfortable. Allow yourself to settle into this position so that the whole body feels fully present where it sits or lies.

Bring your attention to the area of sensation that has been uncomfortable. Let your attention come wholly to that area. Let the awareness be present, moment to moment, to receive the sensations generated there.

Allow the discomfort to be felt.

Moment to moment new sensations seem to arise.

Does the flesh cramp against the pain? Feel how the body tends to grasp it in a fist, tries to close it off.

Begin to allow the body to open all around that sensation.

Feel the tension and resistance that comes to wall off the sensation.

Don't push away the pain. Just let it be there. Feel how the body tries to isolate it. Tries to close it off. Picture that fist. Feel how the body is clenched in resistance.

Feel how the body holds each new sensation.

Begin gradually to open that closedness around sensation. The least resistance can be so painful. Open. Soften. All around the sensation. Allow the fist, moment to moment, to open. To give space to the sensation.

Let go of the pain. Why hold on a moment longer?

Like grasping a burning ember, the flesh of the closed fist is seared in its holding. Open. Soften all around the sensation. Let the fist of resistance begin to loosen. To open.

The palm of that fist softening. The fingers beginning to loosen their grip. Opening. All around the sensation.

The fist loosening. Gradually opening. Moment to moment, letting go of the pain. Release the fear that surrounds it.

Notice any fear that has accumulated around the pain. Allow the fear to melt. Let tension dissolve, so that the sensations can softly radiate out as they will. Don't try to capture the pain. Let it float free. No longer held in the grasp of resistance. Softening. Opening all around the sensation.

The fist opening. The fingers, one by one, loosening their grip.

The sensation no longer encapsulated in resistance. Opening.

Let the pain soften. Let the pain be. Let go of the resistance that tries to smother the experience. Allow each sensation to come fully into consciousness. No holding. No pushing away. The pain beginning to float free in the body.

All grasping relinquished. Just awareness and sensation meeting moment to moment. Received gently by the softening flesh.

The fist opened into a soft, spacious palm. The fingers loose. The fist dissolved back into the soft, open flesh. No tension. No holding.

Let the body be soft and open. Let the sensation float free. Easy. Gently.
Softening, opening all around the pain.
Just sensation. Floating free in the soft, open body.

From 'Who Dies?' by Stephen Levine.

It may become necessary to relieve pain by means of intravenous or intramuscular injections. The latter can be given by the carer once instructed by a doctor or nurse. Better still might be for your medical helper to obtain a subcutaneous syringe driver – this has revolutionised pain control at home. It provides a continuous infusion of painkiller, so that there is no need for injections, and is thus very practical for home use.

Music

The astounding power of music to soothe a person who is dying has been most dramatically demonstrated by the work of Therese Schroeder-Sheker in the United States, who runs the Chalice of Repose project and is bringing harp music, Gregorian chants and other spiritual music into hospice and other settings. Here she describes the beginnings of her work:

Musical midwifery for the dying

The first time that I was ever actually present and alone with someone who was in fact dying is the first time that I ever really experienced silence, and an indescribably delicate kind of light. The man was struggling, frightened, unable to breathe. No more respirators, dilators, tracheotomies or medicines could resolve his disintegrated lungs. He could take no more in, could swallow no more, and in his complete weariness, there was almost nothing he could return to the world. I climbed into his hospital bed and propped myself behind him in midwifery position, my head and heart lined up behind his, my legs folded near his waist, and I held his frail body by the elbows and suspended his weight. At first I held us both in interior prayer, but soon began leaning down to his left ear and singing Gregorian chant in an almost pianissimo.

He immediately nestled in my arms and began to breathe regularly, and we, as a team, breathed together. The chants seemed to bring him balance, dissolving fears, and compensating for those issues still full of sting. When his heart ceased to beat, I stayed still for long moments. Almost twenty years later, the silence that replaced his struggle and that was present in his room has continued to penetrate the core of my life.

People ask if a midwife knows fear or sorrow: none of that exists if you are with the dying person. It's their time, not yours. Any burden or sorrow or wounds of your own disappear.

From 'The Luminous Wound' by Therese Schroeder-Sheker.
The Chalice of Repose is at 554 West Broadway, Missoula,
MT 59802, USA (tel 001 406 542 0001 ext 2810; fax 001
406 728 2206; e-mail: <71151.522@compuserve.com>).

Arts

A family doctor in Kent, Dr David McGavin, gave over the top floor of his surgery to three therapists treating patients (who were terminally and seriously ill) with music, singing, movement and art:

> He hired them out of his own salary four years ago to help patients who had reached the end of the NHS road.
>
> Above Dr McGavin's surgery, Alan Baker and Ellen Bishop, both in their fifties, are exploring the use of colour on a wet canvas under the guidance of an art therapist, Hazel Adams. The walls are decorated with the artwork of other patients and the quiet concentration of Alan and Ellen produces a tranquil atmosphere.
>
> Alan was diagnosed as having Parkinson's Disease seven years ago. He says he is no artist, but the weekly sessions have a deeply relaxing effect. He also had nine months' intensive eurhythmics – rhythmic movement to music – which helped him recover balance and flexibility lost through the disease.
>
> Dr McGavin believes much of the success of the therapies lies in the cooperation of the patient. 'The problem in general practice occurs when you just see the body as a complex machine, and call in the doctor to fix the part that goes wrong,' he said. This merely encourages the patient to wait passively for the doctor to make him or her better. 'I ask the patients if they would like to have a go.'
>
> Therapist John Logan treats patients in the last stages of cancer. He said: 'Cancer patients suffer tremendous fear and anxiety. The music and movement helps that, putting something healthy and life-giving in the face of the illness.'
>
> *From The Independent (Feb. 12th 1988).*

Hospice Arts is an organisation which promotes the arts as 'an essential component of the hospice philosophy of ensuring that people really experience as much as life can offer right up to the very moment they die':

Hospice Arts

Taking part in creative arts activity can be a vital component of whole-person care, and can be therapeutic in a number of ways. By making something worthwhile, you can restore a feeling of self-esteem and a sense of purpose at a time when life may seem confusing and of little value. The piece created can become a treasured memento for family and friends, charged with important emotions. The arts may encourage communication, and stimulate mobility and concentration. The act of creativity, incorporating both mind and spirit, can be a means of exploring and resolving strong and difficult emotions, and those who care for terminally ill patients can also benefit in this way.

For some hospice patients, it may be a case of reviving a long-ignored skill or enthusiasm which had been forced into the background by the business of day-to-day living. For others, the creative arts may be a new experience, yet they too can enjoy making their own works of art, discovering hidden talents and abilities.

From the Hospice Information Service Bulletin (May 1990 –
for contact details see the Resources chapter).

Yvonne Malik suggests the creation of Memory Box personal museums by the elderly or the terminally ill, and has made a beautiful prototype of her own, shoebox size. She writes:

Memory Boxes

Many of us have keepsakes – nostalgic mementoes which stimulate our memories, such as old photos, letters, trinkets, holiday souvenirs, scarves, medals. Individually they may seem small or insignificant, but put together in a display, these same objects could become a decorative and pleasing Personal Museum.

The arrangements could be displayed inexpensively in, for instance, sewing boxes, tool boxes, circular tea trays or shallow suitcases.

Memory Boxes leave something precious behind for our relatives and children. They are the opportunity to communicate in nonverbal ways that 'I was here; I did this; I learnt that', or personal letters can be placed there.

See final chapter for Malik's address,
under Organisations and Individuals.

Barnados have now made a Memory Book – a yellow loose leaf folder – which fits inside a Memory Store – a large yellow empty box containing six drawers. They can be ordered for £15 and £29-95 respectively, plus £2-95 p&p, from Dispatch Services, Barnados Child Care Publications, Paycocke Road, Basildon, Essex SS14 3DR (tel 01268 520 224 ext. 267).

The final days

Janet Stevenson wrote to the Natural Death Centre about the death of her Gran:

Passive not active

In a book about childbirth, I read that you need to give the child peace and quiet to be born, without being rushed or troubled. The most important thing at the other end of life is just sitting quietly with the dying and being there, and holding her hand, that was what I learned. Or so it was with Gran. Passive not active.

Josefine Speyer of the Befriending Network describes how each day those who are dying may sleep more and awake less. They may become unable to hold up the head, and be too weary to speak. During sleep, the time between breaths may increase to 12 to 15 seconds. They may appear to be forgetful and muddled. Then, typically, the hands and feet become colder, the colour fades from the skin, the breathing stops, the eyes gaze into space, colour drains from the lips – the person has died. (Do not be alarmed, writes Dr Lee, in 'A Good Death', if there is later a slight gurgling or sighing noise of air escaping from the throat or a sudden shifting of a limb as the muscles relax.)

For some, this can be a moment of great peace and silence, with no rush to leave the bedside – 'this time is immensely precious' writes Josefine Speyer, 'almost sacred and to be respected.'

Chapter 4

INEXPENSIVE, GREEN
FAMILY-ORGANISED
FUNERALS

Almost everyone who has tried it advocates wherever possible looking after at least some aspects of the funeral of friends and relatives oneself, with the assistance of family and neighbours, without depending entirely on funeral directors. This chapter, parts of which are not for the squeamish, aims to help you find the courage to organise and design such a funeral, by arming you with the essential information and with tales from some pioneers. The next chapter, however, gives advice about getting professionals in to help you. The suggested advantages for a 'd-i-y' funeral are that:

• Participating in this way, according to psychotherapists, helps people to begin to come to terms with their loss;

• You have the option of trying for a greener funeral if you so wish;

• It can be far less expensive – and potentially free if the body is buried in a shroud on your own land, or from about £200 if cremation is used (whereas a Manchester Unity Friendly Society survey found that the average cost of a burial in 1996 was £1,523, with cremation's average cost being £1,024. These figures tend to be 22% higher in the South East);

• You have more control over every aspect of the funeral, which can as a consequence be a much more personal and less 'assembly-line' affair.

Below are some of the stories from the front line, with a discussion of the points they raise; first, a letter that appeared in The Times from the Reverend Canon Raymond Wilkinson of Warwick, who looks back nostalgically to the past and urges relatives not to hand over funerals entirely to the trade:

Personal involvement in funerals

Two of the ancient parish churches where I served as incumbent (one of them as recently as 1970) still possessed the parish bier, whereon in past days parishioners had themselves placed the body of the deceased member of their family, in a coffin made by the local joiner, before pushing it solemnly to their church. They were then met by the parson at the lych-gate before the service in church and the subsequent burial in the churchyard, again performed by friends and relatives.

Undertakers were – and are – neither necessary nor obligatory; but we in this country increasingly divorce ourselves from this last service to our relatives by handing everything over to the professionals – often to the choice of sadly overused hymns.

One of the most memorable funerals I have conducted (from a total of about 5,000) involved no undertakers. The relatives laid out the body; the coffin was made by friends; the family bore it from their own car; after the church service, they lowered the coffin into the grave which they had dug.

A few weeks ago (without, of course, the grave) I conducted just such a funeral at the local crematorium. Could it be that an uncommon but godly sense of what funerals are about is returning? Personal involvement may be painful, but it represents reality and personal accountability – as well as a proper reminder of our own mortality.

The dramatic increase in crematorium disposal of the dead in this century is said to be largely in the interests of convenience, cleanliness and conservation. Where convenience is an overriding factor that may well be so. But ashes (eds: consisting mostly of calcium, with a similar alkaline effect to lime) are useless to growing plants, and I have yet to read of a health risk proven regarding burials.

Churchyards remained relatively small until the 19th century because the usual small wooden memorials decayed, families died out, bones discovered were placed in the charnel-houses built in churchyards, and God's Acre was reused. On the Continent today, such economy of land is general. Grave space there is reused, unless further leases are paid for.

It seems to me that journeys to distant, and often somewhat ugly, crematoria have added expense and detachment where death is concerned. Any enquiry into spiralling costs of undertaking needs to be linked to our increasing detachment from involvement domestically and parochially with our departed friends and relatives.

From a letter to The Times (April 25th 1991) from the Reverend Canon Raymond Wilkinson, 42 Coten End, Warwick.

The recycled coffin

The parish burials of the past that Wilkinson refers to were originally ecologically sound affairs: back in the 15th Century, the body was wrapped in a shroud and the parish coffin, stored in the church, would be reused time and again – in some parts of the country, indeed, town councils decreed that funerals should be 'shroud only' with coffins for the privileged few who could obtain special permission (see the fascinating account in 'The English Way of Death' by Julian Litten, pages 123 to 129). The Natural Death Centre has visions of a similar green funeral service in the future, where the coffin could be reused (and often delivered directly to the next family needing it) with a body covering preventing any leakage into the coffin.

Wilkinson questions whether crematoria are environmentally friendly. So which is better for the environment, being buried or cremated?

Which is greener, burial or cremation?

In the UK cremation was originally presented as the environment-friendly option, with the anti-burial slogan of 'keeping the land for the living'. Nowadays cemeteries and churchyards help protect the land *from* the living, preventing land being used for development and often acting as a refuge for wildlife. Some of the few bits of green space left in Tokyo are graveyards – although some bodies in Tokyo now have to be kept in special warehouses close to the railway stations until burial space can be found in country graveyards. In some countries, in the early days of cremation, the body was taken out of its coffin before being incinerated; nowadays, however, the coffins are all wastefully burnt and we are in the realms of European regulations concerning the pollution of the atmosphere and ground water from the glues used, from the plastics in artificial joints and other implants and from the metals, hydrogen chloride (the cremator's pollution control systems do not catch these emissions), carbon dioxide, formaldehyde and furans emitted in the burning process. A report from Warren Springs Laboratory in Stevenage found that even one of the crematoria updated to bring it into line with the new standards, emitted far more dioxins than permitted – dioxins can cause cancer and other illnesses at low concentrations. Ken West, in his report 'Woodland Burial', writes that a heavy concentration of mercury from tooth fillings has been identified around crematoria.

The conclusion must be that burial is a greener option than cremation, particularly if the burial can be in a nature reserve, with a tree planted instead of having a headstone, as discussed later in this chapter. If cremation is chosen, coffins entering cremators should contain no substances that will pollute when burnt – for instance, no plastics, PVC, fibreglass, styrofoam, rubber or metals such as zinc.

Jane Spottiswoode, who lives near Bala in North Wales, shares similar doubts to those of Raymond Wilkinson about the encroachments of the funeral industry, and has written a spirited book, 'Undertaken with Love', describing the funeral of her husband:

Undertaken with Love

When Jane Spottiswoode's husband Nigel was diagnosed as having lung cancer in 1986, she began to put into operation a plan they had made long before (when both were in perfect health) which was to be buried as cheaply as possible. Indeed her husband had said he would happily be consigned to the compost heap, any funeral money being put towards a slap-up party.

Jane set about arranging Nigel's funeral during his second period in hospital. Immediately, she came across the first of numerous hurdles – that of purchasing a coffin. Armed with the Yellow Pages, she settled down to try to find one but was soon met with much hostility. No manufacturer would supply her with one; she was told they only supplied to funeral directors. So she turned to the undertakers themselves, but the results were the same. They would only supply a coffin as part of their full service.

Jane grew cunning. She was, she said, a theatrical producer, intending to tour village halls with an amateur production of 'A Scent of Flowers' by James Saunders, a play she knew well and one which had a coffin on the stage throughout. 'Oh no we couldn't possibly supply one of our coffins for that sort of thing!' said the lady on the telephone. 'Why not?' asked Jane. 'It might offend our customers,' came the prim reply. Surely not the audience in distant village halls? 'They are all our potential customers,' said the lady, but before putting down the receiver on this incontrovertible truth, she revealed the name of a firm which Jane will always hold in great regard – that of S S Joinery, Stoke on Trent, who would supply a coffin in veneer chipboard for £34-50 plus VAT as long as she could collect it herself.

At a total cost of £197-97 against the £700 or so charged by the Co-op, Nigel Spottiswoode's funeral was certainly cheap. But that wasn't the main point. From start to finish she regarded it as an act of affectionate respect, as did his pall-bearing friends. 'My husband was just taken to the crematorium by his friends, instead of employing a stranger to do it. That was all it amounted to, really, and if more people realised how comparatively easy it can be with a little forethought, they might like to consider it for themselves.'

Although in excellent health, Jane Spottiswoode has already purchased her own coffin which she keeps in the loft, tucked away in the shadows behind the water tank to avoid alarming the plumber.

> *From publicity material for 'Undertaken with Love'*
> *by Jane Spottiswoode.*

Incidentally, Jane Spottiswoode subsequently discovered that SS Joinery denied all knowledge of having supplied a coffin to her. In China, many elderly people share her desire to have a coffin ready in advance (they get the children to buy one for them). And as for putting the body on the compost heap, a letter writer to The Independent quoted with approval an advertisement in James Joyce's 'Ulysses': 'Well preserved fat corpse, gentleman, epicure, invaluable for fruit garden. A bargain £3-13-6.'

Andrew Kerr has suggested further research into how body composting could work:

Composting bodies

I suggest compost funerals. Animal wastes (and the human body belongs to the animal kingdom) are an integral part of the process by which the vegetable kingdom is sustained. If animal remains are mixed with vegetable wastes to the proportion of one in four, in a controlled system, turned and dampened correctly, the result will be a perfect product to be fed to any kind of plant. Most dangerous pathogens are dealt with in the process.

The corpse could be taken to the Compostorium and placed in a specially constructed autoclave or pressure cooker. The corpse would have already been disembowelled and that material placed into a methane digester; this would have averted the potential danger of pathogens. The gas so generated would contribute to the slow and steady heat required to render the remains to a condition ready to be ground up to a kind of slurry to be 'intimately mixed' with straw and other vegetable wastes.

The whole process would be completed in about twelve weeks or so: a decent time for mourning. The finished compost could then be incorporated into the family memorial garden.

This would be far better than burial which is too deep for aerobic processes, or wasteful incineration which is damaging to the environment.

From a letter from Andrew Kerr, Oak Tree Cottage, 89 Netherton Road, Appleton, Abingdon, Oxon OX13 5LA (tel 01865 862237).

Keeping the body at home

Jane Spottiswoode's book about her husband's funeral came in for criticism in the journal of the National Association of Funeral Directors, where the following somewhat value-laden and insensitive comment was made: 'She found that when she needed a mortuary in which to leave her husband until the time of the cremation, she was forced to resort to hijacking the municipal mortuary. Luckily for her she lives in a quiet rural area and as a consequence that facility was otherwise not in use. However, in a busy urban area the use of the municipal mortuary would neither be possible nor desirable.'

Keeping the body cool

So how is the city dweller to manage without the municipal mortuary? Whether or not the person has died in hospital, the hospital mortuary there might be willing to look after the body for a few days, most probably without charge or for a donation; or a funeral director might be willing to provide just this facility without the complete package (certainly many of those listed in the next chapter are willing to do this). If the person has died at home, the body could be kept in a room with the window open, in the coldest room in the house or even in the cellar if preferred. Salt water washing used to be the practice in some cultures. The A. B. Wildlife Trust Fund suggests having a refrigerator with its door open and a cover taped around the door to form a tunnel around the body. In rural France, a special refrigeration plate is often placed under the body so as to make it possible for the body to remain in the house whilst relatives come to pay their respects. Wrapped ice cubes could be placed by the body (but not placed against bare skin where they may burn). It is more important to keep the trunk of the body cool than the head or limbs. Dry ice (which gradually sublimates to a carbon dioxide mist without leaving a wet puddle) could be bought – it has been used on occasion by mortuaries, when their equipment breaks down; and is widely used in Japan in hot weather to allow the body to be remain on a futon at home before the funeral. One supplier in London of dry ice in pellet form is BOC Hackney Ltd, 59 Eastway, London E9 5NS (tel 0181 985 5544), where 10kg, approximately three days' supply, can be collected (from 8-15am to 4-30pm, weekdays only) for £32-16 including VAT, or it can be sent to you express by TNT for an extra £20 or so.

Why keep the body at home?

In some religions, such as Tibetan Buddhism, it is argued that it is best to leave the body undisturbed for several days after death, to allow the complete departure of the soul. And in the West, there are many who emphasise the importance of allowing family members and relatives to see the body – and of giving young children such opportunities, but not insisting on any occasion if they prefer to stay away.

Bereaved parents denied the opportunity to see and touch the bodies of their dead children often deeply regret this. The purpose of concealing grief seems to be to protect other people, not the griever.

The need to hold one's dead child

My child was killed in a road accident. He was 17.

We arrived at the hospital just after 10.15 pm: no one was expecting us. 'Everybody has gone and I should have gone too by now,' a social worker said. My friend and I were put in a small anteroom and the door was closed. We had been put into a box with the lid closed to spare us the sight of panicky people rushing to and fro, telephone calls being made, while the system was reassembled for us.

Apparently there was great rushing about preparing Timothy for viewing. Putting a piece of gauze over a graze on his head was regarded as important so that I should not be offended or frightened or disgusted. We walked along a corridor. We arrived at a door. It was opened. No more hope; no more thinking it might not be Timothy. Incredibly, it was my Timothy, my lovely boy.

He was lying on an altar covered by a purple cloth edged with gold braid and tassels. Only his head was visible. Such was the atmosphere of constraint I either asked or was given permission to enter. I can't remember. I entered alone. The others watched through the open door. I stroked his cheek. He was cold.

Timothy had not ceased to be my child. I desperately needed to hold him, to look at him, to find out where he was hurting. These instincts don't die immediately with the child. The instinct to comfort and cuddle, to examine the wounds, to try to understand, most of all to hold. But I had been told not to do 'anything silly'. They were watching to see that I didn't. So I couldn't move the purple cloth. I couldn't find his hand. I couldn't do anything. I betrayed my instincts and my son by standing there 'not doing anything silly'. I knew that if I did my watchers would immediately lead me away.

Why? No doubt they thought they were acting for the best. We, as a society, have lost contact with our most basic instincts. We marvel at cats washing and caring for their kittens. We admire the protection an elephant gives her sick calf and are tearful and sympathetic when she refuses to leave her offspring when he dies, when she examines and nuzzles him and wills him to breathe. This is exactly what the human mother's most basic instinct tells her to do. And we deny her. She is being denied her motherhood when in extremis.

We have come to think we are protecting her when we are really protecting ourselves. We have forgotten that this is the mother who has cleaned up the vomit, washed his nappies, cleaned the blood from his wounds, kissed him better and held him in his distress. She has done all this since the day he was born. If he has been in hospital she has possibly fed him by tube, she may have changed his dressings and given injections. She will certainly have washed him, helped him to dress and combed his hair. She will have held him. Who are we protecting when we deny her this last service which she can do for her child? We are not protecting the child. We are not protecting her. The fact of her child's death is not altered by the denial of her instincts.

Having nursed my mother through her last illness, I was privileged to bathe her after death, put clean dressings on her wounds, remove her catheter. It was a tearful and loving last service that my sister and I were privileged to perform for her. It helped to heal our grief. But my lovely boy was draped on an altar, covered with a robe, and all expressions of love and care I had were denied to me. And I don't know when that wound will heal. The caring services should think again about how we serve the bereaved. A cup of tea and an aseptic look at the body does not serve. If it is our wish and instinct to hold and wash the body and to talk to the dead loved one, we should be helped to do this. We will be distressed and may frequently need to stop and wipe the tears, but we will be helped in our healing.

From an article by Sheila Awoonor-Renner
in The Guardian (Mar. 15th 1991).

Even if the bereaved accept that a body is too damaged to be seen, there can be intermediate measures. The Child Bereavement Trust told the Guardian the story of the father of a very damaged stillborn baby. The father had a photograph taken of the baby's hand curling round his fingers – 'it was the most beautiful picture, and having something like that can make the difference to whether you can cope or not.'

From a more academic perspective, one researcher, Therese Rando, has written, with reference to adult deaths as well as children's:

Visits to the body

Give the bereaved adequate private time to be with, touch, caress and hold the body, as time with the deceased may be very critical in helping them settle unfinished business and accept the reality of loss.

Those who did not view the body or had arranged for immediate disposal of the remains (excluding the normal Jewish custom of not viewing the body) reported the greatest hostility following the death, the greatest increase in consumption of alcohol, tranquillisers and sedatives, the greatest increase in tension and anxiety, the lowest positive recall of the deceased and greater problems in adjustment to the death, particularly among male respondents.

From 'Grief, Dying and Death' by Therese Rando (Champaign,
USA; Research Press Co., 1984) quoted in 'Caring For
Your Own Dead' by Lisa Carlson.

The Natural Death Centre has proposed that the phrase 'visiting the body' could replace 'viewing', as visiting could include the idea of touching the body. As Stephen Briggs has noted, 'the word "view" is coldly impersonal and conveys a sense of distance and slight distaste. It perpetuates the "keep at a distance and do not touch" inclination.'

Fear of being buried alive

A surprising number of people are frightened that they will be buried alive. Indeed this has occasionally happened. Back in 1912, the Funeral Service Journal reported:

> In Galicia, the body of George Masug, a rich landowner, was being interred, and the last prayers were being said by the officiating priests at the open grave amid weeping, when, as the bereaved relatives were dropping earth on the coffin, ghastly sounds were heard to proceed from it. The cover was lifted and a panic arose among members of the family when the supposed-dead man was found to be alive. He was at once freed from his terrible position. Masug, who was supposed to have died from apoplexy, soon recovered and was able to walk home with the mourners.

More recently, the same journal told of a case in America:

> The Herald Tribune of May 1994 reported that Elenor Marks from New York, apparently dead and being taken in her coffin to the graveside, alarmed the men carrying it by a faint tapping from its interior. When the lid was removed, it was found that the supposed corpse was alive. She was then moved back to her residence and is recovering. She says that she had full knowledge all the time of what was passing, whilst arrangements were made for her burial, but was unable to give any sign of consciousness until the fear of being interred alive aroused her to action.

One perhaps over-suspicious correspondent has complained to The Natural Death Centre about 'the unsavoury practice of removing people from nursing homes to undertakers' parlours before being certified or seen by a doctor, even though a qualified nurse may have expressed an opinion that the person was dead. The reason why it is unsatisfactory is that most undertakers either embalm, sew the gums together or refrigerate the person immediately they arrive on the premises. The consequences of a person not being actually dead are horrific.'

These are not wholly unrealistic fears in Western society today – in 1996, two women in the UK were found alive after being pronounced dead and a study of 150,000 exhumed American war-dead from World War II in Europe it was revealed that no less than 6,000 (4%) showed signs of having been buried alive.

Doctors, if very concerned to avoid, for instance, mis-diagnosing a profound barbiturate- or morphine-induced coma as death, are advised to listen to the heart and lungs with a stethoscope for up to five minutes; to feel the carotid pulse at the side of the neck; to shine a light in the eyes (to see if the pupils stay dilated) and to check there is no blink reflex when the eye is touched. Other situations that can lead to mistakes include hypothermia, near-drowning, unconsciousness from electric shocks, alcohol intoxication and shock following blood loss. In any case, keeping the body at home for several days can reassure all concerned that the person is truly dead.

Laying out the body

If you have a nurse helping you, she or he will normally help with laying out the body. Traditionally whoever is attending to the body closes the eyes after death – and coins on the eyelids can help with this. The chin is propped up with a pillow to keep the mouth closed, or a piece of cloth can be tied under the chin and over the head. To prevent seepage from the body, it may in exceptional cases be prudent (depending on the risk of infection, the likely rate of decomposition and the aesthetics of the situation) to plug the natural orifices (rectum, nasal passages, throat). This is simply done with cotton wool using disposable gloves and some lubrication such as soap or KY jelly if required. An alternative, if there is seepage, is to use incontinence pads from the chemist, replacing them as necessary. The correct procedure when laying out is to press upon the lower abdomen thus ensuring that the bladder is drained. A waterproof dressing should be put on any body ulcers or leaking wounds. As soon as the doctor has certified the cause of death, the body can be washed and dressed, as this is easier in the first six hours or so after death, before the body stiffens. The head is left raised on a pillow – as the embalmers put it, 'this helps prevent the expanding internal contents from purging.'

One correspondent wrote to The Natural Death Centre that she felt 'somewhat unnerved' when washing the body of her husband an hour after he had died, 'to see the purple/bluish state of his back and buttocks, due to the blood draining into it, once circulation stopped'.

For some religious communities, such as Sikhs and Muslims, preparing the body for the funeral by gently washing the body is an act of devotion that family members insist on, even if they have to go to do it in the funeral director's premises. For many Jews, the body should remain untouched for twenty minutes after death, with all washing and preparation the prerogative of the Jewish community.

Forms and procedures

The bureaucracy facing newly-bereaved relatives who are arranging a funeral is fairly minimal, although there will be many more forms to fill in for those looking after probate of the estate. The Consumers' Association devotes two books to the subject ('What To Do When Someone Dies' – the 1994 edition is unreliable, especially on the laws surrounding private land burial – and 'Wills and Probate' – which is excellent); and there is a free Benefits Agency pamphlet 'What To Do After A Death' (see the Resources chapter). We can help the survivors before our own deaths by following the advice in this present book in the 'Preparing for Dying' chapter: by leaving a will, telling people where to find it, and putting in the same place all our financial and other details, and with it the information and documents that will be needed for the registration of death (again listed in that chapter); and by simplifying our affairs.

When the person is dying at home, it is as well to ensure that the doctor (not just the nurses) sees the patient within 14 days of the death (28 days in Northern Ireland). This will normally avoid the death being referred to the coroner (see below). After the person has died, the doctor will (without charge) fill in a medical certificate as to the cause of death. (If cremation is wanted, the doctor charges for the relevant form – and will need to know about any operations in the past year – and the doctor gets another doctor to fill in a similar form, for a total charge of £66, known in the trade as 'ash cash'; the forms are issued by crematoria and also stocked by funeral directors.)

If the person dies in hospital, you can refuse permission for a postmortem (to learn more about the cause of death) if you wish. The coroner will have to issue a certificate as to the cause of death (and may insist on a postmortem) if there were unusual circumstances surrounding the death. But the coroner can issue an interim certificate to allow the executors to begin work on sorting out the deceased's affairs.

Going to the Registry Office

As the next-of-kin or the person arranging the funeral, you take the medical certificate (if the doctor does not send it for you) to the Registrar of Births and Deaths. You have to do this within five days (eight days in Scotland – the five days is extendable to 14 by agreement) or within 42 days in the case of a stillborn child. Find out which registrar covers your area by looking up under 'R' in the phone book, 'Registration of Births, Deaths and Marriages', and checking by phone with whichever seems to be the nearest office to you and asking whether or not they have an appointments system. In Scotland the registrar will want to know the time of death as well as the date and place of death.

Make certain the registrar has correctly recorded all the details in the registry as it is complicated getting them altered once it has all been signed.

Take with you if you can not only the items listed in the Preparing for Dying chapter but also information about the deceased's banks, friendly societies, life insurance and so on, and then the Registrar should be able to estimate how many copies of the various types of death certificate you will need to be able to claim these assets. Sometimes, however, banks and other institutions will simply take a copy of the certificate and give you back the original. It is easier and cheaper to obtain as many copies as you may need and an extra one in case, at the time (or within a month), for £2-50 each (£7 Scotland), rather than later when it can cost £5-50 (£10 Scotland).

The basic white certificate that you will also be given is free and contains a social security form for claiming benefit arrears and widow's benefit.

For burial, you need either a free Burial Certificate from a registrar of births and deaths or a free Burial Order from a coroner. Both have tear-off slips to send to the registrar within 96 hours of the burial having taken place. Cemeteries may want the Certificate or Order 24 hours before the burial. For burials in private land, give the Certificate or Order to the landowner or land manager. (The registrar can issue the free Burial Certificate for the burial to go ahead even before the death has been registered.)

For a cremation, the forms permitting it may be required by a crematorium at least 24 hours in advance of cremation.

In law, the responsibility for 'disposal' of the deceased's body rests with the executors of the will. If the executor has died, the responsibility passes to his or her executor. If the person died with no valid will, then the responsibility devolves onto the next-of-kin: first the surviving spouse; then the children of the deceased (or, if they died during the deceased's lifetime, their offspring); then the parents of the deceased; then the siblings (or their children); then the half-siblings; then the grandparents ... and so on, down to half-uncles and aunts (or their children). Long-term partners have no legal rights in this instance.

Ashes must be given by the crematorium to the person who applied for the cremation (these details are from the Funeral Director journal, November 1994).

Sudden death

The following is based on notes sent to the Natural Death Centre by PC Rick Jones of the Coroner's Office in Essex.

GPs may issue a death certificate even if they have not seen their patient in the 14 days prior to death, provided that the person died from a disease for which the doctor was previously treating them. This would be acceptable for burial. However, the registrar at the crematorium would generally want a coroner's involvement in such cases. The patient's doctor contacts H. M. Coroner who may then agree to issue a Coroner's 'A' Certificate, a certificate without a postmortem.

Where the person died unexpectedly but 'naturally', the coroner would issue a 'B' Certificate to the Registrar of Births and Deaths, giving the cause of death as found at postmortem. For cremation, the coroner would also issue an 'E' Certificate.

For so-called 'unnatural' deaths (suicide, road and industrial accidents, deaths from industrial or notifiable diseases), an inquest has to be held. Once this is officially opened (although it may actually take place at a later date), the coroner issues a cremation form 'E' or a Burial Order.

The bodies of those who died abroad of 'unnatural' causes, when repatriated to this country, have to be referred to the coroner.

Anyone seeking to take a body out of England and Wales (even for sea burial) must obtain a coroner's Out of England Certificate.

Moving the body

Jane Spottiswoode had problems moving her husband Nigel's body after he died:

> There was no way that Nigel in his coffin and with the coffin in a horizontal position, could be carried out of the room and around all the corners and

down the stairs to where the Volvo was waiting. Since then I have learned that the way it is done by the professionals is in a body bag, which is much easier to handle, and then transferred to a coffin either in the pick-up vehicle or at the undertakers.

From 'Undertaken with Love' by Jane Spottiswoode.

A wide range of body bags can be bought from Lear of London (for details see the Good Funeral Guide chapter for the London region) who have a minimum order of £30. You can also go through Green Undertakings (see the next chapter for the North East region). Make sure you get one that is long enough for the body.

If you do not have access to a suitable estate car or van for transport, and cannot find a friend with one, it may be possible to persuade your local funeral director to help or to use a firm that hires out a chauffeur-driven hearse and bearers. See the section on Transport in the next chapter – this is liable to cost from about £80. Or a transit van can be hired through the Yellow Pages for a few hours from about £30 to £60.

One correspondent to the Natural Death Centre found that fixing handles on the two ends of the coffin, helped to get it through the living room and front door, for a burial on their own land.

Stretchers

For the carrying and burial of bodies in shrouds or bodybags, Green Undertakings (tel 01984 632285) have designed some wicker stretchers, costing about £22. These have handles no longer than the stretcher, so that the body can be lowered into a normal-sized grave whilst still on the stretcher. This could appeal to those organising simple and woodland burials, since the stretchers will completely biodegrade.

Sheila Page suggests that an ordinary stretcher can perhaps be borrowed from the local Red Cross or St Johns Ambulance to help move a body to the mortuary. Such a stretcher is long, however, and is likely to need a van.

Carrying the coffin

Coffins are normally carried feet first.

Professional pallbearers tend not to use handles, which are decorative. The coffin is lifted from below and carried on the shoulders. However, handles are useful for burial, to thread the lowering webbing or straps through, so as to prevent the coffin from slipping.

When carrying a cardboard coffin with no handles, the A. B. Wildlife Trust Fund uses lowering straps, by placing them over and under for a secure hold, or a large curtain or blanket folded up all four sides.

Wooden lathes can also be used to carry it a coffin, but on the flat only (unless you have people before and after to prevent the coffin slipping). Sheila Page writes (from the experience of organising her husband Jan's funeral):

We bought three four-foot long pieces of planed 2" by 1" wood, sanded down about 6" at the ends. Slipped under the coffin, these provided a very satisfactory way for six of us to carry the coffin...

The gravediggers had put 2" by 2" wooden bars across the grave with the lowering straps laid neatly along these. We lowered the coffin on to these, our own wooden lathes fitting between, and, being only 1" deep, they were slipped out easily by a nominated friend. Then at a word from our previously appointed chief bearer, we picked up the coffin a few inches, using the straps, and the friend removed the wooden bars. At another word from the chief bearer, we gently lowered the coffin on to the bed of cut grass laid in it by the grave diggers. We placed the ends of the straps by the edge of the grave.

Family-organised cremation

This next account, by Judith Wilson in Torquay, about the funeral of her mother, illustrates how a determined family can make all their own arrangements, without using funeral directors.

A family-organised cremation – 'no stranger touched her'

The idea came from my sister Jean who lives in Lincoln with her family. She had seen 'This Morning' on Breakfast TV and one of the items up for discussion was The Natural Death Centre. She was so impressed that she sent for 'The Natural Death Handbook' and afterwards phoned me and my brother Gordon to say 'Get the book, it's a lovely idea'. So I did get it.

Mum lived in a residential home in Torquay. I also live in Torquay, in a small flat. Gordon and his family live in Worcester, so it was a case of keeping in touch by phone. Mum's health was fading and every day there was a deterioration. The arrangements had to be made.

Mum died on Monday 24th April 1995 at 12.45pm at the age of 90. Gordon and I were with her as she passed peacefully away in her sleep. We were prepared for her funeral, it went very well and I know she would have been proud of the way we came together in total unity to give her a gentle and loving sendoff. No stranger touched her.

I have tried to set out a sequence of events. On the whole there were very few small problems, which we managed to overcome by going further afield – the Torbay funeral directors completely shut their doors, which of course made us more determined to succeed.

Following the suggestions in 'The Natural Death Handbook' we advised the doctor and the crematorium that we were arranging our own funeral. The doctor's first words were 'Is it legal?'; he was soon put right. The crematorium was absolutely wonderful and gave us a lot of advice. It is a very busy crematorium so our main problem was storage. Torbay hospital and mortuary only cater for those who have died in hospital and for coroner's cases so we had no luck there. The funeral directors were most reluctant to hire out anything including their storage facilities or trolleys. Our last resort was to approach the matron of the residential home – she was wonderful and couldn't do enough for us. Mum could stay in her room. We were still apprehensive about the time factor and phoned around to find out about dry ice, eventually finding someone in Exeter who could sell some if the need arose.

The laying out

When the doctor had been to certify the death, he had the forms all prepared and contacted the second doctor required for cremation. After he had left, the matron, Gordon and I gently washed and changed mum and prepared her for her journey. We turned off all the heating, opened the window and had a rotating fan going night and day. On reflection it would have been better to have laid her on something cool, as if we had had to leave her any longer it would have required dry ice. We did have one panic when we unwrapped the bodybag that had been sent to us by a funeral director in Bolton – it was the wrong size. My fault, as I should have checked it on arrival. However one quick phone call ensured that we received the correct size the next day. We heaved a big sigh of relief.

The forms

The necessary paperwork which we obtained for the crematorium was amazingly easy. In fact, as far as administration goes there is nothing to it. We collected forms A, B and C from the crematorium which were self-explanatory and the crematorium staff helped to fill out the others required by themselves. Once the doctor signed the death certificate, it was then taken to the local Registry Office, where we obtained four copies in all. The cost of these was £2-50 each in this area. Forms B and C were all completed by the doctors and their fees paid; we took them back to the crematorium where they checked them over and everything was in order. They then invited us to view the chapel; the attendant was so helpful and gave us some good hints about carrying and lifting the coffin onto the rostrum as it was quite high. The service was arranged for Thursday 27th April at 9.30am. The rest of the day was already booked up, but, as it turned out, this was the best time as we were the first of the day and able to take our time.

The coffin

The coffin was made by a friend in another friend's garage with myself as the helping hand and designer. It was a first for everyone. After about a week's discussion we took the plunge and bought the wood. We overestimated a lot on the materials and had stacks left but it won't go to waste. In some ways it was just as well as we had to cut another lid. We decided on plywood – it is a light wood. Mum, bless her, was a big lady, and we wanted something light and strong. We bought half inch for the base and quarter inch for the sides, ends and lid; with 2" by 2" to join the sides and ends to the base using one and a half inch screws. As her hips were quite large, the shape had to accommodate this.

Ornate beading was put along the sides, top and bottom (to take off the plainness) and up the joins at the top and bottom, (mostly to cover up the defects, but it had the desired effect). No handles were put on, but we did put a 'grip strip' of wood one inch by a quarter inch along the sides at the base for easy carrying – which worked quite well. It was then stained with mahogany wood stain and wax polished. We tested it for strength and also tried it in the estate car which was going to carry her to the crematorium.

We used broom handles for the coffin to glide into the car, advice gratefully received from the Natural Death Centre. An engraved brass plaque with her name, year of her birth and year of her death with the inscription 'With Love' was placed above a cross, which was made of the same beading round the coffin, but left unstained. A small cross was put at the foot end, basically for identification purposes. The brass plaque was later transferred to the box for her ashes by the crematorium staff at our request.

The ashes box

This was made by my brother-in-law Bob from pitch pine and lined with mahogany, brass hinges and brass clips on the front. It is now established as 'The Family Ashes' box – smaller plaques can be added to it and will be passed around the family as necessary. I collected Mum's ashes the day after the funeral from the crematorium.

The funeral

The funeral took place on Thursday 27th April at 9.30am.

Gordon with his son Simon left at 7.55am for the Residential Home and, with the help of two male staff who knew her, lifted and placed Mum into her coffin. The estate car arrived at 9.00am and drove her to the crematorium. The rest of the family were already there in the waiting room. She was carried into the chapel by Gordon (her son), Simon, Anthony and Nicholas (her grandsons), and placed on the rostrum. I placed the flowers around her. The family and friends then took their places in the chapel. The service was conducted by Bob, her son-in-law, who is a lay preacher. It was a lovely service with one hymn and an address. After the funeral we gave the flowers to the matron of the residential home, with our love. They had been marvellous with her. The family all gathered for coffee and biscuits at a designated venue and for 'a chat'. Some of us had not seen each other for years.

My brother and sister (who has been my support throughout) and I have all gained 'something wonderful' from this experience. It is difficult for me to put it into words but it will be with me always. As my brother said when we were gently preparing her, 'it seems the right thing to do', and I shall never forget it.

I hope this will help a lot of people who want to do their own funerals. I for one have no regrets. It is a subject that should be discussed. Just as we prepare for a birth, a christening, a wedding or a confirmation, so should we prepare for a burial. Society seems reluctant to discuss the financial side of things, but it is no disrespect to the departed to talk about it. I have listed below a breakdown of the cost. We did overspend on the coffin but that was personal choice with a big bit of ignorance thrown in. It turned out great in the end, but could be made a lot more cheaply.

Death certificate + 3 copies	£11
Doctors' fees	£64
Body Bag	£15
Brass plaque and engraving	£20
Wood and materials – well overestimated	£205
Organist	£15
Crematorium and hire of organ	£157
TOTAL COST	£486

Wood and materials included glue, screws, broom handles, stains, wax and rope for handles which we did not use. (The beading was very expensive and cost about £35); plus a shroud and a blanket.

From an article in 'Before and After' by Judith Wilson, Flat 2,
4 St James Road, Torquay, Devon TQ1 4AZ
(tel 01803 325702 or 61508).

Burial on private land

Organising a burial on private land is much simpler than most people tend to think, although it can be hard work physically, as the following account demonstrates.

A grave that took four days to dig

Four weeks before my friend Marcelle died, I asked her: 'Just in case I should live longer than you, and in case I should be asked to help with the funeral arrangements, what is it you would like, as I have absolutely no idea?'

'I would like a community service in St Marks Church over the road,' Marcelle replied, 'and a little service with the 90-year-old priest back in my village in France, for my relatives there. Apart from that, I'm not bothered.'

'Do you want undertakers and a posh coffin?'

'No, I want you to organise it ... But I'm not dead yet you know.'

Marcelle died as she lived, with great fortitude. Her husband John and their three children – Pierre, John-David and Marie, all young adults – along with John-David's girlfriend Stephie, had been on duty in a 24-hour rota caring for Marcelle during her last days, and in the event they proved quite capable of organising everything for the funeral too. John-David and Pierre helped the local furniture maker to make a beautiful coffin out of one inch pine, with a wooden cross pattern on top and wooden handles wide enough for webbing to slip through, all covered with a light matt varnish. Pierre went down to the piece of land the family owns in the Cotswolds, and there a handful of friends spent no less than four days hacking with pickaxes through stony ground to dig a grave – a grave so deep, John remarked, that there would be room for him too in due course.

John-David collected the death certificate (with six copies for banks and institutions) and we noted the green form's tear-off slip which you have to return with details of where the burial took place and the date. The Gloucestershire County Council planning department confirmed that there was no need for permission from them, and that they had no concerns about a private land burial so long as no archaeological ruins were to be disturbed.

My friend Nicholas drove his Toyota van with me and the boys on board, to the hospital mortuary to pick up Marcelle's body. We had a funeral director's release form which the hospital nurse had given John-David, and which we had filled in with our own names as the funeral directors. The hospital porter had never dealt directly with a family before, so for this special occasion he decided to leave Marcelle's body wrapped like a mummy taped up in their mortuary sheet, and helped us to put the body into the biodegradable body bag which Green Undertakings had sent us, and to lift this unexpectedly heavy weight into the coffin.

Now I was glad that we had six strong bearers. We'd had a rehearsal in church with the empty coffin the evening before, when it had all seemed easy. But now we carefully repositioned the bearers so that they were all paired off in size and were all taking some of the weight.

A local woman had typeset the service sheets without charge, and Instant Print had also kindly printed them for free. And so the requiem mass began. 300 people crowded into the church. We followed the bishop in, with the coffin, and we left it in the centre of the chancel, on a low dais. Everyone had been invited to bring one flower only, which they all came up to place in front of the coffin.

Pierre read a bible extract. John, who is an assistant priest, made a moving address about his wife and his family, urging neighbours not to stop dropping by. The bishop outlined some of Marcelle's good works, forgetting to mention that it was largely thanks to her efforts that the beautiful church we were in had been saved from being turned into a block of flats.

The coffin stayed in the side chapel overnight, and the next day, in the afternoon, a small convoy of cars (which would have displeased car-hating Marcelle) drove to the Cotswolds.

We hauled the coffin up the steep hill, using webbing to lift it. Green Undertakings had run out of proper funeral webbing, but John-David had found furniture webbing in John Lewis department store which worked just as well.

John was both the priest conducting the service and husband for this final gathering, with 50 of us crowded round. He read some prayers and he recalled a touching poem by Vikram Seth:

All you who sleep tonight
Far from the ones you love,
No hands to left or right,
And emptiness above –

Know that you're not alone.
The whole world shares your tears,
Some for two nights or one,
And some for all their years.

Betsy played some Schubert on her flute, people wept and shared their memories of Marcelle and we sang Blake's Jerusalem from memory ('And did those feet ...'). We followed on from John's words 'ashes to ashes, dust to dust ...' with the African custom of everybody helping to fill the grave. We were throwing in very stony soil, which crashed down so hard I feared the coffin would split open.

It was, it is, all very sad. But I think the funeral helped.
From an article in 'Before and After' by Nicholas Albery.

Rural parts of Montana in the United States can include an extreme form of 'recycling' of the body after burial, according to Stephen Levine, who writes:

Fruit tree planted over body

Often, in the back country of Montana, a hole will be dug and the body, in a plain pine coffin or perhaps just wrapped in a tie-dyed cloth, will be lowered into the ground. Instead of a tombstone, a fruit tree is planted over the body. The roots are nourished by the return of that body into the earth from which it was sustained. And in the years to follow, eating the fruit from that tree will be like partaking in that loved one. It touches on the ritual of the Eucharist.

From 'Who Dies?' by Stephen Levine.

In the UK, from the mid 17th century, the early Quakers were often buried in their gardens – indeed William Penn, the founder of Pennsylvania, is buried in the garden of the Friends Meeting House in Jordans, Buckinghamshire. But nowadays, how do people in the UK go about arranging a funeral on their own land? One of The Natural Death Centre's contacts arranged this after the sudden death of her husband from a heart attack by asking her lawyer to set aside a part of the large back garden for the grave, with its own access, so that this part would not be sold with the rest of the house and grounds. Some council officials still do not know how limited the laws are surrounding private burial – see Ian Alcock's struggles, below – so if you approach them for their blessing, go armed with the information in this chapter.

Planning permission for private burial?

Ian Alcock in Aberdeenshire wants himself and his wife to be buried in their wildflower pasture on their own hill in a special conservation area (SSSI).

He was told to approach the Nature Conservancy Council for Scotland for initial permission and then had to pay £77 for a planning application for 'change of use of hill land to private burial ground' and £60 for a small ad in the local newspaper under 'developments which may cause concern in the neighbourhood'. 'There is no obligation to seek the approval of neighbours,' he writes. And the environmental health officer confirmed that the burial was not likely to cause pollution.

Alcock has built his own coffin: 'It cost me £40 for the plywood and is big enough for two (in case my wife and I go at the same time) and on account of my lack of carpentry expertise, has a certain "rustic charm". The postman refused to believe that it was a coffin until I put rope handles or slings round it (to avoid the corpse falling out of the bottom) and sprayed "RIP" on it with a black sheep marker. It is now in store in a building awaiting me. The dogs peed on it when it was outside, but I had a strong friend help me to move it. Incidentally, a friend has told me that she has recently paid a £1,000 undertaker's bill (and it is cheaper up here) for the "simplest possible" funeral for her father.'

Ian Alcock, Shannel, Ballogie, Aboyne, Aberdeenshire AB34 5DR
(tel & fax 03398 84207).

Ian Alcock subsequently successfully appealed against the need for planning permission. The Scottish Office, in the person of the Deputy Chief Reporter R. M. Hickman (Ref. P/PPA/GD/342, Nov. 25th 1992), ruled that 'a limited number of unmarked and unfenced graves would not constitute a material change of use and I conclude that the planning consent issued to you by the district council is superfluous'. The decision letter also noted that the square area in the middle of grazing land, identified by Ian Alcock for the burial ground, was about 50 metres by 50 metres, and that Ian and his wife wished to be buried there, and to be able to 'afford this opportunity to another close member of the family, family retainer, or perhaps a close friend. ... As there would be no change in the surface land use, nor any upstanding physical features resulting from the intended burials, I am satisfied that a limited number of private graves would not result in a material change of use. If the ground were to be fenced off to become a cemetery, I would agree with the district council that a material change of use would have occurred. ... I have also considered whether the burials would constitute "engineering ... or other operations in, on, over or under the land" ... However, I am satisfied that the digging of a very limited number of graves by hand ... would not amount to a significant engineering or other operation. If there were a large number of burials, perhaps involving an access track or mechanical excavation, the situation would perhaps be different but that would be a matter of fact and degree to be considered on its merits.'

More cautiously, a spokesman for the Department of the Environment wrote to the Natural Death Centre on May 15th 1994: 'May I confirm that planning permission is not required for the burial of one or two persons in back gardens, it would only be required if there was an intention to bury a larger number of people.'

On one occasion, a case was won on appeal, a Certificate of Lawfulness having been refused. The A. B. Wildlife Trust Fund reports that, in May 1996, a man in East Sussex won his appeal to the Department of the Environment against the local authority, who had turned down his application for a Certificate of Lawfulness to have two burials in his half acre garden.

Applying to a local authority for a Certificate of Lawfulness is a way of determining whether something is legal in planning law, without having to apply for planning permission. John Bradfield of the A. B. Wildlife Trust Fund, who has been the Natural Death Centre's main source of information on the laws surrounding funerals, and who is now the UK's acknowledged expert on private land burial law, describes the following two cases in *Green Burial* (in the out-of-print 1994 edition):

• No planning consent was required for a private burial ground in the Harrogate area to be used for 'non-commercial' burials. There would be no fences or gravestones, and the site was within an organic smallholding that would continue to be grazed as before.

• No planning consent was required for 'private non-commercial burial of the householder, those resident with her at the time of their deaths and her relatives only' – for burial in a 300 square metre garden also near Harrogate.

This, then, is the Natural Death Centre's conclusion: planning permission is not required for non-commercial sites, for a limited number of burials for family, friends and those living in the house.

In Eire, by contrast, it is claimed that permission is required from the environment ministry. One correspondent writes, however, that people have been taking the law into their own hands: 'In Eire, the way an inexpensive, green and d-i-y funeral is done is that you bury the remains on your own or the deceased person's property.' If the police later take action, with a prosecution and the courts, they will not exhume the corpse. Depending on how long it has been since the burial, a small fine could be imposed, but this would be unlikely.

Legal requirements concerning funerals

The A. B. Wildlife Trust Fund hopes to publish a new edition of 'Green Burial – The D-i-y Guide to Law and Practice' during 1997. John Bradfield, its author, put an immense amount of research into the first two editions, and generously donated all the proceeds from sales to the Natural Death Centre. He demolished many legal myths that have surfaced in funeral guides, resulting in changes to the 'Encyclopaedia Britannica', 'Penguin Guide To The Law', the 1994 Which? Consumers' Association book 'What To Do When Someone Dies' and several other books. He has persuaded officials at the highest levels to alter their advice.

In urgent cases, and until a new edition is published, the Natural Death Centre will lend out its only library copy of 'Green Burial' on payment of a refundable deposit of £15 – or a local library may be able to obtain a copy for you through the inter-library loan scheme. What follows is the Centre's understanding of some of the A. B. Wildlife Trust Fund's key findings, but readers are advised to refer to 'Green Burial' or the Trust for the full details:

• 'Subject to any restrictive covenants affecting the use of the land (see below), a place of burial may be established by any person without statutory authority, in private land, provided no statutory or other 'nuisance' such as smell or pollution is caused ...' (Halsbury's Laws of England, 1975:504, Butterworths). 'The statute law on burial is archaic ... and does not apply ... to private burial grounds' (Hickman, R. M. Deputy Chief Reporter in the Alcock case, see above).

• There may be very rare instances where a property's restrictive covenants prevent the creation of graves, but application can be made for such covenants to be lifted on the grounds that they have ceased to serve their original purpose.

• Although cemeteries and crematoria may have their own particular rules or guidelines, there is no law requiring a coffin. It is, however, an offence for a dead body to be exposed naked in a public place, if this causes shock or disgust or is intended to do so.

• There is a common law right for Christians to have a Christian burial, otherwise it is not legally necessary to have a Christian or other religious service or any officiant presiding over a funeral; or to be buried in a formal cemetery or consecrated land.

• Consecration by the Church of England alters the legal status of the land, whereas consecration by other religions may 'bless' a piece of land but has no legal implications. Even the Church of England is moving away from consecrating its own property.

• 'No Church of England minister' writes John Bradfield, 'can be criticised for holding a religious service in an unconsecrated burial place. This includes a garden or house ... .'

• Some people organising funerals without using funeral directors have had trouble getting the hospital to give them the body. Unless the coroner is making an investigation into the cause of the death, it is a common law offence for a hospital to refuse to release a body to the executors. As one trial judge put it in 1882: 'executors have a right to the custody and possession of [the] body'.

If you are having problems getting the body released to you, contact the Natural Death Centre and they will willingly send a stiffly-worded fax to any hospital proving obstructive, citing chapter and verse as to their offence and its possible consequences.

• It is a myth that there must be no neighbours within a hundred yards of a burial – a misreading of the 1855 Burials Acts (Ch. 128, S.9 and now repealed and Ch. 68, S.7 which still applies to Scottish public burial grounds).

• An 1847 Act may apply to some old cities or towns, requiring 30 inches of soil between the coffin top and the ordinary surface of the ground. Council cemeteries are governed by a 1977 Order requirement that there be 2 or 3 feet from the coffin top to the surface. But for any other burial grounds there is no minimum depth specified by law.

• There is no requirement to inform the council's environmental health officers of plans for burial on private land, nor do such burials require their advance permission. These officers have no powers to order exhumations.

However, they do have legal powers to prevent any 'deposit' which might be 'prejudicial to health or a nuisance'.

The health risks from burial are very remote. Bradfield quotes a professor of forensic pathology and a consultant to the Home Office as concluding that 'the risks [from the] exhumation of ... recent burials are no greater than those of gardening. Antibiotic [precautions are] not required'.

• The Environment Agency (formerly National Rivers Authority) is entitled to carry out works to prevent pollution of 'any controlled waters', but there is no legal obligation to consult them in advance of a burial.

• There are no laws which can force you to move a body in private land from one grave to another.

• Under the Anatomy Act 1984, S.4(9), a hospital, nursing home or other institution has the right to send a body for anatomical use, without consent, if no friend or relative takes possession of the body.

The fear that the bodies of paupers would be used for dissection purposes has haunted the poor ever since the 1832 Anatomy Act (as described by Ruth Richardson in her book 'Death, Dissection and the Destitute' published by Pelican, 1989). It may well be true that hospitals nowadays do not take advantage of this legal power, but it is ethically unacceptable that they should have the potential right to do so.

• There must be a land burial register for all graves in England. Unless some other law applies, it is necessary to comply with the 1864 Registration of Burials Act, Ch.97, even for an isolated grave in a garden. It requires that Christian laws be followed, even by non-Christians, on the layout and storage of registers. It is difficult to make proper sense of this law and only if noncompliance is 'wilful' can a prosecution take place. Private burial grounds would be expected by any court to do their utmost to comply.

This durable burials register must record, in columns, the 'Entry No., Christian name and surname in block capitals, Address, Date of Birth, Age, Date of Burial, Plan Ref. No., Officiating Minister', with each entry separated by a printed line. The register must be kept in a specially protected steel cupboard.

• Within 96 hours of any burial in England or Wales, the tear-off slip on the burial authorisation must be completed, giving the date and place of burial, and sent to the Registrar of Births and Deaths. This slip will either be on a form issued earlier by the same Registrar (a 'green form' or Burial Certificate, also known as a Disposal Certificate) or by a coroner, if an inquest will be or has been held (a white form called a Burial Order). Who fills in the slip is explained on the form.

• Exhumations in England and Wales, unless only from one legally conse-crated place to another, require a licence from any Secretary of State (licences are issued by the Home Office for a current fee of £10, maximum fee £20).

• Exhumation from or to legally consecrated land requires a Church of England document called a 'faculty'.

• In theory, a funeral pyre that causes no 'nuisance' (ie pollution or smell) seems to be legal, as long as no construction is made which could be defined as a crematorium. There has been no recent instance of an outdoor cremation. However, according to reports in the Funeral Service Journal, the body of a Nepalese diplomat was cremated on a funeral pyre within the grounds of Brookwood in the 1940s. In the First World War, the bodies of Hindu soldiers who died in the Kitchener Hospital in Brighton were cremated on funeral pyres on a specially prepared site at Patcham, on the Downs.

• A body can be transported across county boundaries without permission. Details can be found in an article by John Bradfield in the Funeral Service Journal. Consent, given free of charge, must be obtained to move a body out of England/Wales (treated as one area), Northern Ireland or Scotland – which includes from one to the other.

Burial recommendations (not requirements)

The above summarises the laws. The following are merely the Natural Death Centre's recommendations for good practice:

• Farmland can be used for private land burial. The Ministry of Agriculture has written to the Centre that set-aside land can be used, 'provided there was no return to the farmer in cash or kind ... and the land remains croppable and in good agricultural condition.' Farmers could run green burial grounds in association with wildlife charities, as in the case of Oakfield near Manningtree.

• A large garden can be used for burial. The Natural Death Centre helped one couple in their nineties choose a spot for burial on the edge of their ten acre garden where their beloved boxer dogs were buried, with a way to reach the graves from the public footpath, in case the remainder of the property were later to be sold by the family. The couple also ordered cardboard coffins which they stored in their garage. They felt prepared for their deaths, but their plans were cruelly disrupted when increasing disabilities forced them to move to a residential home, and to sell their home to cover the costs.

The Natural Death Centre advises careful thought before creating a grave in a small urban garden. It is easier to bury a body than it is to exhume it; a garden burial can cause dissension amongst relatives; neighbours may feel offended; and one estate agent has estimated, probably pessimistically, that a back garden burial would substantially reduce the value of a property. In 1995, the body of the playwright Robert Bolt was buried by his family in their garden. It seems possible in such cases that burials of the famous might even increase a property's value.

• You do not need a Certificate of Lawfulness. If you nevertheless wish to have one to set your mind at rest, you may want to ask the council to keep the decision-making stage confidential – the outcome, however, must be recorded on a public register. The cost of applying for a Certificate is approximately half the cost of applying for planning permission (the full cost is payable if one or more burials have taken place). If the Certificate is refused or specifies unsatisfactory conditions, a free appeal can be made to the Department of the Environment, although their findings will then definitely be made public.

• In general, the Environment Agency suggests that the grave should not be within 250 metres of any well or borehole (sometimes reduced to 50 metres) or 10 metres from any standing or running water or 1.5 metres from any underground cables and pipes. And note that animal carcasses in a field normally have to be buried 250 metres from any human-consumption water supply, 30 metres from any other spring and 10 metres from any field drain. A suitable grave would have no water at the bottom when first dug and one metre of subsoil below the base. It could be a good idea to consult the Environment Agency (which has taken over from the National Rivers Authority) by phoning 01454 624400 and asking for the number of their office closest to you. This body may well be less prejudiced against your plans than the local environmental health officer. In practice, the Environment Agency is unlikely to have objections, provided that the grave is not within ten metres of any standing or running water.

• It would be wise to avoid burial in very sandy soil, as it is unsuitable for shallow graves and digging a deep grave can be dangerous.

• The burial needs to be deep enough to prevent foraging animals from trying to dig up the body.

• It would be sensible to store a detailed plan of where the body is buried (or a copy of any exhumation licence) with the deeds of your property. One council's Environmental Services Division arranged for an informal notice to be attached to the Land Charges Register, so as to inform prospective purchasers of the private graves on the land.

Making the coffin

The Oregon-based novelist Ken Kesey (author of 'One Flew Over the Cuckoo's Nest') wrote to his friends about the death in a traffic accident of his twenty year old son Jed: 'It was the toughest thing any of us has ever had to go through, yet it also had and always will have a decided glory. There was also the support we got from friends and family, from teachers and coaches and schoolmates. Without this support I don't think we would have attempted the kind of funeral we had. A home-made ceremony is legally possible. All you need is the land, the determination and the family.'

Jed Kesey's funeral

We built the box ourselves (George Walker, mainly) and Zane and Jed's friends and frat brothers dug the hole in a nice spot between the chicken house and the pond. Page found the stone and designed the etching. You would have been proud, Wendell, especially of the box – clear pine pegged together and trimmed with redwood. The handles of thick hemp rope. And you, Ed, would have appreciated the lining. It was a piece of Tibetan brocade given Mountain Girl by Owsley fifteen years ago, gilt and silver and russet phoenix bird patterns, unfurling in flames. And last month, Bob, Zane was goose hunting in the field across the road and killed a snow goose. I told him be sure to save the down. Susan Butkovitch covered this in white silk for the pillow while Faye and MG and Gretch and Candace stitched and stapled the brocade into the box.

It was a double-pretty day, like winter holding its breath, giving us a break. About 300 people stood around and sang from the little hymnbooks that Diane Kesey·had Xeroxed – 'Everlasting Arms', 'Sweet Hour of Prayer', 'In the Garden', and so forth. With all my cousins leading the singing and Dale on his fiddle. While we were singing 'Blue Eyes Crying in the Rain', Zane and Kit and the neighbour boys that have grown up with all of us carried the box to the hole. The preacher is also the Pleasant Hill School superintendent and has known our kids since kindergarten. I learned a lot about Jed that I'd either forgotten or never known – like his being a member of the National Honour Society and finishing sixth in a class of more than a hundred.

We sang some more. People filed by and dropped stuff in on Jed. I put in that silver whistle I used to wear with the Hopi cross soldered on it. One of our frat brothers put in a quartz watch guaranteed to keep beeping every 15 minutes for five years. Faye put in a snapshot of her and I standing with a pitchfork all Grantwoodesque in front of the old bus. Paul Foster put in the little leatherbound New Testament given him by his father who had carried it during his 65 years as a minister. Paul Sawyer read from 'Leaves of Grass' while the boys each hammered in the one nail they had remembered to put in their pockets. The Betas formed a circle and passed the loving cup around (a ritual our fraternity generally uses when a member is leaving the circle to become engaged) (Jed and Zane and I are all members, y'unnerstand, not to mention Hagen) and the boys lowered the box with these ropes George had cut and braided. Zane and I tossed in the first shovelfuls. It sounded like the first thunderclaps of 'Revelations'.

The following is adapted from a postscript by George Walker about the making of Jed's coffin:

We selected some clear white boards for the sides and top. Nice looking and easy to work with, pine is also traditional.

It was a very good coffin, as coffins go, very beautiful everybody said, and certainly a labour of love. But I don't really believe that is the point. The real value of that coffin was in the doing, in the building of it ourselves. Not in the coffin, as a thing, but in the act of creating it, as an event. It made us all feel better to do this ourselves, to take charge of things as much as we could, not just the coffin but the burial as well. Perhaps it's because, when we lose someone close, particularly someone young and in the prime of life, we feel more than a little burned that things have been jerked so irrevocably beyond our control. Anything we can do to regain our handle on events is gratifying.

Whatever the reason, all who kept themselves actively involved in getting Jed buried agreed: we all gained something through our efforts. We felt better about it than if we had just turned it all over to the professionals, and gone about our business of feeling bad. So, I would say to anybody who feels that they might want to give it a try when someone close dies, absolutely yes; build it yourself. Even if you can't do basic carpentry, you can nail together a kit. If you do have skills, you can make something that will make you feel good long after it's buried out of sight. It doesn't have to be fancy; simple and neat is just fine, but do make it strong. You'll be surprised by the weight.

> *From an article in CoEvolution Quarterly (Summer '84; now called*
> *Whole Earth Review, 27 Gate Five Road, Sausalito, CA 94965,*
> *USA; subs. $32).*

The Huelin d-i-y coffins

If expense is the main consideration, it is worth noting that making a coffin yourself will probably work out as expensive just for materials as the cheapest coffin available from a funeral director (see the next chapter).

Nevertheless the Huelins, a couple in Oxford, gained a great deal of satisfaction from making their own coffins and found themselves quite a centre of media attention as a result. Barbara Huelin outlines the story:

> My husband (now in his eighties) has built our coffins. We spent a most enlightening few months organising and preparing for our deaths; the idea has caught on amongst our friends in Oxford.
>
> The coffins are made in blockboard at a cost of about £50 each (not including our time). They are painted green and have nautical-looking rope handles (from the boat chandlers). The coffins are stored in the workroom. We have bought a double-decker site in the local Council cemetery for £150 to which we intend that family and friends shall physically bear us. We are leaving the commemorative gravestone for our survivors to add if they wish, so that they have something they can do.

There were a number of interested enquiries from members of the public so her husband David sent the Natural Death Centre the following detailed description and drawings of the design that he used:

> **Materials:** The most convenient, though possibly not the cheapest, material is three quarter inch (18mm) blockboard; it is lighter and stronger than chipboard, and is much easier to work. It is normally sold in sheets measuring 8ft x 4ft (2.44m x 1.22m); each sheet costs about £30 (March 1992). The half inch (12mm) version is cheaper but seems rather flimsy for a coffin, and the one inch (25mm) appears unnecessarily heavy, and costs more.
>
> Three sheets of 8ft x 4ft blockboard are enough for two coffins, with a little fiddling. It is possible, though more difficult, to make one coffin with a sheet and a half, though it is not always possible to buy half-sheets. The following suggestions are for making two coffins with three sheets of board.
>
> **Other Materials (for two coffins):**
> • 36ft (11m) wood strip 35mm x 10mm (rim round lid)
> • 42ft (12.8m) batten 25mm x 25mm; this is not needed if the joining is by dovetailing – see below

Coffin A (woman)

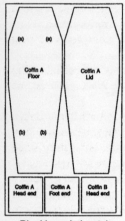

Blockboard sheet 1

Coffin B (Man)

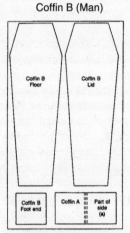

Blockboard sheet 2

Coffins A & B

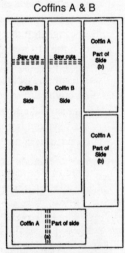

Blockboard sheet 3

- 400 (2 boxes) steel wood-screws, gauge 8 x one and a quarter inch
- 100 panel pins three quarter inch
- 250ml (quarter litre) wood-working glue, e.g. Evo-Stik Wood Adhesive
- 1 litre paint (optional)
- Handles: special subject dealt with separately below.

Tools: A hand-held electric circular saw is invaluable for cutting the basic shapes in the blockboard, which by hand would be arduous work. If dovetailing is intended a coping saw is useful; beyond that, a tenon-saw, chisel, angle-gauge, and sanding equipment for finishing off.

Method: Take the measurements of the future occupant of each coffin, not forgetting the hip width; allow extra space for the possibility of putting on weight before the coffin is needed.

With these measurements the main components for the two coffins can be drawn out on the blockboard: floor and lid, sides and ends (see the illustrations). Since the basic measurements are internal, allowance must be made for the thickness of the wood when drawing the basic shapes.

It is advisable to defer cutting out the lids until the main boxes are built (see below).

Joining: Attaching the sides and ends to the floor of the coffin, and to each other, can be done in several ways; the simplest would seem to be one of the following:

1. With internal battens or corner-blocks, using the 25mm x 25mm batten listed above. With plenty of glue and screws this can be quite satisfactory; the batten joining the sides and ends to the floor of the box can be fixed below the floor for extra strength. As the four corners are not right angles, the internal block or batten will have to be shaped to the actual angle.

2. With dovetailing (so called, though it is not true dovetailing); that is by cutting alternating tongues and recesses all along the edges to be joined, so that they fit together. Each tongue and recess can be 3 or 4 inches long; once the whole thing fits snugly together, the joins can be glued and screwed with a one and a quarter inch screw through every tongue. The recesses need to be a whisker over three quarters of an inch (19mm) deep to match the thickness of the board.

This system involves more work and precision than the batten method, but the result is neat and very strong.

Shaped sides: To achieve the bends in the sides of the coffins, the inner surface of the board should have five or six saw-cuts made across it, to a depth of about three quarters of its thickness; it will then bend to the shape of the floor. The saw-cuts can be filled with glue to add to their solidity, but this is not essential. If the batten method is used, the batten itself can be treated in the same way.

In this particular layout for three sheets of board it has been necessary to divide the sides of coffin 'A' into two sections; they can be joined together by dovetailing at the appropriate angle. With four boards this dividing would not be necessary.

Lid: The precise shaping of the lid of each coffin can be left until the main body of the box is complete; this can be placed inverted over the piece of board reserved for the lid, and its outline drawn straight onto the wood. The lid should have a rim or lip all round its edge, made from the 35mm x 10mm strip listed above; this can be fixed with glue and panel pins.

Once it fits nicely, the lid can be drilled for screws, about 8 inches apart, using gauge 8, length one and a quarter inch screws, and pilot holes can be drilled in the main box. The thoughtful coffin builder will provide a bag of screws for the purpose, and possibly a screwdriver too.

Headrest: A dead person's head falls back unbecomingly unless it is supported. The coffins should therefore have a small platform across the head end, slightly sloping, some two to three inches from the floor of the box.

Packing: Though not strictly part of the construction, there is the question of packing or lining. A very economical, attractive, and adequately absorbent packing is wood-shavings. If shavings of nice-smelling woods, such as cedar or pitch pine, can be obtained, so much the better. One dustbin-liner-full is probably enough.

Paint: Blockboard is not a very interesting colour; a litre of matt emulsion paint will make the two coffins look much more interesting; they can also be embellished with paintings of flowers, or boats, or castles, to taste.

Handles: The importance of handles depends on how the coffins are to be carried: if at shoulder height by skilled men, then no handles are required at all (professional bearers never use them). If the intention is that a coffin should be carried by family and friends, with their hands, then the handles are necessary and should be functional.

Metal or tough plastic handles, such as are used on swing and sliding doors, are inexpensive, but great care is needed in fixing them. It may be advisable to use one and a half inch screws going through the comparatively soft blockboard into a hardwood block inside. Note that if cremation is chosen, then no large metal parts such as handles should be employed.

Another method is with nylon rope of half inch diameter. Half inch holes, some five inches apart, in three pairs, to be drilled in the sides of the coffin; the rope (must be nylon) is cut into lengths of 12 or 13 inches (30 to 33cm) and the ends are threaded into the holes from the outside, so that at least one inch projects on the inside of the box. Next a metal washer with exactly a half inch hole is fitted over the projecting end of rope, which is then melted with a hot-air gun so that it flattens down and spreads over the metal washer; when it cools and hardens it is very firm.

This method is easier than it may seem; it is extremely strong, and the rope loops on the outside of the coffin look attractive and appropriately modest.

Materials: 4 metres (2m each coffin) half-inch nylon rope obtainable at boat chandlers' shops. 24 half-inch washers.

Tool: Hot-air gun.

Barbara and David Huelin, 69 Kingston Road, Oxford OX2 6RJ.

A simple burial box

Ernest Morgan in his excellent book about funerals in the United States, 'Dealing Creatively with Death – A Manual of Death Education and Simple Burial', describes the making of a simple burial box, which has top and sides of quarter inch plywood, and the bottom and ends of three quarter inch plywood. Two reinforcing battens, three quarters of an inch thick, run the length of the box on the inside, attached to the side pieces at the top edge, so the top of the box rests on them – as in this illustration. Ernest Morgan writes:

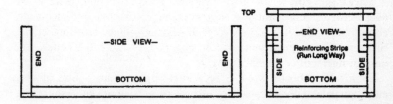

Using nails or screws (eds: the latter, say gauge 8, length one and quarter inch, would give extra strength, particularly for the ends. Wood glue, such as Evo-Stik Wood Adhesive, would also give additional strength):

• Attach the reinforcing battens to the side pieces, flush with the edge and the end, making sure to have the good side of the plywood facing outwards;

• Attach the side pieces to the bottom.

• Attach the ends, again with the good sides out, to the bottom and to the side strips.

Four chest handles, two screwed to each end, could be useful for ease of carrying when going through doors (eds: or rope handles could be used, as in the Huelin coffins, above). The handles could be stored in the box and screwed on when needed. Likewise, the cover could be tacked lightly in place until the box is needed, and then when the time comes fixed firmly down.

A birch coffin

For those who would like something finer, and who have the skills, a coffin made of birch or pine planks dovetailed together could look good, with the name carved into the wood and patterns around the edges as desired, and a final polish with beeswax or linseed oil.

Reusable coffin design

A cabinet maker has written to The Natural Death Centre with ideas for coffin-making workshops, mail boxes in the sides of coffins and reusable coffins:

I run courses in creative woodwork and have long-term plans for running workshops where people could design and make their own coffin. With professional guidance people could design and build a coffin in exact accordance with their wishes. Family members and close friends could be invited to contribute, thus enhancing the quality of the process.

This could also be a family project. Each family member could participate in designing and building a family coffin that could be reused as the need dictated. When it was not being used as a coffin, it could have a functional use, perhaps as a coffee table or even as a plant trough.

There could be a cheap, sealed inner box within the outer shell of the coffin that could be disposable. This would mean that the body does not have to be wrapped up or disturbed. And why the regular shape? Why not pyramid shape or even dolphin shape!

Reusable Coffin Plan

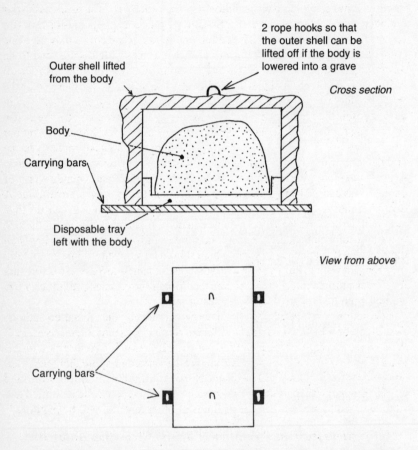

2 rope hooks so that the outer shell can be lifted off if the body is lowered into a grave

Cross section

Outer shell lifted from the body

Body

Carrying bars

Disposable tray left with the body

View from above

Carrying bars

Another of my ideas is to provide some form of mail box either in the coffin or as a small container that could be buried or cremated with the body. The plan would be for there to be a period of silence during the funeral service when those attending the service could write out their final farewell message to the deceased which would then be posted in the box. This could add a valuable dimension to the grieving process.

A spokesman for the National Association of Funeral Directors has been concerned at the prospect of reusing coffins, of hauling bodies in and out of coffins. In answer to this I suggest a false and disposable bottom to the coffin that would allow the main shell to be removed with the body being left respectfully at peace. Maintaining dignity is very important and I feel that there are many ways in which this can be honoured.

From a letter to The Natural Death Centre.

Coffins for cremation – avoiding pollution

If the coffin is destined for cremation rather than burial, there are various requirements for avoiding air pollution. The best approach is to check with your intended crematorium as to whether first, they would accept a home-made coffin (see next chapter); second, what the maximum size of the coffin may be – one crematorium in the United States has said that home-made coffins tend to be made larger than they need be (Lisa Carlson in 'Caring for your own Dead' writes that 'two feet wide and 18 inches deep is sufficient for most bodies'); third, whether the particular construction you are planning needs modifying in any way; fourth, whether any lining or handles you are planning for the coffin or clothing for the body are unacceptable (for instance, PVC linings and rubber soled shoes are discouraged); and fifth, whether any medical implants in the body will be problematic. A pacemaker would need to be removed, for instance, in case it explodes during cremation. In 1996, five thousand pounds worth of damage was caused by an exploding pacemaker at the Morden crematorium. A doctor, a mortician at your local hospital or a funeral director can do this, although, writes Lisa Carlson, 'anyone can do it. A pacemaker is about the size of a small coin, embedded just under the skin, usually near the neck or lower on the rib cage. It is attached to wires which should be snipped.' Some crematoria may also not want to burn a body with silicone implants – in Southern California the silicone turned into a sticky goo on the floor of the cremator, although a UK crematorium had no difficulties in a test it ran.

Instructions for funeral directors have been issued by the cremation authorities, many of which would apply to those running a funeral themselves. P. J. Wilson, the secretary of the Federation of British Cremation Authorities, writes to the Natural Death Centre that 'Crematoria invariably require that bodies are conveyed to the building in a reasonable manner. A rigid coffin able to withstand any handling or transportation problems, adequately secured and identified and suitably lined to prevent leakage of fluids or other material will be required.'

Instructions from the Federation of British Cremation Authorities

• **Bearers:** Sufficient bearers should convey the coffin reverently from the hearse to the catafalque.

  • **Coffin construction:** The coffin must be made of wood or a wood by-product which, when placed in a cremator and subjected to the accepted cremation processes, is easily combustible and which does not emit smoke, give off toxic gas or leave any retardant smears or drips after final combustion. No metal furniture or fittings whatever shall be used on a coffin for cremation. No metal of any kind shall be used in the manufacture of such a coffin except as necessary for its safe construction and then only metal of a high ferrous content [eds: eg use ferrous screws]. Cross pieces must not be attached to the bottom of the coffin. If it is desired to strengthen the bottom of the coffin, wooden strips may be placed lengthwise for this purpose. The coffin must not be painted [eds: water-based paints may be allowed] or varnished but may be covered with a suitable cloth. Products manufactured in polyvinyl chloride (PVC) must not be used in the construction of the coffin or its furnishings. The use of polystyrene must be restricted to the coffin nameplate only, in which case it must not exceed 90 grams in weight.

No coffin shall be accepted unless it bears adequate particulars of the identity of the deceased person therein [eds: normally this would include the name, age and date of death of the person].

• *Lining of the coffin:* The use of sawdust or cotton-wool must be avoided. If circumstances require, suitable sealing material may be used, but no metal, rubber or polyvinyl chloride (PVC) will be permitted and on no account must pitch or a similar substance be used. [Eds: no lead-lined coffins would be permitted.]

• *Size of the coffin:* Where the external dimensions of a coffin are likely to exceed length 81 inches (206 cm); width 28 inches (71 cm); depth 22 inches (56 cm) the proper officer of the crematorium must be given advance notice.

• *Cremation of infants:* In cases when bereaved parents desire the cremation of the body of an infant, they should be warned that there are occasions when no tangible remains are left after the cremation process has been completed. This is due to the cartilagineous nature of the bone structure.

If the warning is not given the parents may have been denied the choice of earth burial and thereby been subjected to understandable distress.

• *Cremated remains:* An urn or casket for cremated remains should be of sufficient internal dimension to provide a minimum of 200 cubic inches (3,280 cubic cm) and securely labelled. The container should be strong enough to resist breakage in transit. The lid must fit tightly and the fastening should be strong enough to prevent the lid being forced open by distortion of the container through maltreatment in transit.

> *Adapted from a text sent by the Federation of*
> *British Cremation Authorities.*

Deidre Martin has sent the Natural Death Centre an encouraging description of the funeral of her mother, Dorothy, which they organised themselves and for which they made the coffin. The description, adapted extracts from which appear below, ties together many of the elements previously discussed in this chapter.

In memory of Dorothy Miller – a simple funeral

My mother died in the Royal Sussex Hospital, Brighton, at 11.20am on Friday February 21st, 1992, at the age of 85. Early that morning my husband and I were called to the hospital and she died when we were both present. She was quiet and peaceful and looked very calm. A young nurse and I laid her out, and I placed some flowers by her before we said goodbye.

My mother had always said she wished to be buried 'simply', and we had already told the hospital matron that we would like to make the arrangements ourselves. She was extremely sympathetic and very helpful. She made an appointment for my husband and me to see the hospital registration officer that afternoon, and told us the hospital would be able to keep my mother's body until we had made adequate arrangements. She also advised us to speak to the crematorium, and to ask them for advice.

At 12.30 pm that day we visited Brighton's Woodvale Crematorium. The staff were marvellous. We asked if we could make the coffin, and deal with all the funeral arrangements ourselves. 'Certainly.' They provided us with a leaflet 'Information and specifications for an interment or cremation arranged without the guidance of a funeral director'. [Eds: this present chapter covers everything in the leaflet that is of more than local significance.] They told us how to make the arrangements, but my main worry was what to do with Grandma. They said she can be kept as long as convenient in the borough mortuary for up to three weeks at no charge – after that a small sum would be necessary. I feel this is always a problem with death – everyone seems to want to dispose of the person too soon! The fact that we had time to think, and time to make arrangements was the first step. The staff said they would help with carrying Grandma into the chapel. We went to look at the chapel to see how high the platform was for the body to be placed on. They told us to telephone and come at any time if we wanted more help or information. At 3 pm that afternoon we were with the hospital registrar. She was delighted someone wished to arrange their own funeral – the ward sister had arranged for my mother to be taken to the hospital mortuary, and the registrar spoke to the mortician on our behalf. He was happy to keep my mother until the day of the funeral – no problem – no charge. He gave us the dimensions of the coffin. Width and length: 5' 9" by 18" wide. All we had to do was to let him know the time for collection and they would help us lift her in and to seal the lid. So my mother's last resting place was the hospital mortuary until March 3rd.

This gave us time to make the coffin and sort ourselves out. I telephoned the Natural Death Centre for some information, which came very promptly, and for which I am grateful. Also I wrote to the British Humanist Association who sent me a booklet 'Funerals without God'. It was very reassuring getting information from various sources, showing us that we could do this ourselves and that it would be very personal and that our mother's passing had not been taken away from us and dealt with by strangers. She had very rarely attended a church and we had been to a number of funerals – in 1989 twelve members of our family and friends had died – and none of the funerals seemed to have been satisfactory for the bereaved. Something appeared to be missing.

The coffin was made in our garage in a day. My husband enlisted the help of George Haines, a friend who is in his seventies, who said he always wanted to make his own coffin, so was delighted to have the chance to practise. Much tea and merriment went into the work, and chipboard and timber arrived from the local yard. Most of the neighbours and friends came to have a look and to try it out.

Really it was the fun bits that started to emerge, such as finding music that my mother liked. On a checkup trip to the crematorium to speak to them about the tapes and how to set them up, they told me they had loads of tapes available. They set all the taping up for us, again giving us every assistance. They also suggested that the funeral should be the last one of the day, to be able to give us assistance and extra time in case we had any hiccups.

The registrar was fascinated; she advised me to take several copies of the death certificate at £2 each as she pointed out that any further copies would cost £5-50 each. That was wise advice as my brothers and the solicitor and crematorium all wanted copies. We dealt with all the paper work which had come from the mortuary, hospital, etc, and that is usually handled by the Funeral Directors – it was simple. We needed burial certificates, doctors' certificates and one or two other certificates mentioned in the interment leaflet from Woodvale, and again we were assisted by everybody.

I tried to involve the family as much as possible. My eldest daughter made a lovely cake for the funeral tea, and also put together a wonderful photographic display, with photos of my mother's life, and the paintings she did in her later years. My brother's estate wagon was measured for the coffin – it would fit in OK. As a precautionary measure, we also hired an estate car for £42 in case of emergencies. Fortunately it was not required to carry the coffin, but it could have been used if necessary. The rest of the family prepared readings from my mother's favourite books and we prepared a programme containing readings, remembrances and music. We timed this for approximately 30 minutes. It was enough. We requested no flowers, but did in fact have a lovely display of everlasting flowers made by my sister-in-law, in a basket, which was placed on the coffin with an Indian rug from my brother, and this looked really great.

So at 4 pm on March 3rd we were ready to conduct the service. What went wrong? Not a lot – one late-arriving relative wanted to view her grandmother and we did not think to let the mortician know in advance of collecting the body. The body was not prepared and obviously did not look its best for the occasion and there was an upsetting reaction. My husband, the friend who made the coffin, George, my brother from Kent, and his two children (a son and daughter) and another grandson from Wales, all went to fetch the body. Lesson number one – double check who knows who is coming, when and where. At the crematorium it was difficult getting the coffin out of the car – nobody realised quite how heavy it would be. One granddaughter wished to help carry the coffin, which was great, but this needed a rehearsal. The crematorium staff helped and it was OK. We made a mess-up of getting everyone into the chapel, and in the end they went in after the coffin was placed on the rostrum. The staff worked the tape recorder and I compered the show. My husband videoed the event and Mother would have been very, very pleased, because basically it went off OK. And it did – it dealt with a lot of emotions, and people were able to work on their own grief; mainly, I felt, because they had helped to get the show on the road.

We collected the ashes the next day from the crematorium, free of charge. We later gave the mortician a bottle of wine and the crematorium staff a Christmas box, saw to the nurses and staff at the hospital for their Christmas fare and hoped we had not forgotten anyone.

A hundred days after her death we held a Celebration for her death and life at the Chithurst Monastery, where a Dhana was given to the monks, and family and friends came once again to join with us in the memorial.

All this activity has helped me to deal with my grief and my feelings of guilt and resentment at having to look after quite a difficult lady. I feel I was also able to deal with my father's death – he died in 1961 at the age of 54 and the funeral was too quickly dealt with, with little time to realise how we all felt at that time. So I was able to lay to rest some unresolved grief over his loss.

Many people have spoken to us regarding making their own coffins and are surprised at how little we spent. For the record the absolutely necessary expenses were:

Fee for the crematorium £105; fees for the doctors £57; death certificates £8; purchase of chipboard and timber £30. Total: £200.

In fact we spent a further £42 on the reserve car, for a grand total of £242. Several people asked, did we do this because we couldn't afford it? The answer to this is, No. I felt doing this ourselves was very rewarding, it helped to deal with our grief and the resentments that we had, and which had built up through the years as a result of some of the difficulties of looking after my mother during her lifetime. The main thought seemed to be that it was just as she would have wanted and this came over very strongly from all who helped and were present.

Dorothy Miller's coffin

Deidre's husband adds this note and the illustration below about the coffin:

We made the coffin from half inch chipboard and 2" by 1" finished battens. First we cut the base and used this as a template for the lid. Although the hospital mortician gave us the width of 18" we erred on the generous side, at 20", to make sure the shoulders would go in all right. On reflection, it would have been ample to make the sides and top with quarter inch chipboard or even hardboard if one really wanted to economise on expense and weight. Below the bottom (and flush with the edges) we fixed battens. We then cut the side pieces 12" high and fixed these on to the battens so that the battens were concealed. Then we fixed battens on the inside of the side pieces a half inch from the top to accommodate a flush-fitting lid. We found

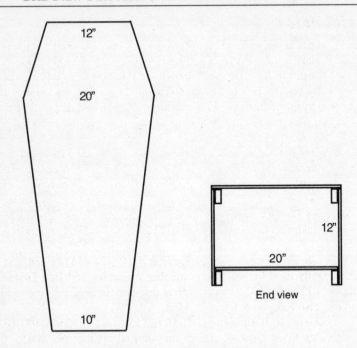

End view

it necessary to strengthen the joining to the lid-battens at the junction of the angle at the widest part of the coffin. We pre-drilled the lid so that it was simple to screw down after putting the old lady in at the mortuary.

We used ferrous screws throughout because after the cremation they were removed from the ashes with a magnet. In the foot end we fixed a small rope handle to use in pulling the coffin out of the car. It was not necessary to fit any other handles.

The mortician said that the coffin was one of the best he had seen.

Helping with 'd-i-y' funerals

Several volunteers have offered to give what advice or assistance they can to those organising funerals without funeral directors in their regions:

• Helen Berrett offers support to those in the Oxford area (tel 01865 727882 evenings; no media calls please).

• Sheila Page offers support in the Hampshire area (tel Lymington 01590 671205, not after 10pm).

• Deirdre Martin offers support in the Brighton region (tel 01273 507644).

• The A. B. Wildlife Trust Fund, based in Harrogate, offers support and legal advice on conventional and unconventional funerals (tel 01423 5309000).

If you have successfully carried out a funeral in this way, please tell the Natural Death Centre if you might be willing to be publicised as part of this network. Please also send in an account of any unusual funeral for publication, again as an encouragement and aid to others, with your tips and advice.

Burial at sea

In theory, burial at sea seems an attractive proposition: the body becomes food for the fish, and it is just a matter of getting a free licence (for England and Wales) from the Ministry of Agriculture, Fisheries and Food (MAFF) and then finding a person with a suitable boat to take the coffin out. In practice, sea burial is mildly discouraged by the authorities (with only about 20 such burials a year) and there are quite complex guidelines. On two occasions recently, bodies buried off the Cornish coast were washed up on shore. There are concerns about commercial fishing trawling the bodies back up – these are busy shipping lanes and foreign trawlers do not always know the areas to avoid. There are now only two places around the coast where sea burials are allowed: one near Newhaven, and the Needles Spoil Ground, to the West of the Isle of Wight. You need to contact your local fisheries District Inspector for the free licence. Either go via Marine Environmental Protection at MAFF (tel 0171 238 5872 or 5868) or make contact directly:

• *Newhaven, East Sussex:* Angus Radford (tel 01424 424109/438125). The vessel normally used for this site is the Tug Meeching (tel Bob Domin, the skipper, on 01273 514131). Local funeral directors in Seaford have used this ground and also Kenyon & Co in London.

• *Poole, Dorset:* R. H. Bushell (tel 01202 677539; fax 01202 678598). His site is the Needles Spoil Ground, shown on Admiralty Chart No 2045, 'Outer Approaches to the Solent'. The vessel normally used for the Needles Spoil Ground is hired from Hurst Castle Ferries of Lymington (tel Sean Crain on 01425 610784). Funeral directors who have organised sea burials there include: J. Bevis & Son in Southampton (tel Mrs M. Bailey, 01703 772120); Davies Funeral Services of Milford-on-Sea (tel G. R. Davies, 01590 644664); Bennett in Essex (tel Jane Arnold, 01277 210104); the Co-op in Weymouth (tel Allan Quatermain, 01305 772789); and A. H. Roger (tel 01703 612435).

Sea burials organised by funeral directors tend to cost between £2,000 and £3,000.

A private yacht can be used if it has accurate positioning equipment and if its skipper has a yacht master's certificate.

You should tell the registrar when registering the death that you plan a sea burial and you can then obtain from the registrar a 'Coroners Out of England Form' (Form 104) – and the local coroner's address to which this should be sent.

The Poole Fisheries Officer, Mr Bushell, has dealt with families making their own arrangements, without using funeral directors, and seems helpful. Guidelines vary slightly between the two regions, but, by talking to Mr Bushell and Mr Radford, and reading the various documents, the following consensus emerges – the aim of these conditions being to ensure that the coffin and body stay down on the sea-bed, that marine life has ready access to the body and that the body is readily identifiable should it be washed up:

• The coffin should not be made of any persistent synthetic material, nor of a species of timber, such as oak, which would endure in the marine environment. It may not include any lead, zinc or copper. (They recommend a chipboard or a softwood such as pine, with the coffin as strong as possible, reinforced on the bottom corners, and large enough to fit extra weights. Even the screws must not be zinc.)

• The wooden coffin should be weighted with at least 2cwt (3cwt Hastings, 4cwt MAFF) of iron, steel or concrete. (They recommend chain or pig iron, and that the weights be put inside the coffin.)

• Holes of at least three quarter inch diameter are to be drilled to allow rapid ingress of water and escape of air, so that the coffin may reach the sea-bed quickly and stay there. (They recommend two dozen holes in the side and lid.)

• The body should also be weighted. (They recommend that the body should have chain wrapped round it, with the chains weighing about 20 kilos, or about 10% more than the body)

• The coffin should effectively retain the body on the sea-bed without unduly preserving it.

• The body may not be embalmed. (The body may be dressed, although the MAFF specifies a cotton sheet or paper substitute – or a biodegradable body bag may be used, but not a canvas shroud.)

• A certificate of freedom from fever and infection should be obtained from the GP or hospital doctor, and this certificate, together with a copy of the death certificate and the form releasing the body for removal out of England, should be submitted to the district fisheries office.

• The body should have a plastic tag around any two limbs (although Poole recommends a tag around the torso and one around the ankle) with a permanent inscription showing the deceased's name and date of burial and the telephone number of a funeral director or solicitor or similar permanent number.

The MAFF reserves the right to inspect the coffin prior to the burial, although this rarely happens in practice. Normally, the local MAFF office must be informed on the day prior to the date of burial and immediately after. An at-least-verbal amendment to the licence is needed if adverse weather or other circumstances delay the burial beyond the week of the licence.

Non assembly-line funerals

There are indeed many ways that people have found to prevent funerals from becoming assembly-line affairs, including those events for which funeral directors are used. Below are some examples – and the particularly useful books on this topic detailed in the Resources chapter are Tony Walter's 'Funerals and How to Improve Them', 'The Dead Good Funerals Book' by Sue Gill and John Fox, 'Celebrating Life' by Andrew Hill and 'Funerals Without God' by Jane Wynne Willson.

• **Reminders:** Have something on top of the coffin during the service, as a reminder of the person who has died - such as a favourite hat or scarf.

• **Fires, candles, lanterns**: John Fox of Welfare State International ('the celebratory arts company' – see the Resources chapter under Organisations) suggests a funeral or memorial service outdoors, the space framed with poles, bunting and music, tables decorated with cloth, flowers and papercuts, and the use of fires, candles and lanterns. 'The Dead Good Funerals Book' which he wrote with Sue Gill, demonstrates the flair and genius of his group of 'Engineers of the Imagination' in designing innovative rituals (the book's first edition is unreliable on the legal side). Here, for instance, is John Fox imagining the kind of cremation service he himself would like:

Hanging the crem with banners and papercuts

Wrapped in his favourite blanket we placed his body in a deep blue shiny cardboard coffin painted inside and out. On the lid his daughter painted simple seed and tree designs in white lines. The coffin rested on trestles in the front room of his house for a day or two; we preferred not to have an open coffin.

'No incense', he had requested. So we lit a few candles smelling of honey.

The night before the committal his coffin was driven round Ulverston on a flat bed truck. We visited his works and a couple of pubs accompanied by a wild percussion band, with salsa brass and firecrackers; then returned to the house.

We knew he preferred cremation so we negotiated with the crematorium manager for a double slot at the beginning of the day to gain time to decorate the space and take it all down afterwards. We hung the crem with simple big banners in blue and red suspended from theatrical lighting stands and put marigolds and sunflowers in earthenware vases. We framed it all with strings of small white papercuts cut with fire and bird imagery and made it more cosy with pools of warm lighting. Incidentally, we did have to remove temporarily a crucifix and cover up a statue depicting a sentimental Jesus story about the sheep that escaped.

Rather unconventionally, we arranged the seats in a circle and placed the coffin on trestles in the middle. On the floor was a bright red Persian carpet (which we borrowed from a shop in town). It looked fantastic. The white seed decorations, painted on the top of the coffin resembled galaxies and the surrounding banners gave the feeling of a womb-like tent.

The service was a bit longer than usual because many people wanted to read poems and tell stories. We gave out photocopied sheets of some of his poems and later made a few handmade books as presents for those who had helped.

The music was great. His son, a musical director, arranged a few tunes for cellos, trombone and trumpet with a small acapella choir who helped us sing along. 'What is the Life of a Man' was hung up on a song sheet! Bryan always said he wanted a song sheet at his funeral because no one ever knows the words of the hymns, but really because he was theatrical and loved pantomimes. Painting the words and hanging the banner took so long we nearly had to abandon the idea but it was worth it

• **One flower each**: You could ask friends not to buy flowers but to bring one flower each, preferably from their garden, and to place it on the coffin. Here is

Allegra Taylor's description of how everyone brought one daffodil each to the funeral of Claire, an eight year old girl who died of leukaemia:

A grave lined with moss and leaves like a bird's nest

The funeral, organised magnificently by Margot's husband, was a triumph of life over death. Many children from Claire's old school came, as well as some she'd known in hospital. Their drawings for Claire were stuck up all round the church: drawings of butterflies, flowers and big yellow suns. A few children stood up and read poems. Everyone was given a candle to hold - the place was ablaze with the illuminated faces of children - and a yellow daffodil to throw in the grave.

The minister - a friend of the family - held the little coffin in his arms as he spoke of Claire's courage and of the lightness and joy she'd brought into the world during her short life. The grave was lined with moss and leaves like a nest for a baby bird. We stood with our arms around each other as we threw in an avalanche of daffodils and sang 'The Lord of the Dance' together: 'Dance, dance, wherever you may be ...' It was the most beautiful funeral I had ever been to and an inspiring example of how it can be. We have begun to reclaim birth and death from the medical profession after generations of abdication - begun to reinstate choice and personal responsibility. Let's do the same with funerals.

From 'Acquainted with the Night' by Allegra Taylor.

• **A child's burial on a farm**: A boy aged five died at home of cancer after a two year struggle. The parents had expected his death and had previously been in touch with the Natural Death Centre for advice. The parents asked a local farmer to allow his land to be used for the burial – the farmer consulted his wife and they gave their permission. The National Rivers Authority (now subsumed within the Environment Agency), having been told the grid reference for the grave, said that there was no danger of it causing pollution. No local council planning permission or permission from the environmental health officer was required.

The father and friends spent all day digging a four foot deep circular grave in the chalky soil. The parents had ordered a woollen burial shroud from the cemetery in Carlisle, and cut this down to child-size, folding it around the boy's body. On the day of the burial, a week after the death, they conducted their own ceremony, with 70 friends of all ages present, including some of the nurses who had cared for him.

As requested, people came wearing ordinary clothes that the boy would have felt comfortable with. They played his favourite music. They had a spiritual circle spreading light into the earth. A friend, whose girl had died some time before, added her cremated ashes to the grave and spoke in her memory. They put flowers and toys into the grave and built a cairn of stones as a burial mound on top.

The funeral director, recommended by the parents' GP, had initially been shocked, but, once satisfied as to the legality of it all, was very helpful. He took the body away and washed it with the essential oils that the parents supplied, so that the body could be visited on his premises by friends. Everything else, such as the transport of the body to the burial place, was organised by the parents.

When the earth has settled over the grave, the parents intend to add a plaque and a rock spiral.

• **Home funerals**: You could get the priest or humanist officiant to conduct the funeral or memorial service in your home or out in the garden. Amongst ministers, Unitarians are particularly willing to conduct a funeral service in your home or elsewhere and will officiate at very personalised or even humanist (that is, atheist or agnostic) funerals. (See Organisations in the Resources chapter). Anglican priests, too, are increasingly willing to conduct 'life-centred' funerals.

The Rosslyn Hill Unitarian Chapel in Hampstead (tel 0171 431 4160) is committed to allowing people to hire the chapel for non-religious funerals, without strict time limits. An organist can be provided.

The following unidentified newspaper cutting in The Natural Death Centre library records a very exuberant funeral – were at least the drivers sober?

Cortège in 250 mile pub crawl

A 20-car funeral cortège set off from Peterborough General Hospital at 8-30am and arrived in Haverfordwest in Wales, 12 hours later. After drinking the Bull Inn there dry, the 100 mourners, mostly Irish travellers, caught the overnight ferry to Rosslare.

The cortège was following the last instructions of Mrs Johanna Connors, who was buried at the end of the trip in New Ross, County Wexford.

• **Humanist funerals**: For a fee of £75, you can get a trained officiant from the British Humanist Association (see Resources chapter) to act as master or mistress of ceremonies for a humanist funeral. The officiant will normally ask you beforehand about the life of the person that died, so that their speech will be personalised. Or you or a friend or relative can conduct the service yourselves, perhaps referring to the very helpful pamphlet entitled 'Funerals Without God', by Jane Wynne Willson on how to run such services, with its sample texts and poetry (see Resources chapter). The pamphlet explains how a humanist service tends to divide into distinct parts:

First there is about eight minutes' worth of entry music, which is played until people have settled down in their seats – if an organist is not being used, this music should be recorded on side A only of a tape marked clearly 'Entry Music' and should be presented to the crematorium preferably the day before. The service proper opens with thoughts on life and death; then a tribute to the dead person (perhaps by a relative); followed by the committal (where everyone stands, the officiant turns towards the coffin, 'commits the body to its natural end' and a button is pressed to close the curtains). Up to about 40 seconds of slow and solemn music is sometimes used for the committal, with the person operating the machine cued to switch it on the moment specific words are said (a second tape should be clearly marked 'Committal Music' with the tape in position to deliver music the moment the Play button is pressed); and the service ends with closing words, after which the officiant walks over to the main mourners and leads them out of the exit door; a tape (marked 'Exit Music') can be played for about five minutes from the moment the officiant steps down from the lectern. Be sure to ask the crematorium to play the music loudly, if this is what you want.

Michael Rennie in Dundee used the 'Funerals Without God' book to help him design a secular funeral for his father:

> During my father's funeral, after welcoming all present, I dealt with the need to come to terms with death and read some words from Pasternak about the essence of our existence on earth. After a poem by Swinburn about the peace to be found in death, we stood in silence for some moments – moments in which those who had religious faith were asked to pray. I then paid tribute to my father's memory, incorporating anecdotes giving an insight into his character and contribution to life. My daughter played on the violin tunes emphasising my father's links with the sea, with Scotland and with the Tyne, as his coffin was taken from the hall. Later I committed him to the earth, and read a poem by C. Day Lewis, which was sufficiently broad in its humanity to resonate with any secular or religious beliefs.
>
> *From a letter to The Independent (Oct. 28th 1991).*

• **A New Orleans band**: The Eureka New Orleans Jazz Band (tel 0121 449 0119) plays at funerals. The eight-piece band consists of trumpets, trombone, sousaphone, banjo, clarinet and snare drum. They can play a fanfare inside or outside the chapel, or elsewhere. Prices range from £180 (four-piece) to £350 (eight-piece) for one hour's performance within a 30 mile radius of Birmingham; £300 to £500 for the London area.

• **Longer services**: It may be possible to book two or even three sessions at the crematorium, if the standard time is not enough, and if there are many people who wish to speak; and to book the last service of the day, in case your timing is not as exact as the professionals. The Good Funeral Guide chapter details how much, if anything, each crematorium charges for extra time.

• **Other cultures, other times**: In the UK, two world wars made funerary pomp on the home front seem out of place and accentuated our Puritan heritage of simple funerals. Indeed in 1644 the Puritans directed that the dead were to be interred 'without any ceremony'. In 1648, when the body of King Charles I was brought to the Royal Chapel at Windsor, the governor of the castle refused to let Bishop Juxon read the funeral service from the Book of Common Prayer:

The funeral of King Charles I

The Bishop of London stood weeping by, to tender that his service might not be accepted. Then was Charles I deposited in silence and sorrow in the vacant place in the vault about three of the afternoon; and the Lords that night, though late, returned to London.

From 'The History of the Worthies of England' edited by
J. Fuller, Publishers IGWL and WG, 1662, quoted in
'The English Way of Death' by Julian Litten.

There is a beauty of its own in the simplicity expected at a Quaker funeral today, where the disposal of the body is supposed to be done with no unnecessary expense and with no flowers. But the diversity of funeral practices in other cultures and religions around the world and the beauty or intricacy of some of their rituals can widen our vision of the potential of funerals to 'enchant' the participants, raising their consciousness above the mundane. The Ecuadorians, for instance, are buried with their eyes open so that they can see their way to heaven; the Yanonami Indians of the Amazon believe that it is barbaric that Westerners do not drink the ashes of their relatives; the Merina hold periodic 'dances with the dead' where the women dance with the dried-out remains of their next of kin; rural Greeks tend the graves daily for five years before the corpse is disinterred and placed in a communal ossuary, with clean bones being seen as a reflection of a good life; and for traditional Hindus even the grandchildren are closely involved:

The Hindu rites of death

Hindus should arrange for the dying person to be brought home to die. The dying person should concentrate upon the mantram given at initiation, or if the person is no longer conscious, a family member should chant the mantram softly in his or her right ear.

After death, the relatives place a simple cloth on the person. Each of the relatives comes and applies sesame oil to the deceased's head. The body is bathed with the water from nine kumbhas, and is placed in the coffin. Each of the grandchildren takes a small lighted stick and stands around the body and sings.

> *From 'Death and Dying – A Hindu Point of View', £1-50 from*
> *Himalayan Academy Publishers, Rakesh Mathur, 6 Carolyn*
> *House, 95 Larkhall Rise, London SW4 6HR.*

A pagan death

There is a Pagan Hospice and Funeral Trust in the UK – now called the Voyager Trust (see the Resources chapter). In the future it hopes to have a network of counsellors to aid dying pagans, to provide pagan funeral services and to purchase a hospice and burial grounds. At present it has a newsletter and leaflets and provides information on pagan approaches to death and dying, reincarnation and other subjects – and is struggling with the Charity Commissioners, who deny that paganism qualifies as a religion under current but archaic charity law.

Pagans aim to design rituals that bring them very close to nature and the seasons. Here is an eloquent description of a pagan death and memorial ceremony is that by Tony Kelly and his friends, concerning his wife Betty who died from cancer:

> Betty was now lying in a green-covered bed in the sunshine at the window, the window open and the air full of warmth and birdsong, willow and birch branches in front of her and a great leafy birch bough at the foot of the bed and the littler branches by the open window. It looked like a woodland glade

and she was pleased. Among all the greenery were two bunches of daffodils in big jars, and jars of dandelions and celandines and yellow polyanthus on the windowsill. And I put a few little branches of silver birch on the bed where she could take hold of them and handle them and feel them in the way she always liked to do ...

I was sitting at Betty's side, speaking to her softly as she dreamed, saying, 'The Goddess loves you,' and other things that I knew would make her happy, and I was holding her hands. Betty stopped breathing ...

We stripped all the alien words and the glitter off the coffin; the wood was beautiful. We laid Betty naked inside it and dressed her with daffodils, tastefully, beautifully, in her hair and about her body, some of them fresh and a few to speak her fading ...

The cremation was without ceremony and we brought her ashes home and kept them with us in the box I made, its lid scalloped like the waves of the sea, till the Hag Moon of Samhain called us to a distant shore ...

The ceremony for the scattering of the ashes took place seven months later, at a remote spot by the sea:

The Sea-lady came over the grass to where I was standing and she raised the lid of the box, and the ashes, speckled black and grey, lay open to the wide open sky. As I held the box to my breast and she took the lid into her own two hands I spoke the message that for seven moons my heart had borne:

> I am come, beloved Mabh
> To do a thing for Betty
> And to do the thing for thee
> For love of Betty
> And for love of thee

Each spoke their own devotion and to each the priestess responded with the same words that had been Betty's own spontaneous response when their phone calls had been conveyed to her, and they sang a six-verse song they had composed for the occasion:

> ... Green Lady Earth,
> Deep Lady Sea ...
> Carry the ash ...
> Her life has flown;
> Thou dost abide ...

We joined our hands in a ring, all nine of us, and a kiss from the Green Lady passed from lip to hand all around the ring. 'With thee for always, Mabh,' I spoke as the love of the Goddess moved me. At last we loosed our hands.

For a copy of the full 16 page text send £1 incl. postage to Tony Kelly, Can y Lloer, Ffarmers, Llanwrda, Dyfed.

Celebration Box

Yvonne Malik (Sweet Briar, 52 Hornby Road, Wray, Near Lancaster LA2 3QN, tel 01542 21767) is a designer by trade and a decorator of coffins. She has designed a Celebration Box, which could be placed at the back of the church or crematorium or memorial service, or filled before death, as a kind of miniature art gallery, to be filled by the congregation with photographs, letters, poems, keepsakes and small items. One prototype she put together using an old house-painter's box, as described by Fraser Harrison, in an article in Country Living (June 1996): 'It was dedicated to Lilian and Horace Parker and was filled with mementos of them, his on one side, hers on the other. Every part of the box overflowed with photographs, keepsakes and small items connected with the couple, from the jaunty cigarette holder of Horace's youth to a minute, beaded evening bag belonging to Lilian.' The following is an extract from Yvonne Malik's leaflet seeking commissions to produce Celebration Boxes:

> When a relative or close friend dies, we often find it impossible to find words to express our feelings. We remember special times, events and places which we shared together, or recall good deeds and kindnesses. These keys to our special memories have an intrinsic value only between ourselves and the one who has died.
>
> Using the Celebration Box is an opportunity to express and focus on a new way of saying 'goodbye'. Each box becomes unique and special, giving us the satisfaction of having taken part in filling it, as well as the ultimate feeling of something shared. This is a new way of including family and friends in a nonverbal act of celebration and comfort – a celebration of the life and shared experiences with the deceased and a later comfort for the bereaved, as well as something to be treasured by the next generation.
>
> Suggested items which have a private or intimate meaning and could be placed in the box include:
>
> Photographs; postcards which reminds us of a special day together; letters, poems, thank-you notes; birthday cards; tickets from a concert which we shared, souvenir from a holiday; button from their favourite jacket, pair of earrings, pipe; copy of a team certificate, club badge, medal; special scarf or cap.
>
> The events and times which we shared require no explanation from us and the tokens placed within the box are private statements. It is something which can be carried out by ourselves, alongside the traditional services of the funeral director.
>
> The Celebration Box can be filled at home prior to the funeral or placed in an accessible situation at the back of the church or chapel and brought home after the final ceremony.
>
> Each Celebration Box is hand decorated and therefore differs from any other. It also has the advantage of being portable, to suit today's more transient lifestyle.

A simpler approach, described by Tony Walter in the Funeral Director (April 1996) – or one which could work in tandem with the Celebration Box – is to place cards in the church pews inviting mourners to leave a sentence or two about the person who has died – for the later comfort of the family.

Public memorial

Remembering the dead begins immediately after death, and continues after the funeral. One suggestion for improving grieving is to set up 'open houses' for bereaved people who can't face going home. Nowadays, many people hold impromptu wakes after the funeral. The wake or after-funeral gathering is common in most cultures, like the wedding feast. However, it is the tone or style of the wake that is all-important. A feast that is too formal might accentuate the loneliness of the bereaved person once the guests have gone home. On the other hand, an informal gathering of mourners who want to share their feelings may begin a sharing process that will come to be of benefit to the bereaved. Laughter and jokes as well as tears are likely to erupt because remembering the dead person is also recalling the richness of life and relationships through stories and anecdotes.

Holding a memorial service at some time, perhaps months after the death and immediate obsequies, may be a way of bringing out the essential cheerfulness and spirit of life with which most of us would like to be remembered. We want to be celebrated as well as mourned. Here is such a celebration, designed by Margaret Chisman for her husband Stan. There is some human instinct that makes us want to be present at such a celebration of people who were our friends. It is rather like giving wedding gifts. We want to give the gifts, be part of the celebration. Why should we deprive ourselves of being part of such a ceremony, the feasting of a life?

A table of objects to commemorate the person

The celebration and commemoration of Stan was held at our home in the double rooms on the ground floor. About 40 friends and relations were present. It was a beautiful day, the garden was full of flowers and their scent drifted in through the open french doors. After welcoming everyone I took the cloth cover off the table and explained that on it were articles that Stan loved or that exemplified his life.

The first thing that everyone noticed about him was his outstanding physical vigour. By contrast many people seemed only half alive. He was fully and gloriously alive in every fibre of his being. He loved rambling – I held up his walking boots – and whenever he decided to go on a walk he began to get excited and I would know to get his boots out. He loved skiing – I showed his goggles – and sadly had a holiday fixed for January by which time he was too ill. There were several photos amongst those displayed of him enjoying this sport. When living in Ipswich he played in the Post Office Table Tennis Team, and they won the cup one year and each player received a small trophy, here displayed. He also played five-a-side football and his old football boots were still in the cupboard upstairs. He took up sailboarding within the last two years and there were several photos of him displayed. These were taken on our holiday in the South of France. I regret I have no photos of him hang-gliding (whoever heard of a man of 62 taking up hang-gliding?), but George, who also introduced him to this sport describes the last occasion; Stan had become airborne to a height of 50 ft and was looking decidedly unhappy but absolutely determined to go through with it.

John White, who could not be present today said that for him he would always remember Stan for playing the glorious voice of Paul Robeson singing 'I thought I saw Joe Hill last night.' We played this record, and as I heard that vibrant voice singing the words of optimism in the face of death I felt once more overcome with grief and loss and wondered whether, despite all my supportive and loving relations and friends, all my active outside interests, my comfortable and satisfying home, I would manage to achieve serenity and full acceptance of his death.

The next part was pure joy. Nearly everyone had an anecdote or memory to share. Some of them were new to me, and I felt as if Stan came alive again for a few minutes.

Alan Mayne commented in the Visitors Book: 'I knew that Stan was a man of many parts but I didn't know how many.'

I asked everyone to end as Stan would have wished – to hug and kiss their neighbours.

> *From 'Interim', a private newsletter*
> *circulated by Margaret Chisman.*

Incidentally, Ernest Morgan warns that those who speak up at memorial services should not allow themselves to be cut short by whoever is conducting the service. 'I have known family members who carried regrets for years that they were cut off from speaking because the service was running too long.'

Memorials by Artists

Memorials by Artists puts bereaved families in touch with artists, for the designing and placing of headstones and other memorials in a style requested by the individual. Themes have included homely domestic items, animals and birds, a typewriter and other symbols suggested by the commissioning person or devised by the artist, as well as epitaphs. The movement was founded by Harriet Frazer.

> The demands for real memorials have proved so great that she has had to employ an assistant. 'The work can sometimes be very sad. Actually, really sad,' she said. 'But what is wonderful is that it is so much to do with life. The artists are so creative, making beautiful things, and celebrating a person is a very hopeful thing to do.'

> *From an article by Mary Greene in*
> *The Sunday Telegraph (April 28th 1991).*

Prices of headstones average from £1,000, including the Memorials by Artists fee. An illustrated booklet is available from Memorials by Artists (see the Resources chapter) for £5, including postage and packing.

Elizabeth Lawlor, who used Memorials by Artists for her husband's headstone, commends them to The Natural Death Centre:

The headstone is up. I wanted a wave on top for symbolic reasons – waves of consciousness, waves being re-absorbed into the ocean, etc – and for my husband's naval and sea-loving connection. The help I received from Memorials by Artists was wonderful.

If you simply need to find a quality person to design the headstone, a free register of artists is kept by the Council for the Care of Churches (tel 0171 638 0971).

A memorial of course need not be a gravestone: you may want to pay for a glass window in church; or to pay for a park bench; or to have a sponsored walk or children sponsored to learn poetry for a recital in aid of the person's favourite charity. If asking for donations to charity, suggest that these be paid by cheque, to help prevent donations going astray.

A lively memorial recently consisted of mixing the deceased's ashes with gunpowder, and launching them into the night sky as a series of giant firework rockets.

A firm called Air Navigation and Trading (tel 01253 345396), based at Blackpool airport, will scatter your ashes over land or sea. They charge £80 an hour.

If you want to plant a tree in a public place in memory of the person, you could ask your local park if this might be possible.

Woodland Creation, The Guildhouse, Tredethick, Lostwithiel, Cornwall PL22 OLE (tel 01208 873618) is an unregistered organisation set up by Tim and Nicky Reed where for £15 you can dedicate a tree in new broadleaved woodland in Cornwall. The tree is tagged on site with the requested dedication, and recorded in a dedication book, with a mapped reference number.

Heritage Conserved Ltd, Afallon, High Street, Llanfyllin, Powys SY22 5AR (tel 01691 648749) sells plots from £25 to £80, where a single tree is planted. Land owners receive legal freehold title to the land and a decorated and personalised Deed is supplied. Each plot is numbered so that individual trees can be identified.

The British Trust for Conservation Volunteers have a scheme where for £12 a paper tag says who the tree was planted for and relatives can get a certificate (but may not know which exact tree it is). They are at 36 St Mary's St, Wallington, Oxfordshire OX10 OEU (tel 01491 824900).

It may have been mainly a publicity gimmick, but a pub in Hereford (The Packhorse) announced a genial offer for regular customers – that of placing their ashes behind tiles in the pub, with a wake in their honour when they die and free drinks all round once a year thereafter, for a price ranging from £50 for a tile in the toilets, to £5,000 for a tile close to the fire. The money was to have been lodged with a local solicitor.

Alternative Urns

John Fox of Welfare State International suggests redecorating the normal small wooden caskets used for ashes: remove the paint with varnish stripper, undercoat with filler and two coats of white wood primer; then paint imagery or words –

he uses fluorescent enamel varnish (Brodie and Middleton); re-varnish, allowing 24 hours for the drying. He adds this story:

> I commissioned a pottery urn from a friend who specialised in throwing decorative slipware. It was for the ceremony to scatter my father's ashes in the Humber Estuary, where he had earned his living as a sea captain.
>
> We ended up with a dome-shaped circular lidded pot about a foot high and a foot diameter at the base. A little like a tiny bee hive.
>
> The lid had to be surprisingly wide too – about six inches, for the ashes to scatter easily downwind.
>
> In white slip on the dark brown of the pot's surface, we inscribed:
>
> 'The last voyage of Captain Fox, MBE. May his spirit be at peace with the sea.'
>
> At the ceremony myself, my wife and our two children then ten and eight played 'Eternal Father' on brass instruments. (My father was a Christian.)
>
> It was memorable and healing for us all.

Welfare State International (artistic director John Fox – see the Resources chapter) offers a consultancy service for those wanting a very special memorial service.

Gemma Nesbitt (Sort, Powerstock, Bridport, Dorset DT6 3TQ, tel 01308 485 273; fax 01308 485 639) is a designer of willow coffins, as described in the next chapter. She has also persuaded Tim Hurn, a potter in Dorset (Home Farm House, Bettiscombe, Bridport, Dorset DT6 5NU, tel 01308 868171) to make little clay pots for ashes, in the shape of beehives or mud-huts (2 to 3 inches high for £10, or a larger size, to contain all one person's ashes, for £25).

Rupert Blamire (Ground Floor Unit, Bannerman Buildings, Bannerman Road, Bristol BS5 ORR, tel 01179 39 3914) has designed a striking neoclassical three-foot-high lidded ceramic urn, made of red terracotta clay from Staffordshire. They can be used for housing the ashes or simply as garden ornaments. The 3' urn costs £95, a 4' model is available for £325. Blamire will deliver the urn for about £40 within his region.

Probate

In chapter two on Preparing for Dying, under the heading 'Simplifying Your Affairs Before Death', it was outlined how someone could leave their estate so that neither probate, inheritance tax nor Inland Revenue account was required. Probate otherwise involves the executors of the will applying to the probate registry for a grant of probate which confirms their power to process the will (if the person died without a will, or if the executors have died or are unwilling to act, the relatives apply for similar powers, known as letters of administration). Solicitors can do the whole thing for you, but in one typical recent instance they charged a rate of £80 per hour, plus half a per cent of all the cash, stocks and shares in the estate and one per cent of the property. To this total they then added 25%.

Shop around for the cheapest appropriate solicitor you can find – for instance, avoid central London and choose a solicitor who specialises in probate work (they are likely to take less time) – perhaps within such a firm you could get a reduction by asking if a trainee solicitor could handle it for you. You could probably reduce the bill further by doing some of the work yourself, such as gathering in the estate's money from the bank and building society.

Likely firms of solicitors that we picked almost at random from the London Yellow Pages included: Jeremy Lawday of V. Barretts Associates (tel 01245 252 353) who charges about £110 an hour; Walford & Co (NW2, tel 0181 452 3000) who charge £95 per hour plus 0.75 per cent of the gross value of the estate. Grant Argent & Co (NW2, tel 0181 452 7651) who charge £90 per hour plus 0.5 per cent of the gross value of the estate; and a trainee solicitor at Nigel Broadhead Mynard (tel 01245 269909) who charges £60 an hour. The Will Consultancy, Old Bank Chambers, Market Square, Pontypridd, Mid-Glamorgan CF37 2SY, Wales (tel 01443 485147), who can draw up wills, also specialise in probate work nationwide and will tend to quote a fixed price.

But assuming the estate is relatively straightforward (with no business partnership, self-owned business, agricultural land, insurance syndicate or family trusts) it can be done by anyone businesslike, with patience enough to wade through all the fiddly details and to write the many formal letters. Again, as when preparing one's will, the most useful book is the Consumers' Association's 'Wills and Probate'. The following is merely a sketch of what is involved:

You will need forms for a personal application for a grant of probate from your local Probate Personal Application Department – if you were not given this address in a booklet at the time you registered the death, you can find it out from the Probate Registry (see the Resources chapter). You can get Form PA2 from the local office which tells you how to do things without a solicitor and the Citizens Advice Bureau may be able to help further. Once you have filled in and returned these forms, you will be given an appointment to go to your local office in person to swear that the information is true. At this point you will need to pay the probate fee (if the estate was worth £250,000 net, for example, the fee would be about £350); and a couple of weeks later you will need to pay any inheritance tax owing (although inheritance tax on land or buildings can be paid over a ten year period at – currently – eight per cent interest).

If the deceased's funds were in a bank these will be frozen until after probate is granted (you could try asking the bank to put any current account amount on deposit, so that at least it earns interest; the bank also has discretion to let the executors continue operating the account, if indemnified by the executors against loss). Because the account is frozen, the executors may have to get an expensive overdraft from the same bank to pay the inheritance tax (although a helpful bank may be willing to set any assets in the deceased's accounts against the required overdraft – and a prudent person might enquire of their bank before death whether they are helpful in this regard). It might have saved money if the dying person were to have transferred sufficient money to National Savings (see Chapter Two for the other advantages) as they will pay inheritance tax directly out of the deceased's assets and in advance of probate (as may some of the bigger building societies and a few of the more helpful banks).

The executors will also need to deal with the Land Registry to transfer any property (form 56 from an Oyez shop) and with the Income Tax people – their forms Cap 30 (to show that any inheritance tax has been paid), form 59 (an income tax return for the year in which the person died) and form R185E (income tax deduction certificates).

Valuing stocks and shares with the exactitude required for probate purposes (your bank may be willing, without charge, to find out the shares' value at the date of death), filling in the probate schedule of them and handling their transfer or sale are small bureaucratic nightmares. To repeat Chapter Two: any dying person who has accumulated the odd lot of shares in privatised BT, etc, would save their executors a great deal of trouble by selling them before death.

Executors will also need to deal with the deceased's mortgage company, house insurance company, district valuer (it is usually acceptable to get sales particulars for similar houses locally and to base your valuation on these), bank, building society, life insurance company, pension company, Benefits Agency and local post office (for forwarding of mail) – plus in some cases advertising in the newspapers for any unknown creditors.

Anyone appointed as an executor who, understandably, cannot face the work involved, can fill in a renunciation form or a form appointing an attorney to do it (both forms are available from an Oyez shop); or you can hand over to a professional part of the way through, but you will have to pay if there are insufficient assets in the estate.

Chapter 5

COFFINS &
PROFESSIONAL SERVICES

The previous chapter told how people could organise a funeral themselves. This one is for those who want help from the trade. It is for those who may be trying to buy funeral goods – such as a cardboard or a regular coffin; a painted coffin or a recycled coffin; a collapsible coffin, a willow coffin or a coffin as bookcase; a body bag or lowering webbing. It describes the goods on offer from coffin shops and coffin manufacturers. It will also enlighten you if you are seeking just one service rather than a complete package – such as cold storage facilities, or a hearse or horse-drawn carriage you can rent, or where to hire extra bearers. This chapter serves as an introduction to the detailed listings in the next chapter (the Good Funeral Guide), giving the results of the Natural Death Centre's nation-wide survey of the funeral trade. It describes not only the Natural Death Handbook Award Winners, but which local authorities supply a cheaper municipal funeral service; how to get a free funeral; why embalming may not be necessary; the snags that go with prepaid funerals; and the high standards being laid down by the best funeral directors, crematoria and cemeteries.

Natural Death Handbook Awards

On Sunday April 20th 1997, as part of the English Day of the Dead ceremonies organised by the Natural Death Centre, the following 16 Awards will be publicly presented:

• The Natural Death Handbook Award for the **Best Woodland Burial Ground** run by **farmers** or **private companies** or **individuals**. This award goes to Greenhaven Woodland Burial Ground near Rugby (tel 01788 860604), who provide exceptional value – a complete funeral, including the grave, the digging, a cardboard coffin, a tree and collection from London, costs from £399. (See the East Midlands section of the Good Funeral Guide chapter for their details.) Highly commended were also the Oakfield Wood Green Burial Ground near Manningtree in Essex and the Hinton Park Woodland Burial Ground near Christchurch in Dorset. Peace Burials, who run the South Yorkshire Woodland Burial Ground, were commended for their imaginative promotions, which include railway funerals.

• The Natural Death Handbook Award for the **Best Woodland Burial Ground** run by a **local authority**. This award goes to the woodland burial ground in Seaton, run by the East Devon District Council (Mr Kane, on 01395 516551 ext 376). The site offers panoramic views out over the valley and sea and a grave costs a mere £57 (digging extra). (See the South West section of the Good Funeral Guide chapter for their details.) Highly commended were also the Carlisle woodland burial ground in Cumbria (the 1993 Award winner) and the Woodvale woodland burial ground in Brighton.

• The Natural Death Handbook Award for the **Best Woodland Burial Ground** run by a **wildlife trust**. This award goes to A. B. Wildlife Trust Fund in Harrogate (tel 01423 530900) for its pioneering work in registering a welfare and wildlife charity which helps those who are dying and gives free advice on a full range of funeral choices. The Trust has used pastures for burial and now has an 8 acre wood-pasture in a Site of Special Scientific Interest for 25 burials. (See the North East section of the Good Funeral Guide chapter for their details.)

• The Natural Death Handbook Award for the **Best Funeral Shop**. This award goes to Heaven on Earth in Bristol (tel 0117 9421836) for their imaginative range of coffin designs. (See page 169 for their details.) Highly commended were the two shops run by Green Undertakings. The latter, for instance, sell the same cardboard coffin by mail order as Regale, the funerals supermarket in London, but at less than half the price. All these shops can also help arrange funerals.

• The Natural Death Handbook Award for the **Best Funeral Director in the North West**. This award goes to Edwards Funeral Directors Ltd in Wigan (tel 01942 821215). They offer a basic funeral for £615 (including disbursements) and an inexpensive municipal funeral service for local residents.

• The Natural Death Handbook Award for the **Best Funeral Director in the North East**. This award goes to D. J. Screen & Sons Ltd of Huddersfield (tel 01484 452220). They offer a fully-fitted coffin for £50, delivered locally free, and nationally at 50 p per mile, and a basic funeral at £385 (disbursements extra).

• The Natural Death Handbook Award for the **Best Funeral Director in the Wales**. This award goes to W. O. Williams in Anglesey (tel 01248 430312). They offer a 'D-i-y Funeral' for £287 (disbursements extra) where the family provides its own bearers, and collects all the forms and certificates.

• The Natural Death Handbook Award for the **Best Funeral Director in the West Midlands**. This award goes to Beechwood Funeral Services in Cheltenham (tel 01242 228208). They offer a fully-fitted coffin for £55 and a basic funeral for £650 (including disbursements).

• The Natural Death Handbook Award for the **Best Funeral Director in the East Midlands**. This award goes to E. M. Dorman in Uppingham (tel 01572 823976). They offer a fully-fitted coffin for £55 and a basic funeral for £480 (disbursements extra).

• The Natural Death Handbook Award for the **Best Funeral Director in the East Anglia**. This award goes to Peter Taylor Funeral Services in Norwich (tel 01603 760787). They offer an 'ecology' funeral for £600 (disbursements extra) and have a horse-drawn hearse available for about £500.

• The Natural Death Handbook Award for the **Best Funeral Director in the South West**. This award goes to the innovative Green Undertakings people in Somerset (tel 01984 632285). They are beginning to offer funerals throughout the region in association with partner firms, and are forcing competitors to lower their prices. Their basic funeral starts at £430 (disbursements extra), they sell a full range of coffins and funeral supplies, they are agents for several woodland burial grounds and they have an all-woman funeral team that can be called on.

• The Natural Death Handbook Award for the **Best Funeral Director in Southern England**. This award goes to Mr Harwood of Harwood & Wallis in Fordingbridge, Hampshire (tel 01425 656944). His firm make about ten coffins a week, the cheapest one selling for £100 fully-fitted, and his cheapest funeral (including all the disbursements) costs £850.

• The Natural Death Handbook Award for the **Best Funeral Director in the Greater London region**. This award goes to E. M. Kendall in Hackney (tel 0171 254 6519). They offer a fully-fitted coffin for £55 and a basic funeral for £375 (disbursements extra). Also highly commended is also Haji Taslim in London, a firm who give free funerals in deserving cases and mainly serve the Muslim communities; and J. E. Gillman & Sons Ltd, whose headquarters are in Tooting (tel 0181 672 1557), with branches in Surrey, Battersea, Balham and West Norwood – and whom several readers have recommended for their sensitivity and helpfulness.

• Readers are asked to recommend funeral directors in Scotland and Northern Ireland. At present, the Natural Death Centre knows of none prepared to sell just a coffin at a reasonable price to the general public and to provide other services on an à la carte basis.

• The Natural Death Handbook Award for the **Best Funeral Supplier**. This award goes to Ted Hodge and his firm E. C. Hodge (MF) Ltd (tel 01945 587477 or 01438 357341). They are the first mainstream funeral suppliers to make a determined attempt to allow the public to buy coffins direct. Their prices start at £88 for a chipboard oak veneer coffin. They also supply a solid pine coffin for £108. (See below, page 167, for their details.) Highly commended in this category are Green Undertakings, winners of the 1993 Award.

• The Natural Death Handbook Award for the **Best Crematorium**. This award goes to the Carlisle Crematorium run by the Carlisle District Council (tel 01228 25022). They offer a reduced fee for those choosing a fuel-saving 'Environmental Cremation', which involves a cardboard coffin and cremation the same day or by the following morning, thus saving on pre-heating of the cremator. They publish excellent guidance for those arranging funerals without funeral directors and they can help the public by providing cold storage for the body. They accept a wide variety of body containers from home-made to wicker coffins.

• The Natural Death Handbook Award for the **Best Cemetery**. This award goes, along with the crematorium award, to Carlisle (who won it in 1993 as well). The Bereavement Manager in charge of both places is Ken West (tel 01228 25022) who has been the key figure in getting the Institute of Burial and Cremation Administration to adopt a Charter for the Bereaved. This charter recognises the right of a family not to use a funeral director and the need for nature reserve burial grounds. The cemetery makes available not only cardboard and regular coffins, but its own woollen shroud. Ken West writes: 'We know that funerals arranged without a funeral director are at least as good, and often better, than those that take the conventional path.'

In making these Awards, the editorial team have relied on their own surveys and investigations and on feedback to the Natural Death Centre from the general public, in deciding which services were the most helpful, the most innovative and the best value.

Good funeral directors

In our view, the ideal funeral director is a *facilitator,* one who helps the family to do as much of the funeral arranging themselves as they can bear, as exemplified in the following excerpts from an account by an American funeral director about what he learnt from the funeral of his father:

A funeral director helping with his father's funeral

I was sitting on the hospital bed holding my father's hand when he died. I hated the scene but I wouldn't have been anywhere else. Such helplessness and desperation I have never felt at any other time. When he died, we wept.

Two men came with a cot – men I had never seen before. They didn't know me or my profession. My emotion didn't leave room for explanations, so I simply asked them to stand aside. It was my dad and I would do it. Hesitatingly they obliged, while I took the cover from the cot, positioned the cot and gathered Dad's limp body into my arms. It was my job. I was his son. It was our love.

I felt a sense of desertion as I watched those two strangers disappear down the hall with Dad. Dad didn't know them.

One of my best friends, a funeral director from the next town, came to get Dad and did all the embalming work. I did the rest – the death certificate, the notification of newspapers, cemetery, minister, church, family, friends, neighbours, all the scores of details which accompany the task of being a funeral director.

My family did lots of other things: we tucked Dad in (it's rough but it's real) and closed the casket; we took him to church ourselves. My brother, sister and I carried Dad to his grave, we lowered him into his grave with straps and our own muscle power. We closed the vault and shovelled the dirt ourselves. We closed out his life ourselves.

Later, weeks later, I asked myself: how many sons, daughters, parents and spouses had I delayed the grief work for because I had performed all of the tasks for them, because I, as a functionary, had usurped their role as care-giving family members? How many times had I made decisions for a family without their opinion, because I had assumed 'they couldn't take it?' They have a right to be heard. The focus must be on their needs, reactions and prior experience. Immediately, my role in funeral service shifted to being that of a facilitator and it has remained there.

By Roy and Jane Nichols from 'Death – The Final Stage of Growth'
edited by Elisabeth Kübler-Ross.

Buying a coffin

The last chapter dealt with making a coffin. This one, inter alia, tells you how to buy one ready-made – not always an easy purchase, as Jane Spottiswoode discovered. Many funeral directors refuse to sell just a coffin, or do so at grossly inflated prices.

Cardboard coffins

When the Natural Death Centre was launched in 1991, it called for cardboard coffins to be made available in the UK. Now there are four main models to choose from. The first edition of the 'Natural Death Handbook' in 1993 could identify only a handful of crematoria and cemeteries that would accept cardboard coffins. But by 1994, Jon Luby of The Federation of British Cremation Authorities was writing that 'my advice would be to accept such a coffin if requested'. Now the majority of crematoria do; and most funeral directors are willing to obtain a cardboard coffin on behalf of a client, although they will tend to charge a high price.

Cardboard coffins are most regularly used for burial in nature reserve woodland burial grounds. Some people prefer to use them in conjunction with a body bag or some other covering for the body. Some like to paint the coffin (using water-based paints) or to put a drape over the cardboard coffin during the funeral service to hide its unorthodox appearance. It is as well to be aware that if the soil is clay or very stony, the cardboard lid may get smashed open as the grave is filled. Measures that could be taken to avoid this include: placing planks or a mattress-type filling on top of the coffin; dropping a layer of hay or bracken or whatever is to hand on top of the coffin; wrapping the coffin in some covering such as a rug; filling the grave very gently to begin with, using specially gathered loose soil; or filling the grave only when those who would be most upset have left.

• Almost the cheapest and perhaps the most elegant of the various cardboard coffins is the Compakta Coffin. It is lightweight, relatively strong and slightly tapered, and, unlike some of the other models, it needs no bolts or clips. It would probably be the most suitable one for those wishing to paint their cardboard coffin. The main Compakta model (also sometimes referred to as The Quantock) is in white cardboard, although a brown cardboard version can be ordered. By paying an extra £22, you can ask for the coffin to be painted for you in the colour of your choice (gold or grey models are normally in stock). The snag with this coffin is that it is tricky to remove the lid for those wanting access to the body; and, internally, it is 76" long by 23" wide and 13.5" deep (allow an extra quarter inch for the external dimensions of this coffin and for the measurements of the other coffins below). You may need a van to transport it, as amongst the few estate cars it fits into are the old Volvo 940, the old Vauxhall Carlton and the new Ford Scorpio. The A. B. Wildlife Trust Fund uses a Renault 5 with the passenger seat removed.

This coffin is available to the trade from P. A. Ginns, Compakta Ltd, The Old White Cottage, Desford, Leicestershire LE9 9GS (tel 01455 828642). It can be collected from there or from L. T. & R. Vowles Ltd (tel 01684 592212) in Upton upon Severn near Worcester, who deliver the coffin nationwide for Compakta. Until recently, it was available to the public from Compakta themselves for £52-88 including VAT and delivery – and no doubt Mr Ginns will continue to supply directly in urgent cases (or go via The A. B. Wildlife Trust Fund on 01423 530900, who will get the coffin to you at this price).

Alternatively, members of the public can find out their most appropriate stockist by phoning the Compakta number or the Natural Death Centre. One such firm is Green Undertakings in Somerset (tel 01984 632285). Compakta's recommended price for the public to pay is £54-93 incl. VAT, delivery extra (Green Undertakings charge £25 for delivery nationally).

Compakta are developing a larger version of their coffin, mainly for the German market. This will be 77" long and 23" across the shoulders. Compakta also sell very small containers for foetal remains.

• Larger and less elegant than the Compakta coffin is the Brighton Casket cardboard coffin. Its dimensions are 78" by 25" by 15.75". This looks a bit like a giant brown cardboard shoe box and uses part-plastic bolts to hold it together. It has a 'moisture-protected white liner' inside. The advantage of both the Brighton Casket and the Woodland Coffin (see below) is that they have removable lids, so they are more suitable for viewing the body than the Compakta one. It is made by Derek Williamson and colleagues of Danisco Park Westminster, New Road, Sheerness, Kent (tel 01795 580051).

From this address it is available only in quantities of five or more, at a price of £46-50 each incl. delivery, for five coffins, or £36-50 for 100. They can, however, tell you who your nearest stockist is for single orders – you will probably be charged at least £53 incl. VAT.

• Danisco Park Westminster also market, besides the Brighton Casket, the Woodland Coffin. This is slightly shorter than both the Compakta and the Brighton Casket. Its dimensions are 75" by 25" by 13.5". Unlike the Brighton one, they will sell this to the public direct, as a single order. It comes as a flatpack, in a white oyster colour, and assembles into the normal coffin shape. It has a removable lid, but the flaps that hold it together are visible on the outside, so it is perhaps marginally less aesthetically pleasing than the Compakta one. It is, however, the cheapest on the market, at £51-40 incl. VAT and delivery within England and Wales. Allow five working days for delivery.

• The most expensive cardboard coffin, but the one the public nevertheless seems to choose most often when presented with a wide range to choose from, is the Swiss-made Peace Box, also known as the Ecology coffin. It looks least like a cardboard coffin, with a wood effect finish to it.

It is the creation of Alexandre Haas, a packaging manufacturer in Lausanne, Switzerland, who writes that it weighs 12 kilos, can carry 200 kilos, has a liquid-proof insert and resists temperatures from 250 degrees centigrade to minus 180 degrees centigrade. But it is above all kind to the environment, says Haas, 'and it is easily transported and can be slotted together in five minutes' (using metal clasps). (Alexandre Haas, Sondeur Diffusion, CH-1029 Villars-Ste-Croix, Switzerland, tel and fax 00 41 21 634 70 26.)

In the UK, it is distributed to the trade by PB UK (tel 01285 655953). Stockists selling single orders include Green Undertakings in Somerset (tel 01984 632285) at £115 (delivery nationally £25 extra); the Heaven on Earth shop in Bristol (tel 0117 9421836) at £150; the 'funeral supermarket' in London E17 (tel 0181 925 2010) at a pricey £231; Carlisle Cemetery at £108 (tel 01228 25022); and the Greenhaven woodland burial ground near Rugby at £104 (tel 01788 860604).

• Some local authority cemeteries and crematoria sell either the Brighton coffin or the Compakta one, whether or not you are booking a funeral service with them. Their prices are reasonable – normally about £55 – but they will require you to collect them. The local authorities include:

Ashford Borough Council in Kent, tel 01233 637311; Bretby near Burton-upon-Trent, tel 01283 221505; Brighton, tel 01273 604020; Cardiff (Thornhill Cemetery, with an exceptionally low price of £40) tel 01222 623294; Carlisle, tel 01228 25022; Hastings, tel 01424 781302; Hexham Town Council in Northumberland, tel 01434 609171; Richmond Borough ('Leisure Services') tel 0181 940 8351; Swale Borough Council in Sittingbourne, Kent, tel 01795 424341.

At least three private woodland burial grounds sell cardboard coffins. They are: Greenhaven near Rugby, tel 01788 860604; Hinton Park on the Dorset/Hampshire border, near Christchurch, tel 01425 273640; and Peace Burials, the South Yorkshire Woodland Burial Ground, tel 01704 821900.

The many funeral directors around the country who sell cardboard coffins will probably add considerably more mark-up than any of the above sources.

Funeral directors tend to be ferociously opposed to local authorities selling coffins, sometimes getting together to threaten a boycott of those crematoria and cemeteries who do so. In 1996, the Natural Death Centre reported two such cases to the Office of Fair Trading.

Coffins not of cardboard

As detailed below, coffins can be obtained from some funeral directors, direct from a couple of manufacturers, from carpenters or from coffin shops.

Coffins from funeral directors

If you want to buy a coffin that is *not* made of cardboard, your cheapest option may be to approach one of the recommended funeral directors in your local region, as listed in the Good Funeral Guide chapter. For instance, the six cheapest fully-fitted coffins (fitted with handles and lining) in these regional listings are:

• £50 in Huddersfield: from D. J. Screen & Sons (tel 01484 452220). Delivery locally free; nationally 50p per mile.

• £50 in Bristol: from Peter J. Connell (tel 01275 849239). Delivery locally £15; nationally 50p per mile.

• £55 in Cheltenham: from Beechwood Funeral Services (tel 01242 228208; also 01452 722131). Delivery locally £10; nationally negotiable.

• £55 in Uppingham: from E. M. Dorman (tel 01572 823976). Delivery locally 'at a negotiable price'.

• £60 in Salisbury: from Richard T. Adlem & Stephen Beckwith (tel 01725 552309). A foil coffin. Phone for delivery price.

• £65 in Manchester: from R. Pepperdine & Sons Ltd (tel 0161 881 5363). Delivery locally £15.

Peace Burials near Sheffield (tel 01704 821900) run two woodland burial grounds and help arrange funerals. They also sell coffins to the public, with variable delivery charges depending in part on whether they happen to be going in your direction. They sell cardboard coffins from £60; a biodegradable body bag with board from £20; a wicker coffin for £399 (incl. delivery; 'we decorate these with garlands of fresh flowers'); an unfitted chipboard coffin from £30 ('we have helped families to line them with a favourite blanket or sheet or piece of material and to decorate the outside with fabric'); or an oak veneer coffin for £160.

The Natural Death Centre circulated a questionnaire to 2,250 funeral directors in October 1996. Of the 61 (excluding branches of the same firm) who deigned to reply – mostly the small independent firms – all except one were prepared to sell just a coffin, without other services, at prices ranging from £50 to £290 for the cheapest fully fitted coffin – with a resultant average price of £122. This is a big improvement since the Centre's 1993 survey, which found a mere 53% of respondents willing to sell just coffins.

Coffins direct from manufacturers

The following are the cheapest coffins available from those coffin manufacturers who are prepared to deliver directly to a member of the public. Most funeral suppliers remain unwilling to sell directly to the public, often because they are frightened that their main customers, the funeral directors, will object. Indeed in 1993, the Natural Death Centre's survey showed that there was not a single mainstream coffin supplier in the country prepared to sell direct to the public. But now there are a brave few who will do so, although, surprisingly, their prices to the public tend to be higher than those charged by the funeral directors above. The firms with the cheapest coffins are listed first.

• £88-12 incl. VAT for a chipboard oak veneer coffin, fully fitted (with lining, handles and nameplate). Next day delivery £26 nationally. From E. C. Hodge (MF) Ltd, factory at New Drove, Off Weasenham Lane, Wisbech, Cambridgeshire PE13 2RZ (tel 01945 587477; fax 01945 466063); or Norton Road, Stevenage, Hertfordshire SG1 2BB (tel 01438 357341). They can also supply a solid pine coffin for £108-10 incl. VAT; a solid oak one for £188 incl. VAT; a book shelf for display which can become an oak veneer coffin for £330 incl. VAT; a solid oak casket for ashes from £9-40 incl. VAT. They also do pet caskets with name plates. 'We have over 100 coffins in stock for next day delivery, and solid timber coffins, and caskets for ashes made with a lock and key, and oak grave markers' (Ted Hodge).

• £90 incl. VAT for a small size 'Cask-Kit' 68" by 20" (£95 for medium size 72" by 22"; £100 for large size 76" by 24"). Delivery nationally: £25. From Eco-F Systems Ltd, Unit 3c, Penbeagle Industrial Estate, St Ives, Cornwall TR6 2JH (tel 01736 798893; fax 01736 798737). This is a flatpack coffin made from softwood residues; it has the traditional coffin shape and is assembled with some 38 steel screws – the screw holes remain very evident in the assembled coffin. '100% biodegradable and ecologically friendly, the coffins are finished, ready for you to personalise' (Delia Vosper).

• £120 for an 'oak foil' standard coffin, fitted and lined, for cremation. Delivery locally £20; nationally £50. From Vic Fearn & Co Ltd, Crabtree Mill, Hempshill Lane, Bulwell, Nottingham ND6 8PF (tel 01159 771571; fax 01159 771571). And at Newbarn Farm, Calbourne, Isle of Wight PO30 4JA (tel and fax 01983 531734). The firm also does a solid oak coffin with satin finish for £490; artist-painted coffins using water-based paints (which can be cremated) from £350 to £800. 'All our coffins are of superior quality. We do not make a cheap looking coffin. We sell all funeral items. We refuse no one. Everything we sell is environmentally friendly' (D. G. Crampton).

• £120 for a fully-fitted coffin suitable for cremation and £130 for a coffin for burial – wood veneer on chipboard coffin, with taffeta lining, plastic handles and nameplate. Apparently these prices will be £10 more if you do not say you came through the Natural Death Centre. Delivery locally free. Not delivered nationally. From Henry Smith (Wandsworth) Ltd, 192-194 Garratt Lane, Wandsworth, London SW18 4ED (tel 0181 874 7622/3). Their solid oak Wandle coffin with solid brass fittings costs £705. 'We are a small family firm and we pride ourselves on our ability to manufacture to any specification very quickly' (John C. Smith, director).

• £199 for an oak finish coffin (with lining, handles and nameplate). Delivery nationally £45. From Barry Albin & Sons Ltd, 52 Culling Road, Rotherhithe, London SE16 2TN (tel 0171 237 3637; fax 0171 252 3205). Their top price coffins include the Winchester solid bronze casket for £4,208. 'We are now 214 years old. We sell everything to the trade and to the public. Owned by the family, we accept no pressure [from funeral directors]' (B. Albin).

• From £580 to £900 (incl. delivery within 2 days) for a coffin made from recycled timber. From Earthsource Ltd, Hill Bailey, Wells House, 15-17 Elmsfield Road, Bromley, Kent (tel & fax 0171 771 2645).

Finally, here is a coffin supplier which insists on an intermediary between the firm and the public:

• £76 (incl. delivery) for an oak finish chipboard and (paper) foil coffin (with handles and lining) from David Broadley at Huddersfield Funeral Supplies (tel 01484 652288). He does not wish to deal with the public direct so credit card orders (by phone) or cheque orders (by mail) must come to the Natural Death Centre, 20 Heber Road, London NW2 6AA (tel 0181 208 2853). Please add on a minimum £5 donation to the Centre.

Coffins from carpenters

Another way of obtaining a coffin, but not normally as cheaply, is simply to ask a local carpenter or to pick one at random from your local Yellow Pages.

The following carpenters have been in touch with the Natural Death Centre, indicating a willingness to provide a coffin:

• £81-36 incl. VAT a flatpack plain chipboard coffin with pre-drilled holes, screws, screwdriver and diagram for assembly. From John Tuck and Mick McNicholas of Windmill Shopfitters Ltd, 1 and 1a Windmill Lane, Stratford, London E15 1PG (tel 0181 534 1901, fax 0181 534 7099). The coffin can be assembled for you, in which case the price is £107-95.

• No set price – from Stephen Briggs, 42 Vanbrugh Park, London SE3 7AA (tel 0181 293 3365), who needs a week's notice. Price is secondary to him, he remarks, his interest as a cabinet maker is in helping people get the à la carte coffin they want.

• About £150 for making you a coffin. Carpenter Paul Sherlock, Hammer House, Hammer Lane, Hindhead, Hants GU26 6DE (tel 01428 606501 or mobile 0468 586 290).

• From £150 for making a flatpack coffin. Simon Dorgan, who is connected with Paula at the Bristol Heaven on Earth shop, below (tel 0117 9421836 or 9240972).

Coffin shops

There are at present only a couple of shops in the UK which sell coffins and other funeral supplies to members of the public. All the inexpensive ones are in the South West or Wales, but they will deliver nationally. They are detailed below.

• £95 for a Strandboard coffin – a conventionally-shaped shouldered coffin, made of flakes of pine, spruce and larch, fitted with rope handles. Delivery locally free, nationally £50. From the Heaven on Earth shop, run by Paula Rainey Crofts and Simon Dorgan, Kingsley House, Cotham Road South, Bristol BS6 5TX (tel 0117 9421836 or 0117 9240972; fax 0117 9424972).

This is the most artistic of the funeral shops. They sell attractively stencilled cardboard coffins for £145; the Zimbabwean collapsible coffin from £95; a pure woollen shroud at £115; batik throws, to cover a coffin, from £118; body bags from £18; coffin linings from £35; rope handles at £6 each; conventional handles at £1-50 each; their pet coffins cost from £70; their urns for ashes from £15. Their Medium Density Fibreboard coffin, painted with water-based paints and decorated, costs £395. 'We also make Fantasy Coffins, such as a Red Arrows Jet Coffin which was recently ordered' (Paula Rainey Crofts).

• £98 for a standard oak veneer chipboard coffin, £27 extra for handles and lining. Delivery nationally at cost, about £25. From Green Undertakings, 44 Swain Street, Watchet, Somerset TA23 OAG (tel/fax 01984 632285). Their shop is open from 9.30am to 5pm daily, and from 10am to 2pm at weekends.

Barbara Butler and her colleagues at Green Undertakings won the 1993 Natural Death Handbook Award for the most helpful funeral supplier – they were at that stage the only funeral suppliers willing to sell to the public direct.

Since then, Green Undertakings have expanded mightily and now have a number of funeral directors as partners, mainly in the South West, and they act as agents for several woodland burial grounds.

They also have two other shops, both with the same opening hours as their Watchet one: at 3 Shuttern, Taunton, Somerset (tel 01823 353223); and at Belmont Funerals, Pillmawr Road (Malpas Road end), Newport NP6 6WF, Wales (tel 01633 855 350).

Apart from cardboard coffins, their other funeral supplies include: a (paper) foil mahogany effect coffin at £128; and a solid pine one at £225.

• £134 for the cheapest coffin supplied by the 'funerals supermarket', the Regale Funeral Store, based on the Roc 'Eclerc chain in France, which opened in 1996 at 227 Hoe Street, Walthamstow, London E17 (tel 0181 925 2010) run by Stephen and Sam Weller. Their prices are disappointingly high. They sell the Compakta cardboard coffin for £131, the Swiss cardboard coffin for £231 and urns from £17. Delivery at cost, and sometimes free locally. Their cheapest basic funeral is £609 (disbursements extra), and they will also supply just embalming, hearse or refrigeration.

Willow coffins and clay pots for ashes

In several cultures, 'the weeping willow is an emblem of grief and a symbol of eternity and immortality. Willows thrive on being pruned.' So runs the argument in favour of the willow coffin, called a 'woven willow chrysalis', which is now being made in Norfolk. It can be ordered either pea-pod-shaped or broad-bean-shaped (for a body to be buried in a foetal position). It is produced within a week to order, in sizes from giant to newborn baby, by Tony Carter (The Willow Weave Company, The Goat Shed, Rowancroft, Kenninghall Road, Banham, Norwich NR16 2HE, tel 01953 887107; fax 01953 887201) from about £350, including transport, for the larger size. About 18 have been made to date. They were designed by Gemma Nesbitt (of Sort, Powerstock, Bridport, Dorset DT6 3TQ, tel 01308 485 273; fax 01308 485 639), who was inspired by the baskets she saw used for carrying produce in a West Bengal street market. 'Basket coffins were made in the Middle Ages. Our chrysalis is more natural and informal-looking than a conventional coffin,' writes Nesbitt. 'The body can be wrapped in a coloured shroud and mourners can place their favourite flowers, such as buttercups and daisies or lilies and roses, into the chrysalis, instead of buying expensive wreaths.'

The chrysalis can be kept at home and used for storage. If tightly filled, it can serve as a bench. One bought years in advance 'should be kept completely dry in a large plastic bag' to prevent woodworm. Willow is of varied tints, ranging from white and buff, to green, red and brown, depending on the length of time it is left to steam before being woven.

Collapsible coffins

A collapsible coffin, made in Zimbabwe, and available in the UK from the Heaven on Earth shop in Bristol (address above), is called the Box. It does not have wooden sides or a wooden top, just a wooden base which folds down into thirds and a shroud which is attached to the base. The resulting folded bag can be slung over the shoulder and carried home on a bus.

It is the custom for the urban breadwinner in Zimbabwe to provide a coffin when a relative dies. Private transport is hired for the occasion, since buses will not allow coffins. But with the onslaught of AIDS and thus a high frequency of deaths, the urban dweller's obligations have become prohibitively expensive. The collapsible Box can be carried on a bus, and, besides having potential for a number of developing countries, could perhaps be of slight service in the UK, since many rail companies have rules against allowing ordinary coffins. People who feel very green and who disdain the use of cars, could then use the train to deliver such a coffin from an urban shop to rural relatives, for their use at the funeral.

The coffin is promoted in the UK by Steve Andrews, 71b Shakespeare Road, London SE24 OLA (tel 0171 326 0274; a contact number in Harare, Zimbabwe, is 00 2634 335 395).

Coffins as bookcase

Coffins as bookcases are sold by the Heaven on Earth Shop in Bristol (address above). During your lifetime you can use their coffin 'Embodiment Chest', made to measure by their carpenter (and costing from £295, unpainted), as a bookcase, coffee table or wine rack, as a window seat or for storage. After death, it can be used to store you.

Papier mâché coffin

Andy Moore of Friends of the Earth and the Community Recycling Network (10-12 Picton Street, Montpelier, Bristol BS6 5QA, tel 0117 9420142), exhibited a psychedelic multicoloured papier mâché coffin at the English Day of the Dead exhibition in 1993. This was a one-off – the Natural Death Centre would be interested to hear of any plan to make such coffins commercially available.

Coffins made of flax or cork

A company in Germany is producing biodegradable coffins and urns. The coffins are made entirely of flax, shaped rather like an insect cocoon. The urns are made of cork, and they have a sea urn which dissolves in water. For the garden, they have urns made of chicken excrement.

Helmut Hilger, Dürener Sargfabrik, Industriestr. 18-20, 52459 Inden Pier, Germany (tel 00 49 2428 80712; fax 00 49 2428 80722).

Reusable coffins

In the United States and in Canada, it is possible to rent a decorous outer coffin for the funeral service, with only the cardboard inner coffin cremated (normally a thin piece of pine or plywood is placed under the deceased to keep the cardboard rigid). For instance, Joanna Moorhead in an interview in the Observer (April 14th 1992) spoke with funeral director Kem Timlick who offers Western

Rent-A-Casket Ltd, a 'cheap, no frills' service in Vancouver. His funerals cost about a tenth of the average. 'If you want to spend a lot of money remembering someone who's died,' he says, 'donate money to crippled children or heart-disease research.'

Alexandre Haas, the manufacturer of the Swiss Peace Box cardboard coffin (see above) has a 'patented ground mechanical opening system for a luxury over-coffin' (perhaps a variant of the idea in the previous chapter) and M. G. von Bratt has written to the Natural Death Centre from New Zealand saying that he has patents for the UK, USA and other countries on a disposable cardboard coffin with a reusable outer core:

Cardboard coffin with reusable outer core

The reusable outer represents a standard coffin and is easily removed from the disposable inner at the crematorium or graveside, with no dignity lost. The outer need not be used as the inner is very presentable. If the funeral director had a reusable outer, at say an initial cost of $1,000, and he charged $100 per burial or cremation, his outlay would be recovered after ten funerals. He could charge between a further $100 and $150 for the disposable inner coffin.

The cardboard coffin costs $30 to produce in New Zealand in numbers of 25, plus $20 for the 16mm lightweight wooden base board. If these items were produced in quantity, the prices would be considerably reduced – almost halved.

Cardboard coffins would be ideal for sea burials as there would be instant water absorption and no buoyancy.

M. G. von Bratt, 24 Claremont Terrace, Otumoetai,
Tauranga, New Zealand.

In the UK, Heaven on Earth (for contact details see above) have designed a £500 Eternity Chest that families can reuse for future funerals – this will hold a cardboard coffin for burial or cremation.

Barry Albin & Sons Ltd (52 Culling Road, Rotherhithe, London SE16 2TN, tel 0171 237 3637; fax 0171 252 3205) have a rental scheme whereby you pay £395 for a 'grave liner' and then a rental fee to use a 'superior' coffin that can, for instance, stay overnight in church – the rental fee ranges from £75 for their Victorian Oak coffin to £350 for the American wood casket.

Painted coffins

Yvonne Malik (Sweet Briar, Wray, Near Lancaster LA2 3QN, tel 01542 21767), a designer and a consultant to the Natural Death Centre, has done beautiful decorations on coffins, for instance a coffin covered with butterflies for a child. She would be prepared to take on further commissions, but she would need to be sent the coffin to work on.

Lisette de Roche (164 Westbourne Grove, London W11 2RW, tel 0171 221 8742; mobile 0370 463 1532) who decorates coffins for Vic Fearn coffin manufacturers (who are mentioned above), will also accept independent commissions from members of the public. She can paint a coffin within four days. You can, if you wish, provide her with a cardboard or regular coffin to paint. Alternatively, her prices (including a coffin) start from £250 for a children's coffin, or from £450 for an adult's coffin. Personal commissions are from £650.

Transport

If you are arranging a funeral yourselves but just need help with transport, your local funeral director may well be as cheap as a local hire firm. Those who replied to our questionnaire were no doubt the more enlightened members of the profession; but 95% of these would supply just transport for the body or coffin, without other services, at prices ranging from £30 to £165 locally; and one offered a mileage charge of £1 per mile. All the firms and their prices are detailed in the Good Funeral Guide chapter. Funeral directors also have estate cars – which many people prefer and which are less expensive to hire than hearses.

Renting a hearse and bearers

Alternatively, you could try a car hire firm that rents out chauffeur-driven hearses, cars and limousines, such as Greens Car Hire (tel 0181 692 9200) who charge £85 for a Daimler hearse; or Cardinal Funeral Carriages (G. A. Leonard, tel 0181 520 5340) who charge £55 for a hearse plus driver/bearer for two and a half hours within 25 miles; or O'Brien Car Hire (tel 0181 311 9591) who charge £60 for a Daimler hearse for two hours and £15 per hour thereafter. Their 'full uniform' chauffeurs can also act as bearers for £10, and extra bearers are available at £20 each. A Daimler limousine is available for £54 for two hours. You could find out the phone numbers of other such firms from the main journal in which they tend to advertise, the Funeral Service Journal (tel 0113 284 1177).

Wheel biers

Those readers who are so green that they cannot accept the idea of motor vehicles of any kind being used to transport the body, could try asking a local church or cemetery if they can lend or rent, with a suitable deposit, a wheel bier. For instance, Maldon Cemetery (see East Anglia region below) and Manchester Cemetery (see North West region below) do have such wheel biers – Manchester Cemetery hire theirs out for use within the grounds for £2-50.

Horse-drawn funeral

More feasible, more expensive and more dashing is to arrange for a horse-drawn hearse (which can be hired by the family direct, the use of a funeral director is not obligatory). A number of firms offer such vehicles, complete with black horses: James Gibson (from £400 in London area; they have branches in London, Huntingdon, Nottingham, Bolton and Blackburn; tel 01204 655869 or 01487 830045); Central Ceremonial Carriages (from £200 plus 50p a mile, based in Bonnybridge, Scotland, tel 01324 812435); Foxdell Carriages (from £450 locally to £650 for the London area; based near Bromsgrove, Worcestershire, tel 01527 873865); Mews Carriages (from £550 for the London area, based in

Hitchin, Herts, tel 01438 871622); Peter Taylor (from £500, a funeral director with various branches in East Anglia, tel 01603 760787); Chalfont Carriage Company (from £475, based in Chalfont St Giles, Buckinghamshire, tel 01494 872 304); and T. Cribb & Sons (from £675, a funeral director based in London E16, tel 0171 476 1855).

Trains and canal boats

Peace Burials (tel 01704 821900) can help you to arrange burial in a woodland burial ground at Alfreton in Derbyshire, with arrival there by steam train from the Midland Railway Centre at Ripley in Derbyshire.

The Calder and Hebble Navigation Society took one of their departed members, who lived in Calderdale, on the canal boat 'The Savile' to the crematorium, and are rumoured to be planning to make this a public service, with room on board for a dozen mourners and the coffin. Their phone number is ex-directory, however.

The woodland burial ground in Retford, Nottinghamshire (Cyril Blackshaw, Bassetlaw District Council, tel 01777 713487) has boats passing it along the Chesterfield canal. Mr Blackshaw thinks that it could probably be arranged for a coffin to be delivered by boat.

Cold storage

78% of our progressive respondents were prepared to supply cold storage facilities to families who were not using the funeral director for the funeral. This could be reassuring for those, for instance, who have to wait for relatives arriving from abroad for the funeral. Some of the other funeral directors did not have cold storage facilities, using embalming instead. The price asked for cold storage ranged from £5 per day (in four instances) to £50 per day, with an average price of just over £15 per day. T. Cribb and Sons (tel 0171 476 1855) in London E16 are willing to provide this service without charge. All the firms and their prices are detailed in the Good Funeral Guide chapter.

Embalming

Embalming, which is normally quite unnecessary, involves draining blood from the body, and replacing it with formaldehyde (plus a pinkish dye such as safranine) pumped in under pressure, which has a hardening and disinfecting effect. 'The cheeks become fuller and firmer, and the eyeballs and surrounding skin become harder,' writes Robert Wilkins in 'The Fireside Book of Death'. He describes how the mouth is prevented from hanging open, sometimes by a needle passed from the lower lip up through the nostril, and how the abdomen is suctioned clean. Unlike Egyptian embalmers, modern embalming aims only for a short-term preserving effect. The funeral trade argues that embalming helps prevent the body smelling and removes some of the trauma from the face. As one of our contacts put it: 'I would certainly look better after death pumped full of pink dye, with the lines on my face smoothed away.' Embalming will probably not appeal to those who dislike make-up for the living face; or to those who want the body to be handled only by close family; or to those who want to allow the body to look very evidently dead. But it is, of course, a certain way of ensuring that the deceased is not buried or burnt alive, if you should have this particular fear.

'Do you embalm the deceased as a matter of course or on request?' we asked the funeral directors in our questionnaire. Several firms replied 'Yes, we do embalm as a matter of course', some adding the proviso 'unless asked not to' – so it is important to make your wishes clear in this regard. The majority claimed only to embalm on request, but often again with provisos such as: 'unless the body is to be exported or conveyed long distance' or 'unless the family wishes to view the body'. One firm wrote: 'We embalm when we consider it necessary for hygienic reasons and for viewing purposes. If there is a risk of infection, we will insist on it for our own staff's sake.' At which point, the client may need to insist on a change of funeral directors. Indeed, embalming is not allowed for sea burial or for burial in some of the nature reserve burial grounds.

Using a funeral director

What can people hope for in a good funeral director? Libby Purves in Country Living magazine described Tony Brown of Saxmundham, Suffolk 'whose cheerful sensitivity makes bereavement more bearable' (see the East Anglia region of the Good Funeral Chapter for his details):

A very independent funeral director

If you arrange a funeral in a town or an urbanised country area, you may of course find a humane and sensitive undertaker, but it is more likely that you will end up on a slick, calculatedly inoffensive and utterly bland production line. You will be edged subtly towards the more expensive coffins and trimmings and given assurances about 'hygienic treatment' – ie surface embalming – and the 'tastefully appointed chapel of rest' – all plastic flowers and melamine.

So in celebration of the few independent, cussed, beloved and legendary funeral directors left, it seemed worth listening to the story of Tony Brown of Saxmundham. Burial of the Dead, after all, is listed as the last of the Seven Acts of Mercy in Christian belief, on a par with feeding the hungry and comforting distress. What men like him do, because of the way they do it, is as useful as any social work, but largely unacknowledged.

He was an ambulance driver who started 'moonlighting for a funeral director, digging graves at six in the morning before a shift'. He took over an undertaker's business in 1979. 'I did farmwork to keep going. I'd be ploughing and my wife would come and wave from the hedge and leave me her bike and I'd jump on it and go quick.'

But some refinements of the trade he rejected from the start. 'I don't embalm, not unless a body's going abroad. I don't touch the body any more than I need to. I don't do all that arranging of their hair and face-painting and that, and I don't sell people fancy shrouds because I do not class myself as a salesman.

'I do like singing. I sing good and loud. I've done "The Old Rugged Cross" three times this week.'

A funeral director who accepts, even revels in, the individuality of each corpse goes a long way to easing the misery. 'There was an old Romany horseman, the other week. We dressed him up in his black suit and neckerchief, like he always wore, and put his cap on him. And it was just him, old Tinker. You know, I felt like putting a fag in his mouth!

'Everyone ought to go the way they want. That's why I hate these prepaid funerals and I hate taking money in advance. I'd rather people had insurance in the old way, then it can all be done as a family want. People are always having ideas and saying to me, "Tony, is that silly?" and I always say No. One woman wanted to go in her own Volvo Estate. We got her in. Why not? When I go, I'm going on a horse and cart.'

He is a Methodist, and is shocked by the fact that when people die without any relatives or friends to bury them, the social services merely stipulate that the body be disposed of correctly. 'There's nothing in law saying that anyone's got to say one single word. So I say the prayers. I've taken a whole cremation service. I'm not a preacher, and of course I don't charge anything for it. But you can't just put someone in a hole and walk away.'

Adapted extracts from an article by Libby Purves in Country Living,
reprinted in Funeral Service Journal.

It is hard to find an independent funeral director nowadays – many of the big firms hide behind the name of the small firm they have taken over, and often it takes some persistence to find this out. Many independent firms are members of SAIF, the Society of Allied and Independent Funeral Directors, so look out for their emblem. With other firms, ask outright if the firm's parent company is Service Corporation International (SCI), the American funeral company which has now captured more than 15% of the UK market, and is beginning to buy up UK crematoria. They are best avoided. A BBC TV documentary claimed that this company's internal documents promoted aggressive selling of their most expensive coffins (for instance, they advised their sales force: 'Do not judge the ability of a family to afford a particular coffin by their appearance').

But a bigger problem in choosing a funeral director is that, in the first shock of a relative dying, 97% of people, according to an Office of Fair Trading investigation, sign up with the very first funeral director they contact. Arranging a funeral is not like buying any other consumer service, and people need to be aware that this could lay them open to exploitation, even if most funeral directors are in fact well-meaning and dedicated people. Do not accept, for instance, a funeral director who just happens to be at the hospital, who may have a private 'arrangement' with staff. Ask the staff for a full list of local firms if they have one. Our advice is that you get a friend who is not so emotionally involved to phone around for you and to report back to you when a funeral director has been located who meets your criteria. Do not be wary of looking outside your area – any extra mileage charge is likely to be a small element of the final bill.

It is perhaps worth re-emphasising at this point that, although The Natural

Death Centre is campaigning for improvements in the funeral trade, and advocates that families organise funerals themselves wherever possible, it acknowledges that funerals in the UK are as cheap or cheaper than most countries in Europe; they are cheap compared with what the average family is prepared to spend on a wedding; and they are carried out in the main by sensitive professionals doing a difficult and stressful job which most people would not have the courage to do.

All members of funeral associations are supposed to offer a basic funeral, but this needs asking for by name. In response to our questionnaire, several neglected or refused to fill in the questions about prices, but for those who were willing to state them publicly, a basic funeral costs from £287 to £865, with an average of £530 – an increase of 16.5% since 1993. To this figure need to be added the so-called 'disbursements' paid out for the client by the funeral director: the cremation fee, doctors' fees (£69) and minister's fee (normally £59), an average extra total of £297. (Burial in a Church of England churchyard costs £107.)

The best value basic funeral for those in the London area, for instance, seems to be that offered by the family firm of H. C. Grimstead Ltd (see Greater London region and East Midlands region in the Good Funeral Guide chapter). Their so-called 'Green Funeral Option' needs asking for by name, costs £395 (disbursements extra), and includes a cardboard coffin, normally taken either directly to the crematorium or the cemetery rather than to the church. Even with their £1-15 per mile charge for going outside a 20-mile radius, this firm would probably work out cheaper than most others for the whole of London and the East Midlands.

For those wanting no involvement in the funeral at all, not even to know which crematorium was used, Rowland Brothers (see Greater London region in the Good Funeral Guide chapter) offer what they call a 'disposal service' for £356 (disbursements extra). F. A. Albin & Sons, in London, offer a 'disposal funeral package'; for £519 (incl. disbursements); and J. E. Gillman & Sons Ltd, also in London, offer a similar funeral, more tactfully entitled 'Direct Transfer Service', for £290 (disbursements extra).

If you are genuinely hard-up, many funeral directors are kind hearted enough to make allowances and will not turn you away. One of our contacts offered a funeral director £400 cash on the spot (the most he could afford) for a £795 funeral and was accepted. The highly commendable and distinctive Islamic funeral service offered by Haji Taslim (see London region in the Good Funeral Guide), based at the East London Mosque – 95% of their clients are from the Muslim community – offers free burial to the indigent, besides being prepared to give cheap or free help of various kinds to those planning their own funeral.

If you need to complain about a funeral director, you can report the matter to their trade association, if they have one – normally either the National Association of Funeral Directors, the Funeral Standards Council or the Society of Allied and Independent Funeral Directors (see the Resources chapter for their addresses). In practice, you may get more satisfaction by going to your local county court (under 'C' in the phone book) or even to the local media. Or it may be a matter that could be reported to the Trading Standards Officer at your local council. The Natural Death Centre would be interested in receiving any brief written accounts that could help warn others – and in receiving positive feedback about funeral professionals whom you have found to be unusually helpful.

Less expensive funerals for council residents

It may be worthwhile phoning your local council's cemeteries department (eg for Brent, this would mean looking under 'B' for Brent and then under 'Cemeteries' within the list of Brent's services) and asking if the council has made a special agreement to provide cheaper basic funerals for residents (note that the requirement is normally that the deceased should have lived in the borough, not the person organising the funeral, but check this). Often, however, the prices are not that good. In London, the Co-op Funeral Service has for several years provided a not-so-cheap basic funeral for certain boroughs: the CWS Co-op does one for residents of **Southwark** (tel 0171 732 4165), **Lewisham** (tel 0171 698 3244) and **Lambeth** (tel 0171 703 2803); the CRS Co-op provides for residents of **Hounslow** (tel 0181 570 4741) – or try the local councils for details of these too. The cost excluding disbursements for the CWS ones is £625 in Lewisham; £820 in Lambeth; and £810 in Southwark – yet in Southwark their basic funeral for residents or non-residents is cheaper than this at £675, although including only a hearse and not the following limousine. For the Hounslow CRS funeral, the cost is £895; the Hounslow Council also has a similar arrangement for this 'Hounslow Community Funeral Service' with other local funeral directors: W. S. Bond (tel 0181 994 0277), Holmes & Daughters (tel 0181 893 1860), Andrew Holmes & Son (tel 0181 572 3277), Frederick Paine (tel 0181 994 0056), A. Spicer (tel 0181 574 3186) and Christopher Wickenden (tel 0181 569 8373). In **Stockport**, the 'Civic Funeral Service' is provided for the council by the United North West Co-operative Society (tel 0161 432 0818). They charge £690 for a cremation (including disbursements); and £1,048 for burial in a new grave (again including disbursements). In **Cardiff**, the local authority funeral service provider is D. Caesar Jones (tel 01222 522 644), who charges £485 (disbursements extra). In **Wigan**, the borough council uses the services of a local funeral director, Richard Evans (tel 01942 821 215) to offer cremation for £650 (including disbursements) and burial for £806 (including disbursements and the opening of a new grave), which is about the same price as their ordinary basic funeral. An inexpensive service is offered by the **St Helens** council (tel 01744 456000 and ask for reception) which has an agreement with the Co-op whereby cremation costs £604 and burial costs £623, both prices including disbursements. **Bury** Metropolitan Borough Council has an arrangement with Hardman's Funeral Service (tel 0161 764 4072) offering a funeral for £350 (disbursements extra – burial, for instance, costs an extra £435).

Memorial Societies

There is scope for religious and neighbourhood groups of one sort or another in the UK to help each other with funeral arrangements, just as within some Jewish communities it is considered an honour to be of service to the deceased in this way. Neighbours could help each other with advice, with transport, by providing bearers, by helping with the making of coffins or even by buying a plot of land for a wildlife cemetery (besides of course helping before death with caring for the dying at home, and after the funeral with reintegrating the bereaved into the life of the neighbourhood).

In the United States, communities in many local areas over the last fifty years have formed their own Memorial Societies (some 150 to date) which use the power of their membership numbers to make agreements with particular funeral directors for cheaper than normal services (society members tend to pay less than a fifth the average cost of an American funeral). A lifetime fee of some $25 is charged, many of the staff are volunteers, and some of the societies offer workshops and meetings and informative leaflets and advice. People who join fill in a prearrangement form which indicates their detailed funeral preferences. Anyone contemplating forming a similar society in the UK – a project which The Natural Death Centre would be happy to help publicise – will find useful the American $10 handbook for Funeral and Memorial Societies, which is available from the Continental Association, 6900 Lost Lake Road, Egg Harbor, WI 54209-9231, USA (tel 001 414 868 3136).

Free funerals

10 per cent of all deaths in 1995 resulted in claims to the government's Social Fund for help with funeral expenses. From April 7th 1997, new restrictions, denounced as 'mean' in the media, will probably be in force: up to £600 will be available from the government (it used to be £500) for claims made before or within three months of the funeral. Phone your local Benefits Agency office (under 'Benefits Agency' or 'Social Security' in the phone book) and ask for form SF200. Details and leaflets (but not the claim form) can be obtained from the Benefits Agency Public Enquiry Office (tel 0171 712 2171).

The person organising the funeral must be on Income Support, income-based Jobseeker's Allowance, Family Credit, Housing Benefit, Council Tax Benefit or Disability Working Allowance, although that person's money over £500 (£1,000 if sixty or over) will be used towards the costs, and any money in the estate of the deceased will go towards the costs. The cheque is usually made out to the funeral directors, not the claimant, but is sent to the claimant to give to them.

From April 1997, there will be a greater attempt made to find a relative who could afford to pay for the funeral. As the government puts it: 'Where there is no surviving partner, and where a parent, son or daughter of the deceased exists, and neither they nor their partner are in receipt of a qualifying benefit, it will be considered unreasonable for the person in receipt of the income-related benefit to take responsibility for the funeral expenses.'

The Benefits Agency (see leaflet FB29, 'A Guide to Benefits When Someone Dies') also gives out a Widow's Payment of £1,000 if the husband paid enough National Insurance contributions and was not getting retirement pension, and if the widow is under sixty.

The local authority is obliged (under the Public Health – Control of Disease

– Act 1984 Part III Disposal of Dead Bodies Section 46) to arrange for the disposal of the body where 'no suitable arrangements have been made'. A. C. T. Connolly (of 26 Broadfields Avenue, Winchmore Hill, London N21 1AD) decided to test this Act by refusing to arrange for the disposal of a relative's body (which was in the mortuary at the local hospital). He resisted 'wrongful' pressure from the registrar of deaths to take various forms before he would register the death. Finally a helpful official in the council's Social Services department agreed to arrange the funeral and to register the death in the name of the council, with the Connolly family reimbursing the council for the £315 cost. The family were notified in advance of the time for the service and the committal at the crematorium. Mr Connolly concludes: 'It is a legally imposed duty on local authorities to carry out this public health function *no matter what the financial position of the bereaved might be*. Yet very few people indeed know of this local authority option.'

Organ and body donation

Ernest Morgan quotes a poetic statement by Robert Test in favour of organ donation:

Give my sight to the man who has never seen a sunrise

The day will come when my body will lie upon a white sheet tucked neatly under the four corners of a mattress located in a hospital busily occupied with the living and the dying. At a certain moment a doctor will determine that my brain has ceased to function and that, to all intents and purposes, my life has stopped.

When that happens, do not attempt to install artificial life into my body by the use of a machine and don't call this my deathbed. Let it be called the Bed of Life, and let my body be taken from it to help others lead fuller lives.

Give my sight to the man who has never seen a sunrise, a baby's face or love in the eyes of a woman. Give my heart to the person whose own heart has caused nothing but endless days of pain. Give my blood to the teenager who was pulled from the wreckage of his car, so that he may live to see his grandchildren play. Give my kidneys to a person who depends upon a machine to exist from week to week. Take my bones, every muscle, every fibre and nerve in my body and find a way to make a crippled child walk. Explore every corner of my brain. Take my cells, if necessary, and let them grow so that, someday, a speechless boy will shout at the crack of a bat or a deaf girl will hear the sound of rain against her window.

Burn what is left of me and scatter the ashes to the winds to help the flowers grow.

If you must bury something, let it be my faults, my weaknesses and all my prejudice against my fellow man. Give my sins to the devil. Give my soul to God.

If, by chance, you wish to remember me, do it with a kind deed or word to someone who needs you. If you do all I have asked, I will live forever.

'Dealing Creatively with Death' by Ernest Morgan.

If you feel the same way as Ernest Morgan and Robert Test, you need to persuade your next of kin (who will have charge of your body after death), to tell your doctor and your hospital ward and to get a donor card from your local health centre, doctor or chemist. Or contact the NHS Organ Donor Register, PO Box 14, Patchway, Bristol BS12 6BR (tel 01179 757575) and ask to be sent a form and a donor card. You can choose to donate any part of the body or only the kidneys, heart, liver, corneas, lungs or pancreas. Animal Aid (The Old Chapel, Bradford Street, Tonbridge, Kent TN9 1AW, tel 01732 364 546) issues a Humane Research Donor Card which requests that the body be used for medical and scientific research. Organ donor cards are also available from the Royal National Institute for the Blind, Central Office, 224 Great Portland Street, London W1N 6AA (tel 0171 388 1266); and from the British Heart Foundation, Distribution Dept, 14 Fitzhardinge St, London W1H 4DH (tel 0171 935 0185).

The cornea of the eyes is the only part of the body that can wait up to 12 hours for removal; the rest have to be removed immediately after 'brain-stem' death, with machines keeping the body's blood circulating after death. Normally the body is made available for the funeral within less than 12 hours, once the relatives have agreed. Relatives are still asked for their approval, even if a name is on the register.

It is not possible to guarantee a free disposal of your body by leaving it for dissection by medical students. Only a percentage of bodies are accepted. Medical schools generally accept only bodies that are unautopsied after death, non-cancerous, relatively whole and within easy range of the school. To offer to donate your body, contact the professor of anatomy at your local medical hospital or HM Inspector of Anatomy, Department of Health, Wellington House, 133-155 Waterloo Road, London SE1 8UG (tel 0171 972 4342); or for those in the London area, contact the London Anatomy Office (all hours, tel 0181 846 1216).

Incidentally, whoever is lawfully in possession of the body can donate it to a medical school, even if the person who died made no provision for this, as long as he or she did not object – either in writing or verbally in the presence of two witnesses; and as long as no relative or spouse objects.

Transplants can be authorised as long as there is no reason to believe that the next of kin would object.

Prepaid funerals

It has been estimated that the prepaid funeral market could become as big a business in the UK as in the United States, where about three quarters of all funerals are paid for before death. The advantages claimed include: people planning in advance tend to choose simple funerals; it allows for leisurely comparison shopping; in some of the plans you are protected against inflationary price rises; relatives do not suddenly face a big bill at a time of stress; it provides peace of mind for those who are elderly and without relatives; and it would reduce your capital and thus perhaps entitle you to social security benefits you might not otherwise have received.

In our view, the advantages of some of the schemes could be outweighed by the potential disadvantages: prepaid funerals militate against family participation – what if your family decide that they want to make your coffin or to look after your funeral arrangements? Many of the schemes tend to favour the big chains with their assembly-line funerals and to drive the smaller firms to the wall. They encourage TV advertising and other heavy marketing ploys. One firm in the UK went bankrupt. And there has been at least one horror story in the United States where the money was simply pocketed, and the prepaid cremation bodies were stacked in the basement of the mortuary, with others buried in mass graves.

A first step is to consider questions such as: what happens if you do not need a funeral in the UK after all, for instance if you die abroad or if your ship sinks at sea? What happens if you die before completing payments? What happens if you need that capital sum in an emergency? Would you not have done better to put the money into a form of investment that you could recover? What happens if the trust or foundation backing your prepaid scheme goes bust or proves fraudulent? What if whoever attends your dying is not aware of your prepaid arrangement? If you want such an arrangement, would it not be more interesting to discuss your funeral wishes with your most trusted next of kin or partner and to pay money into an account or investment controlled jointly with them? Or, probably a less financially attractive option, to put regular premiums into a funeral insurance scheme (or to top up your life insurance) which would pay a lump sum to your relatives on your death, leaving your relatives with more freedom of action? **Sun Life** (tel 0800 27 21 27), for instance, offers a funeral insurance scheme whereby a 70 year old male, whatever his state of health, pays £18 a month for life, and, if death occurs during the first two years, the premiums plus 50 per cent are paid back; thereafter it pays out £1,780 on death. **Scottish Friendly** (tel 0141 275 5000) offer a whole life insurance whereby, for instance, a 70 year old male, having satisfactorily answered medical questions, would pay a premium of £13 monthly for 10 years, thereafter having cover lasting until his death. When death occurs, £1,000 with further variable extra bonuses, probably amounting to between £200 and £500, would be paid out. **Tunbridge Wells Equitable** (tel 01892 515353) offer a similar scheme called the Dignity Bond.

Nevertheless, if your circumstances are such that one of the more high profile prepaid plans seems desirable, try to find a scheme which, as well as satisfactorily answering the above questions, is mainly for small independent firms; places at least 90% of the prepaid funds in trust; will not add extras when the time comes; allows a wide range of choice if you move to another part of the country; allows for no-questions-asked cancellation with refund of money *and* interest (less any small administration fees); and returns any unspent money and interest after the funeral. You will not be able to find such a scheme as yet in the UK (although the last two points are required by law in some American states).

The **greenest best buy** for those needing to arrange the funeral in advance might be to set aside sufficient funds in a joint savings account to cover the full costs of one of the less expensive Woodland Burial grounds (described in detail in the Good Funeral Guide chapter below) which have established arrangements for providing a coffin and for collecting the body. These include: Hinton Park in Dorset (tel 01255 503456), Green Undertakings in Somerset (tel 01984 632285), Greenhaven near Rugby (tel 01788 860604) and Oakfield in Essex (tel 01255 880182). But be very cautious about handing over money in advance. It is one thing to buy burial rights, and quite another to hand over money years in advance for digging graves and body collection. It might also be worth approaching the charitable A. B. Wildlife Trust Fund in North Yorkshire (tel 01423 530900) to see if a special prearrangement can be made for one of their sites. Hinton Park, for instance, charge £650 in advance for a coffin and a plot, including the digging and filling of the grave, the planting of a tree, the provision of a small memorial plaque and the collection of the body (in a green Renault Espace). Extra is charged if the body is collected from beyond a 50 mile radius (collection from London costs about £100 extra). Thus for a London family looking for a site within range of the city, the three feasible sites are Hinton Park, Greenhaven or Oakfield, and the total funeral charges, including collecting the body from London, would be £750 for Hinton Park; £750 for Oakfield; and £399 for Greenhaven (£429 if a driver's assistant is also needed). You will not be able to match such prices in any of the plans described below.

Possibly least objectionable of the mass market plans is **Golden Charter** (tel 0800 833800), since it is specifically designed for the small, independent funeral directors and their association SAIF, the Society of Allied and Independent Funeral Directors (some of whom are also members of the larger National Association of Funeral Directors). Golden Charter's cheapest Standard Way plan costs £965, which allows £365 towards the costs of disbursements. If disbursements cost more than this at the time of the plan's purchase, the extra sum can be paid then to ensure full future cover. The Woodland Trust is paid to plant a tree for each plan bought.

Over 120 local funeral directors offer their own prepayment plans, backed by **Funeral Planning Trust** (for referrals to a local firm, phone 01508 532 632).

The next best is probably the **Perfect Assurance Funeral Trust** run by the National Association of Funeral Directors (NAFD) (for details of your local participants, tel 0121 709 0019), which allows you to choose any firm, small or large, that offers the scheme and to tailor-make a plan to your requirements. The firm then pays the money into the presumed safety of the Perfect Assurance trust fund.

The market leader and the first to advertise on TV has been **Chosen Heritage** (tel 0800 525555), whose cheapest Basic Plan funeral costs £970 (disbursements included, as long as they do not rise by more than 1% above the rate of inflation). If the person dies abroad or ends up not needing their funeral, relatives are refunded. All the plan money, less a £65 administration fee, goes into a trust fund. Chosen Heritage allows cancellations at any time, minus interest and the £65 fee. It has a 'personal choice' option for those wanting a nonstandard package. The snag is that a large number of its 960 funeral directors are part of the giant American SCI company, and such huge chains are to be discouraged.

The Co-op's CRS division (tel 0500 112121) offers a **Co-operative Funeral Bond** Funeral Plan, the price of which will be determined by a quote from your local Co-op funeral director. I asked for the cheapest basic funeral in the Hammersmith area of London (Peter Askew, tel 0181 748 2982) and was quoted £640, disbursements £309 extra. Once the full cost, including disbursements, is paid, and the plan taken out, there will be no more to pay at the time of the funeral. Cancellation is 'at the discretion of the society and any repayment is subject to an administration fee'.

The Co-op's CWS division (tel 0800 289120) has a **Co-operative Funeral Bond** too. Its Earl cremation plan costs £839 (including disbursements). One unusual feature of this plan is that it allows two people to be named on the form and the plan can eventually pay for either of them.

The scheme **Dignity in Destiny** (tel 0800 269318) is almost completely tied to the big chain SCI, using independent funeral directors only in those places where it has no coverage itself. It was unable to tell me its cheapest plan since prices depend on requirements. When their 'planning consultant' salesman phoned me back and I asked how much I would be charged for their rock bottom cheapest possible funeral, I was told £895, with all disbursements extra. When I protested that they must have something cheaper than this, I was told £695, with no limousine and all disbursements extra.

Crematoria

In our view, most crematoria are to be shunned. Who wants rushed funeral services in buildings which have been described as looking like newspaper reading rooms in public libraries or waiting rooms in airports? Several people of late have suggested a different approach. Rather than, say, a service in church followed by just some of the family going on to a committal at the crematorium, with consequent confusion and disruption for any party or gathering afterwards, both the service and something similar to a committal can be held in the church (or other preferred location), with the coffin borne out towards the end of the service. Then just one member of the family goes with the coffin to the crematorium (or just the vicar goes if a committal service at the crematorium is wanted). Crematoria will prefer this too, suggests funeral director Philip Tomlins in the Funeral Director journal (Nov. 1991), as they then do not have the difficulty of finding a time that fits with the church service.

Perhaps the ideal crematorium would be a building that was designed to allow the mourners to gather round a high tech version of a funeral pyre. Tony Walter in 'Funerals and How to Improve Them' has suggested a number of slightly less radical design improvements: a coffin visible and central, near floor level throughout the service, which can be touched, kissed, circled round or filed past; a building in which the coffin can be moved by the mourners, possibly by being lowered under the floor; and a building as beautiful and significant as a church, so that the local community will want it for births and marriages too, and which is close to the elements – surrounded by forest and wildlife, rather than manicured lawns and regimented rows of rosebushes.

Of the 90 respondents to our survey of crematoria nationwide, only Great Grimsby crematorium refused to allow a small group of mourners (by arrangement) to witness the coffin entering the cremator. 9% had flexible seating, which might help those wanting a more participatory 'half-moon' seating arrangement, rather than the 'audience facing the front' style – although changing the seating would no doubt mean paying for extra time.

One off-putting aspect of crematoria is the sense of being led along a factory conveyor belt: In – 30 minutes – Out – Next. Four crematoria, as highlighted in the Good Funeral Guide chapter, allowed 45 minute services: Brighton crematorium (see South region); Weeley crematorium (see East Anglia region); Mintlyn crematorium in King's Lynn (see East Anglia region); and Aberystwyth crematorium (see Wales). Of these four, the most helpful is Brighton, which allows still further time, if available, to be booked without charge.

Contrary to myth, crematoria do burn all the coffins (which is a pity, we feel that they should be reused), and the ashes you get back will definitely be the right ones.

Most crematoria are run by local authorities and have very reasonable fees, although these fees are having to be increased in many places to finance the cost of new facilities that meet stringent EC anti-pollution requirements. This will cost the average crematorium at least half a million pounds; as a result, some of the local authority operations are beginning to sell out to the larger private firms. At present, the cheapest one that met our other criteria for inclusion was the City of Belfast Crematorium (£84-20 for 30 minutes – see Northern Ireland in the Good Funeral Guide chapter). The most expensive was the brand new and excellent-sounding Carpenter's Down Woodlands Crematorium, Basingstoke (£220 for 30 minutes – see South region in the Good Funeral Guide chapter). The average price for a cremation was £169.

Our questionnaire was circulated to all 229 crematoria in the country. Our main interest lay in finding out how helpful they were to people organising a funeral without using a funeral director. Of the 90 who replied, every single one was prepared to deal directly with a family, with no funeral director involvement – whereas in 1993, 8% said that they would deal only with funeral directors. An oppressive 9% said that they would not accept a home-made coffin, even if it met all the anti-pollution requirements and if everything were done 'in a dignified manner without disturbance to other mourners or to staff' – however this was an improvement on 19% in 1993. Cardboard coffins are now accepted by 96% of all UK crematoria – as against a mere 15% in 1993. 56% of the crematoria would accept wicker coffins; 37% would accept body bags (if supported on a piece of wood and covered with a drape); 31% would accept a body in a shroud (if the shroud were kept rigid with a piece of wood).

The following is the full set of questions and answers given by Ken West, Bereavement Services Manager at the Carlisle Crematorium (address in the North West region of the Good Funeral Guides chapter), winner of the Natural

Death Handbook 1997 Award for the Best Crematorium. You can use these questions to select the ones which are relevant to your own situation when approaching your local crematoria, and thus can evaluate the extent to which your local findings match the high standards set by this award winner:

Ken West, who runs both the crematorium and the cemetery, is at the forefront of a campaign to improve local authority funeral provision, and has spearheaded the radical new Charter for the Bereaved, published by the Institute of Burial and Cremation Authorities.

What is your parent organisation if any? Carlisle District Council.

How much time is allotted for each funeral service? 40 minutes.

Can extra time be booked if available? Yes.

If so, at what cost per minute? No charge.

What are your minimum charges for a simple service and cremation? £192, or £167 for an 'Environmental Cremation'. This option requires the use of a cardboard or plastic/chipboard-free container; cremation will be completed either the same day or the following morning. This saves on pre-heating cremators and wasting fossil fuels.

Provided the paperwork is correctly done, and any pacemaker has been removed, will you accept a body directly from the family (no funeral director)? Yes

Is a home-made coffin acceptable? Yes.

Is a cardboard coffin acceptable? Yes.

Is a wicker coffin acceptable? Yes.

Is a shroud or body bag suitable for cremation and covered with a drape, acceptable, if rigidified with a piece of wood? Yes.

Can mourners view the coffin entering the cremator? Yes.

How many at one time? The room size is the only limit, perhaps 20 maximum.

How would you describe the immediate surroundings of the crematorium? Our crematorium grounds contain four zones: the Peace Garden; the January to December monthly gardens; the Woods; and the Memorial Wall.

How would you describe the architecture and feel of the crematorium building and interior? Non-denominational, no fixed religious symbols. The seating is flexible and we already move seating and put the coffin elsewhere than the catafalque. One family decorated the chapel with posters based on photographs.

In what ways do you feel that your crematorium excels, either in terms of its services, prices, attitudes, practices, architecture or surroundings? Our crematorium excels because it recognises the different needs of the people who desire cremation. Whether they appreciate beautiful gardens, native trees and woodland, memorials or areas without memorials, they can find something to suit them. There is no commercial pressure or bias towards so-called conventional funerals.

To this needs to be added that the crematorium has a cold storage facility that families can make use of at a very modest charge, and it sells cardboard and other coffins at most reasonable prices – having resisted intense pressure from funeral directors. It also publishes very full guidance for families managing on their own.

Cemeteries

We wrote to over 500 cemeteries, and of the 57 respondents (some administering several cemeteries) every single one will accept burial by the family without involving funeral directors and will accept either a cardboard or a wooden coffin. 34% will accept body bags, if supported on a plank and covered with a drape. 39% will accept kaftans or shrouds. One cemetery wrote: 'The majority of Muslims are buried in coffins or caskets, but there are a couple of Muslim communities who bury their dead in kaftans and then the casket or boards are placed over the top'.

The Natural Death Handbook Award for the Best Cemetery goes to **Carlisle Cemetery** in Cumbria (who are further detailed in the North West region of the Good Funeral Guide chapter). This cemetery also won the Award in 1993. And its associated crematorium wins the 1997 Award. The Natural Death Handbook editorial team would have preferred to distribute the Awards more widely, but Carlisle's efforts have been so outstanding that they demand recognition.

The Carlisle Cemetery (and its two nearby associated cemeteries of Upperby and Stanwix) will accept virtually any kind of body container made of biodegradable material. Carlisle Cemetery also has an exceptionally well-run woodland burial ground. Here are the cemetery's answers to our questionnaire, which, as with the crematorium answers, provide a high standard by which you can judge your own local equivalents:

> *Does your cemetery have chapel facilities?* Yes.
>
> *How long is allotted for each funeral service?* There is no time limit.
>
> *How much does a plot cost, including digging and burial?* £353.
>
> *How long do grave rights last?* 50 years.
>
> *Maintenance of plot?* There is no charge for this.
>
> *Provided the paperwork is correctly done, will you accept a body directly from the family?* Yes. This is a necessity (Right No. 22) as part of the IBCA Charter for the Bereaved.
>
> *Which of the following types of body container are acceptable?*
>
> *Home-made coffin?* Yes, if made of natural materials.
>
> *Body bag or shroud?* Yes, if made of natural materials.
>
> *Cardboard coffin?* Yes.
>
> *Wicker coffin?* Yes.

The Cemetery sells the Brighton or Compakta cardboard coffins at £57 each, the Ecology cardboard coffin with cotton liner/pillow at £108 or the traditional type oak finish chipboard coffin at £123. The Cemetery has also arranged the design and manufacture of a woollen shroud with stiffening board and three cotton carrying ropes, available for £120.

> *What requirements do you have for a memorial?* Traditional graves are not subject to restrictions, lawn memorials must be within size limits. We have added a further choice, the 'recycled' grave, for those who require a simple, inexpensive burial with no memorial.
>
> *What are the surroundings like?* Parkland in wooded setting with conservation zones. Waterfalls on natural beck, squirrel feeder, lichen reserve, nesting herons, etc.
>
> *What is the architecture of the chapel?* Attractive, Gothic design. Warm, with seating for 100. Organ available or electronic music. Atmospheric lighting.
>
> *How do you feel that your cemetery excels, either in terms of its service, prices, attitudes, practices, architecture or surroundings?* We maintain both conservation areas and conventionally attractive cemetery grounds. The secret is in locating conservation areas away from the main drives and putting up signs to explain the purpose of the conservation.
>
> We have arranged many funerals with families and know that funerals arranged without a funeral director are at least as good, and often better, than those that take the conventional path. Indeed, staff members have arranged funerals within their own families using cardboard coffins. Everyone here is committed to improving the participation of the bereaved and listening to their views.

Contrast this approach with the Southern Cemetery in Manchester which has a rule booklet of 56 pages. Articles it prohibits on graves include wooden crosses ('except those supplied by the city council'), sea shells, rockery and other stones. Those bringing the coffin to the cemetery in other than a funeral director's hearse must transfer it at the entrance gate to a wheeled bier. Not unreasonably, it also wants to be notified if the coffin size will exceed 6' 4" by 22" width, 15" depth (the width measurement must allow for any protruding handles. 'It is difficult and may be dangerous to alter the width of the grave once it has been excavated'. There are occasional stories in the various funeral journals of the embarrassment felt by funeral directors and priests when the coffin will not fit the grave).

The Carlisle Cemetery published a leaflet in February 1996 that further demonstrates how seriously it takes its environmental responsibilities:

The greening of a cemetery

Conservation areas. In 1992, Wards 1 and 2 of Carlisle Cemetery were designated as conservation zones. The grass in these areas is mown once each year in October. Reciprocating mowers are used, cutting the grass as if it were hay, and this is raked off and sent to the composting centre. Many wild flowers appeared including pignut, primrose, ox-eye daisy, knapweed and a single cowslip. In 1995, meadow brown butterflies and burnett moths first appeared, and many insects are now evident. Each Summer, spotted flycatchers nest and feed in these areas. Unusually, some favourite

Victorian plants have flourished. These include the wild daffodil and dog-tooth violet. In these and other areas, bird and bat boxes have been created.

Herbaceous beds. Most beds have been replanted with species favoured by butterflies.

Owls. Residents of Richardson Street have recorded how the owls in the cemetery were regularly heard in the 1950s. They have since declined in number and species, and it is proposed to reverse this trend. Initially, the conservation areas will increase vole numbers, the main prey of owls. Owl boxes are being erected and access given to the roof-space in an old chapel.

Carved Owl. Artist Linda Watson carved a barn owl from the trunk of an old sweet chestnut. 'Barnie' sits on Ward 3 looking over the conservation area, watching for voles no doubt! She has also carved an 'oak leaf' seat for the woodland grave site.

The Beck. The Fairy beck runs through the cemetery. Over the years it was straightened, with the banks mown by flymo type machines. This ceased in 1995, and dogrose, hazel and dogwood were planted along the banks in 1996. These are to provide cover for ducks and bank voles. In 1995, a kingfisher was observed on the beck, suggesting that the environment was improving. To help this species, three waterfalls were created in Spring 1996. These will form small pools able to sustain fish and amphibians.

Herons. Herons have nested in the cemetery for some years. We avoid disturbing them during the nesting period. Sadly, the poor Spring weather in recent years has killed some of the young birds.

Red Alert. The council are supporting projects to conserve the red squirrel. As red squirrels appear in the cemetery on occasion, a feeding hopper has been erected. This cannot be accessed by the heavier grey squirrel. The woodland burial area is also proposed as a future reserve for red squirrels.

Hedgehogs. Hedgehogs are safe in the cemetery. To help them hibernate, felled trees and timber are placed in 'habitat' piles, under which they can also nest. A local resident also rescues hedgehogs and, after recovery, these are released in the cemetery. We do not use poisons or slug bait in the cemetery, chemicals which can kill these creatures.

Memorials. The memorials in the cemetery date from 1855 to the current time. They are an important social record, as well as an essential substrata for lichens (see below). Unsafe memorials are never removed, except where a repair or sinking deeper in the ground is not possible. Modern memorials are made of foreign stone and the beautiful local sandstones are rarely used. Only a few stones each year are hand carved, most being produced by computer controlled sandblasting. The development of local sculptors using local stone would be worth promoting.

Lichens. These small plants are composed of a fungus and an algae, and look beautiful under a hand lens. They are disappearing throughout Europe, but grow moderately well in the clean air of Carlisle. Lichens grow on soil, trees and memorials. It is important that memorials are not moved, as the lichens often die in new positions.

Animal vandals. The cemetery sustains wildlife in surprising ways, some of which lead to complaints! Rabbits routinely eat the flowers neatly around the edge of wreaths left at funerals. They also nip off 'pot mums' leaving a neat stub. This leaves the plant looking as if a gardener had clipped the plant with a pair of shears. Carrion crows pull flowers out of vases in order to drink water. The holly berries on Christmas wreaths are also enjoyed by birds. What they think of the plastic berries, it is difficult to know!

Woodland burial. This is the burial option used by those who are concerned with the environment. The graves will create a new oak forest, and, with the planting of scots pine, will create a squirrel reserve.

Recycled grave. This option was developed following requests by those concerned about the wastage of land for burial. It is also the least expensive form of burial. These graves are owned by the council and situated in old, often very attractive parts of the cemetery. They have been used for two burials which occurred over 100 years ago. The remains of these burials have now disappeared into the soil. These graves are only suitable for single burials, and, not being 'private', a memorial cannot be placed. A biodegradable coffin must be used and the grave will be reused for burial, some 75 to a 100 years from now. Further details are available.

Biodegradable coffins. The standard coffin used today is made of chipboard and plastics. These cause pollution when cremated and the materials will not degrade into the earth after burial. A selection of biodegradable coffins, some made of recycled floorboards, and a wool burial shroud, can be seen in the old burial chapel. Please ask for details and free leaflets.

Recycling old wreaths. A recycling scheme for old wreath frames was introduced in Autumn 1995. The wreaths are collected from cemetery tip sites by a special needs group. They strip off the old flowers and these are sent for composting. The old frames and plastic trays, etc, are then sold back to the florists for reuse. The scheme has not been totally successful due to adverse criticism from the National Association of Funeral Directors.

Cemetery walks. Cemetery walks occur during the Spring and Summer. Contact us for current details, or see the East Cumbria Countryside Project walks leaflet.

Just as house prices vary by region, so too do the rights to a burial plot. The Natural Death Centre's survey found that, including the cost of digging the grave, the prices ranged from £120-50 at Mold Cemetery (see Wales in the next chapter) to £3,025 at Highgate Cemetery (see London region in the next chapter). The average price for the cheapest plot in a cemetery was £504 (incl. digging). Some also charge non-residents either extra or double the price.

Woking (see South region in the next chapter) is an example of a cemetery with a pleasantly liberal and enlightened approach to memorials, with virtually any design accepted.

Remember to request, if buying burial rights, that ownership is put in the name of the surviving partner, to ensure the eventual right to be buried together.

Chapter 6

THE GOOD FUNERAL GUIDE

Unless otherwise stated, you can assume that all the funeral directors in this nationwide guide will sell you a fully-fitted coffin without your having to use any of their other services; and that all the cemeteries and crematoria listed are prepared to deal with families not using funeral directors. Abbreviations in bold are as follows:

Cem = Cemetery
Crem = Crematorium
Green Burial = a nature reserve burial ground where normally a tree is planted instead of having a headstone
(Green Burial) = a nature reserve burial ground site not yet open at the time of going to press
FD = Funeral director
• ✪✪✪ = Winner of a Natural Death Handbook Award.

Abbreviations for professional associations are as follows:

BIFD = British Institute of Funeral Directors
BIE = British Institute of Embalmers
CFSA = Co-operative Funeral Services Association
IAFD = Irish Association of Funeral Directors
NAFD = National Association of Funeral Directors
SAIF = Society of Allied and Independent Funeral Directors
FSC = Funeral Services Council

Those crematoria listed as willing to take home-made coffins do so on condition that such coffins meet the anti-pollution requirements of the Federation of British Cremation Authorities, as set out in Chapter Four. Shrouds, if listed as acceptable, are normally required to be made rigid with a plank; likewise bodybags, which would also normally need to be covered with a drape of some kind. These institutions do not want to cause offence to staff or to other members of the public.

Listings are by region, and then by town within the region, except in the Greater London region, which has not been further subdivided. Here services are listed alphabetically. If you wish to nominate others for a future Award, please write to The Natural Death Handbook (20 Heber Road, London NW2 6AA, tel 0181 208 2853; fax 0181 452 6434; e-mail: <rhino@dial.pipex.com>) with your experience of using their services, whether positive or negative, and including as much detail as possible. Our listings are based on information given to us by the services themselves – the name of the informant is given wherever possible.

The North West

Comprising Cumbria, Lancashire, Manchester, Sefton, Wirral, Liverpool, Knowsley, St Helens, Wigan, Bolton, Bury, Rochdale, Salford, Trafford, Manchester, Oldham, Tameside, Stockport and Cheshire.

• **Cem Accrington**: Accrington (Huncoat) Cemetery, Burnley Road, Accrington, Hyndburn, Lancashire BB5 6HA (tel 01254 232933). Plot (100 years) incl. digging and burial £429-35. Maintenance: No charge. They will accept home-made, cardboard or wicker coffins. Length of funeral service: 30 minutes (extra time can be booked for £35-50). Chapel: As crematorium below. Grounds: Well-tended seating areas. Memorials: Standard headstone style and type, within size restrictions. 'There are separate plots for different religious denominations, and an infant memorial area for foetal remains, stillborn children and small infants. Staff are caring and dedicated' (Lindsay Rogers).

• **Cem Accrington**: Dill Hall (Church of Clayton-le-Moors) Cemetery, Dill Hall Lane, Church, Near Accrington, Hyndburn, Lancashire (tel 01254 232933). Plot (100 years) incl. digging and burial £429-35. They will accept home-made, cardboard or wicker coffins. Length of funeral service: 30 minutes (extra time can be booked for £35-50). Chapel: Accrington Crematorium is the nearest available. Grounds: small cemetery with plots for Church of England and Roman Catholics. Memorials: Standard headstone style and type, within size restrictions. 'A "memorial wall" has been built for the burial and memorial of cremated remains of a loved one' (Lindsay Rogers).

• **Crem Accrington**: Accrington Crematorium, The Cemetery Office, Burnley Road, Accrington, Hyndburn, Lancashire BB5 6HA (tel 01254 232933). Price: £131. Time allotted: 20 minutes within a thirty minute period (extra time can be booked for £35-50). They will accept home-made, cardboard or wicker coffins, or shrouds or body bags. Chapel: Church-like; traditional nonconformist, cruciform design seating 80. Grounds: 'Burial plots on all sides of the chapel.' 'We are always willing to assist and be flexible to requests. Good disabled access' (Lindsay Rogers).

• **Cem Askam-in-Furness**: Ireleth Cemetery, Broughton Road, Askam-in-Furness, Cumbria (tel 01229 820119). No Chapel. Grounds: 'A small cemetery next to the local churchyard with superb views of the Duddun estuary' (C.R. Pollard). Other details as for Barrow-in-Furness Cemetery below.

• **Cem Atherton**: Atherton Cemetery, Leigh Road, Atherton, Lancashire. Other details as for Leigh Cemetery below.

• **Cem Nr. Atherton**: Hovebridge Cemetery, Lovers Lane, Near Atherton, Lancashire. Other details as for Leigh Cemetery below.

• **Cem Barrow-in-Furness**: Barrow-in-Furness Cemetery, Devonshire Road, Barrow-in-Furness, Cumbria (tel 01229 820119). Plot (99 years) incl. digging and burial £359. Maintenance: £126 plus VAT. They will accept home-made, cardboard or wicker coffins, or shrouds or body bags. Length of funeral service: 30 minutes (extra time can be booked without charge). Chapel: 1960s crematorium chapel. Grounds: 'On a hillside overlooking the town with views across the

Irish Sea.' Memorials: Natural stone, within size restrictions. 'Several areas are left uncut to encourage wildflowers. Plans for woodland/green burial site in future' (C.R. Pollard).

• **Crem Barrow-in-Furness**: Thorncliffe Crematorium, Cemetery Office, Devonshire Road, Barrow-in-Furness, Cumbria LA14 5PD (tel 01229 820119). Price: £190. Time allotted: 30 minutes (extra time can be booked without charge). They will accept home-made or cardboard coffins. Chapel: Modern, non-denominational with flexible seating. Grounds: 'Surrounded by a glade of remembrance and cemetery.' 'Because we are a smaller crematorium the staff offer a more personal, friendly service' (C.R. Pollard).

• **FD Bolton**: Gibsons Funeral Service, 342 St Helens Road, Bolton, Lancs (tel 01204 655869). Cheapest fully-fitted coffin only: £90 (no delivery anymore). Cold storage only: Not available. Body transport only: Yes (approx. £70). Advice for d-i-y: Yes, normally no charge. Basic funeral: £685 (disbursements extra). Gibsons horse-drawn funerals from about £550. 'We are too busy at present to continue sending out coffins' (Ray Kevill). Prepaid plan: Gibsons' own plan.

• **Cem Burnley**: Burnley Cemetery, 93 Rossendale Road, Burnley BB11 5DD (tel 01282 435411). Plot (40 years) incl. digging and burial £386. They will accept home-made or cardboard coffins. Length of funeral service: Not strictly limited. Chapel: 'Victorian, sombre.' Grounds: 'Woodland to rear. Part of cemetery in tranquil setting.' Memorials: Restrictions vary in different sections of the cemetery; no new sidestones, etc allowed; inscriptions not to cause offence, etc.' 'Separate plots for different religious denominations, infant memorial area, and caring and dedicated staff. Woodland burial area under consideration' (John Cummings).

• **Green Burial Bury**: Woodland burial site, within Radcliffe Cemetery, Cemetery Road, Bury, Greater Manchester (contact Director of Leisure Services, Bury Metropolitan Borough Council, Textile Hall, Manchester Road, Bury BL9 0DG, tel 0161 253 6510). A grave costs £619 (incl. digging; £35 for a tree, £1 for a seedling). They will accept home-made, cardboard or wicker coffins, or shrouds. Family and friends can help with a token amount of filling the grave. The woodland site is on the perimeter of the cemetery, by a housing estate, with green fields on the other side. 'Our service and our staff are excellent' (Martin Fewster).

• **FD Bury**: The Bury Metropolitan Borough Council has an arrangement with Hardman's Funeral Service (tel 0161 764 4072) whereby residents can obtain a funeral for £350 (with disbursements extra – burial, for instance, costs an extra £435).

• ✪✪✪ **Cem Carlisle**: Carlisle Cemetery, Richardson Street, Carlisle CA2 6AL (tel 01228 25022). Plot (50 years) incl. digging and burial £353. Maintenance: No charge. They will accept home-made, cardboard or wicker coffins, or shrouds or body bags. Length of funeral service: No limit. Chapel: 'Attractive, Gothic design. Warm, with seating for 100.' Grounds: 'Parkland in wooded setting with conservation zones. There are waterfalls on a natural beck, a squirrel feeder, a lichen reserve, nesting herons, etc.' Memorials: Traditional graves are not subject to restrictions, lawn memorials must be within size limits. 'Our range of graves and coffins (see the Carlisle woodland burial site below) enable us to meet all religious and personal needs without difficulty. We have added a further choice, the 'recycled' for those who require a simple, inexpensive burial with no memorial. We maintain both conservation areas and conventionally attractive cemetery grounds. We have arranged many funerals with families and know that funerals arranged without a funeral director are at least as good, and often better, than those that take the conventional path.' (Ken West).

• ✪✪✪ **Crem Carlisle**: Carlisle Crematorium, Bereavement Services, Cemetery Office, Richardson Street, Carlisle CA2 6AL (tel 01228 25022). Price: £167 for 'environmental cremation' in a cardboard coffin, normal fee £192. Time allotted: 30 minutes (extra time can be booked without charge). They will accept home-made, cardboard or wicker coffins, or shrouds or body bags. They can provide cold storage for the body at a charge of £8-25 for up to 24 hours, £11-50 for up to 48 hours or £14-50 for over 48 hours. Extra bearers to help the family can be supplied at £6 per person. Chapel: 'Non-denominational with flexible seating. One family decorated the chapel with posters based on photographs, so the feel of the chapel can be significantly changed.' Grounds: 'Four different zones ensure that the different needs and beliefs of individuals do not intrude upon others: The Peace Garden is bedded out and highly-maintained providing the principal view from the Hall of Remembrance; the monthly gardens are planted to a seasonal pattern; the Woods are for those who prefer a return to nature and may oppose high maintenance regimes; and the memorial wall offers the only cremation memorial option.' 'The service complies with the Charter for the Bereaved, offering both traditional and environmental options. The environmental options also prove far less expensive, offering savings against the cremation fee, and the provision of biodegradable coffins. Our attitude is one of complete openness, giving the bereaved complete access to the information they need in order to obtain a meaningful funeral. There is no commercial pressure or bias towards so-called conventional funerals' (Ken West).

• **Green Burial Carlisle**: Woodland burial site, Carlisle Cemetery, Cemetery Office, Richardson Street, Carlisle, Cumbria CA2 6AL (tel 01228 25022). A grave costs £340 (incl. digging and tree, £15 extra for non-residents). This, the UK's first woodland burial ground, is a peaceful site looking out towards the river, with cattle in an adjoining field. A local artist has made an oak seat. They will accept home-made, cardboard or wicker coffins, or shrouds or body bags. Families and friends can fill in the grave if they wish or can help with a token amount of digging. They sell (prices include VAT) the Brighton or Compakta cardboard coffins for £57, the Ecology (Peace Box) cardboard coffin for £108, a standard fully-fitted chipboard coffin for £123, the Alverstone wooden coffin with rope handles for £320 and their own Carlisle woollen burial shroud (complete with board and ropes) for £120. There is a wall for memorials. 'No chemicals are used; there are approximately two hay cuts each year; the oak trees are from acorns off native trees. It is proposed as a site for a red squirrel reserve in the future' (Ken West). Member of the Association of Nature Reserve Burial Grounds.

• **Cem Clitheroe**: Clitheroe Cemetery, Waddington Road, Clitheroe, Lancashire (run by the Ribble Valley Borough Council, tel 01200 425111). Plot (100 years) incl. digging and burial £301-05. They will accept cardboard coffins. Length of funeral service: 'No limit at the graveside.' No chapel. Grounds: A beautiful rural location. Memorials: Hard stone only. Size restriction in the lawn cemetery. 'We maintain a high standard of customer care' (Mrs Janice Tolson).

• **Green Burial Clitheroe**: Woodland burial ground, part of Clitheroe Cemetery, Waddington Road, Clitheroe, Lancashire (run by the Ribble Valley Borough Council, tel 01200 425111). A grave costs £168-75 for burial rights and £110-70 for the digging fees (incl. tree or bulbs, fees doubled for non-residents). The site is on the perimeter of the existing cemetery, adjacent to existing private woodland, in a pleasant rural setting overlooking the River Ribble. Over half the council employees in a survey said that they would prefer this site for themselves. They will accept cardboard coffins 'if to the required specification'. Families and friends can help in a token way with filling the grave. 'The site is managed to ensure maximum tree growth and to create conditions for wild flowers and nature to flourish' (Mrs Janice Tolson).

• **Crem Crewe**: Crewe Crematorium, Crewe Cemetery Office, Market Close, Crewe, Cheshire CW1 2NA (tel 01270 212643). Price: £155 (non-residents £183-50). Time allotted: 40 minutes (extra time can be booked for £28-50). They will accept home-made, cardboard or wicker coffins, or shrouds or body bags. Chapel: Non-demominational, with flexible seating. Grounds: 'Good grounds and flower beds.' 'A woodland area for cremated remains is in preparation' (Mrs M. M. Slinn).

• **Cem Dalton-in-Furness**: Dalton-in-Furness Cemetery, Cemetery Hill, Newton Road, Dalton-in-Furness, Cumbria (tel 01229 820119). No chapel. Grounds: 'Edge of town with views to the neighbouring countryside. It is an old cemetery with graves dating back to 1800' (C.R. Pollard). Other details as for Barrow-in-Furness Cemetery above.

• **Crem Distington**: Distington Hall Crematorium, Distington, Workington, Cumbria CA14 4QY (tel 01946 830561). Price: £196-90 (£209-90 non-residents). Time allotted: 30 minutes. They will accept cardboard or wicker coffins. Chapel: Modern, non-denominational. Grounds: 'A natural woodland setting.' 'Reasonably priced and well maintained' (Mr S. J. Benn).

• **Cem Great Harwood**: Great Harwood Cemetery, Blackburn Road, Great Harwood, Near Blackburn, Lancashire (tel 01254 232 933). Plot (100 years) incl. digging and burial £429-35. They will accept home-made, cardboard or wicker coffins. Length of funeral service: 20 minutes (extra time can be booked for £10 per quarter hour). No chapel. Grounds: Set in quiet side of town. Memorials: Standard headstone style and materials within size restrictions. 'Well maintained with a caring cemetery foreman' (Lindsay Rogers).

• **Cem Hindley**: Hindley Cemetery, Castle Hill Road, Hindley, Near Wigan, Lancashire. Other details as for Leigh Cemetery below.

• **Cem Leigh**: Leigh Cemetery, Manchester Road, Leigh, Lancashire (tel 01942 828507). Plot (100 years) incl. digging and burial £377. They will accept home-made, cardboard or wicker coffins. Length of funeral service: 30 minutes (extra time can be booked without charge). No chapel. Memorials: Lawn memorials only, within size restrictions. 'Wigan Borough Council (see under F. D. Wigan below), with the co-operation of a specified reputable funeral director, is now able to offer a low cost, but nevertheless dignified funeral service to local residents' (A Bassett).

• **Cem Lytham St. Annes**: Park Cemetery, Regent Avenue, Lytham St. Annes, Lancashire FY8 4AB (tel 01253 735429). Plot (100 years) incl. digging and burial £353 (non-residents £706). They will accept home-made, cardboard or wicker coffins. Length of funeral service: 30 minutes (extra time can be booked without charge). Chapel: As crematorium below. Grounds: As crematorium below. Memorials: 'Within size restrictions; no kerbing' (Mr A. Royston).

• **Crem Lytham St Annes**: Lytham Park Crematorium, Park Cemetery, Regent Avenue, Lytham St Annes, Lancashire FY8 4AB (tel 01253 735429). Price: £135. Time allotted: 25 minutes within a 30 minute period (extra time can be booked without charge). They will accept home-made coffins if made from natural wood, cardboard coffins if approved by Federation, or body bags approved for cremation. Chapel: 'Standard 1950s'. Grounds: 'Open view of fields.' 'Saturday services are available' (Mr A. Royston).

• **Crem Macclesfield**: Macclesfield Crematorium, Cemetery Lodge, Prestbury Road, Macclesfield, SK10 3BU (tel 01625 422330 or 422408). Price: £160-50. Time allotted: 30 minutes (extra time can be booked for £160-50). They will accept cardboard coffins. Chapel: 'Fine Victorian nonconformist chapel made from local stone. Movable seating pews.' Grounds: 'Overlooking a pool and stream in an established arboretum valley.' 'We provide a reasonably flexible service' (John J. Thomas).

• **Cem Manchester**: Southern Cemetery, Barlow Moor Road, Chorlton, Manchester M21 7GL (tel 0161 881 2208). Plot (50 years) incl. digging and burial £655. Maintenance: No charge. They will accept home-made coffins, or shrouds in the Muslim section. Length of funeral service: 20 minutes in chapel. Chapel: Victorian Gothic. Grounds: 168 acre site with listed buildings and a great variety of trees and shrubs. Memorials: A rule booklet of 56 pages. Articles it prohibits on graves include wooden crosses ('except those supplied by the city council'), sea shells, rockery and other stones. Those bringing the coffin to the cemetery in other than a funeral director's hearse must transfer it at the entrance gate to a wheeled bier. Not unreasonably, it also wants to be notified if the coffin size will exceed 6' 4" by 22" width, 15" depth. (The width measurement must allow for any protruding handles. 'It is difficult and may be dangerous to alter the width of the grave once it has been excavated'.) 'We pride ourselves on being experienced in all manner of problems associated with burial – and how to solve them!' (Paul Burton).

• **Crem Manchester:** Barlow Moor Road Crematorium, Chorlton, Manchester M21 7GZ (tel 0161 881 5269). Run by the Manchester Crematorium Ltd. Price:

£178 for 30 minutes in the mornings; or £188 for 40 minutes in the afternoons (extra time can be booked for £65 per half hour). They will accept home-made, cardboard or wicker coffins. Chapels: One Romanesque chapel from the late 19th century and one modern one from the late 1950s. Grounds: In the suburbs or Manchester with a 168 acre cemetery next door. 'Families are treated as individually as possible' (Andrew Paul Helsby).

• **Green Burial Nr. Manchester**: New Manchester Woodland Cemetery, City Road, Ellenbrook, Worsley, Manchester M28 1BD (tel 0161 790 1300). This is a privately run concern, a 12 acre site looking across open fields and surrounded with trees. A grave costs £650 (incl. digging; tree £25 extra; flat bedstone only allowed as memorial, costing from £220). They will accept home-made, cardboard or wicker coffins, or shrouds or body bags. Families and friends can fill in the grave if they wish or can help with a token amount of digging. They sell coffins to the public 'when available, prices on request'. They also sell other services, such as collection of the body – 'quotation on request'. 'Money taken in advance is for purchase of burial plots. A trust scheme is being set up. This is a beautiful rural setting, offering an excellent service to the public' (James Broome). Provisional member of the Association of Nature Reserve Burial Grounds.

• **FD Manchester**: R. Pepperdine & Sons Ltd, Alexandra House, 5 Manchester Road, Chorlton-Cum-Hardy, Manchester M21 9JG (tel 0161 881 5363). Cheapest fully-fitted coffin only: £65 (delivery locally £15). Cold storage only: Yes, £15 per day. Body transport only: Yes (hearse and driver £90). Advice for d-i-y: Yes, £25 per hour. Basic funeral: £625 or £395 using a cardboard coffin (disbursements in both cases extra). 'Independent family firm. Our service is excellent value for money and flexible. What a family wants, a family gets' (Frank Barrett). Prepaid plan: Chosen Heritage, Personal Choice, Perfect Assurance. Member of NAFD.

• **FD Manchester**: S. Wellens and Sons Ltd, 121 Long Street, Middleton, Manchester M24 6DL (tel 0161 643 2677). Cheapest fully-fitted coffin only: £145 (delivery locally 'probably free'). Cold storage only: Yes, £10 per day. Body transport only: Yes (from £30 to £58). Advice for d-i-y: Yes, £35 to £55 per hour. Basic funeral: £515 (disbursements extra). 'We are a completely independent family firm. We have cardboard coffins in stock. We provide a bereavement support service' (Frank Barrett). Prepaid plan: 'Our own personal prepayment'. Member of NAFD, SAIF, BIE.

• **Green Burial Morecambe**: A woodland burial ground at the rear of the Torrisholme Cemetery, Westgate Road, Morecambe, Lancashire (contact Cemeteries Service, Lancaster City Council, Town Hall, Morecambe, Lancashire LA4 5AF, tel 01524 582635). A grave costs £425 (incl. digging and tree, £100 extra for non-residents). Funeral directors must be used – 'although d-i-y arrangements may be possible at a later date'. Families are not allowed to assist with digging or filling the grave (George Bowker).

• **Green Burial Nr. Oldham**: A nature reserve burial ground, with space for 150 graves, part of Saddleworth Cemetery, Upper Mill, Saddleworth, Oldham (run by Saddleworth Parish Council, Civic Hall, Lee Street, Upper Mill, Oldham OLE 6AE, tel 01457 876665). A grave costs £215-50 (incl. digging and tree; £323-25 for non-residents). 'This is a fabulous site, high up, in a very rural and hilly area, looking down on at least five villages'. They will accept cardboard coffins or shrouds. Family and friends can help fill the grave and help with a token amount of digging. It is part of the main cemetery which has been open since 1988 and which won a design competition. 'We want to make this a place that people come to see' (Dave Holland).

• **Cem Padiham**: Padiham Public Cemetery, St. John's Road, Padiham, Lancashire. Grounds: 'No adjacent dwellings.' All other details as for Burnley Cemetery (above) to whom any correspondence should be addressed.

• **Cem Preston**: Preston Cemetery, New Hall Lane, Preston, Lancashire PR1 4SY (run by Preston Borough Council, tel 01772 794585) Lawn cemetery plot (75 years): £320. Digging and burial: £201 extra. Time for service: Unlimited. Grounds: Wooded and Victorian in the old cemetery, bleakly formal in the new. 'Memorials of almost any kind allowed' (Miss Brown).

• **Crem Preston**: Preston Crematorium, Longridge Road, Preston (office New Hall Lane, Preston PR1 4SY, tel 01772 792391). Price: £170. Time allotted: 30 minutes (extra time can be booked for £170 per half hour). They will accept home-made or strong cardboard coffins, subject to prior discussion. Grounds: 'Open parkland at the front, woodlands at the rear' (Miss Brown).

• **Green Burial Preston**: Woodland burial ground, part of Preston Cemetery, New Hall Lane, Preston, Lancashire PR1 4SY (run by Preston Borough Council, tel 01772 794585). A grave costs £320, with digging and burial £201 extra (incl. tree; no extra for non-residents). The site is in the old cemetery, the old lodge garden, surrounded by trees and shrubs. They will accept strong cardboard coffins. A native species tree will be planted for each grave. Mourners may help fill the grave. 'It's rather a nice setting' (Miss Brown).

• **FD St Helens**: The St Helens Council (tel 01744 456000 and ask for reception) has an agreement with the Co-op (tel 01744 23675) to provide a municipal funeral for local residents, whereby cremation costs £604 and burial costs £623, both prices including disbursements.

• **Crem Stockport**: Stockport Crematorium, 31a Buxton Road, Heaviley, Stockport SK2 6LS (tel 0161 480 5221). Price: £173. Time allotted: 30 minutes (extra time can be booked for £35 per half hour; £45 on Saturdays). They will accept home-made or cardboard coffins. Church: 1930s and slightly church-like. Grounds: Crematorium surrounded by walled Gardens of Remembrance. 'Staff at the crematorium are very flexible and helpful' (N. Buckley, registrar).

• **FD Stockport**: A 'Civic Funeral Service' is provided by the local authority for residents, run by the United North West Co-operative Society (tel 0161 432 0818). They charge £690 for a cremation, including disbursements; and £1,048 for burial in a new grave, again including disbursements.

• **Cem Tyldesley**: Tyldesley Cemetery, Hough Lane, Tyldesley, Lancashire. Other details as for Leigh Cemetery above.

• **Cem Whitehaven**: Whitehaven Cemetery, Low Road, Whitehaven, Cumbria (tel 01946 692329). They also administer Hensingham, Netherwasdale, Millom and St John's Beckermet Cemeteries. Plot (50 years) incl. digging and burial £257. Maintenance: No charge. They will accept home-made or cardboard coffins. No chapel. Grounds: Natural woodland setting. Memorials: Within size restrictions. 'Reasonably priced and well maintained' (Mr S. J. Benn).

• **FD Widnes**: John M. Austin, 94 Widnes Road, Simms Cross, Widnes, Cheshire WA8 6AT (tel 0151 420 4862). Cheapest fully-fitted coffin only: £120 (delivery locally free). Cold storage only: Yes, £20 per day. Body transport only: Yes. Advice for d-i-y: Yes, £12 per hour. Basic funeral: £595 (disbursements extra). 'A personal service at a competitive price' (John M. Austin). Prepaid plan: Golden Charter. Member of no association.

• **Cem Wigan (1)**: Gidlow Cemetery, Wigan Road, Standish, Wigan. Other details as for Leigh Cemetery above.

• **Cem Wigan (2)**: Ince-in-Makerfield Cemetery, Warrington Road, Lower Ince, Wigan. Other details as for Leigh Cemetery above.

• **Cem Wigan (3)**: Westwood Cemetery, Westwood Lane, Lower Ince, Wigan. Other details as for Leigh Cemetery above.

• **Cem Wigan (4)**: Wigan Cemetery, Cemetery Road, Lower Ince, Wigan, (tel 01942 866455). Other details as for Leigh Cemetery above.

• **Crem Wigan**: Wigan Crematorium, Cemetery Road, Lower Ince, Wigan (tel 01942 866455). Price: £145. Time allotted: 30 minutes (extra time can be booked without charge). They will accept home-made or cardboard coffins. Chapel: Church-like, converted from a nonconformist cemetery chapel. Grounds: Cemetery with Gardens of Remembrance. 'We would assist with any part of a funeral arrangement or provide any assistance to a bereaved family' (Anthony Bassett).

• **(Green Burial) Wigan**: Cemeteries Section, Wigan Metropolitan Borough Council, Trencherfield Mill, Wallgate, Wigan WN3 4EF (tel 01942 828507). 'The borough has plans to establish one, and possibly two, nature reserve burial areas in the future. Since there is no possibility of expansion at any of our existing sites, the facility will be established in a completely fresh, as yet unknown, location, probably selected from countryside land already owned by the borough. At this stage (November 1996) we are unable to say how soon this service will become available ' (A. Bassett).

• **✪✪✪ FD Wigan**: Edwards Funeral Directors Ltd, Holmwood, Dicconson Terrace, Wigan WN1 2AA (tel 01942 821215). Cheapest fully-fitted coffin only: £125 (delivery locally £20; nationally 75p per mile). Cold storage only: Yes, £20 per day. Body transport only: Yes. Advice for d-i-y: Yes, £20 per hour. Basic funeral: £615 (incl. fees for doctors, minister and cremation). Municipal funeral service for local residents only: cremation for £650 (incl. disbursements) and burial for £806 (incl. disbursements and opening a new grave). 'Our family has been associated with quality funeral service in the town for over 110 years' (R. B. Edwards). Prepaid plan: Golden Charter. Member of SAIF.

The North East

Comprising Northumberland, Newcastle-Upon-Tyne, North Tyneside, Gates-head, South Tyneside, Sunderland, Durham, Hartlepool, Stockton-On-Tees, Middlesbrough, Redcar, North Yorkshire, York, East Riding of Yorkshire, Kingston-Upon-Hull, Bradford, Leeds, Calderdale, Kirklees, Wakefield, Barnsley, Sheffield, Rotherham, Doncaster, North Lincolnshire, North East Lincolnshire and Lincolnshire.

• **Crem Barnsley**: Barnsley Crematorium, Doncaster Road, Ardsley, Barnsley S71 5EH (tel 01226 206053). Price: £187. Time allotted: 30 minutes (extra time can be booked for £71). They will accept coffins approved by the FBCA (see the FBCA anti-pollution requirements in Chapter Four). Chapel: 'A mature building built in 1963.' Grounds: 'Peaceful and quiet garden.' 'A service that meets the changing demands of this sensitive subject' (Denis Rhodes).

• **Cem Barrow-on-Humber**: Barrow-on-Humber Cemetery, North Lincoln-shire (tel 01724 280289). (All correspondence to Scunthorpe Woodlands Memorial Park address below). No chapel. Grounds: 'A tranquil cemetery with farmland on 2 sides and screened on one side by a belt of mixed trees.' Memorials: Headstones, without kerbing, within size restrictions. All other details as for Cem Scunthorpe (1) below.

• **Cem Barton-upon-Humber**: Barton-upon-Humber Cemetery, Barrow Road, Barton-upon-Humber, North Lincolnshire (tel 01724 280289). (All correspond-ence to Scunthorpe Woodlands Memorial Park address below.) No chapel. Grounds: 'With farmland on two sides and a fine view across to the Humber Bridge and estuary.' Memorials: Headstones, without kerbing, within size restrictions. All other details as for Cem Scunthorpe (1) below.

• **Crem Boston**: Boston Crematorium, Marian Road, Boston, Lincolnshire PE21 9HA (tel 01205 364612). Price: £152. Time allotted: 25 minutes within a 30 minute period. They will accept home-made or cardboard coffins (must be identified). Chapel: 'Removable Christian symbols'. Grounds: 'Extensive lawns with many trees and formal rosebeds.' 'Our attitude is friendly, and the ambience inviting' (Martin Potts).

• **Cem (Green Burial) Bradford**: Scholemoor Cemetery, Necropolis Road, Bradford BD7 2PS (tel 01274 571313). Plot (100 years) incl. digging and burial £293. They will accept home-made, cardboard or wicker coffins, or body bags or shrouds. Length of funeral service: Open. Chapel: As crematorium below. Grounds: 'Maintained to a high standard.' 'Our highly trained staff are commit-ted to delivering a sensitive service to meet the needs of the service user. We are also planning a woodland burial area at our Thornton branch cemetery' (David Congreve).

• **Crem Bradford**: Scholemoor Crematorium, Scholemoor Cemetery, Necropo-lis Road, Bradford BD7 2PS (tel 01274 571313). Price: £153. Time allotted: 30 minutes (extra time can be booked without charge). They will accept home-made, cardboard or wicker coffins, or shrouds or body bags. Chapel: Non-denominational, converted Victorian chapel. Grounds: 'Well-maintained cem-etery.' 'Low charges and caring, helpful staff' (David Congreve).

• **Cem Brigg**: Brigg Cemetery, Wrawby Road, Brigg, North Lincolnshire (tel 01724 280289). (All correspondence to Scunthorpe Woodlands Memorial Park address below.) No chapel. Grounds: 'On the edge of a pleasant market town, includes an older section with traditional memorials.' Memorials: Headstones, without kerbing, within size restrictions. All other details as for Cem Scunthorpe (1) below.

• **FD Dewsbury**: George Brooke Ltd funeral directors, 27 Bradford Road, Dewsbury, West Yorkshire (tel 01924 454476). Cheapest fully-fitted coffin only: £245 (delivery locally £35). The firm provides a fully-itemised price list. Cold storage only: Yes, £12-50 per day. Body transport only: Yes. Advice for d-i-y: Yes, 'no charge, we automatically help'. 'We are a small family firm and we try to fulfil a family's requests' (Helen Wilson). Prepaid plan: Golden Charter. Member of NAFD, BIFD.

• **Crem Durham**: Central Durham Crematorium, South Road, Durham, County Durham DH1 3TQ (tel 0191 3848677). Price: £114 (non-residents £169). Time allotted: 30 minutes (extra time can be booked for £20 per half hour). They will accept home-made or cardboard coffins. Chapel: Modern, non-denominational. Grounds: 'Open parkland with distant views.' 'Our service is dignified and fitting to the needs of individual families. We are happy to arrange any music (within reason) and have recently hosted jazz bands, trumpet solos, etc at services' (Mr A. S. Jose).

• **Crem Great Grimsby**: Great Grimsby Crematorium, Weelsby Avenue, Great Grimsby, North East Lincolnshire DN32 0BA (tel 01472 324868). Price: £157 (non-residents £224). Time allotted: 30 minutes (extra time could possibly be arranged). They will accept home-made or cardboard coffins. Mourners not permitted to witness coffin entering the cremator. Chapel: 1950s. Grounds: 'Attractive landscaped grounds with a memorial garden.' 'We are keen to work closely with the public and have recently been promoting environmentally-friendly coffins and independent funerals' (Mrs Sarah Mann).

• **FD Grimsby**: Kettle Ltd funeral directors, 135 Granville St, Grimsby, N. E. Lincs DN32 9PB (tel 01472 355395); also 110 Kidgate, Louth, Lincs LN11 9BX (tel 01507 600710). Cheapest fully-fitted coffin only: £205 (delivery locally free, nationally 43p per mile). Cold storage only: Yes, £15 per day. Body transport only: Yes (hearse for funeral £90). Advice for d-i-y: Yes, £10 per hour. Basic funeral: £630 (disbursements extra). 'We even supplied handles, plate and linings to a client who had made a coffin for his mother's funeral' (Michael Chevins). Prepaid plan: Chosen Heritage, Perfect Assurance. Member of NAFD, BIFD.

• **Crem Harrogate**: Harrogate Crematorium, Stonefall Cemetery, Wetherby Road, Harrogate, North Yorkshire HG3 1DE (tel 01423 883523). Price: £204. Time allotted: 20 minutes within 40 minute period (extra time can be booked for £68). They will accept home-made or cardboard coffins, or others if recommended by FBCA. Chapel: Church-like. Grounds: 'In a well-maintained, traditional cemetery setting'. 'We recognise that bereaved people have differing needs and we accommodate these wherever possible' (M.J. Warren).

• **Green Burial Harrogate**: For locals only: a green burial ground at Stonefall Cemetery, Wetherby Road, Harrogate, North Yorkshire HG3 1DE (tel 01423 883523). A grave costs £710 (incl. the digging and tree). They will accept cardboard coffins or shrouds. 'A local authority green burial ground for local residents only, with space for a couple of hundred graves' (Mrs Warren).

• ✪✪✪ **Green Burial Harrogate**: A. B. Wildlife Trust Fund (Charity Reg. No. 1037444), 7 Knox Road, Harrogate, North Yorkshire HG1 3EF (tel 01423 530900). The Trust arranges burials various nature reserves. The latest site where they can help arrange burials is on 8 acres of Brimham Rocks, a Site of Special Scientific Interest, where up to 25 burials can take place, in the Nidderdale Area of Outstanding Natural Beauty. The land is named Kate's Fell, after Kathleen Davies, one of the first occupational therapists and a modern-day pioneer of the therapeutic value of pets in hospitals. It is a mix of semi-natural woodland with pasture, including bilberry and heather on a warm, West-facing slope looking into the valley of Nidderdale. There are about 250 large boulders scattered throughout and each has legal protection. The Trust's adviser is John Bradfield, author of 'Green Burial', and probably the UK's leading authority on the laws surrounding funerals – he is certainly the source to whom the Natural Death Centre refers people with complex questions. The Trust can help arrange funerals paid for by the DSS, or if necessary, a grave can be made available free of charge; other charges are at the Trust's discretion. Grave rights last 50 years – leasehold property rights are sold and they run with the land, regardless of the land ownership or freehold – 'with 1,000 years' access rights *if* the burial rights are used within a 50 year period'. The Trust will accept home-made, cardboard or wicker coffins, or shrouds, but not body bags – 'our experience is that body bags smack of a waste disposal operation'. The Trust makes available the Compakta cardboard coffin for £45. As for collection of the body or other services, 'all aspects of help can be provided free of charge, depending on circumstances'. Family and friends can, if they wish, dig and fill the grave. In some sites, 'burial mounds can be made for wildflowers or small animals'. 'Our priority is to meet the needs of those seeking help, whilst creating or helping to protect a wildlife area. We are experienced conservationists' (John Bradfield).

• **F.D. Harrogate**: W. Bowers funeral director, Birstwith Road, Hampsthwaite, Harrogate HG3 2EU (tel 01423 770258). Cheapest fully-fitted coffin only: £74-25 (delivery £5 locally, nationally £20). Cold storage only: Yes, £5 per day. Body transport only: Yes, £75 for the first 10 miles. Advice for d-i-y: Yes, £25 per hour. Basic funeral: £685 (incl. fees to crematorium, doctors and clergy). Prepaid plans: Golden Charter and Funeral Plans Ltd. Member of no association. (Roger Bowers). Editorial note: One reader found their service insensitive. Further feedback, positive or negative, is requested.

• ✪✪✪ **FD Huddersfield**: D. J. Screen & Sons, 22 Bradford Road, Huddersfield HD1 6LJ (tel 01484 452220). Cheapest fully-fitted coffin only: £50 (delivery locally free, nationally 50p per mile). Cold storage only: Yes, £5 per day. Body transport only: Yes Advice for d-i-y: Yes, free. Basic funeral: £385 (disbursements extra). 'As a small local family business, we try to assist, barter if required, we are not stuck to fixed prices' (Denis Screen). Prepaid plan: Golden Charter. Member of SAIF, BIFD.

• **Cem Keighley**: Utley Cemetery, Skipton Road, Keighley, Bradford BD20 6EJ (tel 01535 643263). Plot (100 years) incl. digging and burial £293. They will accept home-made, cardboard or wicker coffins, or body bags or shrouds. Length of funeral service: Open. No chapel. Grounds: 'Maintained to a high standard.' 'Our highly trained staff are committed to delivering a sensitive service to meet the needs of the service user' (David Congreve).

• **Crem Keighley**: Oakworth Crematorium, Wide Lane, Oakworth, Keighley, Bradford BD22 0RJ (tel 01535 643263). Price: £153. Time allotted: 30 minutes (extra time can be booked without charge). They will accept home-made, wicker or cardboard coffins, or shrouds or body bags. Chapel: Non-denominational, converted Victorian chapel. Grounds: 'Well-maintained countryside cemetery.' 'Low charges and caring, helpful staff' (David Congreve and J Elsbury).

• **Cem Leeds**: Lawnswood Cemetery, Otley Road, Adel, Leeds LS16 6AH (0113 2673188). Plot (50 years) incl. digging and burial £501. They will accept home-made or cardboard coffins. Length of funeral service: 30 minutes. Chapel: Dark stone, built in the late 19th century. Grounds: 'An historic 20 acre cemetery with beautiful old memorials' (Phil Stephenson).

• **Crem Leeds**: Leeds City Council Cemeteries and Crematoria Section, Otley Road, Adel, Leeds LS16 6AH (0113 2673188). Price: £185. Time allotted: 30 minutes (extra time can be booked for £84). They will accept home-made or cardboard coffins. Chapel: Church-like. Grounds: 'A mix of formal and woodland areas' (Phil Stephenson).

• **(Green Burial) Leeds**: Woodland burial site within Lawnswood Cemetery, Otley Road, Adel, Leeds LS16 6AH (0113 2673188). A grave costs £715 (incl. digging and tree). Open from the Spring of 1997, this woodland burial site will be for local residents only, although two further Leeds woodland burial sites are planned for opening before the end of 1997 that will be open to non-residents. They will accept home-made or cardboard coffins. Families and friends can fill in the grave if they wish. 'The site is a flat area within the cemetery near some mature trees' (Phil Stephenson).

• **Cem (Green Burial) Middlesbrough**: Acklam Cemetery, Acklam Road, Acklam, Middlesbrough. All correspondence to Middlesbrough Teesside Crematorium address below. Grounds: Adjacent to crematorium, open space and Botanic Centre, with views of Cleveland Hills. Chapel: Use of two chapels at adjacent crematorium: one 1960s, with central altar and no windows; the other 1980s, with lots of glass. 'A woodland/green burial area is planned' (P. Gitsham). Other details as for Middlesbrough Thorntree Cemeteries below.

• **Cem (1) Middlesbrough**: Linthorpe Cemetery, Burlam Road, Middlesbrough. All correspondence to Middlesbrough Teesside Crematorium address below. Grounds: 52 acres with heavily wooded older areas and a nature conservation area. No chapel. 'A Friends Group has been formed, which arranges walks/talks on the cemetery's history and wildlife' (P. Gitsham). Other details as for Middlesbrough Thorntree Cemeteries below.

• **Cem (2) Middlesbrough**: Thorntree and Thorntree RC Cemeteries, Cargo Fleet Lane, Thorntree, Middlesbrough (tel 01642 246295) All correspondence to Middlesbrough Teeside Crematorium address below. Plot (50 years) incl. digging and burial £355-25. They will accept home-made or cardboard coffins; and will consider wicker coffins, or body bags or shrouds on application. Length of funeral service: Up to 60 minutes. Memorials: Natural quarried stones or wooden crosses to Council specifications. Chapel: 'Victorian/1930s style' (P. Gitsham).

• **Crem Middlesbrough**: Teesside Crematorium, PO Box 68, Melrose House, Melrose Street, Middlesbrough TS1 2QS (tel 01642 264925). Price: £182. Time allotted: 30 minutes (extra time can be booked for £31). They will accept home-made or cardboard coffins and body bags; may consider wicker coffins or shrouds. Chapel: Modern. Grounds: 'Shrubberies and lawn with views of Cleveland Hills' (P. Gitsham).

• **(Green Burial) Middlesbrough**: Woodland burial ground (which should be open before the end of 1997), c/o Mr Gitsham, Middlesbrough Borough Council, Cemeteries Department, PO Box 68, Melrose Street, Middlesbrough TS1 2QS (tel 01642 264 925). This site is an extension of the Acklam cemetery, with views of the Cleveland hills. Graves will cost about £343 (incl. digging, double for non-residents). Family and friends will be allowed to help fill graves and possibly to do a token amount of digging.

• **Crem Newcastle-upon-Tyne**: West Road Crematorium, West Road, Newcastle-upon-Tyne (tel 0191 2744 737). Price: £168. Time allotted: 30 minutes (extra time can be booked for £42). They will accept home-made, cardboard or wicker coffins. Chapel: Very simple and traditional. Grounds: 'Well-kept gardens.' 'All family requests by way of music, etc are accommodated whenever possible' (Mrs Valerie Coombes).

• **Crem North Shields**: North Shields Crematorium, Walton Avenue, North Shields, North Tyneside (tel 0191 2005861). Price: £162. Time allotted: 30 minutes , (extra time can be booked for an additional payment). They will accept home-made or cardboard coffins. Chapel: Church-like, with removable crosses and flexible seating. Grounds: 'Heavily wooded, older part of mature cemetery - one part is a conservation area.' 'Very attractive mature woodland surroundings' (Tracey Harrison).

• **Cem Scawby**: Scawby Cemetery, Scawby, North Lincolnshire (tel 01724 280289). (All correspondence to Scunthorpe Woodlands Memorial Park address below.) No Chapel. Grounds: 'Tranquil, natural setting in open farmland.' Memorials: Headstones, without kerbing, within size restrictions. All other details as for Cem Scunthorpe (1) below.

• **Cem Scunthorpe**: Crosby Cemetery, Ferry Road, Scunthorpe, North Lincolnshire (tel 01724 280289). (All correspondence to Scunthorpe Woodlands Memorial Park address below.) No chapel. Grounds: 'An old cemetery with traditional memorials.' Memorials: Headstones, without kerbing, within size restrictions. All other details as for Cem Scunthorpe (1) below.

• **Cem Scunthorpe (1)**: Woodlands Memorial Park Cemetery, Brumby Wood Lane, Scunthorpe, North Lincolnshire DN17 1SP (tel 01724 280289). Administers Brumby, Barrow-upon-Humber, Barton-upon-Humber, Winterton, Brigg, Scawby and Crosby branch cemeteries. Plot (50 years) incl. digging and burial £367. They will accept home-made or cardboard coffins. Length of funeral service: 20 minutes (extra time can be booked for £30). Chapel: See below. Grounds: See below. Memorials: No headstones; only bronze plaques set at an angle, off the ground, in a garden border. 'Every effort is made to accommodate the wishes of the deceased and family' (Jack Startin).

• **Cem Scunthorpe (2)**: Brumby Cemetery, Cemetery Road, Scunthorpe, North Lincolnshire (tel 01724 280289). (All correspondence to Scunthorpe Woodlands Memorial Park address below.) No Chapel. Grounds: 'An old cemetery with a mix of traditional kerbs and headstones, plus a lawn section set amongst birch trees.'. Memorials: Stone headstones, without kerbing, within size restrictions. All other details as for Cem Scunthorpe (1) above.

• **Crem Scunthorpe**: Woodlands Crematorium, Woodlands Memorial Park, Brumby Wood Lane, Scunthorpe, North Lincolnshire DN17 1SP (tel 01724 280289). Price: £188 (non-residents £215-50). Time allotted: 20 minutes within a 30 minute period (extra time can be booked for £15). They will accept home-made, cardboard or wicker coffins, or shrouds or body bags. Chapel: 'Light and airy, the upper portion in glass, with a non-denominational stained glass window'. Grounds: 'Shrubberies, specimen trees and avenues creating long vistas across close-mown lawns.' 'We strive to provide an excellent service to all our customers and to help them have the funeral of *their* choice. We have an open door policy, and the public may visit without prior booking for a guided tour' (Jack Startin).

• **Green Burial Nr Sheffield**: South Yorkshire Woodland Burial Ground, Turnshaw Road, Ulley, Near Rotherham and Sheffield (run by Peace Burials Ltd, St Peter's Villa, Ridley Lane, Mawdesley, Ormskirk, Lancashire L40 3SX, tel 01704 821900). A grave costs £410 (incl. digging and any native British tree). The rights last 50 years. The 2.9 acre site is surrounded by fields and is located down a lane by a small country village. A stream runs between the boundary with the next field. A hawthorn hedge has been planted. They will accept home-made, cardboard or wicker coffins, or shrouds or body bags. Family and friends can dig or fill the grave if they wish. A4 size Yorkshire stone plaques, laid horizontally, are allowed. Burials of what are technically known as 'non-viable foetuses' are allowed. There is a group for relatives and friends, which discusses the future development of the site and acts as a support group. Peace Burials Ltd, who can also arrange inexpensive funerals nationwide (from £615 incl. disbursements), will sell coffins, from £60 for cardboard to £390 for wicker coffins (see the coffin section near the start of this chapter). They will collect the body from hospital for about £50 (£80 from London). 'A shire horse-drawn carriage will be available soon. A barn is available near the site for funeral services' (Mary Mallatratt). Member of the Association of Nature Reserve Burial Grounds. See also their other 'railway funeral' site in Alfreton, Derbyshire, below.

• **FD Sheffield**: B. C. Funeral Service, 51 Suffolk Road, Sheffield S2 4BX (tel 0114 276 0211). Parent company: Sheffield Co-operative Society. Cheapest fully-fitted coffin only: £110 (delivery locally £40, nationally 45p per mile). Cold storage only: Yes, £10 per day. Body transport only: Yes. Advice for d-i-y: Yes, £25 per hour or part-hour. Basic funeral: £350 (disbursements extra). 'We work within a 15 mile radius of the city centre at no extra charge' (M.R. Bratton). Prepaid plan: Funeral insurance with vouchers. Member of FSC, CFSA.

• **Cem Shipley**: Nab Wood Cemetery, Bingley Road, Shipley, Bradford BD18 4EW. Plot (100 years) incl. digging and burial £293. They will accept home-made, cardboard or wicker coffins, or shrouds or body bags. Length of funeral service: Open. Chapel: As crematorium below. Grounds: 'Maintained to a high standard.' 'Highly trained staff are committed to delivering a sensitive service to meet the needs of the service user' (David Congreve).

• **Crem Shipley**: Nab Wood Crematorium, Bingley Road, Shipley, Bradford BD18 4BG (tel 01274 584109). Price: £153. Time allotted: 30 minutes (extra time can be booked without charge). They will accept home-made, wicker or cardboard coffins, shrouds or body bags. Chapel: Non-denominational, converted Victorian chapel. Grounds: 'Well-maintained cemetery.' 'Low charges and caring, helpful staff' (David Congreve).

• **FD South Shields**: Mr Peter Kerrigan, Tynedale Funeral Services, Tynedale House, Stanhope Road, South Shields, Tyne and Wear NE33 4TB (tel 0191 4550904). Cheapest fully-fitted coffin only: £175 (delivery locally £10, nationally negotiable). Cold storage only: Yes, £10 per day. Body transport only: Yes (£40 one-off payment) Advice for d-i-y: Yes, £10 per hour. Basic funeral: £505 (disbursements extra). 'Full horse-drawn hearse from £400' (Peter Kerrigan). Prepaid plan: Golden Charter. Member of no association.

• **Crem Whitley Bay**: Whitley Bay Crematorium, Blyth Road, Whitley Bay, North Tyneside (tel 0191 200 5862). Price: £162. Time allotted: 30 minutes , extra time can be booked for an additional charge. They will accept home-made or cardboard coffins. Chapel: 'Converted church with very attractive domed ceiling. Removable cross.' Grounds: 'Mature cemetery, off a very attractive main drive lined with memorial seats.' 'Prices have not increased in the last 2 years' (Tracey Harrison).

• **Cem Winterton**: Winterton Cemetery, Cemetery Road, Winterton, North Lincolnshire (tel 01724 280289). (All correspondence to Woodlands Memorial Park address above). No Chapel. Grounds: 'Tranquil cemetery alongside farmland. A Garden of Remembrance for the scattering of cremated remains.' Memorials: Headstones, without kerbing, within size restrictions. All other details as for Cem Scunthorpe (1) above.

• **Cem York**: York Cemetery, The Gatehouse, Cemetery Road, York YO1 5AJ (tel 01904 610578 day, 01904 640949 evening). 'We will take any body container from body bag to home-made coffin, as long as it is all done with dignity.' Plot (99 years) costs £545 incl. digging. Maintenance: £18 per annum. Friends and relatives can dig and fill graves 'with our supervision for safety's sake'. A tree or bulbs can be planted at the request of relatives (with the cost varying, depending on the requirements). Chapel: A very fine Grade IIA listed classical chapel, prizewinning decoration, warm feel. Time for service: Up to one and a half hours if needed. Grounds: Formal, wild, wooded. Ecological management plan to encourage wildlife. Memorials should be large and Victorian in style. 'This is a Victorian park landscape gone wild. There are special butterfly and scented walks and there is a great deal of educational and informal recreational use of the area. We try to put customers' wishes first and empower them so that they can be in control of their funeral' (Bill Shaw, Warden).

• **Crem York**: City of York Crematorium, Bishopthorpe Road, York YO2 1QD (tel 01904 706096). Price: £221. Time allotted: 20 minutes (extra time can be booked for £50). They will accept home-made or cardboard coffins. Chapel: Built in 1962. Grounds: 'Parkland and trees with a small garden of remembrance' (Mr Milsted).

• **(Green Burial) Nr. York**: The Mowthorpe Independent Garden of Rest, c/o Robert Goodwill, Southwood Farm, Terrington, York YO6 4QB (tel 01653 648459, fax 01653 648225) is a two and a half acre site, adjacent to an existing cemetery, with lovely views over the Vale of York, in an Area of Outstanding Natural Beauty. A grave will cost about £450 per grave including a Compakta cardboard coffin (which are also for sale at £40). Planning permission was granted, but a second application was required and then refused by Ryedale District Council. An appeal will be decided, almost certainly in the site's favour, in May 1997. Member of the Association of Nature Reserve Burial Grounds.

Wales

Comprising Flintshire, Wrexham, Denbighshire, Aberconwy and Colwyn, Anglesey, Caernarfonshire and Merionethshire, Powys, Cardiganshire, Pembrokeshire, Carmarthenshire, Swansea, Neath and Port Talbot, Bridgend, Rhondda Cynon Taff, Vale of Glamorgan, Merthyr Tydfil, Caerphilly, Cardiff, Blaenau Gwent, Torfaen, Newport, Monmouthshire.

• **Crem Aberdare**: Llwydcoed Crematorium, Aberdare, Mid Glamorgan, CF44 0DJ (tel 01685 874115). Price: £126. Time allotted: 25 minutes within a forty minute period (extra time can be booked without charge). They will accept home-made, cardboard or wicker coffins, or shrouds or body bags. Chapels: 'The award-winning building fits particularly well into the rural landscape and is in sympathy with the vernacular architecture of the area. Capel Mair seats 120, Capel Tydfil 50.' Grounds: 'Landscaped with trees, shrubs and ornamental pools, and the gardens provide a haven for quiet contemplation in tranquil surroundings.' Llwyncoed stock both the Heaven on Earth and Ecology Peace coffins, and can supply the Compakta coffin to those organising cremations direct. 'We try to cater for all needs as far as possible' (Clive G. Lewis).

• **Crem Aberystwyth**: Amlosgfa Aberystwyth Crematorium, Fford Clarach, Aberystwyth, Cardiganshire SY23 3DG (tel 01970 626 942). Run by the Crematoria Investment Company. Price: £200. Time allotted: 45 minutes (extra time can be booked for £100). They will accept cardboard coffins. Chapel: 'Modern, with a large window overlooking Cynfelyn Valley. Seating can be flexible.' Grounds: 'A wooded hillside above the beautiful and peaceful Cynfelyn

Valley. The Garden of Remembrance is a rare orchid site, and the sea is visible from parts of the grounds.' 'We were recently complimented by the Welsh Language Board for offering a full bilingual service to the community. As well as protecting the rare plant species, we are developing the gardens into a place where trees and flowers can be planted as natural commemorations for the departed. A family open air memorial service is held every year in June and is very well-attended by bereaved families' (Cyril Breeze Evans).

• ✪✪✪ **FD Anglesey**: W. O. Williams, Tan Graig, Llanedwen, Anglesey, North Wales LL61 6PX (tel 01248 430312). Cheapest fully-fitted coffin only: £87-50, VAT extra (delivery locally £10). Cold storage only: Yes, £10 the first day, £5 per day thereafter. Body transport only: Yes. Advice for d-i-y: Yes (no price stated). Offers what it terms a 'D-i-y Funeral' for £287 (disbursements extra) where 'all the forms and certificates are collected and delivered by the client, there is no embalming included and the client provides own bearers (or pays extra). A fully fitted coffin is supplied and a hearse for up to 20 miles' (W. O. Williams). No prepaid plan. Member of no association.

• **(Green Burial) Carmarthen**: The West Wales Woodland Burial Trust, c/o Brian Kingzett, Carmarthenshire Environmental Centre, 3 Llys Ffynnon, Carmarthen, Wales SA31 1RQ (tel 01267 234684). 'Our intention is to create woodland burial sites as areas of quiet contemplation' (Brian Kingzett). Provisional members of the Association of Nature Reserve Burial Grounds.

• **Crem Cardiff**: City of Cardiff Crematorium, Thornhill Road, Llanishen, Cardiff CF4 5LA (tel 01222 623294). Price: £190-75 (non-residents £316-50). Time allotted: 30 minutes (extra time can be booked for £25 per 30 minutes with organist). They will accept home-made, cardboard or wicker coffins, or shrouds or body bags. Chapels: 'Modern, Portland stone building with wonderful organ.' Grounds: 'Formal gardens, informal woods.' 'We make every effort to meet the bereaved to ensure they are fully advised rather than relying on the funeral director's "advice" ' (Brendan Day).

• **FD Cardiff**: A local authority funeral service for Cardiff residents is provided by the firm D. Caesar Jones, 55 Pantbach Road, Rhiwbina, Cardiff (tel 01222 522 644), who charges £485, excluding disbursements. Add to this the crematorium fee of £190-75 and the doctors' fee of £69. Burial costs £251.

• **Green Burial Cardiff**: Woodland burial ground, Thornhill Cemetery, Thornhill Road, Llanishen, Cardiff CF4 5LA (run by Cardiff County Council, tel 01222 623294). The woodland burial ground is on the perimeter of the cemetery, overlooked by Wenault mountain, and looking down over Cardiff Bay. The site has mature oaks. A grave costs £238 (incl. the digging and tree, £138 extra for non-residents). They will accept home-made, cardboard or wicker coffins, or shrouds or body bags. They sell a cardboard coffin for £40. Families and friends can fill in the grave if they wish. 'It is an excellent site, simply the best' (Brendan Day).

• **Green Burial Lampeter**: Informally, burial may be possible on farmland near Lampeter, Dyfed – contact the owner of the land, Elizabeth Russell, or sons John and Henry, c/o Sheila Harkness, 5 Courtnell Street, London W2 5BU (tel 0171

221 9320 or 01570 470891). The two sites that are possible are Hafod, Bwlchllan or Lletty Rhys, Felinfach. Any form of 'low end-impact' body container is acceptable, and people do not have to use funeral directors, but 'everything must be organised by the person seeking the space'. If people wish to have a memorial, the suggestion is that it be 'a stone in its natural state with a smallish part of its surface polished to take the name and message'. 'This could be ideal for green people in the area,' writes Elizabeth Russell, 'Hafod is a beautiful bosky place with rare species. Lletty Rhys is further from the road and higher up. There is a Site of Special Scientific Interest at Hafod. Both farms are organic and do not use pesticides and are mainly for rough grazing. It is fairly awkward terrain to traverse; full of curlews, owls, kites, etc. I offer the space free to those prepared to carry out the operation themselves and to plant the site with a tree and flowers. It would be a good idea for people who take me up on this offer of free space to involve themselves in Hafod's future. I do want to be consulted as to sites' (Elizabeth Russell).

• **FD Merthyr Tydfil**: Raymond Iles and Sons, Glan Yr Afon, Cefn Coed, Merthyr Tydfil, Mid-Glamorgan, Wales (tel 01685 384538). Cheapest fully-fitted coffin only: £143; cardboard coffin £97 (delivery locally £10; nationally £10 per hour plus 39p per mile). Cold storage only: do not have this. Body transport only: Yes, £60 for the hearse. Advice for d-i-y: Yes, £10 per hour. Basic funeral: £700 (including disbursements). 'Privately owned, good service, flexible with the newest fleet of vehicles' (Carwyn R. Iles). Prepaid plan: Golden Charter. Member of no association.

• **Cem Mold**: Mold Public Cemetery, Alexandra Road, Mold, Flintshire, Wales CH7 1HJ (tel 01352 753820). Plot incl. digging and burial £120-50 (minister's fee £5 extra). No time limit for the service. No chapel. Grounds: this is the town cemetery with flower borders and trees, surrounded by a football field and playing ground. Memorials: to be made of stone with reverent wording. Friendly management. 'Family mourners often lower the coffin' (Arfon Llyod Williams-Cooke).

• **Crem Narberth**: Parc Gwyn Crematorium, Narberth, Pembrokeshire SA6Y 8UD (tel 01834 860622). Price: £130 incl. organists' fee (non-residents £165). Time allotted: 20 minutes (extra time can be booked without charge). They will accept body bags. Chapel: 1960s, removable cross. Grounds: 'Beautifully laid out with trees, borders, etc in seven and a half acres of gently rolling country-side.' 'A friendly service in accordance with the wishes of the bereaved' (Revd. Elwyn J. John).

• **FD Newport:** Belmont Funerals (part of Green Undertakings), Pillmawr Road, Newport, Wales NP9 6WF (tel 01633 855350). See Green Undertakings in Watchet in the South West region below for details.

• **Crem Port Talbot**: Margam Crematorium, Longlands Lane, Margam, Port Talbot, Neath and Port Talbot SA13 2PP (tel 01639 883570). Price: £100 (non-residents £133). Time allotted: 30 minutes (extra time can be booked for £13). They will accept cardboard coffins. Chapel: Face-the-front seating. Grounds: 'Natural woodland' (D. Hywel Selway).

• **Green Burial St Asaph**: 'Y Llwyn' Cemetery, Mount Road, St Asaph (contact Mrs Sylvia Jones, Denbighshire County Council, Fforddlas Depot, Rhyl, Denbighshire LL18 2EL, tel 01824 706455). A grave costs £270 (incl. digging, tree and wildlife seeds; double for non-residents). 'They will accept only biodegradable coffins – cardboard, home-made or from a funeral director.' The woodland burial ground is the bottom section of an existing graveyard that is 'very rustic, natural and peaceful'.

West Midlands

Comprising Shropshire, Staffordshire, Wolverhampton, Walsall, Dudley, Sandwell, Birmingham, Solihull, Coventry, Hereford and Worcester, Gloucestershire.

• **Cem Burton-upon-Trent**: Stapenhill Cemetery, 38, Stapenhill Road, Burton-upon-Trent, Staffordshire DE15 9AE (tel 01283 508572). Plot (50 years) incl. digging and burial £125. They will accept home-made, cardboard or wicker coffins, or body bags or shrouds. Length of funeral service: 30 minutes (extra time can be booked without charge). Chapel: Victorian, well-maintained. Grounds: 'Attractive Victorian cemetery rich in wildlife, overlooking flood plain of River Trent.' Memorials: Within size restrictions. 'We have a children's burial area and a "forget-me-not" garden' (Nick French).

• **Crem Burton-upon-Trent**: Bretby Crematorium, Geary Lane, Bretby, near Burton-upon-Trent, Staffordshire DE15 OQE (tel 01283 221505). Price: £155. Time allotted: 30 minutes (extra time can be booked for £50). They will accept home-made, cardboard or wicker coffins, or shrouds or body bags. Chapels: 'Two chapels, seating 80 and 18 respectively, in a natural and uplifting style using Columbian pine and Welsh slate.' Grounds: 'Maintained as a natural woodland and set in open countryside.' 'The crematorium can supply 2 types of cardboard coffin and has a positive attitude to informing the public of the choices that are open to them. Awarded the Civic Trust Award in 1978' (Nick French).

• **Green Burial Burton-upon-Trent:** Woodland burial, Stapenhill Cemetery, 38 Stapenhill Road, Burton-upon-Trent, Staffordshire DE15 9AE (tel 01283 508572). Run by the East Staffordshire Borough Council. A grave costs £265 (incl. digging and tree and bulbs; double for non-residents). They will accept home-made, cardboard or wicker coffins, or shrouds or body bags. They sell the Compakta cardboard coffin for £70. Family and friends may dig and fill the grave. A grave space must be bought if cremated remains are to be buried. 'The woodland burial area is situated on a hillside overlooking the cemetery, above the flood plain of the River Trent. It has been planted with bulbs, wild flowers and a variety of native trees – including ash, oak, cherry, hazel and birch' (Nick French).

• ✿✿✿ **FD Cheltenham**: Beechwood Funeral Services, 66 Albion Street, Cheltenham, Gloucestershire GL52 2RW (tel 01242 228208; also 01452 722131). Cheapest fully-fitted coffin only: £55 (delivery locally £10, nationally negotiable). Cold storage only: Yes, £10 per day. Body transport only: Yes. Advice for d-i-y: Yes, £10 per hour. Basic funeral: £650 (incl. crematorium and chapel). 'Family business, happy to give concessions where needed' (Peter Kerrigan). Prepaid plan: Golden Charter. Member of no association.

• **Cem Coventry**: Canley Cemetery, Cemeteries and Crematorium Office, Cannon Hill Road, Canley, Coventry CV4 7DF (tel 01203 415886 or 418055). Plot (75 years) incl. digging and burial £422. Maintenance: No charge. They will accept home-made or cardboard coffins, and will consider wicker coffins, or body bags or shrouds. Length of funeral service: No limit at graveside. Chapels: As Crematorium below. 'A modern lawn-type layout with Garden of Rest and pond' (Allan Charlsworth).

• **Cem Coventry**: London Road Cemetery, London Road, Whitley, Coventry. 'Designed by Sir Joseph Paxton and opened in 1847. 43 acres of landscaped park with many interesting features' (Allan Charlsworth). All other details as for Coventry Canley Cemetery above.

• **Cem (Green Burial) Coventry**: Renton Lane Cemetery and Nature Reserve, Renton Lane, Walsgrave, Coventry. 'A new cemetery opened in 1994 includes among other things a Woodland Burial area. The cost of a grave, which includes digging and a (Westminster) biodegradable coffin is available on request from the main office' (Allan Charlsworth). All other details as for Coventry Canley Cemetery above.

• **Cem Coventry**: St. Paul's Cemetery, Holbrooks Lane, Coventry. 'Traditional cemetery set in the industrial North of the city' (Allan Charlsworth). All other details as for Coventry Canley Cemetery above.

• **Cem Coventry**: Windmill Road Cemetery, Windmill Road, Foleshall, Coventry. 'A small cemetery serving local people in that part of the city' (Allan Charlsworth). All other details as for Coventry Canley Cemetery above.

• **Cem Coventry**: Walsgrave Cemetery, Woodway Lane, Coventry. 'Small cemetery on outskirts of the city' (Allan Charlsworth). All other details as for Coventry Canley Cemetery above.

• **Crem Coventry**: Canley Crematorium, Cannon Hill Road, Canley, Coventry CV4 7DF (tel 01203 418055 or 415886). Price: No details given. Time allotted: 45 minutes (extra time can be booked without charge). They will accept home-made, wicker or cardboard coffins, or shrouds. Chapel: 'Recently modernised to provide second chapel.' Grounds: 'Three acres of Gardens of Remembrance, with rose gardens, pond, seasonal lawns and English woodland.' 'A flexible interpretation of rules and codes is always applied' (G. P. Marshall).

• **FD Coventry**: Henry Ison & Sons (Coventry) Ltd, 76-78 Binley Road, Stoke, Coventry CV3 1FQ (tel 01203 458665). Cheapest fully-fitted coffin only: £135 (delivery locally free). Cold storage only: Yes, £25 per day. Body transport only: Yes. Advice for d-i-y: Yes, £65 per hour. Basic funeral: £540 (disbursements extra). 'A Christian firm offering the highest standards' (B. Powell). Prepaid plan: Golden Charter. Member of SAIF, NAFD.

• **Cem Dudley**: Gornal Wood Cemetery, Chase Road, Gornal Wood, Dudley DY3 2RL (tel 01384 813970). Also administers cemeteries at Stourbridge, Hales Owen, Cradley, Lye and Wolescote, Brierley Hill and Dudley. Plot (75

years) incl. digging and burial £572 (double to non-residents). They will accept home-made or cardboard coffins. Length of funeral service: 30 minutes (extra time can be booked for £42). Chapel: Modern, light and airy. Grounds: 'Landscaped setting.' Memorials: Only restrictions as regards health and safety. 'Helpful staff' (David Robinson).
• **Crem Dudley**: Gornal Wood Crematorium, Chase Road, Gornal Wood, Dudley DY3 2RL (tel 01384 813970). Price: £192. Time allotted: 20 minutes at half-hourly intervals (extra time can be booked without charge). They will accept home-made or cardboard coffins. Chapel: Modern, light and airy. Grounds: 'Pleasant and spacious landscaped setting; helpful staff' (David Robinson).
• **(Green Burial) Dudley**: A woodland burial ground planned for 1997 at Gornal Wood Cemetery, Chase Road, Gornal Wood, Dudley DY3 2RL (tel 01384 813970) and run by Dudley Metropolitan Borough Council. The site, with space for several hundred graves, is adjacent to an existing copse of hawthorn and birch trees. A grave will probably cost slightly less than for their regular cemetery (see above) and with less financial penalty for non-residents. They will accept home-made or cardboard coffins. Family and friends will be allowed to help fill the grave. (David Robinson).
• **FD Dursley**: L. W. Clutterbuck, 24/26 High Street, Cam, Dursley, Gloucester-shire (tel 01453 542754). Cheapest fully-fitted coffin only: £115, VAT extra (delivery locally £13-60, VAT extra, nationally £13-60 per hour, VAT extra, for the driver, plus 31p per mile). Cold storage only: Yes, £4-99 per day. Body transport only: Yes. Advice for d-i-y: Yes, £13-60 per hour. Basic funeral: 'funerals are not sold as packages; we start with nought and build up.' 'Family, caring service' (K. L. Clutterbuck). Prepaid plan: Golden Charter. Member of no association.
• **Crem Newcastle-under-Lyme**: Bradwell Crematorium, Chatterley Close, Bradwell, Newcastle-under-Lyme, Staffordshire ST5 8LE (tel 01782 635498). Price: £188. Time allotted: 30 minutes (extra time can be booked without charge). They will accept home-made, cardboard or wicker coffins. Chapel: Multi-denominational, timber-clad. Grounds: '13 acres of themed gardens with a multitude of memorial trees and shrubs' (Mr S. P. Wells).
• **Crem Redditch**: Redditch Crematorium, Bordesley Lane, Redditch, Hereford and Worcester B97 5AS (tel 01527 62174). Price: £165. Time allotted: 30 minutes, extra time can be booked for £42. They will accept home-made, wicker or cardboard coffins, shrouds or body bags. Chapel: Timber and slate, without religious symbols except a cross on the descending catafalque. Grounds: 'Spacious, naturally-designed gardens in rolling Worcestershire countryside.' 'Our aim is to say "yes" to mourners' needs' (Ken Elliott).
• **Crem Shrewsbury**: Emstrey Crematorium, London Road, Shrewsbury, Shropshire SY2 6PS (tel 01743 359883). Price: £150. Time allotted: 40 minutes (extra time can be booked for £150). They will accept home-made, cardboard or wicker coffins, or shrouds or body bags, subject to FBCA conditions. Chapel: Modern, church-like. Grounds: 'A quiet restful atmosphere with private formal

gardens set in open countryside.' 'The Chapel of Remembrance contains an 'on-screen' memorial cabinet where personalised memorials including photographs and drawings can be viewed' (Mrs E.A. Seabury).

• **Crem Stoke-on-Trent**: Carmountside Crematorium, Leek Road, Milton, Stoke-on-Trent, Staffordshire ST2 7AB (run by Karen Deaville for Stoke-on-Trent City Council, tel 01782 533911). Price: £200. Time allotted: 30 minutes (extra time can be booked for £42-50). They will accept home-made or cardboard coffins. Chapel: Old listed building. Grounds: Varied gardens including some woodland. The crematorium has a new viewing room where up to 12 people can have a sideways view of the coffin entering the cremator.

• **Crem Stourbridge**: Stourbridge Crematorium, South Road, Stourbridge, West Midlands DY8 3RQ (tel 01384 813985). Price: £192. Time allotted: 20 minutes at half-hourly intervals, extra time can be booked without charge. They will accept home-made or cardboard coffins. Chapel: A converted cemetery chapel with a church-like atmosphere. Grounds: 'A pleasant, mature, traditional cemetery landscape' (David Robinson).

• **Green Burial Stroud**: For locals only. Brimscombe woodland burial area, a difficult-to-reach part of a regular cemetery, with no seat to rest on at the top: 'I have never carried a coffin as far under such difficult conditions,' reports one funeral director. It is expensive at £1080 a grave. They will accept cardboard or biodegradable coffins or shrouds, but not chipboard coffins. The site is on a hillside with views across the valley. For those who lived or were born in the area. Contact George Damsell, Stroud District Council, Ebley Mill, Stroud, Glos GL5 4UB (tel 01453 754425).

• **FD Stroud**: Lansdown Funeral Service Ltd, 64 Slad Road, Stroud, Gloucestershire GL5 1QU (tel 01453 762276). Cheapest fully-fitted coffin only: £120, VAT extra (delivery locally £10). Cold storage only: Yes, £50 per week, £50 minimum. Body transport only: Yes (private ambulance £50; hearse – driver only – £104). Advice for d-i-y: Yes, free. Basic funeral: £615 (disbursements extra). 'We are independent and family-owned. Our prices are on a menu basis. We have a 25 seat private chapel' (J. J. Baker). Prepaid plan: Golden Charter. Member of NAFD and SAIF.

• **Crem Walsall**: Streetly Crematorium, Little Hardwick Road, Aldridge, Walsall WS9 0SG (tel 0121 353 7228). Price: £137. Time allotted: 30 minutes (extra time can be booked for £29). They will accept home-made, cardboard or wicker coffins and body bags. Chapel: 'There are two chapels, with interiors in hand-finished straw coloured brickwork and a high, sloping cedar ceiling. Suitable for small or large non-denominational gatherings.' Grounds: 'A 27 acre site in the greenfield fringe to the East of the borough in a pleasant, rural environment well separated from residential development'. 'A friendly, flexible and helpful service to all' (Steve Billings).

• **Crem Wolverhampton**: Bushbury Crematorium, Underhill Lane, Bushbury, Wolverhampton (tel 01902 314992 or 314995). Price: £160. Time allotted: 30 minutes (extra time can be booked for £40). They will accept home-made, cardboard or wicker coffins. Chapels: Modern design. In West Chapel coffin lowers, in East Chapel curtain draws across. Grounds: '40 acre site with planted flower borders, and a wooded area for placing cremated remains.' 'Two chapels allow the family to choose the way the coffin is committed, and the East Chapel allows for a more intimate service' (Clare Yardley).

• **Crem Worcester**: Worcester Crematorium, Tintern Avenue, Astwood Road, Worcester WR3 8HA (tel 01905 22633). Price: £180. Time allotted: 30 minutes (no charge for extra time – 'a double service is available if we are not busy'). They will accept home-made, cardboard or wicker coffins. A leaflet is provided for 'd-i-y' families. Chapel: 1960s building with a conventional layout. Grounds: Attractive lawns and borders with a stream running though. The Garden of Remembrance is adjacent to the old cemetery with its many fine old established trees. 'We will deal with any requests that do not adversely affect other users' (David Seaman).

• **Green Burial Worcester**: A wildflower meadow green burial ground at Astwood Cemetery, Tintern Avenue, Worcester WR3 8HA (run by City of Worcester Council, tel 01905 22633). A grave costs £335 (incl. digging, memorial inscription and planting 'in accordance with development plan'). They will accept home-made, cardboard or wicker coffins. A stepping stone in the grass pathway with an inscription on it costs £137 or there can be a free two line inscription in the nearby crematorium's Book of Remembrance. Bird and bat boxes have been put up. Family and friends can fill the grave if they wish and can help in a token way with the digging. 'The site is a wildlife area surrounded by hedges in an old part of the cemetery, with lots of very large established trees nearby' (David Seaman).

East Midlands

Comprising Derbyshire, Nottinghamshire, Leicestershire, Warwickshire, Northamptonshire, Bedfordshire, Oxfordshire, Buckinghamshire.

• **Green Burial Alfreton**: Golden Valley Burial Ground, Riddings, Alfreton, Derbyshire (run by Peace Burials Ltd near Sheffield, tel 01704 821900). A grave costs £275 (digging £135 extra, unless families do their own digging). Transportation of coffin and funeral party can be by steam train to the track-side cemetery (from the Midland Railway Centre at Ripley in Derbyshire). The funeral would then cost from £800. Meals (from £3-50 per head) and music bands (from £100) are available on the train. There is a tin tabernacle chapel that can be used (for £60) beside the line. The one acre burial ground can only be reached either by this train or through the Golden Valley Country Park. 'A lovely secluded setting' (Mary Mallatratt). Other arrangements as for the South Yorkshire Woodland Burial Ground (see above).

• **Crem Amersham**: Chilterns Crematorium, Whielden Lane, Amersham, Buckinghamshire HP7 0ND (tel 01494 724263). Price: £140. Time allotted: 30 minutes. They will accept home-made or cardboard coffins, and will consider other body containers if they can be inspected in advance. Chapel: 1960s brick-built with copper roof. Grounds: 'A natural woodland setting in open countryside on the edge of the Chiltern Hills'. 'Willing to consider every reasonable request on its merits' (Charles Howlett).

• **FD Amersham**: H. C. Grimstead Ltd, 10 Hill Avenue, Amersham, Buckinghamshire HP6 5BG (tel 01494 434393). They offer a cheap basic funeral for £395, disbursements extra – their 'Green Funeral Option' with a cardboard coffin. See Grimstead in the London region, below, for details.

• **FD Banbury**: Trinder Funeral Service, a branch of Lodge Bros., at 122 Middleton Road, Banbury, Oxfordshire OX16 8QU (tel 01295 272207). See Lodge Bros. in the London region, below, for details.

• **FD Beaconsfield**: H. C. Grimstead Ltd, Tilbury House, Shepherds Lane, Beaconsfield, Buckinghamshire HP9 2DU (tel 01494 672668). They offer a cheap basic funeral for £395 (disbursements extra) – their 'Green Funeral Option' with a cardboard coffin. See Grimstead in the London region, below, for details.

• **Cem Bedford**: Norse Road Cemetery, 104 Norse Road, Bedford, Bedfordshire (tel 01234 353701). Plot (75 years) incl. digging and burial £238. They will accept home-made, cardboard or wicker coffins, or body bags or shrouds. Length of funeral service: 45 minutes (extra time can be booked for £20). Chapel: Modern, secular. Grounds: Modern, heavily wooded. Memorials: Lawn-type back to back. 'Well-kept' (Michael Day).

• **Crem Bedford**: Bedford Crematorium, Cemetery Complex, 104 Norse Road, Bedford, Bedfordshire (tel 01234 353701). Price: £175 (£194 non-residents). Time allotted: 45 minutes (extra time can be booked without charge). They will accept home-made, cardboard or wicker coffins, shrouds or body bags. Chapel: Modern, with wall-hangings and oak seating. Grounds: 'Designed for ease of access and egress.' 'Each funeral an individual experience' (Mr Michael Day).

• **FD Bicester**: L. Hartness, a branch of Lodge Bros., at 11 Victoria Road, Bicester, Oxfordshire OX6 7QD (tel 01869 253282). See Lodge Bros. in the London region, below, for details.

• **FD Biggleswade**: Woodman & Son, a branch of Lodge Bros., at 3 Market Square, Biggleswade, Bedfordshire SG18 8AP (tel 01767 315700). See Lodge Bros. in the London region, below, for details.

• **FD Brackley**: W. J. Franklin & Son, 30 High Street, Brackley, Northants NN13 5DS (tel 01280 702356). See Lodge Bros. in the London region, below, for details.

• **Crem Bramcote**: Bramcote Crematorium, Coventry Lane, Bramcote, Nottingham NG9 3GJ (tel 0115 9221837). Price: £130. Time allotted: 20 minutes (extra time can be booked for £130). They will accept home-made or cardboard coffins. Chapel: Modern, with large window giving view of small enclosed garden. Grounds: 'Parkland with lots of trees, seats and walks with no plaques as well as immaculate gardens.' 'We aim to make each service very personal, and keep costs low to help families' (Mrs Janet Weatherall).

• **Green Burial Buxton**: Green burial ground created by the High Peak Borough Council within their cemetery (contact Mrs Elvidge or Tony Robinson, Environmental Health, Town Hall, Buxton, Derbyshire SK17 6EL, tel 01298 28459). The grave costs £246 (incl. burial).

• **Crem Chesterfield**: Chesterfield and District Crematorium, Chesterfield Road, Brimington, Chesterfield, Derbyshire S43 1AU (tel 01246 345888). Price: £120 (non-residents £180). Time allotted: 20 minutes within 30 minute period (no extra time bookable). They will accept home-made coffins. Chapel: Non-denominational, built 1959, with church-like pews. Grounds: 'A pleasant memorialised garden with established trees, shrubs and roses' (John David Eggleshaw).

• **FD Nr. Gerrards Cross**: H. C. Grimstead Ltd, Churchfield Lodge, Churchfield Road, Chalfont St Peter, near Gerrards Cross, Buckinghamshire SL9 9EW (tel 01753 891200). They offer a cheap basic funeral for £395 (disbursements extra) – their 'Green Funeral Option' with a cardboard coffin. See Grimstead in the London region, below, for details.

• **Green Burial Gerrards Cross**: Parkside woodland burial ground, Parkside Cemetery, Windsor Road, Gerrards Cross, Buckinghamshire SL9 8SS (tel 01753 662426; run by the South Bucks District Council, Environmental Services). Cost of plot and burial fee £128-70 (double for non-residents) (a digging fee has to be arranged with private contractors, such as Mr Hepburn on 0850 650 036; a tree costs £40). They will accept home-made, cardboard or wicker coffins, or shrouds or body bags. Families and friends can fill the grave if they wish and can help with a token amount of digging. A small wooden plaque at the bottom of the tree would be possible, if arranged by the family. The site is an extension of the existing cemetery, with a field beyond with ponies, and woodland behind the field. 'We allow certain areas of long grass to encourage invertebrates and we are not too tough on brambles and nettles. Our prices are very reasonable for this area. The M4 and M40 are readily accessible' (Mr C. Merchant).

• **FD High Wycombe**: G. Smith Ltd, 7 The Green, Woburn Green, High Wycombe HP10 0EE (tel 01628 523566). Cheapest fully-fitted coffin only: £195 (delivery locally free; nationally courier rates). Body transport only: Yes, £90 per vehicle. Advice for d-i-y: Yes, token fee. Basic funeral: £450 (disbursements extra). 'As long as it is legal we will try to fulfil the family's wishes' (Ron Allen, Manager). Prepaid plan: Dignity Plan. Parent company SCI-UK. Member of NAFD.

• **Green Burial Hope:** Green burial ground created by the High Peak Borough Council within their cemetery in Hope, Derbyshire. See Green Burial Buxton above for contact details.

• **Crem Kettering**: Kettering Crematorium, East Lodge, Rothwell Road, Kettering, Northamptonshire NN16 8XE (tel 01536 534218). Price: £162 (non-residents £187). Time allotted: 45 minutes (extra time can be booked for £25). They will accept home-made, cardboard or wicker coffins, or shrouds. Chapel: One modern, non-denominational, the other church-like. Grounds: 'Pleasant gardens with mature woodland areas.' 'Advice and assistance to those wanting more involvement with funeral arrangements is freely given - funerals are viewed as the families', not ours. We are in the early stages of establishing a woodland burial ground' (Alan C. Brook).

• **Crem Leamington Spa**: Mid-Warwickshire Crematorium, Oakley Wood, Bishops Tachbrook, Leamington Spa, Warwickshire CV33 9QP (tel 01926 651 418). Price: £128 (£148 non-residents). Time allotted: 30 minutes (extra time can be booked for £18 per 30 minutes). They will accept home-made, cardboard or wicker coffins, or shrouds or body bags. Chapels: Modern. The North Chapel seats 20 people; the South Chapel seats 80 and has an organ. Grounds: Informal woodland. 'Our crematorium must be one of the most flexible and helpful crematoria in the UK. The atmosphere is extremely peaceful and the woodland is home to many forms of wildlife. We do not have memorials and there is no commercialism' (D. W. Thompson). Winner of the 1993 Natural Death Handbook Best Crematorium Award.

• **Crem Leicester**: Gilroes Crematorium, Gilroes Cemetery, Groby Road, Leicester, Leicestershire LE3 9QG (tel 0116 287 2292). Price: £176 (£186 non-residents). Time allotted: 30 minutes (extra time can be booked without charge). They will accept home-made, cardboard or wicker coffins. Chapel: Traditional, Gothic-cum-Tudor, with large Assembly Hall attached. Grounds: In the middle of a cemetery. 'As well as the architecture, the Assembly Hall is a distinguishing feature of particular interest to Hindu, Sikh and Jain families' (John Dooher).

• **Cem Luton**: Luton Church Cemetery, 26 Crawley Green, Luton, Bedfordshire (tel 01582 22874). Plot (99 years) incl. digging and burial £267. Maintenance: £51 p.a. They will accept home-made, cardboard or wicker coffins, or shrouds or body bags. Length of funeral service: No time limit, given four days' notice. Chapel: 'Private, small and functional.' Grounds: Wooded hillside overlooking Luton. Memorials: No restrictions. 'Understanding and helpful staff' (Ian Williamson).

• **Crem Luton**: Luton Crematorium, The Vale, Butterfield Green Road, Stopsley, Luton, Bedforshire LU2 8DD (tel 01582 23700 or 30761). Price: £150 (non-residents £160). Time allotted: 30 minutes (extra time £150). They will accept home-made or cardboard coffins. Chapel: Modern and functional. Grounds: 'Pleasant.' 'Semi-rural setting. Helpful staff' (N. Schonewald).

• **Green Burial Mappleborough Green**: Wildlife churchyard, Mappleborough Green, Warwickshire (contact Revd. Richard Deimel, The Vicarage, 3 Manor Mews, Studley, Warwickshire B80 7NA, tel 01527 85 28 30). This site can accept burials now, although it will officially open later in 1997 once the thistles have been attended to. Situated 15 miles from Birmingham, with views out onto undulating farmland, and adjoining a Victorian church and churchyard, it is planned as a five acre meadow with trees. They will accept most kinds of biodegradable body container. A grave costs £153 (non-residents £353). Families can either do their own digging and filling of the grave or pay a local digger between about £30 and £50. Families can also provide a tree, although there will be a tree planting plan, rather than a tree for each grave.

• **Green Burial New Mills:** Green burial ground created by the High Peak Borough Council within their cemetery in Thornsett, near New Mills, Derbyshire. See Green Burial Buxton above for contact details.

• **FD New Mills**: Jeremy Unsworth Funeral Service, 67 Church Road, New Mills, High Peak, Derbyshire (tel 01663 742772). Cheapest fully-fitted coffin only: £180 (delivery locally free). Cold storage only: No. Body transport only: Yes. Advice for d-i-y: No. Basic funeral: £500 (disbursements extra). 'We are here to please' (Jeremy Unsworth). Prepaid plan: Golden Charter. Member of SAIF.

• **Cem Oxford**: Wolvercote Cemetery, Banbury Road, Oxford OX2 8EE (tel 01865 513962). Administers branch cemeteries at Headington, Rosehill, and Botley, of similar design and with same pricing and practice. Plot (75 years) incl. digging and burial £335. Maintenance: £35 p.a.. They will accept home-made or cardboard coffins. Length of funeral service: 30 minutes (extra time can be booked for £25). Chapel: Victorian, with fully-equipped organ. Grounds: Late Victorian; wide variety of trees. Memorials: No kerbs. 'Service to the public is paramount' (H. P. Dawson).

• **Green Burial Oxford:** Hugh Dawson, Cemetery Manager, Wolvercote Cemetery, Banbury Road, Oxford OX2 8EE (tel 01865 513962). Woodland burial plots are located at three cemeteries in Oxford: Wolvercote (a corner of the cemetery on the boundary with the recreation ground and sports ground); Headington Cemetery (Dunston Road); and Botley Cemetery (North Hinksey Lane). A grave costs £335 (tree £50 extra; bulbs £25; double for non-residents). They will accept home-made or cardboard coffins. Trees are planted between October and May, and relatives can help, choosing between a whitebeam, silver birch, hazel, field maple or wild service tree. Individual trees are guaranteed for a 20 year period and if a tree is lost during that period it will be replaced free of charge. Beyond that period some coppicing and thinning will be required. In addition, a maximum of 100 wildflowers may be planted from a selection of bluebells, snowdrops, wood anemones or wood violets. Relatives may also sponsor a seat with plaque.

• **Green Burial Retford:** Woodland burial ground, North Road, Retford, Nottinghamshire (enquiries to Cyril Blackshaw, Bassetlaw District Council, Grove House, 27 Grove St, Retford, Nottinghamshire DN22 6JP, tel 01777 713487). Opened in 1997. A grave costs about £200 including the digging and a tree (non-residents 50% extra). They will accept home-made, cardboard or wicker coffins, or shrouds or body bags. The site is within an old cemetery which resembles a country park, and contains established trees. There are boats passing up and down the Chesterfield canal and it could probably be arranged for a coffin to be delivered by boat. The grave area is deep enough for single graves without disturbing any remains that may still be there (the last burial was at least 100 years ago).

• ✪✪✪ **Green Burial Rugby:** Greenhaven Woodland Burial Ground at New Clarks Farm, run by Christine Atkin and Nicholas Hargreaves of Yelvertoft Road, Lilbourne, Rugby, Warwickshire CV23 0SZ (tel 01788 860604). The grave costs £200 (family and friends can dig the grave or it costs £75 extra if dug for you). They will accept home-made, cardboard or wicker coffins, or shrouds or body bags. They sell the Westminster Brighton cardboard coffin for £54 or the Peace Box one for £104. They will collect the body at a cost of 70p a mile (eg about £70 for London collections) with a driver's assistant £40 extra. Wooden plaques are allowed as memorials. 'The site is situated in an elevated position with good views (incl. the A14). It is typical Northamptonshire countryside, at present with not many trees, but lots of old hedges dotted with ash trees, and a pond. All our trees are grown from seed from local trees. Wildflower seeds and bulbs are also planted. Clients' pre-payments are safeguarded as they have a legal deed to their plots and other moneys are kept in a separate clients' account. It is a family-run site, very relaxed, with very reasonable prices and very centrally placed' (Christine Atkin). John Bradfield comments that this site 'puts people and wildlife first and is setting the standards by which to judge other schemes'. Member of the Association of Nature Reserve Burial Grounds.

• **FD Rushden**: A. Abbott & Sons (Rushden) Ltd, Bedford Road, Rushden, Northamptonshire NN10 0LZ (tel 01933 312142 or 410365). Cheapest fully-fitted coffin only: £200 (delivery locally £25; nationally by mileage). Cold storage only: Yes, price negotiable. Body transport only: Yes, £70. Advice for d-i-y: Yes, fee negotiable. Basic funeral: £790 (disbursements extra). 'Family owned and operated. Full bespoke service' (M. Abott). Prepaid plan: Golden Charter. Member of NAFD & SAIF.

• ✪✪✪ **FD Uppingham**: E. M. Dorman, 10 Main Street, Bisbrooke, Uppingham, Rutland LE15 9EP (tel 01572 823976). Cheapest fully-fitted coffin only: £55 (delivery locally 'at a negotiable price'). Cold storage only: Yes, £11 per day. Body transport only: Yes. Advice for d-i-y: Yes, £12 per hour. Basic funeral: £480 (disbursements extra). 'As a small family-owned funeral director, all arrangements are carried out by me' (E. M. Dorman). Prepaid plan: Golden Charter. Member of NAFD.

• **FD Winslow**: Heritage & Sons, 63 High Street, Winslow, Buckinghamshire MK18 3DG (tel 01296 713341). Cheapest fully-fitted coffin only: £140 (delivery locally £25; nationally by carrier depending on distance, with a £45 hessian wrapping). Cold storage only: Yes, £20 per day. Body transport only: Yes, £1.10 per mile. Advice for d-i-y: Yes, £30 to cover home visit. Basic funeral: £428 (disbursements extra). 'Quality funerals at reasonable prices, plus our own flexible funeral plan' (E. M. Dorman). Prepaid plan: Our own Heritage & Sons Plan. Member of NAFD.

• **Green Burial Worksop:** Hannah Park woodland burial ground, Netherton Road, Worksop, Nottinghamshire (enquiries to Cyril Blackshaw, Bassetlaw District Council, Grove House, 27 Grove St, Retford, Nottinghamshire DN22 6JP, tel 01777 713487). Opened in 1997. A grave costs about £200 including the digging and a tree (non-residents 50% extra). They will accept home-made, cardboard or wicker coffins, or shrouds or body bags. The entrance is through a natural copse, opening up into an eight acre cemetery with panoramic views of the town. The site borders the ancient Hannah Park Wood, and will help to extend it.

East Anglia

Comprising Norfolk, Suffolk, Essex, Cambridgeshire and Hertfordshire.

• **Crem Bury St. Edmunds**: West Suffolk Crematorium, Near Risby, Bury St. Edmunds, Suffolk IP28 6RR (tel 01284 755118). Run by Crematoria Management Ltd. Price: £205. Time allotted: 45 minutes between services. They will accept home-made or cardboard coffins. Chapel: Design based on old Suffolk barn. Grounds: 'Peaceful rural setting.' 'A small staff work as a team, united to help the funeral directors and bereaved' (Royna Brunskill).

• **Cem (Green Burial) Cambridge**: Cambridge City Cemetery, Newmarket Road, Cambridge (tel 01954 780681). Plot (50 years) incl. digging and burial £450. Maintenance: £35-25. They will accept home-made, cardboard or wicker coffins, or shrouds or body bags. Length of funeral service: No set limit. Chapel: Traditional, church-like. Grounds: No exceptional features. Memorials: Traditional sections graves are not restricted, but must be agreed; headstone/vase only in the lawn section. 'Well-established cemetery with identified areas for special religious groups, and a separate infants/children's section. It has space for approximately five years only (from 1996). A new cemetery, adjacent to Cambridge City crematorium (see below) is in the planning stage, and will incorporate a woodland/green burial area' (David Giles).

• **Crem Cambridge**: Cambridge City Crematorium, Huntingdon Road, Cambridge CB3 OJJ (tel 01954 780681). Price: £190. Time allotted: 30 minutes (extra time can be booked for £100). They will accept home-made, cardboard or wicker coffins; they would consider shrouds or body bags. Chapel: A more traditional East chapel from 1938 and a modern West chapel from 1991. Grounds: 'Crematorium situated in open countryside of Cambridge green belt.' 'A total flexibility' (David Giles).

• **Cem Clacton-on-Sea**: Clacton Cemetery, Burrs Road, Clacton-on-Sea, Essex (tel 01255 831108). Plot (99 years) incl. digging and burial £335. They will accept home-made and cardboard coffins. Length of funeral service: 45 minutes for the chapel and graveside (extra time is charged at £37). Chapel: 'Late 19th century, small but compact.' Grounds: 'Lawned areas neat and tidy, with rose bushes in between headstones.' Memorials: Within size restrictions. 'The grounds are neat and the staff caring' (Jerry Howe).

• **FD Clacton-On-Sea**: R. Gwinnell & Sons, 351 Holland Road, Clacton-On-Sea, Essex CO15 6PD (tel 01255 815600). See Manningtree, below, for details.

• **Cem (Green Burial) Colchester**: Colchester Cemetery, Mersea Road, Colchester, Essex CO2 8RU (tel 01206 282950). Plot (25 years) incl. digging and burial £170 (non-residents extra). Maintenance: £16 p.a.. They will accept home-made or cardboard coffins. Length of funeral service: 20 minutes. Chapel: Small Victorian Gothic. Grounds: Victorian, with long-established and various trees. Memorials: Within size and materials restrictions. 'Woodland/green burial area planned' (C. Ryland).

• **Crem Colchester**: Colchester Crematorium, Mersea Road, Colchester, Essex CO2 8RU (tel 01206 282950). Price: £170. Time allotted: 20 minutes (extra time can normally be booked). They will accept home-made or cardboard coffins. Chapel: Modern, non-denominational. Grounds: 'Formal gardens in attractive 1850s cemetery with fine, mature specimen trees.' 'Gardens have recently been enhanced by further tree planting' (C. Ryland).

• **FD Colchester**: R. Gwinnell & Sons, 112 Ipswich Road, Colchester, Essex CO4 4AA (tel 01206 868585). See Manningtree, below, for details.

• **FD Colchester**: Hunnaball Funeral Services, York House, 41 Mersey Road, Colchester , Essex CO2 7QS (tel 01206 760 049). Branches in Manningtree (see below) and elsewhere in region. Cheapest fully-fitted coffin only: from £75; the Ecology Peace Box cardboard coffin £105 (delivery locally £20). Cold storage only: Yes, £60 per day. Advice for d-i-y: Yes, £40 to £50 per hour. Basic funeral: £350 (disbursements extra), £500 for those further afield. 'All our branches are linked to family members' (Melanie Hunnaball). Prepaid plan: Perfect Assurance, Chosen Heritage, Golden Leaves, East Anglia Funeral Plan. Member of NAFD.

• **FD Dovercourt**: R. Gwinnell & Sons, 193 Main Road, Dovercourt, Essex CO12 3PH (tel 01255 241900). See Manningtree, below, for details.

• **Cem Frinton-on-Sea**: Kirby Cross Cemetery, Holland Road, Kirby Cross, Frinton-on-Sea, Essex (tel 01255 831108). Plot (99 years) incl. digging and burial £335. They will accept home-made and cardboard coffins. Length of funeral service: 45 minutes for the chapel and graveside (extra time can be booked without charge). Chapel: 'Late 19th century, small but compact.' Grounds: 'Lawned areas neat and tidy.' Memorials: Within size restrictions. 'The grounds are neat and the staff caring' (Jerry Howe).

• **FD Hadleigh**: R. Gwinnell & Sons, 77 High Street, Hadleigh, Essex IP7 5DY (tel 01473 824440). See Manningtree, below, for details.

• **Cem Harlow**: Parndon Wood Cemetery, Parndon Wood Road, Harlow, Essex CM19 4SF (tel 01279 423800 or 446199). Plot (50 years) incl. digging and burial £1052. Maintenance: No charge. They will accept home-made, cardboard or wicker coffins, and shrouds. Length of funeral service: No limit. Chapel: Non-denominational. Grounds: 'Tranquil woodland setting.' Memorials: Within size restrictions; no kerbing. 'Having BSI registration shows that we give an excellent service' (Mrs Chris Brown).

• **Crem Harlow**: Parndon Wood Crematorium, Parndon Wood Road, Harlow, Essex CM19 4SF (tel 01279 423800 or 446199). Price: £180. Time allotted: 30 minutes (extra time can be booked for a variable charge). They will accept home-made, cardboard or wicker coffins, and body bags. Chapel: Non-denominational, with removable cross. Grounds: 'Lovely woodland area.' 'A separate baby and children's area. We are hoping to extend the cemetery and include a natural burial area' (Mrs Chris Brown).

• **FD Harpenden**: Phillips Funerals, Parchment House, 9 Victoria Road, Harpenden, Hertfordshire AL5 4EB (tel 01582 461100). See Phillips Funerals in St Albans for details.

• **Cem Harwich**: Dovercourt Cemetery, Main Road, Dovercourt, Harwich, Essex (tel 01255 831108). Plot (99 years) incl. digging and burial £335. They will accept home-made and cardboard coffins. Length of funeral service: 45 minutes for the chapel and graveside (extra time can be booked without charge). Chapel: 'Late 19th century, small but compact.' Grounds: 'Lawned areas neat and tidy.' Memorials: Within size restrictions. 'The grounds are neat and the staff caring' (Jerry Howe).

• **FD Huntingdon**: T. L. Cobbold, a branch of Lodge Bros., at 54 High Street, Hail Weston, St Neots, Huntingdon, Cambridgeshire PE19 4JW (tel 01480 472398). See Lodge Bros. in the London region, below, for details.

• **FD Ipswich**: Co-operative Funeral Service, 10 Upper Orwell Street, Ipswich, Suffolk (tel 01473 257242). Branches include: Felixstowe (tel 01394 670100); Hadleigh (tel 01473 823117); Stowmarket (tel 01449 612765); Sudbury (tel 01787 372736); Woodbridge (tel 01394 385456); Bury St Edmunds (tel 01284 754017); Saxmundham (tel 01728 604455). For service details see Norwich below.

• **Crem King's Lynn**: Mintlyn Crematorium, Lynn Road, Bawsey, King's Lynn, Norfolk PE32 1HB (tel 01553 630533). Price: £150. Time allotted: 45 minutes (extra time can be booked for £31-73). They will accept home-made or cardboard coffins. Chapel: Modern with lowering catafalque. Grounds: 'Mature woodland glades set with memorial shrubs and trees' (Colin Houseman).

• **FD King's Lynn**: Thornalley Funeral Services, 51-53 St James Street, King's Lynn, Norfolk (tel 01553 771399; will not give price breakdowns over the phone). Cheapest fully-fitted coffin only: £95 (delivery locally £10; nationally £10 plus carrier charges). Cold storage only: Yes, £10 per day. Body transport only: Yes. Advice for d-i-y: Yes, £15 per hour. Basic funeral: £445 (disbursements extra). 'We are a family business' (Raymond Thornalley). Prepaid plan: The Thornalley Funeral Plan. Member of NAFD.

• **Cem Maldon**: Maldon Cemetery, London Road, Maldon, Essex (information from Maldon District Council Offices, Princes Road, Maldon, Essex CM9 5DL, tel 01621 875836). Plot (100 years) incl. digging and burial £420. Maintenance: No charge. They will accept home-made and cardboard coffins. Length of funeral service: 'Any reasonable time is allowed.' Chapel: Simple Victorian chapel, refurbished 1996, seats 40 people. Available without extra charge. Grounds: Rural, on the edge of town, surrounded by farmland. Memorials: All types of memorial are permitted in the traditional cemetery area. Our Victorian hand pull bier has been renovated and brought into service' (David Lobb, Cemeteries Officer). There is also a Primrose Garden for children's burials and a woodland burial ground (see below).

• **Green Burial Maldon:** Woodland Glades, Maldon Cemetery, London Road, Maldon, Essex (information from Maldon District Council Offices, Princes Road, Maldon, Essex CM9 5DL, tel 01621 875836). A grave costs £435 incl. digging and burial (double for non-residents). They will accept home-made and cardboard coffins. Family and friends can do a token amount of digging and filling the grave. The woodland site is an area bordering onto farmland within the walled boundary of an existing mature cemetery. Cardboard coffins are encouraged, and in the longer term will be the only acceptable option. In the short term, very simple coffins of chipboard veneer are permitted, but not more lavish varieties. Use of the cemetery chapel for burial services is free, as is use of their Victorian hand bier. Families are permitted to select a grave space within 'burial islands'. The 'islands' consist of between 20-40 graves, and all tree, shrub, bulb and wildflower planting has been carefully pre-planned to provide a balanced woodland as time progresses. Eventually, the islands will link together and all available groundspace will become used for graves. 'There is a Day of Dedication each autumn when the bereaved are invited to plant trees and bulbs and to form a group who will give practical assistance in enhancing the woodland and who may help each other through bereavement' (David Lobb, Cemeteries Officer).

• **Green Burial Manningtree:** Oakfield Wood Green Burial Ground, Wrabness Hall, Wrabness, Manningtree, Essex CO11 2TQ (tel John Acton 01255 880182; enquiries to the site agent: Peter Kincaid, 256 High Street, Dovercourt, Harwich, Essex CO12 3PA, tel 01255 503456). John Acton, the farmer, manages this seven acre burial ground overlooking the River Stour but has given ownership of the land to the Essex Wildlife Trust. A grave costs £318-75 for 'perpetuity' (incl. digging, tree, wooden plaque, tree guard, entry into Register of Burials with Ordnance Survey grid reference). £750 all-in price incl. coffin, burial and collection within 100 mile radius – this includes London. Interment of ashes costs £268-85. They will accept home-made, cardboard or wicker coffins, or shrouds or body bags. Mourners can assist in digging and filling the grave. A native broadleaf tree is planted at every plot in the dormant planting season. The ground is in set aside farm land. The perimeter is planted with about 22,000 hard wood native hedging plants. Any monies paid in advance go into a Trustee account. 'Our prices are competitive, and it is a special scenic location that will be preserved by a charitable Wildlife Trust for evermore' (Peter Kincaid). Provisional member of the Association of Nature Reserve Burial Grounds.

• **FD Manningtree**: R. Gwinnell & Sons, 24 High Street, Manningtree, Essex CO11 1AD (tel 01206 391506). Cheapest fully-fitted coffin only: from £100 (delivery dependent on mileage). Cold storage only: Yes, £10 per day. Advice for d-i-y: Yes, basic advice free. Basic funeral: £500 (disbursements extra). 'We are happy to perform any task that is ethically and legally correct' (C. J. Doggett). Prepaid plan: Ipswich and Norwich Co-operative Society Funeral Bond. Member of NAFD.

• **FD Manningtree**: Paskell Funeral Service, 15 High Street, Manningtree, Essex CO11 2RS (tel 01206 396 709). Run by Saul Hunnaball. See Hunnaball Funeral Services, Colchester, above, for details.

• **Crem Norwich**: St Faiths Crematorium, 75 Manor Road, Horsham St Faith, Norwich NR10 3LF (tel 01603 898264). Run by Norwich Crematorium plc. Price: £160. Time allotted: 30 minutes (extra time can be booked for £80). They will accept home-made, wicker or cardboard coffins, body bags or shrouds. Chapel: 1930s, church-like. Grounds: '15 acre Gardens of Remembrance said to be some of the best-kept gardens in the country.' 'Saturday and Sunday services. No reasonable request is refused' (P.H. Garrick).

• **FD Norwich**: Co-operative Funeral Service, St Stephens Square, Norwich, Norfolk (tel 01603 625495). Branches include: Norwich (tel 01603 483060); Great Yarmouth (tel 01603 842464); Gorleston (tel 01493 440838). Cheapest fully-fitted coffin only: £122 (delivery locally £30). Cold storage only: Yes, £30 per day. Body transport only: Yes. Advice for d-i-y: Yes, £40 per hour. Basic funeral: £485 (disbursements extra). 'We are the best in our locality and do not cut corners' (Roy Gwinnell). Prepaid plan: Golden Charter. Member of NAFD, SAIF.

• ✪✪✪ **FD Norwich**: Peter Taylor Funeral Services, 85 Unthank Road, Norwich, Norfolk NR2 2PE (tel 01603 760787 or 01603 620298). Branches include: Holt (tel 01263 711992); Halesworth (tel 01986 872204); Bungay (tel 01986 892178); Long Stratton (tel 01508 531806); Dereham (tel 01362 699484); Watton (tel 01953 881229); Diss (tel 01379 642321); Harleston (tel 01379 853094); Horstead (tel 01603 737729); Wroxham (tel 01603 783797); Aylsham (tel 01263 733176); Wymondham (tel 01953 603138). Cheapest fully-fitted coffin only: £82-25 (delivery locally £20; nationally 60p per mile over 20 miles). Cold storage only: Yes, £10 per day. Body transport only: Yes, £60. Advice for d-i-y: Yes, modest, negotiable fee. Basic funeral: £540 (disbursements extra). 'We also offer an "ecology" funeral with the Brighton cardboard coffin at £600 plus disbursements, and a horse-drawn hearse is available for approximately £500' (Nicholas Taylor). Prepaid plan: Own. Parent company: Anglia Funeral services. Member of NAFD.

• **Cem (Green Burial) Peterborough**: Broadway and Eastfield Cemeteries, Eastfield Road, Peterborough, Cambridgeshire (tel 01733 262639). Also administers the Woodston, Stanground and Fletton cemeteries under the same pricing, burial and memorial policy. Plot (100 years) incl. digging and burial £490. They will accept home-made, cardboard or wicker coffins, body bags or shrouds. No chapel facilities. Grounds: 'Broadway cemetery has a conservation area and a superb range of wild flowers.' Memorials: Lawn type (under review). 'A woodland burial area is planned within an existing cemetery' (Cheryl Eva).

• **Crem Peterborough**: Peterborough Crematorium, Mowbray Road, North Bretton, Peterborough, Cambridgeshire PE6 7JE (tel 01733 262637). Price: £185. Time allotted: 30 minutes (extra time can be booked for £110). They will accept home-made, cardboard or wicker coffins (subject to full details in advance). Chapel: Modern, church-like; side wall of glass looking out to semi-woodland. Grounds: Semi-woodland. 'Our attitude is that if we are asked for something out of the usual we consider "why not" rather than just plain "no". One gentleman has had a d-i-y funeral at which he also stayed to watch throughout the whole, three-hour cremation process. This had been his uncle's wish' (Mrs Cheryl A. Eva).

• **FD Royston**: Cecil Newling, a branch of Lodge Bros., at 3 Green Drift, Royston, Hertfordshire SG8 5DB (tel 01763 243048). See Lodge Bros. in the London region, below, for details.

• **FD St Albans**: Phillips Funeral Service, 68 Alma Road, St Albans, Hertfordshire AL1 3BL (tel 01727 851006; fax 01727 841434). There is a branch at

Parchment House, 9 Victoria Road, Harpenden, Herts AL5 4EB (tel 01582 461100). Cheapest fully-fitted coffin only: £125 (delivery locally £115; nationally £1-25 per mile). Cold storage only: £35 per day. Body transport only: Yes, £115. Advice for d-i-y: £50 per hour. Basic funeral: £595 (disbursements extra). 'Personal "care and compassion" for the families we serve irrespective of the value of the goods or services they purchase from us' (Terry Smith). Prepaid plan: Golden Charter. Member of NAFD and SAIF.

• **FD Saxmundham**: Tony Brown's Funeral Service, New Cut, Saxmundham, Suffolk IP16 4HE (tel 01728 603108). (See the description by Libby Purves earlier in this chapter.) Would not supply coffin only. Cold storage only: Yes, £10 per day. Body transport only: Yes. Advice for d-i-y: Possibly, depending on the situation. Basic funeral: £596. Prepaid plan: No – 'privately if required, but I do not believe in it.' Would not give price breakdowns over the phone and does not have a price list for members of the public to take away. 'I conduct a personal family business I like doing and I object to all unnecessary red tape. I give a very good Christian service and treat everybody the same unless they want something elaborate. We probably know 95 per cent of the people we deal with. We still class ourselves as "your local funeral director" ' (Tony Brown).

• **Cem (Green Burial) Southend-on-Sea**: Sutton Road Cemetery, Sutton Road, Southend-on-Sea, Essex SS2 5PX (tel 01702 215015). Plot (50 years) incl. digging and burial £664. Maintenance: Included in fee. Cleaning of headstone £28 p.a. They will accept home-made or cardboard coffins. Length of funeral service: 30 minutes (extra time may be booked for £38). Chapel: Church-like, seats 35. Grounds: 'Attractive, 48 acre site with its own church and chapel.' Memorials: Within size restrictions. 'Environmental awareness and support for conservation. If additional land can be purchased, we plan a woodland burial site' (D. Adams).

• **Crem Southend-on-Sea**: Southend-on-Sea Crematorium, Sutton Road, Southend-on-Sea, Essex SS2 5PX (tel 01702 215018). Price: £200. Time allotted: 30 minutes (extra time can be booked for £65). They will accept home-made or cardboard coffins. Chapels: One church-like, with good acoustics, the other modern. Grounds: 'Gardens back onto open fields. However, busy road at front and small industrial area to the South.' 'Environmental awareness and support for conservation and the general quality and appearance of the crematorium' (D. Adams).

• **FD Thorpe-Le-Soken**: R. Gwinnell & Sons, High Street, Thorpe-Le-Soken, Essex CO16 OEA (tel 01255 861818). See Manningtree, above, for details.

• **Crem Upminster**: South Essex Crematorium, Okendon Road, Corbets Tey, Upminster, Essex RM14 2UY (tel 01708 222188). Price: £182. Time allotted: 30 minutes (extra time can be booked for £49). They will accept home-made, cardboard or wicker coffins. Chapels: The South chapel has flexible seating. Grounds: 'Established formal garden'. 'Flexible to clients as long as they are not disturbing others' (Linda Thoroughgood).

• **Crem Weeley**: Weeley Crematorium, Colchester Road, Weeley, Essex CO16 9JP (tel 01255 831108). Price: £166. Time allotted: 45 minutes for the service (extra time £88 for 45 minutes). They will accept home-made or cardboard coffins. Chapel: Modern, non-denominational, brick walls with wood seating and roof. Grounds: Park-like grounds. Fish pond with waterfall and fountain. Tape recordings of services can be ordered for £11-75. 'We are a small team like a family. I hope that friendliness and a caring attitude are conveyed to our visitors' (Janet Beech).

The South West

Comprising South Gloucestershire, Bristol, Bath and North East Somerset, North West Somerset, Somerset, Dorset, Devon, Cornwall.

• **FD Appledore**: A. D. Williams, Chanters House, Hubbastone Road, Appledore, N. Devon EX39 1LZ (tel 01237 421867). Also a branch in Ilfracombe, see below. Cheapest fully-fitted coffin only: £100 (delivery locally £10). 'No cold storage facilities, but would be able to offer my chapel of rest'. Body transport only: Yes. Advice for d-i-y: Yes, £15 per hour. Basic funeral: £400 (disbursements extra). 'Happy to help people achieve a green burial option' (David Williams). Prepaid plan: Golden Charter. Member of SAIF.

• **FD Ashburton:** F. Christophers & Son, Bridge House, 9 Kingsbridge Lane, Ashburton, Devon (tel 01364 654065). Cheapest fully-fitted coffin only: £125 (delivery locally 80p per mile). Cold storage only: Yes, £8 per day. Body transport only: Yes. Advice for d-i-y: Yes, £25 per hour. Basic funeral: £730 (including disbursements of £260). 'Oldest family firm in Devon, established 1846, covering area of Southern Dartmoor' (Frederic Christophers). Member of SAIF.

• **Crem Barnstaple**: North Devon Crematorium, Old Torrington Road, Barnstaple, Devon EX31 3NW (tel 01271 45431; fax 01271 328116). Price: £160. Time allotted: 30 minutes (extra time can be booked for £38 per half hour). They will accept home-made or cardboard coffins, provided they conform to regulations. Chapels: 'Small but serene'. Grounds: 'Seven acres of secluded grounds with woodland on two sides.' 'Staff on duty 365 days of year for advice and information' (Mrs B. Hilton).

• **Cem (Green Burial) Bath**: Haycombe Cemetery, Haycombe Cemetery, Whiteway Road, Bath BA2 2RQ (tel 01225 423682). Plot (75 years) incl. digging and burial £309. Maintenance: £72 pa, if required. They will accept home-made, cardboard or wicker coffins. Length of funeral service: 30 minutes (extra time can be booked for double price). Chapel: Non-denominational; large window with spectacular views. Grounds: Well-maintained, secure and pleasant site. Memorials: Approved natural stone only, within size restrictions. 'A woodland burial area will be introduced in April 1997' (Rosemary Tiley).

• **Crem Bath**: Haycombe Crematorium, Whiteway Road, Bath BA2 2RQ (tel 01225 423682). Price: £144 (non-residents £175). Time allotted: 30 minutes (extra time can be booked for £144). They will accept home-made, cardboard or wicker coffins, or body bags or shrouds. Chapel: 'Modern, with a glass wall overlooking rural valley'. Grounds: 'Open countryside with beautiful views.' 'The staff have mostly been here for a long time and take great pride in providing a good service to the public' (Rosemary Tiley).

• **Crem Bournemouth**: Bournemouth Crematorium, Strouden Avenue, Bournemouth, Dorset BH8 9HX (tel 01202 526238). Price: No details given. Time allotted: 20 minutes (extra time can be booked for an unspecified charge). They will accept home-made, wicker or cardboard coffins, shrouds or body bags. Chapel: Non-denominational. Grounds: 'Glades, seats, rosebeds, trees' (J. A. Walker).

• **Green Burial Bournemouth:** Bournemouth North Cemetery Woodland Burials, a local authority site, c/o J. A. Walker, Cemeteries, Bournemouth Community Services, Strouden Avenue, Bournemouth, Dorset BH8 9HX (tel 01202 526238 – also the number for info on other local cemeteries). A grave costs £380 (incl. digging and choice of any tree; double for non-residents). They will accept home-made or cardboard coffins. Families and friends can fill the grave. 'The woodland burial ground has a view of the cemetery grounds, there are some large trees, and laurel trees have been planted' (J. A. Walker).

• **Cem Bristol**: The Bristol General Cemetery, The East Lodge, Arnos Vale, Bath Road, Bristol BS4 3EW (tel 0117 9713294 or 0117 9713295). Plot (60 years) incl. digging and burial £500. Maintenance: £30 per cut and tidy. They will accept home-made or cardboard coffins. Length of funeral service: 30 minutes (extra time can be booked for a minimal charge). Chapel: 'Dates back to 1840; homely feel.' Grounds: '45 acres of Victorian park/woodland with much wildlife, many listed buildings and a "welcome home" feel.' Memorials: No restrictions. 'We will reduce the burial fee to accommodate families with cash flow problems' (Beverley Webber).

• **FD Bristol:** Green Undertakings (Knowle West Area Funeral Service), Arnos Vale Cemetery, Bath Road, Bristol BS4 (tel 0117 977 1800). 'Standard traditional funeral, including cremation and doctors' fees, £595.' See Watchet below for details.

• **FD Bristol:** Peter J. Connell, Burlington House, 2 Cabstand, Portishead, Bristol BS20 9HW (tel 01275 849239). Cheapest fully-fitted coffin only: £50 (delivery locally £15; nationally 50p per mile). Cold storage only: Yes, £10 per day. Body transport only: Yes. Advice for d-i-y: Yes, £15 per day. Basic funeral: £495 (disbursements extra). 'We will tailor any funeral to suit the family's requirements' (Peter Connell). Member of SAIF, NAFD, BIE, BIFD.

• **FD Bristol:** Heaven on Earth shop, Kingsley House, Cotham Road South, Bristol BS6 5TX (tel 0117 942 1836 or 0117 924 0972). Paula Rainey Crofts can arrange funerals through her nationwide network of good funeral directors.

• **Green Burial Bristol:** Woodland burial ground, Arnos Vale Cemetery, Bath Road, Bristol BS4 (tel 0117 977 1800). A grave costs £500 (incl. digging; for residents or non-residents). The woodland burial ground is within an existing woodland that is part of the overgrown 48 acre privately-owned Arnos Vale Cemetery. 'Trees already on or near the burial ground can be dedicated in memory of the dead, with a carved oak plaque giving their name, age span and date of burial.' They will accept home-made, cardboard or wicker coffins. Families and friends can help with a token amount of digging or filling the grave. Green Undertakings (see Watchet below) have an office facility here and can arrange funerals. 'We hope to bring in funds towards the restoration and upkeep of these historical grounds and buildings' (Barbara Butler, Green Undertakings).

• **Green Burial Bristol:** Woodland Burial Site, South Bristol Cemetery, Bridgwater Road, Bedminster Down, Bristol BS13 7AS (tel 0117 963 4141). A grave costs £750 (incl. digging and tree; for residents or non-residents). A secluded local authority woodland burial site of several acres overlooking Bristol, the Avon Gorge and the Suspension Bridge. Families and friends can fill in the grave if they wish. A choice can be made from eight native species trees. They will accept cardboard coffins or shrouds. 'Wildflower seeds have been introduced and the grass is cut one or two times a year' (Robin Pope).

• **Green Burial (Nr Bristol)**: Christopher Baker, Rookery Farm, Alveston, (10 miles north of) Bristol BS12 2SY (tel 01454 415495; fax 01454 419081), having been turned down for a larger scheme, has submitted a new planning application for a 20 acre burial ground in the valley. The site is grazing land, small fields with high hedges, with the M5 nearby. Four converted Georgian barns will provide a chapel and function rooms. The cost of the grave (incl. digging, a tree, a small concrete plaque and the use of the chapel and party room) will be between £500 and £600. Families will be able to help with digging and filling and do not have to use funeral directors. Provisional member of the Association of Nature Reserve Burial Grounds.

• **FD Dawlish:** B. G. Wills & Son, 22 Brunswick Place, Dawlish, Devon (tel 01626 862426). Cheapest fully-fitted coffin only: £125 (delivery locally 'no charge'; cardboard coffins 'shortly available'). Cold storage only: 'Not available, but we would hold body in chapel of rest at £20 per funeral.' Body transport only: Yes. Advice for d-i-y: Yes, £15 per hour. Basic funeral: £440 (disbursements extra). 'We are a small family firm. We are willing to assist in any aspect of the funeral arrangements no matter how small' (G. Wills). Member of NAFD.

• **Green Burial Devon**: There are several woodland burial grounds on farms in Devon, with Green Undertakings (see below, under Watchet) as the sole agents.

• **Cem Dorchester**: Dorchester Cemetery, 31a Weymouth Avenue, Dorchester, Dorset DT1 2EN (tel 01305 263900). Plot (100 years) incl. digging and burial £429 (non-residents double). They will accept cardboard coffins. Length of funeral service: No time limit. Chapel: Victorian, with pews and stained glass window. Grounds: Well-maintained, secure and pleasant site. Memorials: No restrictions, subject to approval. 'If current demand continues, the cemetery will be full by 2001, at which point new premises will be sought. Serious consideration will then be given to provision of a woodland burial area' (Sue Cheeseman).

• **Cem Exeter**: Exwick Cemetery, Exwick Road, Exeter, Devon EX4 2BT. Chapel: 'Volcanic stone and brick. Light and airy inside.' Grounds: 'Some fine angels. Attractive hillside setting in the newer areas with views across the valley to the Cathedral and the city centre.' 'A special section for still-born and pre-term babies' (John O'Callaghan). All other details as for Higher Cemetery below.

• **Cem Exeter**: Higher Cemetery, St. Marks Avenue, Heavitree, Exeter, Devon EX1 2PX (tel 01392 265707). Plot (75 years) incl. digging and burial £256. They will accept home-made, cardboard or wicker coffins, or body bags or shrouds. Length of funeral service: No time limit. Chapel: 'Of distinctive red-hued Heavitree stone. Old but cosy.' Grounds: '1860s urban cemetery with Commonwealth War Graves section, an older section laid out as a "quiet garden" and a small area for wildlife.' Memorials: Within size restrictions. 'A typical "town" cemetery which suffers like most from neglect over the years' (John O'Callaghan).

• **Cem Exeter**: Topsham Cemetery, Elm Grove Road, Topsham, Exeter, Devon EX3 OEJ. Chapel: 'Light, airy and comforting atmosphere with lovely stained glass window' Grounds: 'A typical small town cemetery.' 'Small site with old-established trees and nearby allotments make this a very tranquil spot' (John O'Callaghan). All other details as for Higher Cemetery above.

• **(Green Burial) Falmouth**: Volunteers connected to the Falmouth Green Centre (Union Road, Falmouth, Cornwall TR11 4JW, tel Philip Pearce on 01326 375158) and the local British Trust for Conservation Volunteers are trying to find a suitable piece of land for green burials and an appropriate organisation to manage it.

• **FD Ilfracombe**: A. D Williams, 31 Portland Street, Ilfracombe, N. Devon (tel 01271 328218). See Appledore above for details.

• **Cem Paignton**: Paignton Cemetery, Colley End Road, Paignton (tel 01803 327768). Plot (100 years) incl. digging and burial £425 (non-residents £850). No maintenance charges. They will accept home-made or cardboard coffins. Length of funeral service: As required. Chapel: Traditional church setting. Grounds: 'Mature trees, sea views, sense of space.' Memorials: No kerbs, no wood, no metal. 'Staff endeavour to make funerals as personal as possible' (Vivienne D. Foster).

• **Cem Plymouth**: Efford Cemetery, Efford Road, Plymouth, Devon PL3 6NG (tel 01752 264857) Plot (25 years) incl. digging and burial £722. They will accept home-made or cardboard coffins. Length of funeral service: 30 minutes (extra time can be booked for £21). Chapel: Edwardian. Grounds: Formal, with some wooded areas. Memorials: Approved natural stone only, with no kerbing and within size restrictions. 'We produce an advisory leaflet for families organising do-it-yourself funerals' (Mrs Aitchison).

• **Crem Plymouth**: Efford Crematorium, Efford Road, Plymouth, Devon PL3 6NG (tel 01752 264857). Details as for Weston Mill below.

• **Cem Plymouth**: Weston Mill Cemetery, Ferndale Road, Plymouth, Devon PL2 2EP (tel 01752 264837). Details as for Efford Cemetery above.

• **Crem Plymouth**: Weston Mill Crematorium, Ferndale Road, Plymouth, Devon PL2 2EP (tel 01752 264837). Price: £162 (non-residents £190). Time allotted: 30 minutes (extra time can be booked for £20 per half hour). They will accept home-made, wicker or cardboard coffins. Chapel: 1920s, traditional. Grounds: 'Secluded Garden of Rest within cemetery grounds.' 'Experienced, caring staff' (Brian Howells).

• **Crem Poole**: Poole Crematorium, Gravel Hill, Poole, Devon BH12 5DL (tel

01202 602582). Price: £171. Time allotted: 20 minutes in a 30 minute period (extra time can be booked for £171). They will accept home-made or cardboard coffins. Chapel: Fixed seating. Grounds: 'Formal gardens and woodland area with drift planting'. 'We have a "woodland scattering area" based on the four seasons, available free to users of the crematorium' (Steve Carter).

• **FD Poole:** Colin Rogers Funeral Service, 3 Bank Parade, Bryant Road, Wallisdown, Poole, Dorset BH12 5DL (tel 01202 533353). Cheapest fully-fitted coffin only: £150 or £75 (cardboard) (delivery locally £10). Cold storage only: Yes, £10 per day. Body transport only: Yes, from £45 for estate car. Advice for d-i-y: Yes, free usually, but £88 charge for help throughout the process if they wish to use our facilities. Basic funeral: £520 (cardboard coffin, disbursements extra). 'We help families however unusual their wishes and allow them to take an active role, giving backup support. Families will only pay for those elements required, as each is individually priced' (Colin Rogers). Member of SAIF and BIFD.

• ✪✪✪ **Green Burial Seaton:** Green burial ground, Collyford Road, Seaton, Devon (run by Mr Kane and colleagues, c/o the Registrar, Chief Exec. Dept., East Devon District Council, Knowle, Sidmouth, Devon EX10 8HZ, tel 01395 516551 ext 376). This is a site for 160 graves in old meadow land, part of the present Seaton Cemetery, in an Area of Outstanding Natural Beauty, on a hillside with a panoramic view out over the valley, estuary and sea. They will accept a home-made or cardboard coffin. A grave costs only £57 (incl. a tree; double for non-residents), but people must also pay for the digging to be done for them, either privately (at a cost of £80 to £110) or through a funeral director. Friends and family may help with a token amount of digging or filling the grave. 'The site opened in November 1996. The coffin needs to be quite strong as the soil is wet and heavy. Any family-organised funeral must be done properly. A tree is planted for each grave' (Mr Kane).

• **FD Taunton:** Green Undertakings, 3 Shuttern, Taunton, Somerset TA1 4ET (tel 01823 353223). See Watchet below for details.

• **FD Taunton:** Belmont Funerals (associated with Green Undertakings), St Decuman's, Taunton, Somerset TA23 0AX (tel 01984 633673). 'For low-cost funerals anywhere in England South of Worcester and throughout Wales. Even with travelling costs for distance funerals, our charges are likely to cost considerably less than most more local funeral directors.' See Watchet below for details.

• **Cem Thornbury**: Thornbury Cemetery, Kington Lane, Thornbury, South Gloucestershire (tel 01454 412103). Plot (50 years) incl. digging and burial £220 (non-residents £440). Maintenance: £25 to £33-50 pa. They will accept home-made, cardboard or wicker coffins, or body bags or shrouds. Length of funeral service: No limit. Chapel: 'Small and intimate.' Grounds: 'Very well-maintained in rural surroundings.' Memorials: Designs are subject to approval as being 'appropriate.' No kerbing. 'One of the best kept in the West of England' (G.W.H. Jackson).

• **Cem Torquay**: Torquay Cemetery, Hele Road, Torquay, Devon TQ2 7QG (tel

01803 327768). Plot (100 years) incl. digging and burial £425 (non-residents £850). No maintenance charges. They will accept home-made or cardboard coffins. Length of funeral service: As required. Chapel: 'Modern, churchlike.'. Grounds: 'Mature trees, clear views.' Memorials: No kerbs, no wood, no metal. 'Staff endeavour to make funerals as personal as possible' (Vivienne D. Foster).

• **Crem Torquay**: Torquay Crematorium, Hele Road, Torquay, Devon (tel 01803 327768 or 329977). Price: £166. Time allotted: 25 minutes (extra time can be booked without charge). They will accept home-made or cardboard coffins. Chapel: Modern non-denominational with moveable seating. Grounds: 'Set at the top of a hill. Tree-lined drive approach with lawns and gardens surrounding' (Vivienne D Foster).

• **Green Burial Torrington**: Honeywood burial ground (for humans and pets), c/o Julian Wedgwood, Huntshaw House, Huntshaw, Torrington, North Devon EX38 7HH (tel 01805 623765). Open from early in 1997, the site is a South-facing slope above the home of Julian Wedgwood, on which 1,800 Oak trees have been planted – 'a house cannot be seen for miles,' although the church of St Mary Magdalene is nearby. A plot with an Oak tree will cost £140. This gives the right to burial for one human body and one pet, and there is room for four subsequent pets. Beyond a ten-year period, the plot will have to be paid for again, if it is sought to bury further pets. The digging and burial charge is £250 for a human body and between £25 and £125 for a pet. No horses. Parrots and similar free. 'Humans will be buried to the South of the tree, as the Mongols would have insisted. Pets can go to the East, North or West'. Mr Wedgwood will accept any body container as long as it will eventually biodegrade. There will be no grave markers, but a plaque can be hung on the tree. Moneys are held in a lawyer's account with 10% per year allowed to be taken out by the scheme.

• **✪✪✪ FD Watchet:** Green Undertakings, 44 Swain Street, Watchet, Somerset TA23 0AG (tel 01984 632285). Cheapest fully-fitted coffin only: £78 (foil/chipboard), or £55 (Compakta cardboard) (delivery locally free within 20 miles; nationally at cost, about £25). Cold storage only: Yes, not more than £5 per day. Body transport only: Yes. Advice for d-i-y: No charge, but for full pre-planning with forms etc about £25. Basic funeral: Typically about £450 (Watchet & Taunton £430; Newport £475 – disbursements extra; Bristol £595 including cremation fee and other disbursements. A further £20 off for prompt payment; and £20 off for supplying own bearers; with full discounts for families helping, typically around £350, disbursements extra). 'We are specialists in green, earth friendly, low-cost and family-assisted funerals; we charge only for work done; an all-woman funeral team – Martha's Funerals – is available' (Barbara Butler). Prepaid funerals: 'We accept pre-payments in trust for our own funerals but in most cases advise "at need" only.' Member of no association.

• **Green Burial Watchet:** A green burial ground in Somerset, intended mainly for children, run by Green Undertakings, 44 Swain Street, Watchet, Somerset TA23 0AG (tel 01984 632285). This is a paddock of less than an acre with private road access and lovely views. A grave costs nothing for children, £150 is charged for digging a grave for adults. Donations are also sought for a trust fund. They will accept home-made, cardboard and wicker coffins, or shrouds or body bags. Families and friends can help with a token amount only of digging or filling the grave. Subsequent visits by appointment only, because animals may be loose. 'We will be making sheltered garden areas with benches' (Barbara Butler).

• **Cem (Green Burial) Weston-super-Mare**: Ebdon Road Cemetery, Ebdon Road, Worle, Weston-super-Mare, North Somerset BS22 9NY (tel 01934 511717). Administers branch cemeteries at Milton Road, Clevedon, and Portishead. Plot (80 years) incl. digging and burial £400. Subject to inspection, they will accept home-made, cardboard or wicker coffins, or body bags or shrouds. Length of funeral service: 30 minutes in chapel, no time limit at graveside . Chapel: See crematorium chapel below . Grounds: 'Attractive, well-maintained grounds with farmland on two sides.' Memorials: Within size restrictions. 'Will do their utmost to facilitate special requests. There are plans for a woodland burial facility' (Robin Michael Wood).

• **Crem Weston-super-Mare**: Weston-super-Mare Crematorium, Ebdon Road, Worle, Weston-super-Mare, North West Somerset BS22 9NY (tel 01934 511717). Price: £219. Time allotted: 20 minutes for the service, ten minutes for entry and exit (extra time can be booked). They will accept home-made, cardboard or wicker coffins, or shrouds or body bags – 'We may wish to inspect the body container beforehand'. The crematorium opened in 1966. Grounds: 'Set in attractive well-maintained grounds with farmland on two sides.' 'Staff will do their utmost to facilitate special requests' (Robin Michael Wood).

• **Crem Weymouth**: Weymouth Crematorium, Quibo Lane, Weymouth, Dorset DT4 0RR (tel 01305 786984). Price: £203. Time allotted: 30 minutes (extra time can be booked for £20). They will accept home-made, cardboard or wicker coffins. Chapel: Church-like. Grounds: 'Large, lawned Gardens of Remembrance with trees and rose beds'. 'Being a relatively quiet crematorium we can spend time on details and go out of our way to meet the family wishes. We can offer a tape-recording service for family who cannot make it to the funeral' (Catherine Webb).

• **FD Weymouth:** Stockting Funeral Service, 22 Crescent Street, Weymouth, Dorset DT4 7BX (tel 01305 785915). Parent company: Grassby & Sons Ltd. Cheapest fully-fitted coffin only: £120 (delivery locally £20; nationally: 'no'). Cold storage only: Yes, £25 per day. Body transport only: Yes. Advice for d-i-y: Yes, £15 per hour. Basic funeral: £595 (disbursements extra). 'We would be prepared to supply a cardboard coffin if requested' (No name given). Member of NAFD.

• **FD Winscombe:** : C. V. Gower & Son funeral director, The Square, Winscombe, North West Somerset BS25 1BS (tel 01934 842945). Cheapest fully-fitted coffin only: £135 (delivery locally £10; nationally 50p per mile). Cold storage only: Yes, £5 per day. Body transport only: Yes. Advice for d-i-y: Yes, no charge. Basic funeral: £500 (disbursements extra). Member of SAIF, NAFD, FSC.

• **Cem Yeovil:** Yeovil Cemetery, Preston Road, Yeovil, Somerset (tel 01935 76718 or 01935 23742). Plot (75 years) incl. digging and burial £381 (non-residents £762) Maintenance: £22 p.a., in older sections. They will accept home-made or cardboard coffins. Length of funeral service: 30 minutes. Grounds: Formal. (Registrar).

• **Crem Yeovil**: Yeovil Crematorium, Bunford Lane, Yeovil, Somerset (tel 01935 76718). Price: £179. Time allotted: 20 minutes in a 30 minute period (extra time may be booked for £89-50). They will accept home-made or cardboard coffins (Registrar).

The South

Comprising Wiltshire, Berkshire, Surrey, Kent, Hampshire, West Sussex, East Sussex.

• **(Crem) Basingstoke**: Carpenter's Down, Woodlands Crematorium, Crockford Lane, Chineham, Basingstoke, Hampshire (tel 01270 626037). Opens Summer 1997. Owned by Roseholt plc. Price: £220. Time allotted: 30 minutes (extra time can be booked for £200). They will accept home-made, cardboard or wicker coffins, or shrouds or body bags. Chapel: Two ceremony rooms, convertible into a major ceremony room. Spacious reception and private family area. Grounds: '40 acres of mature woodland. Encouragement is given for modern sculptured and natural memorials. Traditional memorials in hedged enclosures to avoid conflict with natural beauty of woodland.' 'The crematorium has been designed to give maximum flexibility and choice in the form of funerals and provides refrigerated body storage facilities within the premises for those not wishing to use a funeral director' (Barry Evans).

• **FD Banstead**: A branch of W. A. Truelove & Son Ltd at 121 High Street, Banstead, Surrey SM7 2NS (tel 01737 212 160). For details see Carshalton, below.

• **FD Battle**: Arthur C. Towner Ltd, 19 Market Square, Battle, East Sussex TN33 0XB (tel 01424 775515). See St Leonards, below, for details.

• **Green Burial Beaulieu:** Beaulieu Woodland Burial Ground, Grindinstone, Beaulieu, Hampshire (enquiries to Mrs Linda Coote, New Forest District Council, Client Services Division, The Town Hall, Avenue Road, Lymington, Hampshire SO41 9ZG, tel 01703 285952). A grave costs £300 (incl. digging and tree or shrub; £475 for non-residents). They will accept home-made or cardboard coffins. 'It is a section within an existing cemetery, in a rural area' (Mrs Linda Coote).

• **Crem Brighton**: Woodvale Crematorium, Lewes Road, Brighton, East Sussex BN2 3QB (tel 01273 604020). Price: £123. Time allotted: 45 minutes (extra time can be booked without charge). They will accept home-made or cardboard coffins. Chapels: One consecrated church with movable seating, one non-denominational Victorian flint building. Grounds: 'Pleasantly landscaped with rockery, water courses, gardens with flower beds, benches etc. Awarded Charter Mark 1994.' 'Services are tailored to meet individual requirements. Brighton Borough Council developed the "Brighton" casket, a biodegradable coffin, which is now used for both burial and cremation' (Stephen Horlock).

• **Green Burial Brighton:** Woodland Burial Ground, Borough Cemetery, Bear Road, Brighton, East Sussex (Office: Woodvale Cemeteries, Woodvale Lodge, Lewes Road, Brighton, East Sussex BN2 3QB, tel 01273 604020). A grave costs £386 (incl. digging and tree; double for non-residents). A local authority woodland burial site, within a large meadow overlooking Brighton and the sea in one direction and the Sussex downs in the other. 50 burials have taken place with a further 79 reserved; there is room for over 2,000. Families and friends can fill in the grave if they wish and can help to plant a tree. A choice can be made from nine native species trees. The Brighton cardboard coffin is available from them for £53. They will accept home-made or cardboard coffins. The meadow is cut only twice per annum to encourage wildlife to thrive. No chemicals are used in maintaining the area. 'Free assistance and advice and a guide to self-help funerals are available. The site and scheme have won three awards' (Stephen Horlock). Member of the Association of Nature Reserve Burial Grounds.

• **FD Calne**: E. Wooten & Son, a branch of Lodge Bros., at 1 North Street, Calne, Wiltshire SN11 OHQ (tel 01249 812258). See Lodge Bros. in the London region, below, for details.

• **FD Carshalton**: A branch of G. E. Gillman & Sons at 16 Green Wrythe Lane, Carshalton, Surrey SM5 2DW (tel 0181 669 0483). See their entry in the London region, below, for details.

• **FD Carshalton**: W. A. Truelove & Son Ltd, 118 Carshalton Road, Sutton, Surrey SM1 4RL (tel 0181 642 8211). For branches, see Cheam (London region), Wallington (London region), Epsom, Coulsdon, Caterham, Mitcham, Sutton and Banstead. Cheapest fully-fitted coffin only: £125, VAT extra. Cold storage only: No. Body transport only: No. Advice for d-i-y: No. Basic funeral: £640 (prompt payment price, disbursements extra). 'Family owned and run. A range of services, simple or elaborate' (Simon Truelove). Prepaid plan: Truelove Funeral Trust. Member of NAFD and National Selected Morticians.

• **FD Caterham**: A branch of W. A. Truelove & Son Ltd at Leslie House, 187 Croydon Road, Caterham CR3 6PH (tel 01883 345 345). For details see Carshalton, above.

• **Crem Chatham**: Medway Crematorium, Robin Hood Lane (Upper), Chatham, Kent ME5 9QU (tel 01634 861639). Run by Medway Crematorium Joint Committee. Price: £138. Time allotted: 40 minutes between services. They will accept cardboard coffins. Chapel: Churchlike, with movable seating. Grounds: Semi-formal rose gardens and woodland. 'We aim to meet all cultural, religious and personal preferences where possible' (Mrs Ruth Winch).

• **FD Chertsey**: Lodge Bros., 7 Windsor Street, Chertsey, Surrey KT16 8AY (tel 01932 565980). See Lodge Bros. in the London region, below, for details.

• **Green Burial Christchurch**: The Hinton Park Woodland Burial Ground, c/o Mike Hedger, Hinton House, Hinton, Christchurch, Dorset BH23 7EA (tel 01425 278910 or 273640; mobile 0385 390817; emergency numbers if no reply: 01425 276413 or 01202 292357). This site is on the Dorset/Hampshire border, a peaceful meadow now containing 60 burials, each with a semi-mature tree, surrounded by mature oaks and scots pine, with red deer in the adjoining meadow. Hinton House is visible, also a lake, horses, sheep and woods. 5,000 small trees have been planted. There are many species of birds. A plot costs £300, and gives a legal right and ownership for burial, covering 99 years from the burial; with an extra £250 for digging and filling the grave, the provision of the tree and the collection of the body within a 50 mile radius (collections from London, for instance, cost about £100 extra); and an extra £25 for a small name plaque. They will accept home-made, cardboard or wicker coffins, or shrouds and body bags. Cardboard coffins can be bought for £55 or a veneered plain coffin for £75. Family and friends can dig and fill the grave if they so wish. The graves can be visited subsequently any time in daylight hours. Catering within Hinton House is possible after the burial, at a charge of £7 per person (for sandwiches, fruit and soft drinks). Bed and Breakfast locally can be arranged, as can church services. 'We can collect the body using our green Renault Espace from home, hospital or nursing home and can look after the body until the funeral. We can make arrangements for newspaper advertisements. About 80 to 90 per cent are pure family burials, doing their own lowering, reading their own thoughts and poems, occasionally prayers and often music, with wine and food in the summer, actually in the meadow. We have had one person saying goodbye alone to her husband, and, on another occasion, 300 people saying farewell to a popular nurse in a local hospital' (Mike Hedger). Full member of the Association of Nature Reserve Burial Grounds.

• **Cem Crawley**: Snell Hatch Cemetery, The Dingle, West Green, Crawley, West Sussex (tel 01293 528744 ext 2503). Plot (50 years) incl. digging and burial £290. They will accept home-made, cardboard or wicker coffins. No chapel. 'Helpful and caring' (Mrs E. M. Crump).

• **Cem Eastbourne**: Langney Cemetery, Hide Hollow, Langney, Eastbourne, East Sussex BN23 8AE (tel 01323 766536). Plot (75 years) incl. digging and burial £243. They will accept home-made or cardboard coffins. Length of funeral service: No time limit . Chapel: Victorian . Grounds: 'Parkland with mature trees.' Memorials: No restrictions. 'We endeavour to be as helpful as possible. In 1995 the service was awarded a Charter Mark for excellent service to the public' (Doug Roderick).

• **Cem Eastbourne**: Ocklynge Cemetery, Willingdon Road, Eastbourne, East Sussex BN21 1TL (tel 01323 766536). Grounds: 'Downland cemetery.' All other details as for Eastbourne Langney Cemetery above.

• **Crem Eastbourne**: Eastbourne Crematorium, Hide Hollow, Langney, Eastbourne, East Sussex BN23 8AE (tel 01323 761093). Price: £200. Time allotted: 30 minutes within a 45 minute period (extra time can be booked for £40). They will accept home-made, cardboard or wicker coffins. Chapels: 1960s chapel seating 80, with smaller family chapel seating 30, open since 1990. Grounds: 'Designed to have the effect of rolling Sussex downland.' 'We endeavour to be as helpful as possible. In 1995 the service was awarded a Charter Mark for excellent service to the public' (Doug Roderick).

• **Green Burial Eling**: Eling Woodland Burial Ground, Eling Hill, Totton,

Southampton, Hampshire (enquiries to Mrs Linda Coote, New Forest District Council, Client Services Division, The Town Hall, Avenue Road, Lymington, Hampshire SO41 9ZG, tel 01703 285952). A grave costs £300 (incl. digging and tree or shrub; £475 for non-residents). They will accept home-made or cardboard coffins. 'It is a section within an existing cemetery, in a rural area' (Mrs Linda Coote).

• **FD Epsom**: A branch of W. A. Truelove & Son Ltd at 14-18 Church Road, Epsom, Surrey KT17 4AB (tel 01372 723 337). For details see Carshalton, above.

• **✪✪✪ FD Fordingbridge**: Harwood & Wallis, 34 Hayters Way, Camel Green, Alderholt, Fordingbridge, Hampshire SP6 3AX (tel 01425 656944). Cheapest fully-fitted coffin only: £100 (delivery locally free, nationally by mileage, about £25). Cold storage: Yes, for those in this area. Body transport only: Yes. Advice for d-i-y people: Yes, no charge. Advice sheets are available. Basic funeral: £850 (incl. crematorium fee, doctors' fees and minister). A fiercely independent firm. 'I started work at the age of 15 in antique restoration, repair and undertaking, where I was taught to make coffins. American-owned funeral firms are getting stronger in this country. They are ruthless business people. We make about 10 coffins a week. We supply transport to the registrar's office. We help with every arrangement' (Mr Harwood). Prepaid plan: None. Member of no association.

• **Crem Guildford**: Guildford Crematorium, Broadwater, New Pond Road, Godalming, Surrey, GU7 3DB (tel 01483 444711). Price: £200. Time allotted: 30 minutes (extra time can be booked for £90). They will accept home-made coffins. Chapel: Modern, non-denominational. Grounds: 'Open-fronted, well-maintained' (Keith Hendry).

• **FD Guildford**: J. Monk & Sons, a branch of Lodge Bros., at 3 Artillery Terrace, Guildford, Surrey GU1 4NL (tel 01483 562780). See Lodge Bros. in the London region, below, for details.

• **Cem Hastings**: Hastings Borough Cemetery, The Ridge, Hastings, East Sussex TN34 2AE (tel 01424 781302). Plot (50 years) incl. digging, burial and use of chapel £443. They will accept home-made, cardboard or wicker coffins. Length of funeral service: 20 minutes (extra time can be booked for £42 per 20 minutes). Chapel: Church-like. Grounds: As Crem below. Memorials: Head-stones only, within size restrictions. 'Unrivalled views' (Richard Peters). See also Green Burial ground below.

• **Crem Hastings**: Hastings Crematorium, 234 The Ridge, Hastings, East Sussex TN34 2AE (tel 01424 781302). Price: £196. Time allotted: 20 minutes (extra time can be booked for £42). They will accept home-made or cardboard coffins. Chapel: 1850s. Grounds: 'Trees, lawns and flower beds in 80 acres of cemetery grounds.' 'On a hillside overlooking Rye Bay to the East, and the Sussex countryside to the North and West' (Richard Peters).

• **Green Burial Hastings**: Woodland Burial, Hastings Borough Cemetery, The Ridge, Hastings, East Sussex TN34 2AE (tel 01424 781302). A grave costs £230 (incl. digging; double for non-residents; £42 extra for use of the chapel). No plots can be sold just for cremated remains, although these may be interred or strewn into existing graves. They will accept home-made, cardboard or wicker coffins.

They sell the Brighton cardboard coffin for £53. Family and friends can fill the grave if they wish. Graves are seeded with wildflowers and have a tree planted on them (silver birch, downy birch, rowan, crab apple, guelder rose or fastigiate hawthorn). 'The site is a very peaceful spot on the edge of an existing copse in a quiet corner of an 80 acre cemetery, well shielded by banks and trees' (Richard Peters).

• **FD Haywards Heath**: P. & S. Gallagher Funeral Directors, Fraser House, Triangle Road, Haywards Heath, West Sussex RH16 4HW (tel 01444 451166). Cheapest fully-fitted coffin only: £98 (delivery locally £15, nationally at cost). Cold storage: Yes, £15 per hour. Body transport only: Yes. Advice for d-i-y people: Yes, £15 per hour. Basic funeral: £575 (disbursements extra). 'A family-run business with complete facilities' (Patrick Gallagher). Prepaid plan: Golden Charter and own plan. Member of SAIF, BIE.

• **Crem Isle of Wight**: Isle of Wight Crematorium, Station Lane, Whippingham, East Cowes, Isle of Wight PO32 6NJ (tel 01983 882288). Price: £208 (non-residents £312). Time allotted: 30 minutes (extra time can be booked for £43). They will accept home-made, cardboard or wicker coffins. Chapel: 'Nothing attractive about building.' Grounds: 'Rural, wooded, peaceful.' 'We do not excel in anything other than giving what we believe is a first class service' (P. Sheppard).

• **Green Burial Isle of Wight**: Springwood Woodland Burials run by William Hall, Independent Funeral Directors, Winford Road, Newchurch, Sandown, Isle of Wight PO36 0JX (tel & fax 01983 868688). A grave costs £365 (incl. digging and choice of oak, mountain ash or beech tree). They will accept home-made and cardboard coffins, or shrouds or body bags. They sell the Brighton cardboard coffin for £50 or the Alverstone coffin ('uses only recycled and reclaimed timber') for £300. Family and friends can help dig or fill the grave if they wish. The five acre cemetery is in a peaceful setting. Paths lead to a small memorial garden where small bronze plaques can be placed. Extensive tree and bulb planting has taken place and there is a pond with a small marsh area. Bird, bat and kestrel boxes have been erected and a slow worm pit constructed.

• **FD Lindfield**: Masters & Son (Lindfield) Ltd, 4 Denmans Lane, Lindfield, West Sussex RH16 2LB (tel 01444 482107). Cheapest fully-fitted coffin only: £95 (delivery locally £15). Cold storage: Yes, £15 per hour. Body transport only: Yes. Advice for d-i-y people: Yes, £20 per hour. Basic funeral: £495 (disbursements extra). 'Both my wife and I trained as bereavement counsellors with Cruse' (Ian Masters). Prepaid plan: Golden Charter. Member of NAFD, SAIF.

• **Cem Maidstone**: Sutton Road Cemetery, Sutton Road, Maidstone, Kent (tel 01622 738172). Plot (100 years) incl. digging and burial £210. They will accept home-made, cardboard or wicker coffins, or shrouds. Length of funeral service: 90 minutes (extra time may be booked without charge). Chapel: 'Built in 1850, with typical gargoyles, stained glass, spire, etc.' Grounds: '49 acres of parkland with mature trees and a variety of lawn and general sections.' Memorials: Lawn section allows for headstone only, general section permits headstone, kerbs and vase - both are subject to size restrictions. 'Good location, experienced staff and reasonable prices. A tree memorial may be sponsored, without plaques, and not adjacent to the grave' (Tim Jefferson).

• **Crem Maidstone**: Vintners Park Crematorium, Bearsted Road, Maidstone, Kent ME14 5LG (tel 01622 738172). Price: £170. Time allotted: 30 minutes (extra time can be booked for £60). They will accept cardboard coffins. Chapel: 'Modern, formal, bright, accommodating 80'. Grounds: 'Surrounded by a conservation area, with formal gardens and a woodside walk area.' 'Large, well-laid out, interesting' (Tim Jefferson).

• **FD Maidstone**: Doves Funeral Directors, 1 Knightrider Street, Maidstone ME15 6LP (tel 01622 688662). A branch of Doves in Swanley (see below for details).

• **FD Mitcham**: A branch of G. E. Gillman & Sons at 205 London Road, Mitcham, Surrey (tel 0181 685 0349). See their entry in the London region, below, for details.

• **Crem Morden**: North East Surrey Crematorium, Lower Morden Lane, Morden, Surrey SM4 4NU (tel 0181 337 4835). Price: £155. Time allotted: 30 minutes (extra time can be booked for £60). They will accept home-made, cardboard or wicker coffins. Chapel: Converted late Victorian church. Grounds: '400-yard, poplar-lined drive and 3.5 acres of gardens.' 'We have our own trained staff (no contractors) who take a pride in their work and helping relatives' (J.E. Skinner).

• **FD Newbury**: R. C. Smallbone Ltd, Starwood House, 37 Pound Street, Newbury, Berkshire RG14 6AE (tel 01635 40536). Cheapest fully-fitted coffin only: £90 (delivery locally £10; delivery nationally 'variable'). Cold storage only: Yes, £15 per day. Body transport only: Yes. Advice for d-i-y: Yes, £25 per hour. Basic funeral: £785 (including fee for Reading crematorium and CoE minister). 'Small independent family-owned company that strives to carry out every request of the bereaved' (Michael Smallbone). Prepaid plan: Golden Charter. Member of SAIF.

• **Crem Portchester**: Portchester Crematorium, Upper Cornaway Lane, Portchester, Hampshire PO16 8NE (tel 01329 822533). Price: £158. Time allotted: 30 minutes (extra time can be booked without charge). They will accept home-made or cardboard coffins. 'Natural gardens' (J. Clark).

• **FD Portsmouth**: Meridian Funerals, 252 Havant Road, Drayton, Portsmouth, Hampshire PO6 1PA (tel 01705 221299). Cheapest fully-fitted coffin only: £95 (delivery locally £10; nationally £20 plus carrier's charge). Cold storage only: Yes, £30 per day. Body transport only: Yes. Advice for d-i-y: Yes, £25 per hour. Basic funeral: £455 (disbursements extra). 'We believe embalming is not required in most cases. Professionally qualified husband and wife business' (K. L. Thomas). Prepaid plan: Meridian. Member of SAIF.

• **Cem Reading**: Henley Road Cemetery, All Hallows Road, Caversham, Reading, Berkshire RG4 5LP (tel 01734 472433 or 474102). Plot (75 years) incl. digging and burial £517 (£560 extra for non-residents). Maintenance: No charge. They will accept home-made or cardboard coffins. Length of funeral service: 30 minutes (extra time £65 per half hour). Chapel: Same chapels as for Reading crematorium. Grounds: No traffic noise, park and farmland to the rear, mansion on the hillside. Memorials: Tablet and headstone size restrictions for new graves in Park Cemetery. 'Graves are individually numbered, making finding graves very easy' (Mrs Ruth Winch).

• **Crem Reading**: Reading Crematorium, All Hallows Road, Caversham, Reading, Berkshire RG4 5LP (tel 01734 472433 or 474102). Price: £195. Time allotted: 30 minutes (extra time can be booked for £65). They will accept home-made or cardboard coffins. Chapels: Large 1930s chapel is not church-like, and seats 70 with excellent organ and interior of dome visible. Small, modern brick and pine chapel seats 30. Grounds: 'Set in centre of 50 acre cemetery, with 5 acre Gardens of Remembrance secluded by tall hedges.' 'We aim to meet all cultural, religious and personal preferences where possible' (Mrs Ruth Winch).

• **FD St Leonards**: Arthur C. Towner Ltd, 2-4 Norman Road, St Leonards on Sea, East Sussex TN37 6NH (tel 01424 436386). Branch in Battle also, see above. Cheapest fully-fitted coffin only: £99 (delivery locally £20). Cold storage only: Yes, £20 per day. Body transport only: Yes. Advice for d-i-y: Yes, £50 per hour. Basic funeral: £470 (disbursements extra). 'We strive always to provide our clients with the funeral they need, not what is most convenient for us to provide' (Edward Towner). Prepaid plan: Golden Charter. Member of NAFD, SAIF and National Selected Morticians.

• **FD Salisbury**: Richard T. Adlem & Stephen Beckwith, 17 Paddock Close, Sixpenny Handley, Salisbury, Wiltshire SP5 5NZ (tel 01725 552309). Cheapest fully-fitted coffin only: £60 (foil), £68 (veneer), £78 (cardboard), phone for delivery price. Cold storage only: Yes, as long as no other funeral director is involved, £40 up to 8 days, then £12 a day. Body transport only: Yes, £1 per mile, with no minimum charge. Advice for d-i-y: Yes, no charge if they phone or call on us, otherwise a transport charge. Basic funeral: £840 (incl. church fees, doctors' fees and cremation fee). 'Our large estate car plus wheeled bier etc is available for hire. Families who have used us are willing to discuss the high level of service they have received from us. We do not have to satisfy shareholders or directors so we charge the lowest prices we can afford' (Stephen Beckwith, partner with my wife). Prepaid plan: Golden Charter. Member of no association.

• **FD Salisbury**: H. A. Harold & Son, funeral directors, 77 Estcourt Road, Salisbury, Wilts SP1 3AX (tel 01722 321177). Cheapest fully-fitted coffin only: £195 (free delivery locally, nationally at cost). Cold storage only: Yes, £5 per day. Body transport only: Yes. Advice for d-i-y: Yes, £40 management fee. Basic funeral: £500 (disbursements extra). 'Manager conducts non-religious funerals' (Paul Harris). Prepaid plan: Dignity and Chosen Heritage. Parent company SCI-UK. Member of the NAFD.

• **FD Sevenoaks**: Doves Funeral Directors, 112 St John's Hill, Sevenoaks TN13 3PB (t el 01732 740444). A branch of Doves in Swanley (see below for details).

• **FD Sidcup**: Ashdown Funeral Services, 232 Blackfen Road, Sidcup, Kent DA15 8PW (tel 0181 294 2115). Cheapest fully-fitted coffin only: £106 (delivery locally £20). Cold storage only: Yes 'if space available', £5 per day. Body transport only: Yes. Advice for d-i-y: Yes, £5 per hour. Basic funeral: £336 (disbursements extra). 'Having only one premises and one permanent employee, our overheads are small. If our clients wish to add or subtract services, we can do so, and we alter the charges accordingly' (Mr E. Micallef). Prepaid plan: Golden Charter. Member of SAIF.

• **FD Southsea**: Mayfields funeral directors, 90 Elm Grove, Southsea, Hampshire PO5 1LN (tel 01705 875575). Cheapest fully-fitted coffin only: £75 (delivery locally £10, nationally 75p per mile). Cold storage only: Yes, £5-75 per day. Body transport only: Yes. Advice for d-i-y: Yes, £25 per hour. Basic funeral: £779 (including disbursements). Prepaid plan: SAIF. 'Small family business with bereavement centre and trained counsellors' (David Colbourne).

• **Cem Sutton**: Sutton Cemetery, Alcorn Close, off Sutton Common Road, Sutton, Surrey SM3 9PX (tel 0181 644 9437). Plot (50 years) incl. digging and burial £515. Maintenance: £28 to £77. They will accept home-made, cardboard or wicker coffins, or shrouds or body bags. Length of funeral service: 60 minutes between bookings (extra time free with sufficient notice). Chapel: Victorian Gothic, warm and intimate with seating for 50-60.' Grounds: Well-maintained, secure and pleasant site. Memorials: Approved natural stone only, within size restrictions. 'Experienced and caring staff with our priorities given to the bereaved and the funeral service' (Mr Don Ward).

• **FD Swanley**: Doves Funeral Directors, 35 Station Road, Swanley, Kent BR8 8ES (tel 01322 669000. Cheapest fully-fitted coffin only: £85 (delivery locally £25, nationally from 80p per mile). Cold storage only: Yes, £15 per day. Body transport only: Yes, for a Daimler hearse £160. Advice for d-i-y: Yes, no charge. Basic funeral: £500. Prepaid plan: Golden Charter. Branches in Maidstone (tel 01622 688662), Bromley (tel 0181 460 1888), Orpington (tel 01689 870030), Sevenoaks (tel 01732 740444), Staplehurst (tel 01580 892125), Larkfield (tel 01732 871188) and Sittingbourne (tel 01795 431300). 'We have grown as a family-run business to nine branches within five years' (Kevin Critcher)

• **FD Swindon**: A. E. Smith & Son, a branch of Lodge Bros., at Queens Drive, Swindon, Wiltshire SN3 1AW (tel 01793 522023). See Lodge Bros. in the London region, below, for details.

• **FD Tonbridge**: Abbey Funeral Services, 173 High Street, Tonbridge, Kent TN9 1BX (tel 01732 360328). Cheapest fully-fitted coffin only: £123-60 (delivery locally £25). Cold storage only: Yes, £50 per day. Body transport only: Yes. Advice for d-i-y: Yes, £25 per hour ('form to be provided by client'). Basic funeral: £350 (for deaths attended between 9am and 5pm, and bills settled within 7 days of the funeral, disbursements extra). 'Small independent family business' (Geoffrey Tapp). Prepaid plan: Golden Charter. Member of SAIF and NAFD.

• **FD Weybridge**: Lodge Bros., 36-38 High Street, Weybridge, Surrey KT13 8AB (tel 01932 854758). See Lodge Bros. in the London region, below, for details.

• **Cem (Green Burial) Woking**: The Brookwood Cemetery, Cemetery Pales, Woking, Surrey GU24 OBL (tel 01483 472222). Plot (50 years) incl. digging and burial £1,250. Maintenance: £100. They will accept shrouds or body bags. Length of funeral service: As long as needed. There is a chapel. Grounds: Vast

420 acre cemetery with beautiful trees, many areas overgrown, Victorian monuments. Memorials: Virtually any design of memorial is accepted up to 3ft. 'All graves remain undisturbed for ever, there being so much unused land at Brookwood Cemetery. We may possibly develop a woodland burial ground in future' (E. Mary Cockram).

• **Crem Wokingham**: Easthampstead Park Crematorium, Nine Mile Ride, Wokingham, Berkshire RG40 3DW (tel 01344 4210314). Price: £192. Time allotted: 30 minutes (extra time can be booked for £90). They will accept home-made, cardboard or wicker coffins, and consider shrouds or body bags. Chapels: Modern and well-lit, seating 98 and 16 respectively. Grounds: Set in 22 acres of Berkshire countryside. 'Guidelines are constantly being amended to comply with public demand wherever possible' (Julian Hunter).

• **Crem Worthing**: Worthing Crematorium, Horsham Road, Findon, West Sussex BN14 0RQ (tel 01903 872678). Price: £210. Time allotted: 40 minutes (extra time can be booked for £25). They will accept home-made, wicker or cardboard coffins, or shrouds or body bags. Chapel: 1960s, Swedish-style, non-denominational. Grounds: 'Wildlife sanctuary' (Ian Rudkin).

• **FD Worthing**: Monumental Funeral Service, 92-94 Broadwater Street West, Broadwater Green, Worthing, West Sussex BN14 9DE (tel 01903 235353). Cheapest fully-fitted coffin only: £215 (delivery locally £10 within 10 miles). Cold storage only: Yes, £10 per day. Body transport only: Yes. Advice for d-i-y: free, £25 arrangement fee. Basic funeral: £450 (disbursements extra). 'Privately family-owned and managed' (Kenneth Blaylock). Prepaid plan: Golden Charter. Member of SAIF.

Greater London region

Including old Middlesex. See also South region.

• **FD**: **F. A. Albin & Sons** Funeral Directors, Arthur Stanley House, 52 Culling Road, London SE16 2TN (tel 0171 237 3637); also at 164 Deptford High Street, London SE8 3DP (tel 0181 694 1384). Cheapest fully-fitted coffin only: £199 (delivery nationally £45). Basic funeral: £687 for burial at Nunhead cemetery and £822 for cremation at Honor Oak crematorium (both incl. disbursements). Also offers a 'Disposal Funeral Package' with no viewing, no service and no one in attendance for £519 (incl. disbursements). For the coffins they sell and the display coffin they rent, see Chapter Five. 'Owned by the family, we are now 214 years old' (B. Albin).

• **FD**: **H. J. Bent & Co** Funeral Directors, 343 Ladbroke Grove, London W10 6HA (tel 0181 969 1170); also at 1c Westminster Court, London NW8 8JN (tel 0171 723 1186); and 3 Pavilion Parade, Wood Lane, London W12 0HQ (tel 0181 743 3338). Cheapest fully-fitted coffin only: £90 approx. (delivery locally £1 per mile; nationally from 50p per mile above 50 miles). Cold storage only: No. Body transport only: Yes (£50 estate car; £100 hearse). Advice for d-i-y: Yes, £10 per hour. Basic funeral: £500 (disbursements extra). Provided no price list ('reprint in action'); would only be prepared to give prices over the phone 'with reservations'. 'We were the first company to be BS5750 registered' (Shearsmith).

Prepaid plan: Chosen Heritage 'and our own'. Member of no association.
• **Cem: Camberwell** New Cemetery, Brenchley Gardens, London SE23 3RD (tel 0171 639 3121). Plot (50 years) incl. digging and burial £671 (non-residents £1773). They will accept home-made or cardboard coffins. Length of funeral service: 30 minutes or 45 minutes if chapel being used (extra time can be booked for £50). Chapel: Church-like. Grounds: Formal gardens. Memorials: Natural stone, within size restrictions. 'We may perhaps introduce a woodland burial facility in the future' (Mr Buckley).
• **FD: Chelsea Funeral Directors**, 260(b) Fulham Road, Chelsea, London SW10 9EL (tel 0171 352 0008). Cheapest fully-fitted coffin only: £175 (delivery locally £10). Cold storage only: Yes, £25 per day. Body transport only: Yes. Advice for d-i-y: Yes, £30 per hour. Basic funeral: £575 (disbursements extra). 'Independently owned, sensitivity to personalised funeral requests' (Neil Cocking). Prepaid plan: Golden Charter. Member of SAIF, NAFD.
• **Cem: Chingford** Mount Cemetery, Old Church Road, Chingford, London E4 6ST (tel 0181 524 5030). Plot (75 years) incl. digging and burial £638 (new graves for residents only). They will accept a wooden home-made coffin. Length of funeral service: 30 minutes (extra time can be booked without charge). No chapel. Grounds: Large, older cemetery with lots of trees. Memorials: Lawn-type headstones only, within size restrictions. 'We will accommodate all families' wishes to the best of our abilities within the limits of cemetery regulations' (John Billson).
• **Cem: City of London** Cemetery, Aldersbrook Road, London E12 5DQ (tel 0181 530 2151). Plot (50 years) incl. digging and burial £816. They will accept home-made, cardboard coffins or wicker coffins, or shrouds or body bags (subject to approval). Length of funeral service: 30 minutes (extra time may be booked without charge, subject to availability). Chapel: Victorian Gothic. Grounds: Formal. Memorials: Lawn-type only, in hard stone and within size restrictions. See woodland burial entry (Pat Clark).
• **Cem (Green Burial): City of London** Cemetery, Aldersbrook Road, London E12 5DQ (tel 0181 530 2151). At time of the time of going to press pricing policy was still being finalised, but – assuming the decision is made to sell grave rights, which would run for 50 years – the cost is likely to be in the region of £600. They will accept home-made, cardboard or wicker coffins – all coffins must be biodegradable. Since the site already has established trees, they may not always plant new ones for each burial. Families may help fill the grave if they wish. No memorials will be permitted on the woodland site, although families may, if they wish, sponsor a bench or some other memorial elsewhere in the cemetery. 'The site is attached to the existing, world-renowned, City of London Cemetery, whose 200 acre site has very well-kept grounds and excellent security. The woodland burial area, which features a variety of mature trees, will be managed as a conservation area, complementing the cemetery's existing nature reserve. We are happy to advise d-i-y families' (Ian Hussain).
• **FD: T. Cribb & Sons** funeral directors, 112 Rathbone St, Canning Town, London E16 1JQ (tel 0171 476 1855). Branch at Victoria House, Woolwich

Manor Way, Beckton, London E6. Cheapest fully-fitted coffin only: £137 approx. (delivery locally free). Cold storage only: Yes, no charge for reasonable time span. Body transport only: Yes. Advice for d-i-y: Yes, no charge – within reason. Basic funeral: £563 (disbursements extra). 'Free legal and medical helpline; probate and will service; DSS help, Victorian horse-drawn hearse available (from £675)' (J. Cribb). Prepaid plan: Golden Charter. Member of SAIF.

• **Crem: Croydon** Crematorium, Mitcham Road, Croydon CR9 3AT (tel 0181 684 3877). Price: £176. Time allotted: 30 minutes (extra time can be booked without charge). They will accept home-made, cardboard or wicker coffins, or shrouds or body bags. Chapels: One churchlike and one modern. Grounds: 'Landscaped, with award-winning water gardens'. 'A caring and professional service for all members of the community who are bereaved' (Mike Stride).

• **FD: Rowland Brothers**, 301 Whitehorse Road, West Croydon CR0 2HR (tel 0181 684 1667). Cheapest fully-fitted coffin only: £150 (delivery free locally; nationally £1 per mile). Cold storage only: Yes, £25 per day. Body transport only: Yes, £250 for hearse and four bearers. Advice for d-i-y: Yes, no charge for a quick call, substantial advice £100. Basic funeral: £465 (disbursements extra). 'We also have a disposal service which costs £356 for those who want no involvement at all' (Tony Rowland). Prepaid plan: Golden Leaves. Member of NAFD, SAIF.

• **FD: Doves Funeral Directors**, 1 Simpsons Road, Bromley BR2 9AP (tel 0181 460 1888) Also 19 Carlton Parade, Orpington BR6 OJD (tel 01689 870030). Branches of Doves (see Swanley in South region above for details).

• **Cem: East Finchley** Cemetery, East End Road, London N2 0RZ (tel 0181 567 0913). Plot (100 years) incl. digging and burial £720. They will accept home-made coffins. Length of funeral service: As required. Chapel: Recently renovated. Grounds: Collection of mature decorative trees. Memorials: Within size restrictions. 'Night-time security service and weekend patrols' (R. G. Bradfield).

• **Cem (Green Burial): East Sheen** Cemetery, Sheen Road, Richmond, Surrey TW10 5BJ (tel 0181 876 4511; fax 0181 878 8118). Administers similar cemeteries in Hampton, Mortlake, Teddington and Twickenham. Plot (50 years) incl. digging and burial £390. They will accept home-made, cardboard or wicker coffins (subject to approval of cemeteries manager). Length of funeral service: As long as required. Chapel: Non-denominational. Grounds: 'Rural in an urban environment.' Memorials: Natural stone, within size restrictions. Can be either lawn-style or traditional kerbed. 'We supply a d-i-y funeral guide and cardboard coffins (for £60). A woodland burial ground is planned for 1997' (Kate Towers).

• **Crem: Enfield** Crematorium, Great Cambridge Road, Enfield, London EN1 4DS (tel 0181 363 8324). Price: £185-50. Time allotted: 20 minutes (extra time can be booked for £100). They will accept cardboard coffins. Chapel: Pre-war, red brick. Grounds: 'Attractive rock and water gardens'. 'The best possible service given the very restricted budget available' (Nigel Morgan).

• **FD: J. E. Gillman & Sons Ltd**, 971 Garratt Lane, Tooting, London SW17 OLW (tel 0181 672 1557). Branches: Mitcham, Surrey (tel 0181 685 0349);

Carshalton, Surrey (tel 0181 669 0483); Tooting, London SW17 (tel 0181 672 6515); Battersea London SW11 (Edwin Bassett Funeral Service, tel 0171 228 0360); Balham High Road, London SW12 (E. A. Godfrey, tel 0181 673 8719); West Norwood, London SE27 (J. B. Wilson, tel 0181 670 4126). Cheapest fully-fitted coffin only: £90 (delivery free within a seven mile radius; nationally 'not possible'). Cold storage only: Yes, £10 per day. Body transport only: Yes. Advice for d-i-y: Yes, 'price depends on many factors'. Direct Transfer Service: 'Where there is no service, religious or secular, and no mourners', £290 (disbursements extra). Basic funeral: £595 (disbursements extra). 'Independent family firm, very experienced, qualified and flexible staff' (Brian Parsons). Prepaid plan: Golden Charter. Member of NAFD, SAIF.

• **FD: H. C. Grimstead Ltd**, 58 Swan Road, West Drayton, Middlesex UB7 7JZ (tel 01895 431000). The firm also has branches in Ruislip (tel 01895 822297), Eastcote (tel 0181 866 0688) and Harefield (tel 01895 822297) – and see the East Midlands region above for its branches in South Buckinghamshire at Beaconsfield, Amersham and Gerrards Cross. Cheapest fully-fitted coffin only: £200. Cardboard coffin £90. Cold storage only: Yes, £10 per day. Body transport only: Yes, from £60. Advice for d-i-y: Yes, probably no charge. Basic funeral: £395 for the 'Green Funeral Option' with a cardboard coffin (disbursements extra; and £1-15 extra per mile, each way, outside a 20 mile radius); otherwise £495. 'We are one of the few independent funeral directors, the third generation of the family' (Colin Thompson). Prepaid plan: Own plans and own trust fund. Member of NAFD.

• **FD: Haji Taslim Muslim Funerals**, East London Mosque, 45 Fieldgate Street, London E1 1JU (tel 0171 247 2625 or 0171 247 9583). Cheapest fully-fitted coffin only: £100 approx. Cold storage only: Yes, no charge. Body transport only: Yes, £60 for two hours with a driver within a 25 mile radius. Prices can be reduced for those in financial difficulty. Although 95% of the firm's business is Islamic, it is not exclusively so.

• **Cem: Hanwell** Cemetery, 38 Uxbridge Road, London W7 3PP (tel 0181 567 0913). Plot (100 years) incl. digging and burial £720. They will accept home-made coffins. Length of funeral service: As required. Chapel: Recently renovated. Grounds: Collection of mature decorative trees. Memorials: Within size restrictions. 'A night-time security service and weekend patrols' (R. G. Bradfield).

• **Crem: Hendon** Crematorium, Holders Hill Road, London NW7 1NB (tel 0181 346 0657). Price: £107. Time allotted: 30 minutes (extra time can be booked for £35). They will accept home-made or cardboard coffins. Country churchyard set in 40 acres of naturally wooded cemetery grounds. 'Practical, sympathetic and sensible service to the recently bereaved' (George Nash).

• **Cem Highgate** Cemetery, Swains Lane, London N6 6PJ (tel 0181 340 1834). Plot (70 years) incl. digging and burial £3025. They will accept home-made or cardboard coffins. No chapel. Grounds: One of the most famous cemeteries in the world, with many eminent Victorians buried in grand style in a beautiful woodland setting. Memorials: 'Any memorial installed must reflect some sympathy with Highgate's historic status.' 'As a privately-run charity, Highgate is able to offer a much more flexible service than most. For instance, within the limits imposed by limited space, we would arrange woodland burial on individual request' (Mr Richard Quirk).

• **Crem: Honor Oak** Crematorium, Brockley Way, London SE23 3RD (tel 0171 639 7499). Price: £183. Time allotted: 30 minutes (extra time can be booked for £91). They will accept home-made, cardboard or wicker coffins. Chapel: Neoclassical, Byzantine. Grounds: 'Garden of Remembrance, sports field and cemetery.' 'The coffin is lowered on a catafalque to symbolise the lowering of a coffin in a grave' (T. M. Connor).

• **FD Hounslow**: The local authority in Hounslow has an arrangement with local funeral directors to supply a 'Hounslow Community Funeral Service' to residents, at a cost of £895 (disbursements extra), which is not particularly cheap. The firms taking part are: The CRS Co-op (tel 0181 570 4741), W. S. Bond (tel 0181 994 0277), Holmes & Daughters (tel 0181 893 1860), Andrew Holmes & Son (tel 0181 572 3277), Frederick Paine (tel 0181 994 0056), A. Spicer (tel 0181 574 3186) and Christopher Wickenden (tel 0181 569 8373).

• **Crem: Islington** Crematorium, High Road, East Finchley, London N2 9AG (tel 0181 883 1230). Price: £165. Time allotted: 30 minutes (extra time can be booked for £100). They will accept home-made or cardboard coffins. Chapels: 'Light and warm 1930s, with movable seating.'. Grounds: Garden of Remembrance. 'Families are left to do their own thing' (D Pryor).

• **✪✪✪ FD**: **E. M. Kendall** funeral directors, 46 Dalston Lane, London E8 3AH (tel 0171 254 6519 and 0171 249 2884). Cheapest fully-fitted coffin only: £55 (delivery locally £10; nationally 'negotiable'). Cold storage only: Yes, £10 per day. Body transport only: Yes. Advice for d-i-y: Yes, £10 per hour. Basic funeral: £375 (disbursements extra). '24 hour service, moderate charges, every assistance given, distance no object' (E. M. Kendall). Prepaid plan: Own and Avalon. Member of BIFD and FSC.

• **Cem: Kensal Green** (All Souls) Cemetery, Harrow Road, London W10 4RA (tel 0181 969 0152). Plot (perpetuity) incl. digging and burial £1,040. Maintenance if required £38 p.a., VAT extra. They will accept home-made, cardboard or wicker coffins, or shrouds or body bags. Length of funeral service: Up to an hour, or longer if no following service. Chapel: Greek style (Doric) with a grandiose 'feel' and Victorian ambience. Grounds: Much wildlife; Gothic, with a honeycomb of catacombs underground. Memorials: Very few restrictions, except in two lawn grave areas where size and type of stone are regulated. 'Beautiful setting, historic architecture, polite and friendly staff' (David Burkett).

• **FD Lambeth**: A municipal funeral service for local residents, by arrangement with the local authority, is provided by the CWS Co-op (tel 0171 703 2803) at a cost of £820 (disbursements extra).

• **FD Lewisham**: A municipal funeral service for local residents, by arrangement with the local authority, is provided by the CWS Co-op (tel 0171 698 3244) at a cost of £625 (disbursements extra).

• **Crem: Lewisham** Crematorium, Verdant Lane, Catford, London SE6 1TP (tel 0181 698 4955). Price: £198. Time allotted: 30 minutes, extra time can be booked for £198. They will accept home-made, cardboard or wicker coffins. Chapel: Non-denominational. Grounds: 'Landscaped Gardens of Remembrance, featuring central pond which attracts wide variety of wildlife.' 'We will always try to accommodate specific requests' (Julie Dunk).

• **FD**: **Lodge Bros. (Funerals) Ltd**, Ludlow House, Ludlow Road, Feltham TW13 7JF (tel 0181 751 3361). Branches include: Feltham (tel 0181 894 9731, 0181 890 2231 and 0181 890 7902); Yiewsley (tel 01895 446686); Uxbridge (tel 01895 233018); Sunbury-on-Thames (tel 01932 785402); Shepperton (tel 01932 220081); Hounslow (tel 0181 570 0118); Hillingdon (tel 01895 234011); Hampton Hill (tel 0181 977 3127); Ashford (tel 01784 252226); West Ealing (tel 0181 567 0227); Brentford (tel 0181 567 0227). Cheapest fully-fitted coffin only: £134 . Body transport only: Yes. Advice for d-i-y: Yes. Basic funeral: £718 to £865 (varying between branches, disbursements extra). 'Our family business has been established 200 years and offers a very full range of services' (J. R. Lodge). Prepaid plan: Family Funerals Trust. Member of NAFD, BIFD.

• **Crem**: **Manor Park** Crematorium, Manor Park Cemetery Company Ltd., Sebert Road, Forest Gate, London E7 0NP (tel 0181 534 1486). Run by the Manor Park Cemetery Company Ltd. Price: £195. Time allotted: 30 minutes (extra time can be booked without charge). They will accept home-made or cardboard coffins. Chapels: 'Free church design. Homely.' Grounds: 'Wide drive-through cemetery. Large area for flowers.' 'Installation in July 1996 of England's first electric cremator' (Brian O. Kuhrt).

• **FD**: **Mears & Cotterill**, 169 Merton Road, Wandsworth, London SW18 5EF (tel 0181 874 7698). Cheapest fully-fitted coffin only: £105 plus VAT (delivery locally £30). Body transport only: Yes. Advice for d-i-y: Yes, £50 set fee. Basic funeral: £340 (disbursements extra). 'We are family owned. We supply coffins, hearse, embalming and advice as required, without insisting that we complete the whole of a funeral' (John William Mears). Prepaid plan: Golden Charter. Member of FSC.

• **Cem**: **Mill Hill** Cemetery, Milespit Hill, London NW7 2RR (tel 0181 567 0913). Plot (100 years) incl. digging and burial £720. They will accept home-made coffins. Length of funeral service: As required. Chapel: Recently reno-vated. Grounds: Collection of mature decorative trees. Memorials: Within size restrictions. 'Night-time security service and weekend patrols' (R. G. Bradfield).

• **Cem**: **New Southgate** Cemetery, Brunswick Park Road, London N11 1JJ (tel 0181 361 1713). Plot (50 years) incl. digging and burial £1,250. Maintenance: No charge. They will accept home-made, cardboard or wicker coffins, or shrouds or body bags. Length of funeral service: 30 minutes (extra time £50). Chapel: Built 1858, with a high steeple and (screenable) ornate oak altar. Grounds: One of best selections of conifer in London, together with native trees. Cemetery used by Jews (Reformed) and the Cypriot community. The shrine of Yogi Effendi in Bahai section has 100,000 visitors a year. Memorials: No restrictions, provided no offence is caused to others. The cemetery has made contributions of up to £2,000 'for modernistic designs by an approved designer'. 'All graves have flower heads covering the bottom of the grave and flowers on the surface at the head and at the corners. Clean dry soil and flower petals provided for strewing. Special facilities provided as and when required, such as tables for traditional Cypriot food and wine' (Barry Evans).

• **FD Southwark**: A municipal funeral service for local residents, by arrangement with the local authority, is provided by the CWS Co-op (tel 0171 732 4165) at a cost of £810 (disbursements extra).

• **Crem: Putney Vale** Crematorium, Stag Lane, Putney, London SW15 4ED (tel 0181 788 2113 or 0181 789 8734). Price: £150 (non-residents £210). Time allotted: 20 minutes (extra time can be booked for £60). They will accept home-made or cardboard coffins. Grounds: Formal garden, fountain, lily ponds, extending into wooded glade (Anne O'Connell).

• **FD**: **Regale Funerals**, based on the Roc 'Eclerc chain in France. This UK 'funerals supermarket' opened in 1996 at 227 Hoe Street, Walthamstow, London E17 (tel 0181 925 2010) run by Stephen and Sam Weller. Cheapest fully-fitted coffin only: £134 (delivery at cost, and sometimes free locally). Cold storage only: Yes, £5 per day. Body transport only: Yes, from £106 for a removal, £138 for a funeral. Basic funeral: £609 (disbursements extra). 'We are independent and give value for money' (Mr Fuller). Prepaid plan: None, but can help organise funeral insurance with United Friendly.

• **Crem: South London** Crematorium, The Garden of Remembrance, Rowan Road, London SW16 5JG (tel 0181 679 4164). Price: £151. Time allotted: 30 minutes (extra time can be booked for £90-50). They will accept cardboard or home-made coffins, and will consider wicker coffins, shrouds or body bags. Chapels: Edwardian, churchlike. Grounds: 'Formal gardens with 3 new mausoleums at the front of the building.' 'Services are available on both Saturdays and Sundays. There are very few restrictions and we will offer whatever the families want so long as it's legal' (Mrs A. T. Munns).

• **Crem: South West Middlesex** Crematorium, Hounslow Road, Hanworth, Feltham, Middlesex TW13 5JH (tel 0181 894 9001). Price: £150. Time allotted: 30 minutes (extra time can be booked for £83). They will accept home-made or cardboard coffins, or body bags. Chapel: Three traditional chapels seating 25, 80 and 120 respectively. Grounds: 'Both formal and informal.' 'Very striking architecture and the grounds give a feel of tranquillity and peace' (Peter Alan Cronshaw).

• **Crem: Southwark** Crematorium, Bockley Way, London SE23 (tel 0171 639 3121). Price: £183. Time allotted: 30 minutes (extra time can be booked for £50). They will accept home-made, cardboard or wicker coffins. Grounds: Formal gardens, shrubbery, wooded area, Garden of Remembrance (Mr Buckley, Clerical Officer).

• **FD**: **W. A. Truelove & Son Ltd**, a branch at 31 High Street, Cheam, Greater London SM3 8RE (tel 0181 642 3300); also at 55 Chipstead Valley Road, Coulsdon, Greater London CR3 2RB (tel 0181 660 2620); also at Donald Drewett & Sons, 49-51 Upper Green East, Mitcham, Greater London CR4 2PF (tel 0181 648 2905); also at 20 Mulgrave Road, Sutton, Greater London SM2 6LE (tel 0181 642 0089); also at 109 Stafford Road, Wallington, Greater London

SM6 9AP (tel 0181 647 1032). See their entry above, under Carshalton, South region, for details.

• **Crem: West London** Crematorium, Kensal Green Cemetery, Harrow Road, London W10 4RA (tel 0181 969 0152). Price: £153 (£155 non-residents). Time allotted: 20 minutes within a 30 minute period (extra time can be booked for £78). They will accept home-made, cardboard or wicker coffins (home-made coffins must comply with FBCA standards); they would need to see shrouds or body bags first. Chapels: 'A beautiful classical building. The East Chapel is in art deco style with oak pews and solid marble catafalque; the West is modern and light with light oak fixtures and catafalque.' Grounds: 'Surrounded by beautiful Gardens of Remembrance, with over 4,000 dedicated roses, and columbaria in the colonnades at the rear of the building.' 'The superintendent is a qualified funeral director who will assist people to arrange funerals without recourse to a funeral director' (Celia Luetchford Smith).

• **FD**: **Willow Independent Funeral Service**, 21 Wellington Street, Woolwich, London SE18 6PQ (tel 0181 854 6222). Cheapest fully-fitted coffin only: £285. Cold storage only: Yes, £5 per day. Body transport only: Yes. Advice for d-i-y: Yes, £15 per hour. Basic funeral: £535 (disbursements extra). 'We are independent and give value for money' (Mr Fuller). Prepaid plan: Golden Charter. Member of SAIF.

Scotland

• **Crem Edinburgh**: Mortonhall Crematorium, 30, Howdenhall Road, Edinburgh EH16 6TY (tel 0131 664 4314). Price: £190 (non-residents £190). Time allotted: 30 minutes (extra time can be booked for £30). They will accept cardboard coffins. Chapel: Modern, church-like. Grounds: 'Mature woodland, lawns and mounds.' 'Flat granite memorials in rose borders only type allowed' (George Bell).

• **FD**: **Barclay's Funeral Services**, 4 Taylor Gardens, Edinburgh EH6 6TG (tel 0131 553 6818). Parent company SCI. Cheapest fully-fitted coffin only: £195. Cold storage only: Yes, no charge. Body transport only: Yes, £70 hearse, £50 limousine. Advice for d-i-y: Yes, no charge. Basic funeral: £695 (disbursements extra). 'We go above and beyond the call of duty' (Peter Deery). Prepaid plan: Dignity. Member of NAFD.

• **Green Burial Edinburgh**: Woodland burial ground, Costorphine Hill Cemetery, Edinburgh, Scotland (contact Bereavement Services Manager, Morton Hall Crematorium, Howden Hall Road, Edinburgh, Scotland EH16 6TX, tel 0131 664 4314). A grave costs £300 incl. the digging, burial and tree (the same for non-residents). They will accept cardboard coffins, or shrouds or body bags. Mourners may help fill the grave. Subsequent visits to the graveside are discouraged – there can be a memorial on a pathway. 'There is room for 500 graves. Silver birch trees are planted, and bluebells and wild flowers. It is a quiet woodland side' (G. P. Bell).

• **Crem Masonhill**: Masonhill Crematorium, Masonhill, By Ayr, South Ayrshire KA6 6EN (tel 01292 266051). Price: £140. Time allotted: 30 minutes (extra time can be booked for £70). They will accept home-made, cardboard or wicker coffins, or shrouds. Chapel: 1960s non-denominational. Grounds: In open country with established trees. 'The service will adapt to meet the needs of the bereaved' (Howard Greenoff).

• **Crem Perth**: Perth Crematorium, Crieff Road, Perth PH1 2PE (tel 01738 25068). Price: £166-20. Time allotted: 45 minutes between each service (extra time has never been asked for). They will accept rigid containers as long as draped with a cloth. Grounds: formal and wooded.

Eire and Northern Ireland

• **Crem Belfast**: City of Belfast Crematorium, 129 Ballygowan Road, Crossnacreevy, Belfast, Northern Ireland BT5 7T2 (tel 01232 448342). Price: £84-20 (non-residents £168-40). Time allotted: 30 minutes (extra time can be booked without charge). They will accept home-made, cardboard or wicker coffins, or shrouds or body bags. Chapel: Modern, church-like – but without religious symbolism. Grounds: 'Beautiful lawns and memorial trees.' 'Nothing is too much trouble and every family is treated with respect whether they are on low income or very rich' (Mrs Sharon McCloy).

• **(Green Burial) County Down**: Natural Undertakings, Patrick McEvoy of 22 Kinnegar Road, Holywood, Co. Down, Northern Ireland (tel 01232 426484). Patrick McEvoy is actively researching the possibility of starting a woodland burial ground in Northern Ireland or getting the North Down Borough Council to do so and he writes: 'I would be grateful if you would direct any enquiries about any aspect of natural burial in my direction.' Provisional member of the Association of Nature Reserve Burial Grounds.

• **FD County Leitrim**: Luke Early, Main Street, Mohill, County Leitrim, Eire (tel 078 31081 or 087 470795). Cheapest fully-fitted coffin only: £290 (delivery locally £30; anywhere in Eire for £90). Cold storage only: No. Advice for d-i-y: Yes, £15 per hour. Basic funeral: £495 (disbursements extra). 'No parent company, Personal contact with bereaved family' (Luke Early). Prepaid plan: None. Member of IAFD.

Isle of Man

• **(Green Burial) Isle of Man**: W. P. Kreen of Lhie Ny Greiney, Surby Mooar, Port Erin, Isle of Man IM9 6TD (tel 01624 834104) is planning to try to start a green burial ground on the Isle of Man.

Chapter 7

WOODLAND BURIAL GROUNDS

The Natural Death Centre, the A. B. Wildlife Trust Fund and others have for several years publicly promoted the concept of woodland burial grounds where a tree is planted by the grave instead of having a headstone. Such a site provides a very elegant solution to a number of problems:

• Cemeteries in many areas are filled to capacity – and when visits to graves cease, the cemeteries could be destroyed to make way for building development.

• It would not be desirable to continue for centuries into the future covering the countryside with row upon row of headstones. Furthermore, headstones can become dangerous to children and are very costly to maintain.

• Burial has become pricier than cremation, particularly in and around cities.

• Cremation causes pollution and adds to the greenhouse effect.

• Crematoria are bleak places in which to hold funerals.

• Woodland burial grounds are less costly to develop than crematoria.

• The planet needs more trees and the UK has a policy of increasing its forest cover.

• People are seeking less expensive funerals and ones which they can organise themselves, without necessarily using funeral directors.

• Farmers need to diversify to bring in more sources of income – many have land for which they are paid very little under set aside.

• People would like beautiful rural settings for the burial of their family and friends.

• Woodland burial grounds provide a refuge for wildlife.

• The Green generation as it gets older – Friends of the Earth supporters and the like – will not want to cause pollution with their deaths. They will be attracted by the concept of 'giving the body back to nature'. As Jonathon Porritt puts it: 'The combination of built-in fertiliser, plus unlimited tender loving care from the relatives, would pretty well guarantee a thriving woodland in next to no time.'

The Centre made these points in a number of media interviews from 1993 onwards. Farmers were not slow to respond to the challenge. The Centre also gave a talk to the Institute of Burial and Cremation Authorities, urging that every local authority should follow the example of Carlisle and set up a green burial ground within its area. Again, progress has been rapid.

It was also hoped that charitable and non-profit bodies such as the National Trust, the Woodland Trust, the Forestry Commission and the new planned national forests would all start making provision for memorial groves. In this instance, however, progress has been more cautious, with the Woodland Trust, for example, deciding not to develop any such burial grounds within its land for the time being.

Incidentally, 'woodland burial grounds' has become the popular term for these new sites, but it should be noted that woodland is just one sort of habitat and that 'green burial grounds' or 'nature reserve burial grounds' better conveys the diversity of meadows and pastures that are being used.

The Carlisle woodland burial ground

As mentioned, the first woodland burial ground was the one set up by the City of Carlisle. Ken West, the manager there, wrote during the planning stages in 1993:

> The creation of a memorial woodland resource would benefit the environment and could be returned to the community after the expiry of grave rights. It could then form part of a country park or a green lung, for walking, pony trekking or similar. Part of the intangible benefits are a return to nature and the need to encourage insects, birds and mammals.
>
> For the layout of the graves, I prefer a double grave with burials side by side, at a depth of 4' 3". This allows, after a burial, the planting of a tree on the used portion of the grave. There will be space for 900 graves to the acre, about 9% less than our current setting out. This is more than compensated for by the reduced excavation costs, drainage problems, backfilling, reinstatement of sunken graves, etc. Additionally, the cost of a traditional new graveyard had to include new roads, deep drainage, etc, which will not apply in the same degree with this scheme.
>
> People choosing the woodland concept before death will have gained a real psychological benefit – a piece of woodland and a real, living memorial instead of a dull, dead stone. Perhaps the test of any product is 'Would you use it yourself?' I can state clearly that I would and refer you to these lines from 'Drummer Hodge' by Thomas Hardy:
>
> > His homely Northern breast and brain
> > Grow to some Southern tree
> > And strange eyed constellations reign
> > His stars eternally.

> *Adapted extracts from an article by Ken West,*
> *Carlisle Bereavement Services Manager.*

The rate at which new woodland burial grounds are opening is impressive. In January 1996, there were 17 such grounds known to the Natural Death Centre; by July, there were 33; by January 1997 there were 52.

Of these 52 woodland burial grounds (all of which are detailed in the Good Funeral Guide chapter), 34 are run by councils, 12 are run as businesses by farmers or private individuals, and 6 are run as non-profit concerns either without charging or, for instance, asking for donations to a wildlife trust. At least 19 more sites are about to open, and 30 more are at an early planning stage. The cost of a grave, including the digging and the tree, ranges from £57 at Seaton in Devon (see South West region below) to £1,080 at the Brinscombe woodland burial ground in Stroud. The average cost is £362. The average cost for the sites run as businesses is £445.

Association of Nature Reserve Burial Grounds

In 1994, the Natural Death Centre set up an Association of Nature Reserve Burial Grounds to promote these grounds to the public, to increase networking between them, to advise them about planning and other hurdles, to defend their interests with the authorities and to help set standards that will benefit the public. Membership, whether full or provisional, costs £20 per annum, although members are also encouraged to pay 1 per cent of the ground's gross income to the Natural Death Centre charity.

To be allowed to become a full member of the Association, a green burial ground must be willing to allow the use of cardboard coffins; it must allow families to organise a funeral without a funeral director if they so wish; it must safeguard funds paid in advance; and it must manage its site ecologically.

The Association is still at a very early stage, relying primarily on the probity of statements made by its members and on feedback from the public, as it does not yet have the resources for site inspections.

Code of Practice

The following is the Code of Practice (updated August 19th 1996):

• Association members agree to take all reasonable steps for the conservation of local wildlife and archaeological sites and to manage their sites according to sound and consistent ecological principles.

• Association members accept for burial bodies whether wrapped in a shroud or placed in a cardboard or wooden coffin or alternative container or wrapping, provided these are environmentally acceptable.

• Association members will not require that a funeral director be used. Those using the Nature Reserve Burial Ground will be informed that they may organise the funeral themselves, including conducting any service. They may dig a single depth grave, subject to any equipment, training, safety or regulatory constraints; and they may help with filling in the grave.

• Association members will keep a permanent record of exactly where each grave is. A copy of the burial ground register entry will be made available to the client.

• Association members will either sell coffins and shrouds to clients or provide information as to where these can be obtained.

• Association members, whose charges must be fair and reasonable, will provide fully itemised price lists for potential clients on request, and will also reveal these prices on the telephone on request.

• Association members will provide a copy of this Code of Practice to clients using their services, and will have copies available on request for others.

• Association members will provide each client using their services with a feedback form asking for their comments on the service provided and for any suggested improvements. This feedback form is to include the address and phone number of the Association for any complaints.

• Association members, if taking money in advance, agree to abide by the Office of Fair Trading's recommendations on prepaid funerals.

• Association members accept that in the event of a complaint from a client that is not dealt with to the Association's satisfaction within three months of the complaint being made, the Nature Reserve Burial Ground's membership will cease without refund.

• Before membership is granted or renewed, the Association may require further evidence on the above or any other relevant matters.

The Association of Nature Reserve Burial Grounds, c/o The Natural Death Centre, 20 Heber Road, London NW2 6AA (tel 0181 208 2853; fax 0181 452 6434; e-mail: <rhino@dial.pipex.com>).

Advice for those setting up green burial grounds

The main obstacle facing any farmer, company or individual wanting to set up a relatively large scale commercial green burial ground is likely to be obtaining planning permission. Several grounds have only won permission on appeal. Local objections can be ferocious and irrational, fuelled by fear of death and the taboos surrounding the whole subject. Applicants who want to spare themselves a long-drawn out process and the hostility of their neighbours would do well to choose a site not overlooked by neighbours and where neighbours will not even see the funeral cars. Even to be invisible may not help them sufficiently however: the landscape officer in one application reported that even though the site could not be seen from the road, the mere knowledge that the site was there, would make driving past it a 'depressing experience' – what a contrast with Victorian days when to have picnics in cemeteries was a quite normal occurrence.

Applicants might also be well advised, if they have a choice between forecasting for 700 burials a year or for 50 burials, to go for the smaller number initially; likewise, if there is a choice between applying for the whole property of 50 acres to become a burial ground, or for a mere 7 acre field within it, to apply for the smaller site. The burial ground will take many years to fill up and by then the momentum in favour of such developments will be that much greater than it is now. In the meantime, a small site may arouse fewer passions.

Applicants should also choose a site where the council cannot claim that access from the road will be dangerous or the car-parking inadequate and they should seek the advice of council officers at an early stage.

But even when the council officers support an application, the applicant should be wary if there is local opposition. Local petitions and letters against the applicant need to be matched by petitions and letters in favour – the Association of Nature Reserve Burial Grounds and the Natural Death Centre get many thousands of requests for information about green funerals each year and could perhaps be commissioned to write on behalf of the applicant to local members of the public who are likely to be sympathetic.

It could also be good tactics to arrange a five minute individual meeting with every councillor on the relevant planning committee to show them your plans, to answer any doubts that they may have and to let them see that you are not the devil incarnate.

Produce a detailed landscaping plan and illustrate how the site will look when the trees are mature. At one planning meeting a site was rejected, with one councillor remarking: 'The trees are small, it doesn't look like a wood', not seeming to realise that it is in the nature of trees to grow bigger.

John Bradfield of the A. B. Wildlife Trust Fund in Harrogate (tel 01423 530900) offers commercial applicants detailed ecological, legal or planning advice, with or without on-site visits, on a fee-paying basis. (He can also advise charitable projects on how best to proceed.)

To find a green burial site to buy, it might be worth approaching an agent dealing in woodland such as John Clegg & Sons (tel 01494 784711) or the Woodlands Centre (tel Margaret Hanton on 0181 693 4000) or Woodland Investment Management (tel 0181 693 4000).

Additional tips have been sent in by existing green burial grounds:

Julian Wedgwood of the Honeywood burial ground suggests that the first person to get on your side is the local vicar, then the chair of the parish council, before approaching bodies like the Environment Agency. Once you have an outline letter from the latter saying that they cannot see any immediate objection, you can then spend the money on a planning application.

Mr Rodney Hill, the Wigan Cemetery Registrar, adds that, at the earliest opportunity, groups should meet not only with council people and local clergy but with the local authority cemetery and crematorium people – you need to explain that you are not in competition but are offering an alternative service. When choosing a site, groups should consider whether the area floods or has water problems. Have a colour plan drawn up and put on display, with permission, in local authority buildings and the town hall, hold meetings with the press and public to smooth out problems before a planning application is submitted.

James Broome of the New Manchester Woodland Cemetery has slightly different advice on timing, suggesting that just before the planning application is lodged, or within one week of doing so, make sure local people are aware of your plans. They must clearly understand the difference between your scheme and a traditional cemetery. If you rely on the standard notices sent out by the local authority to inform people, it gives a chance for substantial opposition to arise, and you may find a local do-gooder organising a petition against you. 'While the planning committee tend to ignore petitions,' Broome writes, 'they do take notice of well-constructed logically argued objections in the form of an individual letter, and some of these will no doubt also enter the system.'

In their own case, once they had addressed these problems and had arranged a meeting on site with a cross-section of local people – giving a project presentation followed by a question and answer session – opposition dwindled.

Barbara Butler of Green Undertakings say that they will help people in any way they can to get their sites going (they already act as sole agents for several farmers). Be sure, she says, that the site you choose is acceptable to the Environment Agency (which has taken over the National Rivers Authority). Apply for a change to mixed use if the site is presently farmland. And she emphasises the points made above that 'local people need to know what is happening or they will imagine the worst – always!' and that access must be easy and acceptable to the highway authorities.

Charitable green burial grounds

The trailblazing green burial charity has been the A. B. Wildlife Trust Fund in Harrogate (see the North East region of the Good Funeral Guide chapter for their full details). Already in 1993, John Bradfield of the A. B. Wildlife Trust Fund was writing that: 'After two and a half years of correspondence with the Charity Commission, I've finally got agreement in principle to create a registered charity that combines nature reserves and human (and pet) burial grounds. I believe that by being able to select burial in land in which nature has a prior claim, there will be a qualitative shift in emotional experience, away from the "warehousing of the dead" in cemeteries and churchyards.' In his letter to The Natural Death Centre, John Bradfield added:

The A. B. Wildlife Trust Fund

I'm concerned that we should be able to take *full* control over dying and death. This means being able to avoid the use of funeral directors (et al) or to buy only those services required from them. It could mean digging the grave oneself having chosen the location, or digging it with a group of friends and relatives. Health and safety factors need to be fully taken account of, but are not barriers in themselves. Risks can be reduced by making shallow graves, which are also more environmentally benign.

There is no minimum depth for graves in national laws for private land, unless the Towns Improvement Clauses Act 1847 applies, in which case the minimum is 30 inches from the ground level to the top of the coffin, if a coffin is used. The minimum for public cemeteries is 24 inches and we know of a hospital burial ground, closed in 1969, where coffins were at ground level.

I'm also keen that coffins not be used unless environmentally benign, such as second-hand timbers from doors, floors and pallets. A ban will be placed on tropical hardwoods, even those from assumed sustainable sources. A coffin is wrongly said by some to be required for transporting the body, but a choice may be exercised simply to use a shroud, the person's own clothes, or some other alternative, such as basket from willow or sustainable osier beds, cardboard or carpet.

My only real concern is how to keep a precise plan of the site, noting the exact position of each grave. There will have to be some fixed points of some sort, from which to take measurements, without them being a visual intrusion.

For a donation of £5, the A. B. Wildlife Trust Fund will send any group trying to start a charitable nature reserve burial ground a copy of its constitution – or no doubt a copy could be obtained from the Charity Commission library at 57 Haymarket, London SW1 (tel 0171 210 4477). The Trust is also seeking donations of land and money to run further burial grounds under its own aegis. (Green Undertakings are registering a charity based on a similar constitution, called Butler's Trust.)

John Bradfield noted in 'Green Burial' that the Charity Commission agreed that the trustees of the Harrogate Trust for Wildlife Protection had power to allow a small numbers of burials within its nature reserves, without having to mention burials in its constitution. Such burials have since taken place.

A Certificate of Lawfulness (also known as a Lawful Development Certificate or 'LDC'), he adds, which costs about half the fee for applying for planning permission, could be sought to ascertain how many graves your local authority would permit without requiring planning permission.

If the graves are dug by hand, and there are none of the various identifying signs of a cemetery, such as roads, sale of burial rights, gravestones and large fencing, John Bradfield argues in 'Green Burial' that there will have been no 'substantial' or 'material' change of use and therefore the local authority should not require planning permission to be sought. Woodland burial grounds should make it clear that they have no interest in setting up cemeteries.

John Bradfield prefers to rely, not on tree planting, but on allowing woods naturally to plant themselves, or using a good seed supply from near at hand, thus promoting local strains and genes, and conserving genetic diversity. Burials should be on parts of the site with the least ecological importance, rather than in areas of existing wildlife value such as old woods with woodland flowers, bogs, marshes or wild flower meadows or pasture. 'It is too easy to overlook important wild flower areas, so it is worth asking someone with a trained eye to study the area between early Spring and late Autumn.'

Burials should happen only exceptionally, Bradfield adds, in Sites of Special Scientific Interest – but even these may have areas with little ecological value such as old refuse tips or nettle beds, areas once churned up by heavy machinery, large areas of bracken, old bonfire sites, areas where topsoil may need to be stripped off, or agriculturally 'improved' grassland where the aim is to recover some degree of species diversity.

In one planning appeal by a burial ground in Oswestry, monitored by John Bradfield, the inspector pointed out that 'cemeteries are not "inappropriate" development in terms of the guidance on Green Belts (contained in Planning Policy Guidance note 2 (PPG2) or local planning policies)'.

The A. B. Wildlife Trust Fund has sent in a number of other tips for those seeking to set up charitable green burial grounds:

> Persuade a local and well-established wildlife charity to agree to one or more burials in existing nature reserves, so as to begin the process and start changing attitudes (see 'Green Burial' 1994, page 61) but to avoid complex charity law, do not sell access or burial rights.

Work with a local wildlife charity to extend an existing nature reserve, by purchasing adjacent land for burials. Ask that charity to agree, from the outset, to take over the project after a number of years (as the Essex Wildlife Trust will do at Wrabness) or when burials have ceased.

Even if an established wildlife charity is wary of involvement, it is still worth buying land which it is likely to accept as a gift at some distant date.

Don't accept unsuitable land just to get started, as the land can't be sold or exchanged for a better site – burials are permanent. Small life rafts of wildlife in seas of barley and sugar beet, will be of no interest to most wildlife charities. They would take over small sites if adjacent to existing nature reserves, so the total area is increased.

If you are aiming for more than a handful of burials in the long-term, decide whether or not to have a few burials first, before applying for planning permission.

You must get a Certificate of Lawfulness or planning permission, if graves will be sold in advance of need, to make the arrangement watertight.

To avoid complex charity law, it can be easier for an individual or non-charitable group to own the land and agree to burials, if reasonable donations are made to a named charity, with ownership passing to that or some other charity at a later date (as with Kate's Fell, which is owned by John Bradfield, but with all money going to the A. B. Wildlife Trust Fund).

So that there is no doubt when questions are asked, have a clear and long-term plan from the outset on (a) the protection of graves, (b) access to the land for visits to graves, and (c) the conservation of existing wildlife or how wildlife will be established and managed over time.

Perpetual rights and perpetual protection cannot be guaranteed by non-charitable landowners, unless covered by some aspect of law, such as the Cemeteries Clauses Act 1847. The maximum length of time in law which public cemeteries and the Church of England can guarantee is 100 years, but even these rights can be ended if the correct steps are taken.

The A. B. Wildlife Trust Fund will not accept embalmed bodies. It has also banned hearses for its Kate's Fell site, partly to keep the planners happy (no one will know a funeral is taking place if no hearses are around) and partly to encourage people to use their own vehicles.

A. B. Wildlife Trust Fund (Charity Reg. No. 1037444), 7 Knox Road, Harrogate, North Yorkshire HG1 3EF (tel 01423 530900)

Local authority woodland burial grounds

Dawn Eckhart, the Community Development Officer at the Seaton cemetery in Devon, suggests that the quickest and simplest way for a local authority to begin a woodland burial ground is to set it up as a pilot project within an existing cemetery. The cemetery will already have planning permission and so there are no negotiations needed with other agencies about health and safety or water pollution. If Dawn Eckhart had more time, she would like to research a source of coffins produced from local and sustainably-managed forests.

The disadvantage of a small scheme, she says, is not being able to allow people to buy adjacent plots in advance. The site has no sign of the graves on the surface, so graves are being dug in sequence to avoid error.

Brendan Day, who runs the Thornhill Cemetery in Cardiff, advises that a woodland burial section is a good way of utilising cemetery ground where only a depth of 4'6" can be obtained. Families do not expect two depth graves in a woodland burial ground, once they are aware of the need for the body to be as close to the surface as possible so as to encourage the bacterial action and decay. Thus a local authority may be able to make use of a site with a relatively high water table or with a rocky layer beneath it.

David Lobb, Maldon Cemeteries Officer, wrote in the Funeral Service Journal (November 1996) that their woodland burial glades are being created within an existing mature cemetery. Families choose a grave space within burial islands. Each island consists of between 20 to 40 graves, and the islands will eventually link up together. Pathways constructed from bark with log edgings will be developed as the need arises. The grounds are managed as wildflower meadow. For the wildflower planting, they use pre-grown plant plugs, 'these being of much more immediate impact and far easier to establish. Species include red campion, ragged robin, white campion, harebell and ox-eye daisy'. John Bradfield of the A. B. Wildlife Trust Fund cautions, however, against indiscriminate use of wildflower seed – 'no wildflowers should be grown without obtaining advice from a credible wildlife charity on the species and genetic origin.'

Hugh Dawson, Oxford Cemeteries Manager, writes that all register records are now kept on computer, with many packages available. The woodland burial grounds, he comments, will design themselves, depending on the types of trees which families select to be planted on the graves.

This chapter ends with suggestions and adapted extracts from a long feasibility study and update prepared by Ken West, the pioneer of woodland burial. The full book-length set of papers, entitled 'Woodland Burial – A Return to Nature', is available for £20 from Carlisle Cemetery, The Cemetery Office, Richardson Street, Carlisle CA2 6AL (tel 01228 25022).

The Woodland Burial – A Return to Nature

• Local authority cemeteries all lose money. In Carlisle, for instance, all cemetery income simply covers the grave digging and associated administrative costs. There is no surplus whatsoever for subsequent grave maintenance – a deficit of £273,500 for 1990/91. Maintenance costs, when viewed over a 50 year period, average £86·15 per year. The woodland burial site, by contrast, will have insignificant maintenance costs and long term liabilities. Income from coffin sales and plaques on the Memorial Wall offers the possibility of woodland cemeteries actually making a profit.

• The format of the funeral has been changed by those favouring the woodland concept. The number of secular funerals is slightly above average. One funeral has already occurred with the family requesting that all staff attending, both from the cemetery and the funeral director, should wear jeans and tee-shirts. A further funeral is being planned along these lines for the future. I have not previously experienced this request in my 35 years in this work.

- Chipboard coffins are lined with a plastic sheet. Expert opinion suggests that although chipboard acts like a sponge and breaks down very quickly in damp or wet soil, the plastic wraps itself around the body and may cause mummification. This will be avoided if a biodegradable coffin is used.

- Woodland burial is perceived as being much more successful than it really is. Woodland burial represents only 1.5% of the total funerals we complete, including cremation ... (although), for the period October 1995 to March 1996, 19% of our grave sales were in the woodland.

- If a new woodland burial scheme reduces memorial or other sources of income, either to the funeral director or associated memorial outlet, it may be opposed. A advance reservation scheme for graves may defeat negative advice the bereaved may receive from funeral directors at the time of death.

- Graves are marked with a concrete block sunk level with the ground, engraved with a number from 1 upwards. Each twentieth grave marker will be erected 24" high to facilitate measurement to locate other grave markers in dense vegetation.

- The graves take up more space than in conventional cemeteries, as two coffins are put side by side. But the graves are shorter length and width per coffin than usual, because they are dug to a shallow depth and collapse will not become a problem.

- We initially planted many of the unused graves with an oak whip, mainly to give the site a 'woodland' appearance. Subsequently, we find that these trees are easily moved and replanted onto graves which have recently been used for burial. This is useful as it generally allows the partner or family to plant the tree on their grave during the summer months.

- Reports of some other woodland burial schemes have been disappointing. One had graves located around cemetery perimeters, creating a line of trees rather than woodland. Another was situated on a compost heap formed by the cemetery grass mowings accumulating over years. At another location, the staff had little idea about the concept.

The woodland should replicate the type of woodland which exists naturally in the area. One woodland scheme offers a choice of three tree species, one of which is Mountain Ash (Sorbus). Unfortunately, most people using the scheme are choosing this and creating a Mountain Ash wood. Such a wood is rarely found naturally, particularly in lowland, and these trees are often short lived.

Other schemes are using the typical garden centre type tree, the 'lollipop' tree, with a cleared stem up to (say) 4' to 5' and the branches radiating from a single apical point. These trees never attain the typical forest tree appearance and they often possess structural weaknesses. They may also be grown from European rather than native seed.

In Carlisle, we located some landowners who have been growing Oaks from acorns harvested from old trees growing on their land. These young trees cost £1 each and are about 2' to 2'6" high and with a good fibrous root system. Any seed trees you use should be old enough to predate the period of potential introduction from abroad. About 100 years should suffice.

Oak offers many benefits – the number of insect species found on the oak is 284, which exceeds any other tree. Lichens number 324, which well exceeds any other tree. Oak is not suited, however, to chalk soils or industrial spoils.

• Tree shelters (translucent polypropylene tubes) would look unattractive across burial areas. Spiral guards (loosely coiled plastic tubes which wrap around the stem) are used instead. They are only suitable on feathered whips with a stem diameter of at least 25mm.

• Weeds around the tree are controlled by mulching using black polythene mulching mats (600mm by 600mm square), minimum 500 gauge with ultra violet inhibitor. The mat is dug in around its edges and covered by leaf mould or wood chips.

• Evidence from existing crematoria memorial planting schemes shows that trees, which, on the woodland burial ground will be only 1.5 metres apart, can be thinned after five years, with few, if any people, concerned.

• The Forestry Commission 'Woodland Grant Scheme' gives money per hectare for Oak woodland, if a minimum 0.25 hectare is planted within a five year period. This figure can be reached by including shelter and other types of planting achieved for the opening of the burial area.

• 20 weeks after burial (depending on the time of year), the grave will be forked/rotovated and levelled approximately 75mm below the normal ground surface. Approximately 210 bluebell bulbs will be laid evenly over the grave surface, covered by 75mm of top soil. The Oak tree whip will be planted and the plastic mulch mat at its base will be covered with 65mm of leaf mould. The remaining soil surface will be levelled and wildflower seed sown and raked into the soil.

• Environment Agency objections to the setting up of a cemetery may be based on reports of watercourse pollution from cemeteries in the USA. This is apparently due to the high percentage of bodies treated with embalming fluid, and formaldehyde has been found in the water. If this objection arises, it might be sensible to prohibit the embalming of bodies accepted for burial for the woodland burial site.

• The types of people using the woodland graves include those who seek an alternative to cremation; those who like the no-memorial anonymity; single people who do not need to buy the conventional double grave space; the broadly green – gardeners and those who love birds, countryside, trees and wildflowers; those liking the low cost aspect; and those wanting secular or independent funerals.

• A dedication ceremony can formally open the burial area. This involves a religious ceremony jointly performed by representatives of all the churches.

• Although I coined the phrase 'return to nature', other fertile minds are already improving on this. I particularly like 'leave the world a better place', devised by a funeral director operating his own woodland site in the Isle of Wight.

Chapter 8

'Improving' Grieving

Anything written about grieving is unlikely to suit everybody because grief is an intensely personal emotion. It can be bewildering and surprising and make us do unexpected things. Grief can knock us sideways. The absence of grief, too, can be stunning. It is not always there when we expect it and need it. Grief is a volatile emotion: one moment we are engulfed in it, the next we are coping with everyday life, driving the car, calling on a friend, laughing at jokes over lunch. Like being in love, grief is something that is just there, it happens, it makes us feel we are somehow different from people who are not in that condition. For that reason, anyone who is suffering bereavement might read this chapter differently from someone who isn't. The title, for example: of course we cannot 'improve' your grieving. But society can improve the way it reacts to those who are grieving, and there are certain attitudes and practices, some of them reported below, which obstruct the natural expression of feeling and which could be improved upon, and certain evolving customs in modern life that may be worth sharing.

This chapter is built around the experience of grieving. Academic references and sources are given a secondary position. See also the Organisations listed in the Resources chapter – for in many particularly hard bereavements, such as when grieving over the loss of a child, a support group can be a great help in gradually learning to cope.

The different levels of grief we experience can be very surprising. A dear friend dies and after the funeral we resume normal existence with an appetite that makes us almost guilty. Where has that person gone? Why don't we feel it more? We probably will experience the sorrow when reminders of past times crop up, but meanwhile the fact that life just goes on as before can seem almost unreal. And then someone dies who has shared our most intimate life and it is as if a part of the self has been removed without warning. Hence the wisdom of saying that when we mourn the other, we mourn the self. Such grief reaches into the part of us where the roles played in our identity by the self and the other – the partner, the mother, the child – seem indistinguishable. One mourner, just when he thought he was recovering from his wife's death, broke out in a violent rash. It took him a further eighteen months to realise what had happened:

Debilitating grief

I was much debilitated; the body had to excrete the accumulated stress of several years. Some mourners, I was to discover, are prey to nervous

breakdowns, ulcers and much much worse: chronic arthritic conditions, heart attacks, even cancer. This is probably what accounts for so many instances, in centuries gone by, of persons dying of grief or 'a broken heart'.
From an article by Libby Purves in The Times (April 3rd 1992).

The potential phases of grieving are recorded in many textbooks, the results of professional and academic study of individual experiences. But here is Margaret Chisman's own personal and courageous account. In the first extract she expresses her immediate reaction to the death of her husband Stan.

Picking up the threads

When the hospital phoned at 3am on March 24th to say he had died I was alone in the house as my daughter, by chance, was away that night. After a short bout of numbed weeping I phoned near relatives and then made a cup of tea – remembering to add extra sugar for shock. I asked myself what I should do with the rest of my life now that the bottom had dropped out of it, and told myself that the most important thing was how to get through the rest of the night, and the next few weeks.

Later she wrote about the emotions of the first week:

During the first week after his death I made myself, in the privacy of my home, keep on saying out aloud 'My husband is dead and I'm a widow' until I could say it without weeping.

I am still weeping daily but it is mercifully lessening as I begin to pick up the threads again just a little.

After a few months she was able to write about the experience in a structured way and to begin to share with others and include a view of the future:

It is probable that most survivors experience similar phases of grief. First comes a numb inability to believe it. The reality of the loved one's presence is still so strong inside you that you know they are still alive and that they will return.

This is gradually replaced by an agonising acceptance of irretrievable loss bringing with it almost overwhelming grief. Never again to see, to hear or to touch your loved one. Oh, the unbearable pain of it all! You cry a lot, your face crumples uncontrollably, your whole torso shakes with hollowness, your throat aches with constriction and grief holds you in its iron grip.

Gradually the incidence of these attacks lessen; your horizon begins to open up a little and you begin to enter phase three. This is shot through with conflicting emotions. It is similar to the early stages of convalescence after a major accident or operation (such as the loss of a limb or of a sense resulting in blindness or deafness). You may feel resentment, 'Why should this happen to me?' You may try to reject the whole thing and suppress your feelings; you may be filled with self pity. There is one thing certain, however, about phase three, you have to fight! You have to confront your anger, resentment, rejection, self-pity – to realise that you won't get through to phase four unless you take these negative reactions and, with determination, turn them into something positive. This could include doing some things in a different way, doing new things, taking up a new hobby – you may have to fight a sense of disloyalty. Towards the end of this phase you feel you want to hurry things along, like a child picking away at its scab, only to be dismayed at the still unhealed flesh below. In many life processes there seems to be a natural flow that cannot be hastened, but neither should it be thwarted. You have to steer between nurturing grief beyond its proper bounds, and yet encouraging the first new shoots of post-bereavement independence, not feeling disloyalty to your loved one when you do something different or new.

Phase four shows a calm and serene acceptance of your bereavement and a need to build for the future, but even here there will be occasions when a trigger flashes fiercely your grief into life again – 'They're playing our tune,' a verse of poetry, a flower, a turn of phrase will bring your memories flooding back – even when your love is but a dream on the horizon of the past.

I see the process of bereavement, grief and recovery in pictorial terms. The black centre is the death of your loved one, phase one is shown in purple, two in red, three in orange and four in green. The grey smudge round the edge is your own death which, with the spiral revolution of time, will coalesce into a dense black dot at the centre of someone else's grief. The lesson we would do well to learn is that no previous phase is ever completely finished. You will get flashes of phase 1 even after years of being in phase four, but it is the balance that changes one phase to the next.

Time does heal if we let it. The scar will always be there, but we must not become like medieval beggars who hawked their festering cicatrices. We must do all we can in phases three and four to help the natural healing processes in ourselves and others.

From 'Interim', a private newsletter
circulated by Margaret Chisman.

How long does it take to 'overcome' grief? Margaret Chisman quotes one widower in her newsletter:

How long till grief is 'overcome'?

You say that I am further along the path to recovery as my wife died over three years ago. I was told that it would be six months before I would get over the grief. It was much longer than that, about eighteen months before I stopped bursting spontaneously into tears, when driving, preparing lectures, etc. Now after three and a half years the emotions are still there, but more controlled. No doubt other people respond differently.

From 'Interim' by Margaret Chisman.

There is an element of grief we should perhaps not even try to overcome but instead build into our lives. If there is a meaning to life, it is amply demonstrated in the emotions we feel for that which we have lost. Yes, there was a meaning after all, if only I could have seen it at the time! What is missing in our lives is not meaning but the ability to perceive it while it is there.

The academic structuring of grief does, after all, have a purpose. It may help us to deal with the overpowering aspects of the emotions we experience in that strange country. Other people have been there before us. We have not been singled out. There are maps. There is a geography of grief and loss:

A tentative 'map' of grieving

Grieving takes place after any sort of loss, but most powerfully after the death of someone we love. It is not just one feeling, but a whole succession of feelings, which take a while to get through and which cannot be hurried.

Although we are all individuals, the order in which we experience these feelings is very similar for most of us. Grief is most commonly experienced after the death of someone we have known for some time. However, it is clear that people who have had stillbirths or miscarriages, or who have lost very young babies suffer a similar experience of grieving and need the same sort of care and consideration.

In the few hours following the death of a close relative or friend, most people feel simply stunned, as though they cannot believe it has actually happened. They may feel like this even if the death had been expected. This sense of emotional numbness can be a help in getting through all the important practical arrangements that have to be made, such as getting in touch with relatives and organising the funeral. However, this feeling of unreality may become a problem if it goes on too long. Seeing the body of the dead person may, for some, be an important way of beginning to overcome this. Similarly, for many people, the funeral or memorial service is an occasion when the reality of what has happened really starts to sink in. It may be distressing to see the body or attend the funeral, but these are ways of saying goodbye to those we love. At the time, these things may seem too painful to go through and so are not done. However, this often leads to a sense of deep regret in future years.

Soon though, this numbness disappears and may be replaced by a dreadful sense of agitation, of pining or yearning for the dead person. There is a feeling of wanting somehow to find them, even though this is clearly impossible. This makes it difficult to relax or concentrate and it may be difficult to sleep properly. Dreams may be extremely disturbing. Some people feel that they 'see' their loved one everywhere they go – in the street, the park, around the house, anywhere they had spent time together. People often feel very angry at this time – towards doctors and nurses who did not prevent the death, towards friends and relatives who did not do enough, or even towards the person who has left them.

Another common feeling is guilt. People find themselves going over in their minds all the things they would like to have said or done. They may even consider what they could have done differently that might have prevented the death. Of course, death is usually beyond anyone's control and a bereaved person may need to be reminded of this. Guilt may also arise if a sense of relief is felt when someone has died after a particularly painful or distressing illness. This feeling of relief is natural, extremely understandable and very common.

This state of agitation is usually strongest about two weeks after the death, but is soon followed by times of quiet sadness or depression, withdrawal and silence. These sudden changes of emotion can be confusing to friends or relatives but are just part of the normal way of passing through the different stages of grief.

Although the agitation lessens, the periods of depression become more frequent and reach their peak between four and six weeks later. Spasms of grief can occur at any time, sparked off by people, places or things that bring back memories of the dead person. Other people may find it difficult to understand or embarrassing when the bereaved person suddenly bursts into tears for no obvious reason. At this stage it may be tempting to keep away from other people who do not fully understand or share the grief. However, avoiding others can store up trouble for the future and it is usually best to try to start to return to one's normal activities after a couple of weeks or so. During this time, it may appear to others as though the bereaved person is spending a lot of time just sitting, doing nothing. In fact, they are usually thinking about the person they have lost, going over again and again both the good times and the bad times they had together. This is a quiet but essential part of coming to terms with death.

As time passes, the fierce pain of early bereavement begins to fade. The depression lessens and it is possible to think about other things and even to look again to the future. However, the sense of having lost a part of oneself never goes away entirely. For bereaved partners there are constant reminders of their new singleness, in seeing other couples together and from the deluge of media images of happy families. After some time it is possible to feel whole again, even though a part is missing. Even so, years later you may sometimes find yourself talking as though he or she were still here with you.

These various stages of mourning often overlap and show themselves in different ways in different people. Most recover from a major bereavement within one or two years. The final phase of grieving is a letting-go of the person who has died and the start of a new sort of life. The depression clears completely, sleep improves and energy returns to normal. Sexual feelings may have vanished for some time, but now return – this is quite normal and nothing to be ashamed of.

Having said all this, there is no 'standard' way of grieving. We are all individuals and have our own particular ways of grieving.

From the Royal College of Psychiatrists' free leaflet
on 'Bereavement' (available for SAE from
17 Belgrave Square, London SW1X 8PG).

This basic structure is fleshed out in many books. Some of it has, however, now been questioned by five different studies of widows and widowers, studies which have found that between a quarter and two thirds of the bereaved are not greatly distressed, and that severe depression need not necessarily follow a loss. Dr Camille Wortman, a psychologist at the University of Michigan who has reviewed recent research in an article in the (American) Journal of Clinical and Consulting Psychology, comments that the absence of extreme distress 'can be a sign of resilience. Many have world views – often a spiritual outlook – that lets them see the loss in a way they can accept.' Those who are most upset after a loss tend also to be among the most upset a year or two later – findings which question the widespread assumption that a period of severe distress leads to a more balanced adjustment. Dr Barnardo of the Catholic University of America reported in the Journal of Personality and Social Psychology that, of the 42 people in his study, those who tended to 'let their grief feelings out' had more physical symptoms and negative emotions 14 months after a death than those who repressed their feelings.

There is no such thing as 'The Good Grieving Guide'. There is no reason on earth why the bereaved person (ie each and every one of us at some time or another) should become the passive consumer of someone else's advice. We all have our own experience. As Toby Young wrote, after the death of his mother: 'The fact that I was expected to be grief-stricken in public made me even less inclined to be so. I wasn't going to start grieving just because it was the socially acceptable thing to do.'

Tony Walter has argued (in Mortality, March 1996) that people need permission to retain the dead person, not to let them go. Some bereaved people begin to recall more and more memories of their lost spouse, a process described (in Jane Littlewood's delightful phrase) as 'falling in love backwards'. The essence of grieving, Walter believes, is for the community of people that knew the deceased, to discuss and elaborate an accurate and durable 'biography', a shared condensation of the person, to integrate the memory of the person into their lives, mainly through conversation, so as to move on with, as well as without, the deceased. Is it because we do not share memories like this, he asks, that the demand for bereavement counselling has arisen? In Bereavement Care (Spring 1991), he wrote:

> The Jews understand this. Like the Shona, they bury the body within a day or so and then the close family 'sit shiva'. They sit in the living room at home for a week, while friends, relatives and neighbours come to visit, bringing food, talking about the departed. Talking endlessly. Laughing, crying, sharing memories. And then, after that week, the family slowly get back to ordinary life.

Grief is a very active emotion – among other things it contains anger and even aggression, it can be sharply critical, and has its own sense of humour! Many of the books about bereavement in the Resources chapter are a mixture of impersonal wisdom and highly personal attitudes. Some come from the heart and offer comfort, however idiosyncratic. Others profess vigorous solutions and guidance. Some are biased towards research, others might touch a personal chord in one's own experience. They are all useful. Browse among them, and choose what is to your own taste. Reject what you don't like.

Suicide

Particularly difficult can be facing grief after a murder or a suicide, and this may require specialist help.

Feeling responsible for a suicide

The toughest question to ask Jill Winters is: 'How many children do you have?' Her son James killed himself when he was 34. If she says she has two children, she feels she is denying his existence. If she says she had three but one died, more searching, and unwelcome, questions may follow.

Eight years after her son jumped from a third-floor window, Mrs Winters has finally stopped blaming herself for his death. The sense of liberation has been, she says, remarkable. But it has taken her a long time to accept what happened and to feel at peace with herself again.

The families of those who have taken their own lives have to cope with feelings of distress which go far beyond normal grief. Unlike other deaths, suicide carries with it a heavy social stigma. Those left behind may see it as a violent statement that the love they provided was not enough. Families can become ensnared in a hopeless search to find out why a child, or a parent, felt so desperate; there are profound feelings of guilt to cope with.

'When it happened it was completely unexpected, although looking back I could see it was on the cards,' Mrs Winters recalls. 'We were devastated by it. We were numb to start with. We found it very difficult to talk about; there was a feeling of isolation.'

Her husband came to terms with their son's death better than she did. 'I felt that I hadn't done the right things, that I had been a terrible mother,' she says. 'I wished I had done everything differently. I kept looking for ways that I could have prevented it. I took full responsibility.'

Mrs Winters went to a group for bereaved parents but felt out of place. 'These were people who had lost their children in the normal way. I didn't feel I was one of them,' she says. 'Suicide didn't seem acceptable.'

James was unmarried and had been a solicitor. A psychiatrist had been treating him for schizophrenia. Mrs Winters now realises she was not responsible for his actions. 'I think he was finding life so difficult and stressful that he could not stand it any longer. He was afraid of having another breakdown.'

Support agencies are waking up to the fact that families bereaved in this way often need specialist help. CRUSE, the national bereavement care group, has set up a number of support groups specifically for families of suicide cases and plans to establish more. Forbes Craig, a former nurse and now a counsellor with CRUSE, says that while all families feel loss on the death of someone close, with a suicide there is 'the intensity of the feelings, the inherent violence, the statement being made that whoever is left can't help any more. If it's a natural death we can take it because we all die. But when it's suicide there's a whole history of culture against it.' Suicide was only decriminalised in 1961, she points out. She says that there is no time limit to when someone who has experienced a suicide might need help. One woman sought help nineteen years after her mother killed herself.

Rose Hampton, the director of CRUSE, had a close friend who took her own life many years ago. 'The experience lives with you for years and years,' she says. 'I can still see her now as clear as day. In the end you have to realise that you can't be responsible for other people.'

> *From an article by Bernadette Friend in The Independent (Aug. 11th 1992). See also the 'Shadow of Suicide' organisation in the Resources chapter.*

The bereaved parent

To lose part of yourself ... Perhaps the loss of a child brings this aspect of grieving into real focus more than any other experience. Here is an account, quoted in full, of the experience of a stillbirth and the fierce reactions it provoked towards our modern attitude to death.

The experience of a stillbirth

Four years ago this summer, I was happy, healthy, seven and a half months pregnant and full of expectations. Within the space of 12 hours, struggling to shake off the effects of a general anaesthetic and an emergency Caesarean section, I was left holding my seemingly perfect stillborn daughter, Laura.

The four days that followed were spent being studiously avoided in a corner of the antenatal ward, desperately trying to shut out the sight of pregnant women and the sound of newborn babies crying. Still quite poorly and in a state of shock, I leapt at the opportunity for the hospital to make all Laura's funeral arrangements for me – anything to have the whole nightmare taken away.

The result was a totally meaningless cremation service taken by a stranger exactly one week to the minute after her birth; there was no gravestone, no special place of hers that I could visit and care for. Most importantly, there was the guilt and regret: I felt I had failed my daughter in the one and only thing I was ever going to be able to do for her.

Four years on, I know that my experience and feelings are not uncommon. I run a local branch of Sands, the Stillbirth and Neo-Natal Death Society. The aim is to support people whose babies die at or around birth by offering a listening ear and a shared experience. I want to make some good come out of the tragedy of Laura's death by trying to ensure that others don't end up with the same regrets as I did.

For example, I had absolutely no idea that I could have asked to hold Laura again a few hours or even a day or more later – at a time when I could have taken her in better and stored my memories of her. As it was, the only time I spent with her I was so dopey that I could barely lift my hand to stroke her face. I had no idea that I could have asked for a lock of her plentiful hair. Things are much better now, professionals much more thoughtful and aware that information may need to be given several times before it sinks in, but there is still room for improvement.

A national Sands survey showed that while some hospitals handle the situation well, others do not. Many foetuses, or 'foetal material', are incinerated with other hospital waste. Parents are not consulted and are totally unaware that they have any choices to make, totally unaware of the fate of their baby's body. Obviously it would be wrong, and in some cases quite inappropriate, to suggest that all babies lost through miscarriage should be held by their mothers. However, babies can be perfectly formed little beings long before they reach 28 weeks; I would suggest that they are most definitely not 'hospital waste fit for incineration only' and it is not the right of hospital staff to decide whether or not a mother should hold her child or decide upon the fate of its body; she should at least be told that she has a choice.

Just as holding your dead child plays an important part in the grieving process, so does saying a formal goodbye in the shape of a funeral or some other social ritual, be it religious or not. It is a way of sharing, of acknowledging the existence of, the child you have lost. This is especially true in the case of babies because society is keen to pretend they never existed ('Oh well dear, you can just have another one' ... 'At least you've got your other children' ... 'As soon as the next one's born healthy everything will be all right'). The more people around me negated Laura's existence, the more they implied that other things would make up for her loss, the more I fought to keep her memory alive.

For women who have had miscarriages or terminations for abnormality, society offers even less opportunity to say goodbye – after all, the baby didn't really ever exist, did it? But a loss is a loss and needs to be grieved for, needs to be acknowledged. Women who lost babies several years ago or more have to live with the fact that they were simply wrapped up and incinerated; there was no choice.

Our society is still singularly bad at dealing with death or allowing for the fact that the grieving process is a necessary part of carrying on with life. In China, they have an annual day set aside for national mourning: people tend graves or simply focus their thoughts on loved ones who have died. God forbid that the stiff British upper lip be subjected to such a public display of emotion!

Feelings of grief (often quite frightening in their ferocity and variety) must be hidden away behind closed doors; until, that is, they burst out, unleashing all sorts of problems and you end up, as I did, crawling desperately to a psychotherapist.

Whenever and however the death of a child occurs, it means shock and disbelief. It may mean regrets about decisions taken at the time; it may mean missed opportunities; it may mean guilt; it may mean anger. One thing is certain; it always means being scarred for the rest of your life.

From 'In Living Memory' by Caroline Jay in The Guardian.

'The Bereaved Parent' by Harriet Sarnoff Schiff and 'Beyond Endurance, When a Child Dies' by Ronald J. Knapp are sensitive explorations of the complex of emotions and realistic living circumstances surrounding the bereaved parent, offering both insight and comfort in great measure. Another book which deals explicitly with this area of loss is 'On Children and Death' by Elisabeth Kübler-Ross. The intensity of grief for the loss of a child is likely to be prolonged and may take half a year to reach its zenith and longer still if it was a violent death. There is an entire subculture of shared feelings created by men and women who have suffered the loss of a child from a wide range of causes. Nowhere is this more fully expressed than in the extraordinary and moving series of pamphlets and newsletters issued by The Compassionate Friends (address under Organisations in the Resources chapter – they even do a special newsletter called Sibbs for bereaved brothers and sisters). Here is an explanation of their policy of 'Befriending, rather than counselling':

Befriending

What do we mean by befriending? The Pocket Oxford Dictionary defines it as 'act as a friend; help in need'. Within The Compassionate Friends it takes on a greater meaning. Befriending is also sharing. We are all befrienders. We all share when we write a letter, make a phone call or talk with another bereaved parent at a meeting. We share when we read the Newsletter. Prayer, meditation and positive loving thoughts are a form of sharing.

The necessity to 'share' and talk about our loved ones and emotions is a need within all bereaved parents that requires to be met. As the pain of grief recedes, so the need to talk endlessly diminishes. We are then in a position to 'share discriminately'. To let the newly-bereaved talk – to be willing to share with a few sentences – to encourage expressions of feelings: 'Yes, I felt that and I also felt...' This is why those who have first contact with the newly-bereaved have been bereaved themselves for at least two years.

Grief is a natural reaction to the death of a loved one/ones. Talking about our dead child/children and the emotion let loose within us is the way forward along the path of grief. Being able to befriend from the time of a death, giving the newly-bereaved permission to grieve, should mean that counselling will be needed by a small minority only: those who become stuck in their grief; people who have other problems within their family; or difficulties within themselves due to past experiences. For these, bereavement counselling is very beneficial and could be viewed as complementary to befriending.

From 'Thoughts on Befriending' by Margaret Hayworth, in The Compassionate Friends Newsletter (Spring '89).

A child's understanding of death

Young children are curious about death. They have to negotiate the reality of death and fit it into their scheme of things. In a child's world, the loss of a pet can assume enormous emotional significance. When Grandma or Grandad dies, or a parent or a sibling, the loss has to be explained in ways the child can come to terms with. Otherwise there may be a hidden morbid element that will affect development and grownup life. In the following extract, a hospice counsellor helps a father and son to speak about their joint loss. The little boy displays a mixture of childish expression (drawing a picture, as he would at school) and very realistic concerns. These show his awareness of how his dependency has shifted with the loss of his mother.

Coming to terms with a mother's death

A seven year old had been bereaved of his mother a week before. Father sought help for his son. There seemed to be a great deal of apprehension, not just for the boy. However, he happily accepted a large glass of squash – it was a hot day. Father sat slightly apart. In order to understand the outcome of this brief intervention, something of the father's manner and bearing needs to be known. He was a large man who worked with animals. A man who was used to being obeyed by animals and humans alike; this was the tension, I felt. He gave his son instructions to answer my questions honestly. After introductions about who I was and what I did, and the purpose of his visit to the Hospice, I asked about his mother's funeral, including Father in the conversation. Father refused to be drawn, prompting his son instead. The small boy looked at his father as he spoke with a mixture of fear and defiance in his eyes. He spoke of the funeral but quickly went on to say he had visited the grave earlier on his way here. He and his father had discussed the sort of stone they would put on the grave during the drive to the Hospice. I wondered if he would like to draw it for me; he wasn't particularly good at drawing, he said, but he agreed he would have a try when I said I wasn't either.

As he drew, he spoke of his dog which had recently died and the circumstances of its death; 'being put down'. He asked, 'Where was he?' looking all the while at his father. It seemed very hard for the father to be honest about where the body of the pet dog was, though his son did know where his mother's was. This was the theme of the picture. Two tombstones, one a slab and one a cross, drawn very small in the corner of the paper, with a bird in flight above. He spoke very naturally about what was going on the stone and referred to his father for help with the precise detail. I wondered about the cross in the picture.

'Well, that had been part of the talk in the car, about the shape.' The slab seemed to be preferred by the father so that the wording could be better managed.

I wondered what the cross meant.

'That Mummy had gone to be with Jesus.'

'What does that mean for you?' I responded.

'That Mummy no longer suffered great pain and she had left her poor body and was now in Heaven,' he replied.

'Do you know where that is?'

'No – not really.'

I wondered, 'Could you tell me about the bird you have drawn so cleverly?'

He said 'I thought it would make a nice picture. It reminds me of the churchyard in the country with trees around.'

I allowed a pause and then, 'So you are not sure where Heaven is – nor is anybody if they are really honest – none of us is sure – even grownups – but the bird is important to you. Could the bird be Mummy's spirit flying free, out of pain, able to go where she liked to the place we are not quite sure where which is called Heaven?' He liked this idea very much and repeated it.

His father softened and tears ran down his cheeks. His son watched.

I asked, 'Do you and your Dad cry together?'

'Yes,' he said, 'we do when we go to the churchyard, to the grave.'

'That's good,' I said, giving lots more permission in my voice.

There was something in the way he watched his father that prompted me to ask him if there was anything he found very hard to say to his Dad which he might like to say if he found courage here. It seemed as though he had been longing for this opportunity. There was so much, he was worried about his dad working with bulls – he might get hurt; he was worried when his dad drove too fast – he might crash. He didn't want the goats or the calves to be slaughtered, they were his friends and he missed them. He wanted his bedroom to be the same room when he came home, not to be changed around. It was easy to see how insecure, worried and angry this small boy was towards his father, and how he was asking him to take care of himself in order to care for him. A brief interruption allowed him to say more about a visit to the grandparents which was planned and how dad would be in his absence. All his concerns came tumbling out and his anger was acknowledged.

From 'Brief Interventions in Anticipatory Grief and Bereavement'
by Lizette Pugh, in Counselling (Feb. 1992).

What do children need? They need society to open up about death in much the same way as we all do. Children are no problem so long as we try to understand them. Adults are the problem, as one man discovered when he openly shared his bereavement with his children:

'Remembering Mum' book

After Adrian Crimmin's partner, Mandy, died of pneumonia, he made no attempt to conceal his pain from their two boys, Sam, five, and Eddy, three. The children went to Mandy's funeral, sang her favourite Jackson Browne songs at the service, drew pictures on her headstone and shared their father's tears.

But when the family sought to share their grief outside, it was a different story. They met with a wall of silence. Even best friends wouldn't talk about Mandy, close relatives suggested they should have recovered from the death after only three months.

'My kids were confused by other people's strange reactions; a child can't understand that society is conditioned to be embarrassed by death.'

At school children who knew of the death displayed signs of anxiety.

'One child was so upset that he couldn't bear to let his mother out of his sight. If she was a minute late at home time, he broke down in tears. Some of the kids suffered nightmares, others just didn't want to come to school. There was obviously a need to talk about death and to help them to understand.'

It was one of the teachers at school who suggested the idea of collaborating on a children's book about bereavement.

'It was an idea I'd had in my mind for some years,' explains Sam's teacher Ginny Perkins. 'I'd taught classes before when parents had died and I'd felt totally helpless. Although I felt I had no problems now in talking to the children about Mandy's death, I could have done with a prop when I was younger, and I'm sure there are other teachers who wouldn't feel comfortable about tackling the subject by themselves.'

The initial stages of finding a publisher were simple, but again 'grownup' obstruction was encountered before the book was accepted.

'I could get the idea past the editors, who were mostly young and female,' Perkins explains, 'but as soon as the word "bereavement" was mentioned at a board meeting, that would be the end of it.'

After months of persistence, the book was accepted. The result is a sensitive, true story called 'Remembering Mum'. Using large, colour photographs, it follows the family through a typical day, showing how Mandy's memory still touches every aspect of their lives. There are poignant reminders of her, like the daffodils she loved blooming for the first time since she died. At school, Sam and Eddy are seen making a model to take to her grave. At the cemetery, they are pictured hugging by her headstone. Before bed, the boys pore over snapshots of Mandy, immortal-ised one sunny afternoon at Hampstead Heath.

From an article by Fiona Cumberpatch in The Guardian (Dec. 17th 1991).
'Remembering Mum', A & C Black, 35 Bedford Row, London WC1R 4JH.

Hopefully this is one of many cases of 'improving' grieving by listening to children, supplying their needs and perhaps learning from them as well! The adult need to 'get rid of' death, to deal with bereavement by 'getting over it' quickly, is countered in that story by a clear demonstration of the fact that the bereaved child has to grow up with his loss. The pain may be lessened, but the reality is still there as part of his life, as a tailpiece to that story shows:

'Three years after Mandy died, they still have some anger and they still ask questions. A month ago Sam said, "I didn't even think she was going to die, Daddy. Why didn't you tell me?" I'd much rather they expressed their feelings now, than carried them on through their lives. But they need other things, too. Sam and Eddy told me that photos of Mandy were very important to them and so was listening to the music she liked, which they used for dancing to.'

Private grief

'We mustn't intrude on private grief,' is a common, jokey saying we use when we want to be a little unkind about the misfortunes of others. Behind the saying, unfortunately, is the assumption that grief is something that should be draped and shrouded from view, and that the rituals of grief are designed to conceal rather than to express feeling. Nothing could be further from the truth.

Listen and be compassionate

My close friends and family were absolutely wonderful when Ernest died. But other people I knew well would cross the road if they saw me coming, and if they did have to speak and ask me how I was, I learned to my cost that I mustn't really tell. They wanted me to say just, 'I'm fine'.

Some people seem to delight in telling me of another bereavement. They asked how my husband died and when I said from a sudden heart attack, immediately told me about a heart attack that killed someone else. I had enough nightmares about my husband's death and I didn't need the harrowing details of anyone else's.

The most helpful thing people can do is listen, just let you talk and be compassionate. People think it will hurt you to talk, but talking keeps the person alive for you. Or they fear they will be reminding you – as if you had forgotten.

It is an absolute safety valve to be allowed to talk, which is why I joined CRUSE, the support group for widows and widowers. There people can cry because everyone understands, but you'll hear gales of laughter too.

Jean Baker, quoted in an article entitled 'Please Don't Say That' in
The Sunday Times magazine.

Those who don't know what to say may feel inspired by a lovely Irish tradition, described by Danny Danziger in The Independent (Jan. 27th 1992):

> At the very end of the service, before the funeral, the people come up and they hold your hand, and they say a phrase that will ring many bells in Irish ears: that is, 'I am very sorry for your trouble.'

Or, as Elsie Sieben wrote in The Compassionate Friends Newsletter (Spring 1985):

> Hug me, tell me you care and that you're sorry this has happened.
> Be available to me – often if you can – and let me talk and cry without judging me.
> Just love me and I will always remember you as a true friend.

And Virginia Ironside in The Times (July 29th 1992) related how surprised she was to be consoled by letters after her father's death:

> I will never let another death go by without dropping the relatives a line. Letters that say things like: 'He will live on for ever in your heart' – trite lines I'd usually wrinkle a lip at – seem to have huge significance, laden with meaning. 'I am down the road if you want an ear,' came from an old schoolfriend I barely know. And a lovely line from my son's godfather: 'These sad deaths are like signposts which direct you into a new and unknown route. I can only wish you well.'

Simply helping the bereaved person with household tasks can be important. Dr Colebrook, who lost his son in a motorbike accident, wrote in the British Medical Journal (Dec 31st 1983) that he felt that he had experienced outstanding support from a local girl, an old college friend of his wife, who simply took over the housekeeping and looked after arrangements at home.

Consolations

Jenny Kander offers consolation of a sort in The Compassionate Friends paper (No. 16) on 'The Death of an Only Child':

> Grief, for a time, can seem larger than life. Your anguish is your response to that, but do not relate solely to your pain; remember your child, however painful the memories at first; recall your lives together, however short or long they were, so that restoration may take place and, in time, you will realise that he or she is still with you in the deepest sense, bonded to you and living within your heart. You are parents of your child for eternity. Nothing can alter that. Nothing can take that away.

At some stages of bereavement the sense that the dead person is present is powerful and disturbing. Of course it is psychologically quite accurate to say that someone we love is within us, an indwelling presence. This is in itself a comfort. But when the longed for appearance of the person in the flesh does not occur, then there is anguish. Where is that physical, substantive presence that we miss? To contain the spirit of the dead person within the self is at once a comfort and an agony, but the bereaved person often wants a larger context for this containment, a context that will take some of the burden away and at the same time be soothing and healing. In this sense the child may feel nearer to a dead person whilst up in an aeroplane because he or she has been told that the spirit is 'up there'. The more sophisticated adult may feel the same soothing presence, inside himself or herself, yet enclosed in something larger, in a religious building for example, within the uplifting and inspiring confines of a cathedral. Or in music which has the same grandeur and peace of containing the spirit. Or in the chanted words of prayer. The bereaved person, then, craves some form of communion within which he or she can share the agony and beauty of containing the spirit of the dead. We may call this religious, or we may call it therapeutic. The distinction only matters to the observer. If the bereaved person is religious, the practice of religion will have a therapeutic effect. If he or she seeks comfort in a conventional therapeutic setting, it is likely to have the intensity of a religious experience. Religion, after all, is largely about reconciling life and death.

Professional mourners, women who attend a funeral service and wail or keen, are traditional in many cultures, and this is one way of sharing the burden of the dead spirit. In Crete this method of joining the living to the dead has been brought to a fine art.

Keening

An essential element in the lament singing is that women identify with each other. Each woman's recollection of her own grief serves to remind and intensify the grief of others. A skilled lamenter has to move her audience to 'ponos' (pain) and thus, symbolically, to lead the living to the dead. The depth of these laments has thus a metaphysical dimension.

From a paper by Sonia Greger, sent to The Natural Death Centre, entitled 'Woman – Man – Peasant – Central Administration'.

There are many who claim to join the living to the dead in a more direct sense, through psychic guidance and evocations, or through the gift of vision.

Help from the spirit world?

Suddenly I gasped, as a flash of headlights shot over the hill – the old man was going to walk right out in front of a car. But just then, something strange happened – I stood transfixed, as a ghostly gleaming-white mist appeared behind him. It quickly condensed into the radiant form of a middle-aged spirit woman. Strangely unruffled by the gale, her hair was completely unmoved, not a drop of rain had wet it, and her flowing white spirit robes were bone-dry.

All at once she stooped down, drew back her arm and delivered a swift blow to the back of the man's knees. My heart jumped into my throat as he fell backwards like a collapsing house of cards, landing on the pavement with his legs in the gutter. Just a second later, a reckless car hurled around the blind bend at over 50 miles per hour, missing his feet by half an inch – then zoomed past the bus queue, splashing us with muddy water.

Brushing the rain from my eyelashes, I watched the ghostly woman kneel down, kiss the old man's troubled brow, smile, and then vanish into the dark night – fading back into the spirit world, from whence she came.

I've had these psychic abilities from my earliest years, visions of other worlds beyond death.

From 'Voices from Heaven' by Stephen O'Brien.

There is no reliable guide to life after death. Guidebooks abound, but the paths they indicate are varied to the point of confusion. A theologian asks the question, Where do the dead go when they pass over? He reviews the possibilities, beginning with nowhere:

Living in God

Perhaps there is nowhere to go. Perhaps people, burdened with fear, want and sorrow, just dance into the arms of death, as Schopenhauer said, wondering what the tragic comedy of life is supposed to mean – and finding out it ends in nothing. Those who have died are then shadows of the past. Nothing remains of them except for the loving scratches or hideous scar they etched on our world, and our memories.

Then, he considers the opposite option, that of reincarnation:

Perhaps our inner Atma is made of incorruptible stuff, as Hindus maintain. At death the spark of our soul then divests itself of one mortal body to start life again in another disposable shell. Our deceased relatives and friends could then be at any station on the spiralling track of reincarnation. They might even have reached their destination, nirvana, where they merge back into the infinite ocean of Atmas.

Or maybe the dead await judgement:

Perhaps the dead roam as shades in the netherworld, populating the Old Testament *She'ol*. The psalms describe this abyss under the earth as a house of darkness, a bottomless pit, a land of forgetfulness. All the dead can do is bide their time till their fate will be sealed at the universal judgement.

He ends by advocating a truly spiritual understanding:

We can meaningfully speak of heaven and hell, as long as we remember that they are dimensions of life, not locations in outer space. We can say the dead merge back into God if we realise She/He is an ocean of love who does not swamp our littleness. Properly understood, the time-honoured phrase coined by Kohelet puts it rather well: those who have died live in God.

From 'Learning to live with life after death' by John Wijngaards in The Times (Nov. 4th 1991).

Stephen Levine talks of the comfort to be had in facing up to the worst that human life can bring.

Fierce journey towards freedom

I've been with many people whose grief has been beyond bearing. And in some ways it has been the best thing that ever happened to them. For they come to plumb the depths of their being.

When we experience grief, we are not just experiencing the loss of our son or daughter, our husband or wife, our parent or loved one. We are dropped into the very pit of despair and longing. We are touching the reservoir of loss itself. We experience the long-held fear and doubt and grief that has always been there. It is not an experience that most would choose, though the confrontation with this area of deep holding seems to be an initiation often encountered along the fierce journey toward freedom.

> *Stephen Levine, quoted in Raft, The Journal of the Buddhist Hospice Trust.*

Sogyal Rinpoche in his helpful book 'The Tibetan Book of Living and Dying' advises helping your dead friend and the healing of your own grief by invoking, perhaps with a mantra, any enlightened being who inspires you, and imagining tremendous rays of light streaming out towards you from that being, filling up your heart. And then: 'Imagine you are sending this blessing, the light of healing compassion of the enlightened beings, to your loved one who has died.'

If the hardest death to bear is an untimely one, and the hardest untimely death is a child's death, and the hardest child's death is one that is accompanied by feelings of great guilt amongst the survivors, then we can surely trust the parents who report their thoughts and feelings in The Compassionate Friends publications. Yes, Margaret Hayworth warns, if death causes *persistent* self-accusatory thoughts, then probably professional therapeutic help should be sought (Newsletter, Summer 1992). But a way that helps is to give yourself permission to forgive yourself, by writing a letter to your child listing regrets and stating your need for forgiveness. For the rest, she shares Kübler-Ross and Levine's spiritual perspective on suffering as an opportunity for the soul to develop. The American spiritual teacher Ram Dass developed these arguments in a public talk where he was responding to a father whose son had drowned. The father was in despair: 'They say that God is perfect but all I can think is that God made a mistake. I cannot believe there would be any good reason for Him to allow this to happen.' Ram Dass replied, in part:

> I feel such pain for the loss you and your wife have suffered. The grief that parents experience over the loss of a child is perhaps the deepest grief of all because it seems to upset the natural order of things.
>
> What I can share with you from a spiritual vantage point cannot really allay your grief. Perhaps however it may allow you and your son to know each other in a new way, and that other way of knowing may give balance to the grief.
>
> Because your son was attractive and was your son, and so warm and vibrant, you got to know him through his uniqueness and his separateness.

There is another way of knowing a person, which we know through our intuitive heart. This way of knowing one another is subtle, so it is often hidden behind the more obvious ways of knowing people through senses and thought. But if we know what to look for and cultivate that intuitive way of knowing, we find out for ourselves that we are each indeed more than just bodies and personalities.

The soul has an agenda in taking birth itself as a human being. It has certain work to do and complete while on the earth plane and it uses the body and personality to carry out that work. And when the work is finished it leaves this plane. The wisest beings with whom I have made contact in this lifetime all assure me that a soul leaves the physical plane neither a moment too early nor a moment too late. Human birth is a bit like entering in the fourth grade, and we stay just as long as it is necessary to achieve what we need from that specific grade or form, and then we are naturally ready to go on for further evolution by leaving this plane.

I can sense from the description and pictures of your son, the purity of his heart and the beauty of his soul. And I suspect that though you considered his work on earth just at the beginning, for his soul the work was completed. Even the manner of his leaving was part of his work. For your personality, the pain is shattering and seemingly unbearable. You wake crying and find life now meaningless. Such suffering is what the personality would avoid at all costs if it were able. For your soul, however, it is an entirely different matter. For your soul, suffering is that which forces you to grow spiritually, and brings you closer to awakening to whom you in truth are. I realise even as I say all these things to you, that it is really too much for me to ask of you that you understand the way in which the manner of your son's death was his soul's gift to your soul. I suspect all that seems topsy-turvy to you. But you did ask me how I understand such tragic events, and this is my truth that I am honoured to share with you.

Probably your suffering and attachment to him and sense of loss is felt by his soul. Although he now understands what has happened, why it had to happen the way it did and why you are suffering as you are, I am sure he is surrounding you with healing energy; and as you are able to quiet your mind, I suspect that you will feel it. It of course acts to your benefit even if you don't feel it . To the extent that you are able, sit quietly and just hang out with your son, talking to him as you normally would about the many experiences you shared together. In doing so, look to see the thread of spirit that pervaded each experience. Imagine that you and he are souls who met on earth this time as father and son. How many times in your years together did the love between you nearly rend the veil of mystery that would have allowed you to recognise the truth of soul that lay at the root of your relationship? It takes only a moment for two people to recognise their bond as souls. Souls know no time. And now, even though your son is no longer embodied, you and he can recognise each other.

Chapter 9

THE POLITICS OF DYING

The Natural Death Centre has drawn up the following provisional Declaration of Rights of the Person Dying at Home. The attainment of many of these rights lies in the Utopian future, and would require a fairly drastic redirection of NHS resources and a reanimation of Neighbourhood Care type schemes in both urban and rural areas. The statements that follow are thus perhaps more in the realm of desirable goals than enforceable rights; and are limited by how much a family can cope with, since so much of the caring depends on the family at present. Your suggested improvements to this Declaration would be welcomed. It could be made into a more personal declaration by crossing out bits that do not apply to you or by adding others.

A Declaration of the Rights of the Person Dying at Home

• I have the right to sufficient support from the National Health Service and the community to enable me to die at home, if I so wish, whether or not I have relatives to care for me.

• I have the right not to die alone; although with the right to be left alone, if desired.

• I have the right to expect the local priest or other community leader to ask the neighbourhood to support me and those caring for me.

• I have the right to have 'midwives for the dying' or their equivalent to attend to my physical, emotional and spiritual needs.

• I have the right to the same expertise of pain relief as I would obtain if occupying a hospital or hospice bed.

• I have the right not to be taken without my consent to hospital as my condition deteriorates, or, if a hospital operation is required to relieve pain, I have the right to be brought home again afterwards.

• I have the right to have any Living Will I have signed respected and, if not fully conscious myself, to have the wishes of my appointed proxy respected.

• I have the right to reject heart stimulants, blood transfusions or other medical interventions to prolong my life.

• I have the right, to the extent that I so wish, to be told the truth about my condition and about the purposes of, alternatives to, and consequences of, any proposed treatments.

• I have the right to fast as death approaches, if I so desire, without being subjected to forced feeding in any form.

• I have the right to discuss my death and dying, my funeral or any other related matters openly with those caring for me.

• I have the right to as conscious and dignified a death as possible in the circumstances.

• I have the right, if I so express the wish and if the circumstances allow, for my body to remain undisturbed at home after death for a period, and for my funeral to be handled by my relatives and friends, if they so desire, without intervention by funeral directors.

All comments please to The Natural Death Centre, 20 Heber Road, London NW2 6AA (tel 0181 208 2853; fax 0181 452 6434).

Policy changes needed

This book and indeed the above Declaration have implied the need for a number of changes in policies and practices relating to dying and death. These are summarised here:

Education

• Children need less exposure to violent death on television and in the media and yet they need to be more involved in the natural dying of their relatives and friends; to have the opportunities to visit the body if they wish and to participate in the funeral. Teachers in schools can help where appropriate by introducing relevant literature to do with bereavement or, for instance, by helping the children to make Memory Books or Memory Boxes that compile their thoughts and memories and photos of the dead or dying person.

• A number of people learn first aid, which they may or may not ever need to use. But everybody would benefit from learning the basics about preparing for dying and about looking after the dying person, if only to be better prepared for their own death. A one day (or weekend) first-aid-style course in practical care for those who are dying should be popularised, and open to the general public, not just to the nursing profession.

• Death needs to become less socially invisible. Towards this end, the Natural Death Centre promotes an annual English Day of the Dead, along the lines of the Mexican Day of the Dead, both as an opportunity for rituals in remembrance of friends and relatives who have died, with a flavour of festival to it, and also as a chance for debate, discussions and exhibitions related to death and dying. The English Day of the Dead is on the third Sunday in April each year.

The National Health Service and the community

• The natural death movement must be as insistent as the natural birth movement in pressing for changes in the NHS. First, there needs to be a feasibility study leading to a pilot project that would look at the relative costs for a particular region if the policy were to become one of enabling those who are terminally ill to die at home rather than in hospital or elsewhere; and the study would encourage and collect suggestions from carers about how services for those who are dying could be improved. Second, the Marie Curie, Macmillan and other nursing and hospice home-care services need to be adapted, or new organisations founded, for extending services to people dying of other causes besides cancer, motor neurone disease and AIDS. Third, there needs in the long term to be a new holistic profession of 'Midwives for the Dying', trained to look after the physical, emotional and spiritual needs of the dying and their carers; backed up by a nationwide network of volunteer befrienders for those who are dying, who will sit with them, carry out errands for the carers, provide transport, etc. Fourth, we need the Canadian experimental brokerage scheme, whereby those with handicaps or those who are terminally ill, together with their carers, identify their own financial and other needs, interviewing and selecting would-be helpers, with generous funding coming from the state. Carers taking time off work should receive an allowance equivalent to their net salary. Fifth, respite breaks for carers should be frequently and flexibly available, preferably through a vast extension of the Crossroads-type arrangements, whereby a replacement carer comes into the home and takes over all the tasks involved. Sixth, night nurses need to be routinely available for all those receiving home palliative care.

• There are many Neighbourhood Watch anti-crime schemes that have provided the foundations for neighbours to get to know each other. There need to be grants for pilot projects to extend these into Neighbourhood Care schemes where neighbours would gradually begin to care for each other in crisis, including helping those who are dying, their carers, and the bereaved. It would be natural in many areas for the local doctor, priest or other respected figurehead to provide the impetus to get such schemes going. For example, Harriet Copperman writes in 'Dying at Home' of an instance where the vicar 'organised a rota of people to sit with a patient who lived alone, in order that he could die at home'. Indeed, a great deal of neighbourhood care already takes place, often under the aegis of church groups, but formalised Neighbourhood Care schemes, receiving funding from Social Services and others, could encourage such activity in neighbourhoods where it is currently lacking.

Spirituality

• There needs to be an English Book of the Dead (there are already several American ones) that would translate Tibetan insights into the experience and psychology of dying and the reports from those who have had Near-Death Experiences into anglicised and even Christian rituals that could become part of a prearranged Dying Service for those wanting it – for instance an elaboration of the 'go towards the light' message whispered into the ear of the dying person, along with breathing and other meditations; and perhaps accompanied by music such as that offered by the Chalice of Repose at a hospice in the United States. People could be encouraged to design their own Dying Plans specifying the kind of material of this nature that they might like.

• People seem to appreciate dying close to nature, as near outdoors as the elements will allow. Either the patient needs to be able to get a taste of the outdoors or nature needs to be brought into the house or even the hospital – not only flowers, but branches, trees and animals.

Hospital

• A hospital palliative care ward should have as much a 'home from home' atmosphere and design as possible – imagine, for instance, a country house hospital with open fires and meals around long tables, with patients' interests accommodated, whether for pets, music or complementary treatments.

• Dr Marie Louise Grennert's excellent palliative care work at the Malmo Geriatric and Rehabilitation Clinic in Sweden (tel 00 46 40 33 10 00) deserves copying. To encourage patients to talk freely, she has an informal discussion with each one at the outset and asks: 'What are your most pressing problems right now? What do you want from the care provided here? What is your outlook on the future? Where do you get your strength or inner resources from? How do you feel about entering this palliative care ward?' Next-of-kin also talk with the doctor about anything that is on their mind, not just medical matters – and are invited back to the hospital two weeks after the death for a further talk. Two hours or so after the death, all the ward staff gather briefly to discuss the patient who has died, any problems that arose and any lessons that can be learnt.

• In the hospital setting, the partner needs acceptance as part of the caring team (that is, if both partner and patient would like this). Ideally, just as a parent can sometimes stay with a child in hospital, the partner should be able to share a bed with the dying person, as is possible at home, or to have another bed alongside.

• The medical carers need to maintain reassuring physical contact with the dying. One American hospital renowned for its excellent palliative care was filmed looking after a dying woman who was rigged up to the most high tech equipment. She died with the medical team in full attendance and with an accurate record kept of the exact time of her death. But nobody held her hand or had anything to do with her as a person or even said a word of blessing over her dead body.

• The nursing staff could show carers and visitors simple techniques such as scalp massage and Boerstler's breath relaxation method which can be helpful to the dying person and which give family and friends a feeling of involvement.

• Patients need to be allowed to acknowledge the deaths of fellow patients and to say goodbye in some way – rather than the drawing of ward curtains around each bed, so that no patient is disturbed by seeing the dead body moved away. Dr Elizabeth Lee, in her book 'A Good Death', describes, in contrast, a death in a small Kenyan hospital. The patient's mother stood and, raising one arm above her head, began to sing a hymn. All the other young women on the ward stood by their beds, faces turned to the dead woman, and singing with her mother. They faced her death and bade her goodbye.

• Where it suits their particular style, doctors and nurses in hospital could evolve a brief religious or humanist ritual (depending on their own belief systems and that of the patient) to say together over the body of someone who has just died.

• How to support the dying person and a knowledge of NDEs and of the various kinds of basic information in this Handbook should become an integral and important part of the training of doctors and nurses. (Project 2000 nurses should not be able to use their 'supernumerary status' to 'opt out' of this subject in their training.) Medical staff need encouragement to recognise the difference between healing and curing, and to acknowledge that a peaceful death is an achievement rather than a failure on their part. All Accident and Emergency department staff should be trained in dealing with those who are bereaved, and each such unit should have a counsellor on call (as suggested in the Nursing Times, Jan. 8th 1992). Counselling help, discussions groups, talks by experts and other support must be available to all personnel caring for the dying (as suggested by Pam Williams, see the booklist).

• Doctors should use tests that are completely reliable indicators of death, for the reassurance of those who are worried that they might be buried or cremated whilst still alive.

• Some hospitals incinerate miscarried foetuses with the hospital waste. A better approach is that of the Aberdeen Maternity Hospital where, since 1985, a service is held at the local crematorium every three months attended by the hospital and those families and friends who wish to come. The main point that parents should have some choice about what happens to the body – and about viewing the body.

• Permission needs to be granted for the resumption of research into the use of the psychoactive and empathogen drugs with the terminally ill – drugs that in the right setting apparently not only relieve pain, depression, tension and anxiety, but help the patient gain a perspective on their situation. Mescaline, LSD, ketamine and MDMA have all produced promising results in these areas. Readers are referred particularly to the Bethesda Hospital work with terminally ill cancer patients written up by Dr Stanislav Grof in 'The Human Encounter with Death', where 71% of the patients rated an improvement in their emotional condition after participation in the experiment.

• Whilst mindful of the exceptions – Mother Teresa, for instance, with her great zest for life, who had a heart pacemaker fitted at the age of 82 – and whilst accepting that the patient's own wishes come first, we believe it would be helpful in some cases if doctors were to take any evidently frail and elderly patients (and their carers) through a detailed series of questions aimed at ascertaining the person's perceived quality of life, before pressurising the patient to accept a major operation and the subsequent stresses and strains of 'maximum recovery' treatment.

• A doctor seeing a very elderly person peacefully dying in a residential home may need to resist the temptation to rush the patient by ambulance to hospital, just so as to guard against claims of negligence.

• When dealing with those who are very elderly and dying, cardiopulmonary resuscitation given by emergency teams should be reserved for those patients who want it, or whose relatives request it on their behalf, or who stand a good chance of surviving and being discharged (currently about 6% of those patients to whom it is given). This routine assault on those who are very elderly and dying should be something a patient has to be 'opted in' for, rather than 'opted out' from as at present. (See 'Whose Life Is It Anyway?' by nurse Pam Williams, an unpublished paper in The Natural Death Centre library.)

• The legal standing of Living Wills should be confirmed by an act of parliament, if only to give more secure legal protection to any medical carer who follows a patient's requests.

• All patients should be offered the opportunity of drawing up a Living Will before entering hospital for serious treatment. Indeed, GPs need to discuss the Living Will concept with all their patients who reach pension age, and should encourage them to lodge a copy of their Living Will at the surgery, and to carry on their persons a summary credit-card-size Living Will card, giving the doctor's phone number. The US government in 1987 concluded that Living Wills could save its health service $5 billion a year ('one out of every seven health care dollars are spent on the last six months of life'). Here then is a reform that would not only save the NHS money, but that would improve the quality of living and dying.

• The hospital should endeavour to leave the body undisturbed for a period after death, if so desired by the next-of-kin, for religious or other reasons.

• The Natural Death Centre backs the proposal made by the A. B. Wildlife Trust Fund that postmortems should be performed only in exceptional cases, so as to reduce the trauma for relatives and friends. In cases where the coroner knows that death was natural, bodies should be swiftly released to the families.

• The Anatomy Act 1984 needs amending, to remove the right of hospitals and similar institutions to send unclaimed bodies for anatomical use, irrespective of whether these institutions at present make use of these powers. Under S.4(9) 'in the case of a body lying in a hospital, nursing home or other institution', any person acting on behalf of the management has legal powers to decide whether to send the body for anatomical use. This only applies when no friends or relatives take lawful possession of the body. (Information from 'Green Burial' by John Bradfield, 1994, page 42.)

• Hospitals need to make available leaflets for families explaining how they can organise funerals inexpensively and without funeral directors. All staff need to know that the next-of-kin have the legal right to take possession of the body.

Euthanasia and suicide

The word 'euthanasia' comes from the Greek for 'good death' and in the Shorter Oxford English Dictionary has the definition of 'a quiet and easy death or the means of procuring this or the action of inducing this'. With such a definition it seems hard to imagine who could be against it – even to enter a hospice could count as slow euthanasia. It may reassure relatives of those who have taken their own lives to know that our culture's present stand against suicide and euthanasia has not been shared at other times and in other cultures. For Christians (as The Compassionate Friends outline in a paper on suicide) it stems from a decision of the church Council of Braga in AD 562 to refuse funeral rites to all suicides. This in turn came about because early Christians were killing themselves in worrying numbers – martyrs had all their transgressions wiped out and were glorified by the church, and Christian suicide was very prevalent and acceptable in the fifth century. The Christians had inherited the Roman attitude to suicide. They saw it as a virtuous act if undertaken with dignity, just as the Greek stoics before them viewed death and suicide with equanimity. Plato too felt that if life became 'immoderate' through disease, then suicide was a justified and reasonable act.

The arguments in favour of doctor-assisted active euthanasia include the following: that a small percentage of terminal pain cannot be controlled by drugs; that some patients are either insufficiently mobile or conscious to take their own lives unassisted; that the drugs required for a swift and painless exit are unobtainable without a prescription; and that, as a democracy, we should accept the verdict of the overwhelming majority of people – 82% of respondents to a recent UK survey agreed that 'doctors should be permitted to end a life when someone requests it'. (The first legislature in the world to legalise euthanasia was Australia's Northern Territory; but, in December 1996, Australia's federal house of representatives overturned this, leaving the final say to the senate.)

The arguments against euthanasia include: that pain relief as practised in hospices is a very advanced art; that it is against the Hippocratic Oath for a doctor to kill a patient; that it is not for the doctor to play God and to decide that a patient's time is up; that the soul may have lessons to learn from the body's helplessness, dependency and suffering – the 'labour pains' of dying; and, most powerfully, that it is a slippery slope – once mercy killing is legalised, where will it end?

The Inuits and the Japanese used to practise euthanasia by hypothermia – the elderly person lost consciousness in the freezing cold and died within hours. In nature, some animals who realise their time has come refuse all food, just as, traditionally, American Indians who had decided that 'now is a good time to die' thereafter refused all food. Hindus who are taken to muktibhavans (hospices) in Benaras consider it appropriate and natural not to eat. The *slowness* of this kind of dying seems to be the crux of the matter. Rather than a possibly impulsive decision regretted in the event – a regret implied, for instance, by the positive and almost mystical transformations experienced by those few who survived suicide jumps from Golden Gate Bridge – fasting to death requires commitment and perseverance.

In its early stages, fasting can sometimes have an almost meditative effect, helping people to feel centred and spiritual. If they then change their mind when viewing their condition from this new perspective, they can simply start accepting food again. Death by fasting has been described in this book as a 'gentle way to die' (in the case of Caroline Walker) and as being 'like a leaf falling from a tree' (in the case of Scott Nearing). Da Free John (in 'Easy Death') has talked of it as 'a kind of traditional yoga for conscious death; people who traditionally died in this way were philosophically disposed toward intuitive transcendence and gradual transition'.

President Mitterrand, suffering from terminal cancer, called his wife to his bedside and told her that his end was near – he would take no more medicines and no more food. Such a death can be a slow, orderly and graceful process that allows the person time to come to terms with his or her exit. (Derek Humphry, however, warns in his book 'Final Exit – The Practicalities of Self-Deliverance and Assisted Suicide for the Dying' – on public sale in the UK or $16-95 from the Hemlock Society, PO Box 11830, Eugene, Oregon 97440, USA, tel 001 503 342 5748 – that self-starvation can sometimes lead to severe indigestion, muscle weakness, mental incapacity and painful dehydration. Among the self-adminis-tered methods he recommends instead are 4.5 grams of secobarbital in combi-nation with brallobarbital, mixed with alcohol and pudding, taken on an empty stomach, followed by a plastic bag secured by rubber band over the head. Hardly a slow, conscious or dignified death.) As a way of dying, fasting is tough on the relatives, watching the patient become more and more skeletal. But perhaps the fact that it is hard on the relatives is an additional safeguard against pressure on the elderly person from potential beneficiaries from the estate. Fasting is also a way that absolves doctors or nurses from ethically problematic involvement, as long as the terminally ill person makes clear his or her rejection of enforced feeding, preferably through filling in a Living Will.

Our tentative conclusions, therefore, are:

• Euthanasia actively assisted by doctor or relative should remain illegal, but judges should be given more scope for leniency in their sentencing, should such cases come to court. We support the recommendations of the Committee on the Penalty for Homicide, chaired by Lord Lane, which called for an end to compulsory life sentences for murder.

• The Natural Death Centre would like to see research into alternatives to active euthanasia, such as better relief of pain, anxiety and depression in terminal care. Our guess is that the breakthrough will come through the use of drugs that enhance the circulation of the neurotransmitter 5-HT.

Funerals and procedures

• Given that our investigations show that few of the mainstream coffin manufac-turers will sell a coffin directly to a member of the public and that funeral directors do not see themselves as 'coffin shops' – if they grudgingly sell just a coffin they tend to add an extravagant mark-up – The Natural Death Centre recommends that the Office of Fair Trading issue a requirement that funeral suppliers and directors sell coffins to the general public without undue profit.

• Just as funeral directors are required by their associations to offer a basic funeral as one of their options – although only 10 out of 18 in one small study informed the member of the public of this option – so they should also be obliged to offer a basic container for those not wanting a coffin. This could be, as in the United States, either an unfinished wood box or a cardboard coffin or other rigid container (supported by a plank of wood if necessary).

• Given that 97% of people are 'hooked' the moment they contact an undertaker, and do not shop around, The Natural Death Centre recommends the adoption of regulations similar to the 1984 funeral rules of the American Federal Trade Commission, whereby funeral directors are obliged:

(a) to give a price breakdown over the phone (several of the funeral directors in our survey refused to do so).

(b) to give a written and itemised breakdown of prices, to be displayed on the premises and to be readily available for visitors to take away. In 1996, the National Association of Funeral Directors inspected 172 member firms and found that 32.5% were still failing to display a price list, despite the fact that such display is required by the Association's Code of Practice. The Office of Fair Trading should seek a Price Marking Order, legislating as to the composition and distribution of price lists, and making noncompliance a criminal offence. Of the replies to our questionnaire to over 2,000 funeral directors, the most fully itemised price list came from George Brooke of Dewsbury in West Yorkshire (the normal funeral director's price list hides many of the funeral costs behind an inflated price for the coffin). Colin Rogers in Dorset is also to be commended – he offers specific percentage reductions for nine processes that families may wish to do for themselves.

(c) to give an *itemised estimate* before the funeral, so that you can add or subtract items to get what you want.

(d) to charge a fee for embalming only if authorised by the family or required by law – eg for transport out of the country.

(e) to disclose in writing what service fee, if any, is being added by the funeral director to the cost of disbursements, and whether he or she is getting a refund, discount or rebate from the disbursement supplier.

• There should also be an enforcement of the requirement that funeral directors reveal clearly on their paperwork and premises if they are part of a larger firm. (The latter, unlike most chains in other businesses, have pushed up prices, and they will tend to bring about a bland uniformity of style.) One small firm complained in the Funeral Service Journal that 'certain multinationals openly admit they do not display ownership on the premises or paperwork, which is against trading law. Even those that do, go under a pseudonym to fool the public.' Some chains claim to be 'family funeral directors', meaning only that they serve families, a fraudulent use of words which the Disciplinary Committee of the National Association of Funeral Directors has nevertheless explicitly condoned.

• The government should take up Jonathon Porritt's suggestion (reported in the D-i-y chapter) that Memorial Groves (where a tree is planted by the body) should be included in its Community Forests.

• The Benefits Agency, the Births and Deaths Registrar, the Citizens Advice Bureau and many crematoria should make printed information available to the public about what happens after a death. This information should include the fact that it is possible to organise a funeral without using undertakers and a summary of how to go about it – or at least should refer readers to The Natural Death Centre and similar organisations.

• The Funeral Service Journal carries fairly regular reprints of news items about funeral directors who have been found guilty of crime or fraud. Whilst we are against the registration of funeral directors – it would tend to leave trade associations such as the National Association of Funeral Directors (NAFD) with a near-monopoly of power – the rules on prepaid funeral plans need tightening.

For instance, a funeral director with an unspent record for any crime involving fraud should not be able to take cash from the public for prepaid funeral plans.

• The various funeral directors' associations need to improve their self-policing and in particular their complaints procedure. All complaints should be acknowledged within ten days and dealt with within three months.

• Members of the public do not shop around in the trauma of bereavement. We recommend in this book that they get a friend who is less involved do so on their behalf, so as to find a funeral director that suits their particular requirements. But it would also be of assistance to the public if there were regularly published comparative surveys of price and services, drawn up on a regional basis, naming particular establishments. This book is a step towards such a goal.

• Many people have written to The Natural Death Centre wanting what amounts to a 'disposal service' for their body after death. All local authorities should make agreements with undertakers to supply a cut-rate basic funeral to residents. As an experiment, some might want to go further and offer a 'disposal service', with a simple body container and no hearse, for those members of the public who want this. One correspondent has taken the idea to an extreme and writes that he feels strongly that any such disposal service should not charge 'more than £25 for 60 kilos of rubbish'. This does not fit with the Natural Death Centre's view of the mystery and dignity of death – and of the importance of the rite of physical farewell to a person's body – but we accept that for some people a disposal service is all that they want.

• Funeral directors and funeral shops should make available to the public the type of refrigeration plate that is placed under the deceased's body in rural France, so that the body can more easily be kept at home.

• Local authorities, church authorities or the government should offer financial incentives to churchyards to reopen their graveyards and any impeding legislation should be amended. At the moment it can be to a church's financial advantage to declare a graveyard closed, and to pass its maintenance over to the local authority. Cemeteries too, particularly in London, are running out of space. The Belgian practice, outlined by Tony Walter in 'Funerals and How to Improve Them', needs to be adopted, whereby a short-term grave is bought. We believe that a minimum period of 25 years would be suitable – then if a further 25 years were not paid for, a notice would be pinned to the grave, giving one year's grace before the grave would be made available for reuse. In this way, local burials remain possible and graves are well tended.

• New crematoria buildings should be adaptable, with flexible seating arrangements. Some might like to follow Tony Walter's design proposals for 'theatre in the round' with the coffin stage centre (see The Good Funeral Guide chapter for more on this).

• UK crematoria and cemeteries should offer cardboard and other coffins and shrouds for sale to those who are not using funeral directors, and could consider having a vehicle available for hire for the collection of bodies and cold storage facilities. The Office of Fair Trading should take action against groupings of funeral directors threatening to boycott such places. Likewise, all coffin manufacturers should be willing to sell direct to the public, with the Office of Fair Trading investigating those which are threatened by funeral directors as a result.

• Crematoria, cemeteries and others in the funeral business are urged to adopt the Charter for the Bereaved (published by the Institute of Burial and Cremation Administration), which is more innovative and challenging than the otherwise similar Dead Citizens Charter (published by the National Funerals College).

• Cemeteries should allow family and friends to help dig and fill the graves if they so wish, subject to any safeguards.

• Only one doctor should have to sign for cremation, as recommended by the Brodrick Committee in 1971. In many cases at present, the second doctor neither examines the body nor positively identifies it, yet a second fee is charged.

• There are many commercial opportunities that entrepreneurs could seize on within the UK funeral trade, particularly as the Green movement's sixties generation ages and becomes responsible for organising the funerals of parents and friends. The first undertakers to offer an entirely green funeral might do rather well – one option could consist, for example, of a horse-drawn cart (or wheel bier for short distances), the body in a cardboard coffin or similar, followed by burial in a wildlife burial ground. Another option would be to offer a posh rentable coffin for display, plus a cheap inner coffin that can be cremated or buried.

• Every local authority should encourage the development of nature reserve burial grounds in its area. Every county wildlife trust and other environmental charities should set one up and conscientious farmers could do so.

• The d-i-y superstores could offer flatpack coffins. Sainsbury's Homebase wrote to Jane Spottiswoode to say that they would not sell coffins as their stores were intended for family shopping 'based on the future and therefore not associated with death', whereas of course death in the future is one certainty that every family faces! Argos wrote to say that the sale of coffins would require a 'truly personal service' – in fact all that is required is the assurance that the coffin is big enough: two or three standard sizes should suffice.

• Every town needs its funeral shop, similar to the Heaven on Earth shop in Bristol, where inexpensive or artistic coffins can be bought, along with every other funeral item, from body bags to lowering webbing and urns. These need to offer items with lower mark-ups than do the Roc'Eclerc funeral supermarkets in Europe or the Regale Funeral Store in London.

• 'At present', writes K. A. Gilchist to the Natural Death Centre, 'it is far easier to take time off for having a bad cold than for the death of a close relative.' The entitlement of those who are bereaved to adequate leave of absence needs recognition.

• Probate work should no longer remain an expensive monopoly of the banks and solicitors. Others should be able to offer their services.

• The rules about the styles of memorial permitted in churchyards, cemeteries and crematoria should be relaxed, with any design or type of stone allowed. The disliked Albert Memorial monstrosities of one era become the much-loved tourist attractions of the future. And as one vicar complained in the journal

Funerals: 'I can't tell you how often I deal with clients who are deeply upset because they have set their heart on some appropriate memorial which has then been forbidden. The Church of England court ruling in 1996 that bereaved families should be allowed to attach photographs of the deceased to their tombstones is a positive development.

• Everyone is entitled to an obituary. Even funerals paid for by the state should include a small fee so that the minister or presiding person can help assemble a brief life story of the deceased for publication – if nowhere else, then at least for putting online in one of the free and permanent 'Gardens of Remembrance' on the Internet (see the Resources chapter). All priests should follow the practice of humanist officiants, who talk before the funeral to relatives, a friend and a colleague, so that at the service they can recount the biography of the person who has died.

Perhaps the next millennium will see the emergence of the new profession described by the science fiction writer Orson Scott Card, that of Speaker for the Dead – memorial service orators who provide catharsis for the friends and relatives by painstakingly assembling the unvarnished truth about the deceased's motivations, intentions and achievements. It could be a suitable job for resting novelists.

• Birthdays are recognised social occasions. Deathdays could be recognised too. On the first anniversary of the death, it could become the accepted practice for there to be a meal for close friends and relatives, and at subsequent deathdays just the simple gesture at mealtime of a toast to the person's memory or those present telling a story or memory about the one whose anniversary it is – thus passing on family lore to the next generations.

This may be the appropriate moment to wish you, dear reader, a peaceful deathday. May death for you be as graceful as Walt Whitman imagined it could be:

Come, lovely and soothing Death,
Undulate round the world, serenely arriving, arriving,
In the day, in the night, to all, to each,
Sooner or later, delicate death.
From 'Leaves of Grass' by Walt Whitman.

Chapter 10

USEFUL RESOURCES

Booklist

❁❁❁ = *HIGHLY RECOMMENDED from a Natural Death perspective.*
NDC = *Can be ordered through the Natural Death Centre book service.*

• Ainsworth-Smith, Ian and Speck, Peter **Letting Go – Caring for the dying and bereaved**, SPCK, 1982, 154 pp, £6-99, ISBN 0 281 03861 0.
• NDC❁❁❁ Albery, Nicholas et al (eds), **Before and After – The best new ideas for improving the quality of dying and for inexpensive, green, family-organised funerals**, The Natural Death Centre (see Organisations below), 1995, 80 pp, £5-95 incl. p&p, ISBN 0 9523280 1 1.
• NDC❁❁❁ Albery, Nicholas et al (eds), **Creative Endings – Designer dying and celebratory funerals**, The Natural Death Centre (see Organisations below), 1996, 80 pp, £5-95 incl. p&p, ISBN 0 9523280 2 X.
• NDC❁❁❁ Albery, Nicholas et al (eds), **The Natural Death Handbook**, this present book, published by The Natural Death Centre (see Organisations below for address), 1997, 320 pp, £12-95 incl. p&p, ISBN 0 9523280 3 8.
• Alexander, Helen (ed), **Living with Dying**, £2-75 incl. p&p (cheques to 'BSS') from Living with Dying, PO Box 7, London W3 6XJ.
• Aleksander, Tobe, **A Practical Guide to Coping with Death**, Channel 4 TV, 1992, 47pp for 34p stamp and SAE from Coping With Death, PO Box 4000, London W3 6XJ.
• Arnold, Johann Christoph, **Why Fear Death? – Stories from ordinary lives**, Plough Publishing House (Darvell Bruderhof, Robertsbridge, East Sussex TN32 5DR, tel 0800 269048), 1996, 132 pp, $10, ISBN 0 87486 083 0.
• Barley, Nigel, **Dancing on the Grave – Encounters with death**, John Murray, 1995, 240 pp, £9-95, ISBN 0 7195 5286 9.
• Bell, Lesley, **Carefully – A guide for home care assistants**, ACE Books (Age Concern), 1993, 160 pp, £19-99, ISBN 0 86242 129 2.
• ❁❁❁ Benefits Agency, **What To Do After A Death in England and Wales**, and **What To Do After A Death in Scotland,** Leaflets D49 and D49 S available free from The Stationery Office, Causeway Distribution Centre, The Causeway, Oldham Broadway Business Park, Chadderton, Oldham OL9 9XD. You can order this by phone from the Benefits Agency Public Enquiry Office (tel 0171 712 2171).
• Benn, June (ed), **Memorials – An anthology of poetry and prose**, Ravette, 1986.

• Blackmore, Susan, **Dying to Live – Science and the Near-Death Experience**, Grafton (HarperCollins), 1993, 291 pp, ISBN 0 586 09212 9.

• Boerstler, Richard, **Letting Go – A holistic and meditative approach to living and dying**, Associates in Thanatology, 1985, 60 pp, $3-95 plus $2 p&p, ISBN 0 9607928 0 5 T (see Videos and Tapes below, for address).

• Boerstler, Richard and Kornfeld, R.N., **Life to Death – Harmonizing the transition**, Healing Arts Press (UK Distribution by Deep Books, London), 1995, 240 pp, $14-95, ISBN 0 89281 329 6.

• Boston, Sarah and Trezise, Rachael, **Merely Mortal – Coping with dying, death and bereavement**, Methuen, 1987, ISBN 0 413 15590 0. Out of print.

• British Medical Association, **Advance Statements About Medical Treatments – Code of practice**, British Medical Association, 1995, 30 pp, ISBN 0 7279 09142.

• Brotchie, Jane, **Help at Hand – The home carer's survival guide**, Bedford Square Press, 1990, 148 pp, £6-95, ISBN 0 7199 1281 2.

• Buckman, Dr Robert, **I Don't Know What To Say – How to help and support someone who is dying**, Macmillan Papermac, 1990, 247 pp, £8-99, ISBN 0 333 54035 2.

• N. Callanan, Melly & Kelly, Patricia, **Understanding and helping the dying**, Hodder & Stoughton, 1992, 218 pages, £8-99, ISBN 0340 574 81 X.

• CancerLink, **Caring at Home – Caring at home when cancer cannot be cured**, available from CancerLink (see under Organisations below), 1993, 44 pp, £1-75, ISBN 1 87053436 6.

• Cannon, Geoffrey, **The Good Fight – The life and work of Caroline Walker**, Ebury Press, 1989, 179 pp, £4-99, ISBN 0 7126 3769 9. (Out of print.)

• Carlson, Lisa, **Caring For Your Own Dead**, Upper Access, 1987, 344 pp, $12-50, ISBN 0 942679 01 6.

• Cason-Reiser et al, **Dying 101: A short course on living for the terminally ill**, Pushing the Envelope Publications (1278 Glenneyre Suite 313, Laguna Beach, CA 92651-3103, USA, tel 001 714 497 8176), 205 pages, $19-95, ISBN 0 9649938 0 5. Insights gained from group work.

• Channel 4 TV, **A Child's Grief – Coping with a death in your family**. Send an SAE and two first class stamps for this excellent booklet, to: A Child's Grief, PO Box 4000, London W5 2GH.

• Collick, Elizabeth, **Through Grief**, available from CRUSE (see under Organisations below), £6-95 incl. p&p.

• Copperman, Harriet, **Dying at Home**, Wiley, 1988, 158 pp, £5-50, ISBN 0 471 26278 1.

• Couldrick, Ann, **Grief and Bereavement: Understanding Children**, 1988, available from Sir Michael Sobell House (tel 01865 225860).

• Couldrick, Ann, **When Your Mum or Dad Has Cancer**, 1991, available from Sir Michael Sobell House (tel 01865 225860).

• Davies, Simon, **Death Meditation**, a nonsectarian booklet available from the author at 44 St Gerrard's Road, Lostock Hall, Preston, Lancashire PR5 5TS.

• Dickenson, Donna and Johnson, Malcolm (eds), **Death, Dying and Bereavement**, Sage, 1993, 355 pp, £12-95. This is the reader for the Open University course on death and dying.

• Doyle, Derek, **Coping with a Dying Relative**, Macdonald, 1983, 96 pp, £2-95, ISBN 0 86334 026 1.

• Doyle, Derek, **Domiciliary Terminal Care**, Churchill Livingstone, 1987, £6-95. Aimed at GPs and community nurses but covering pain, diet, equipment and counselling.

• ✪✪✪ Duda, Deborah, **Coming Home – A guide to dying at home with dignity**, Aurora Press (PO Box 573, Santa Fe, New Mexico 87504, USA, tel 001 505 989 9804, USA), 1987, 404 pp, £11-95 from Airlift (tel 0171 607 5792), ISBN 0 943358 31 0.

• Elkington, Gail and Harrison, Gill, **(Teach Yourself) Caring for someone at home**, Hodder and Stoughton, 1996, 200 pp, £5-99, ISBN 0 340 66999 3.

• England, Audrey (ed), **Helping Ourselves**, available from The Compassionate Friends (see under Organisations below), £2. For those who have lost a child.

• Enright, D. J. (ed), **The Oxford Book of Death**, OUP, 1987, 351 pp, £5-95, ISBN 0 19 282013 3.

• Foos-Graber, Anya, **Deathing – An intelligent alternative for the final moments of life**, Nicolas-Hays, 1989, 397 pp, £11-95 from Airlift (tel 0171 607 5792), ISBN 0 89254 016 8.

• Fremantle, Francesca and Trungpa, Chögyam (eds), **The Tibetan Book of the Dead**, Shambhala, 1975, 120 pp, $3-95, ISBN 0 394 73064 X.

• Garsia, Marlene, **How to Write a Will and Gain Probate**, Kogan Page, 1992, 136 pp, £8-99, ISBN 0 7494 0532 5

• Gill, Sue and Fox, John, **The Dead Good Funerals Book**, Engineers of the Imagination, 1996, 192 pp, £11 incl. p&p from The Natural Death Centre (see Organisations below), ISBN 0 9527159 0 2. Good, but unreliable on the law.

• Gold, E. J., **The American Book of the Dead**, IDHHB Publishing (PO Box 370, Nevada City, CA 95959, USA, tel 001 916 272 0180), 1983, $15-95, ISBN 0 89556 051 8. Describes in plain English how to help the person through and beyond death, with readings, from a Tibetan-style perspective. For UK, see also 'Gold' under Videos and Tapes, below.

• Green, J. and Green, M., **Dealing with Death**, Chapman & Hall, 1992, ISBN 0 412 36410 7. Wide coverage of legal, technical and religious aspects.

• Green, Jennifer, **Death With Dignity – Meeting the spiritual needs of patients in a multi-cultural society**, Nursing Times (Macmillan Magazines), 15 pp, ISBN 0 333 54971 6.

• Grey, Margot, **Return from Death – An exploration of the Near-Death Experience**, Arkana (Penguin), 1987, 206 pp, £5-99, ISBN 0 14 019051 1.

• ✪✪✪ Grof, Stanislav and Halifax, Joan, **The Human Encounter with Death**, Souvenir Press, 1978, 240 pp, £2-95, ISBN 0 285 64874 8. Out of print, alas.

• Grollman, E., **Talking About Death**, Beacon Press (Boston), 1970. For parent and child to read together.

• Grosz, Anton, **Letters to a Dying Friend – What comes next, based on the Tibetan Book of the Dead**, Quest, 1989, 169 pp, $9-95, ISBN 0 8356 0640 6.

• Harding, Douglas, **The Little Book of Life and Death**, Arkana (Penguin), 1988, 150 pp, £6-99, ISBN 0 14 019174 7.

• Hastings, Diana, **Crisis Point – A survivor's guide to living**, Papermac (Macmillan), 1989, ISBN 0 333 48267 0. Has a good chapter on dying.

• Hicks, Cherryl, **Who Cares? Looking after people at home**, Virago, 1988, 271 pp, £5-95, ISBN 0 86068 834 8. Well-argued case for better provision for carers.

• Hindmarch, Celia, **On the Death of a Child**, Radcliffe Medical Press (15 Kings Meadow, Ferry Hinksey Road, Oxford OX2 0DP), 1993, 133 pp, £1-75, ISBN 1 870905 19 9.

• ❸❸❸ Hjelmstad, Lois Tschetter, **Fine Black Lines – Reflections on facing cancer, fear and loneliness**, Mulberry Hill Press (Box 425 B, Englewood, Denver, Colorado 80151, USA, tel 00 1 800 294 4714), 1993, 166 pp, $14-95 plus p&p, ISBN 1 9637139 5 7. Includes some fine poems.

• Hockey, Jennifer, **Making the Most of a Funeral**, CRUSE (see under Organisations below), 1992, 54 pp, £3-25, ISBN 0 900321 04 0. Useful suggestions aimed at priests, such as: involve the family, no rushing, use symbols and include the children.

• Huxley, Laura, **This Timeless Moment – A personal view of Aldous Huxley**, Chatto and Windus, 1969, 330 pp, ISBN 7011 1439 8. Tells the story of his dying.

• John, Da Free, **Easy Death – Talks and essays on the inherent and ultimate transcendence of death and everything else**, Dawn Horse Press, 1983, 410 pp, $10-95, ISBN 0 913922 57 9.

• Jones, Mary, **Secret Flowers – Mourning and the adaptation to loss**, Women's Press, 1996, 96 pp, £6-99, ISBN 0 7043 4505 6. About coming to terms with the death of her husband from cancer.

• Justice, Christopher, **The 'Natural' Death While Not Eating – A type of palliative care in Banaras, India**, Journal of Palliative Care 11:1/1995,38–42, Centre for Bioethics. Christopher Justice is at the Department of Anthropology, McMaster University, Hamilton, Ontario, Canada.

• Kamath, M. V., **Philosophy of Death and Dying**, Himalayan International Institute of Yoga, Honesdale, PA, USA, 1978.

• Knapp, Ronald J., **Beyond Endurance – When a Child Dies**, Schocken Books (USA), 1986, £7-95, ISBN 0 8052 0823 2. Records all aspects of the experience of the bereaved parent (including where the child was murdered). Knapp really listened to the 135 families he interviewed.

• Knox, Michael D. and Knox, Lucinda Page, **Last Wishes – A workbook for recording your funeral, memorial and other final instructions**, Applied Science Corporation (PO Box 16118, Tampa, Florida, USA), 1994, 144 pp, $14-95 plus $8 p&p Europe, ISBN 0 9628460 0 7.

• Kohner, Nancy, and Mares, Penny, **Who Cares Now? Caring for an older person**, BBC Education, 1991, £1 incl. p&p from Who Cares Now?, PO Box 7, London W3 6XJ.

• Krementz, J., **How it Feels When a Parent Dies**, Gollancz, 1986. Stories from 18 children.

• Kübler-Ross, Elisabeth, **On Death and Dying**, Tavistock Publications (Routledge), 1973, 272 pp, £9-99, ISBN 0 415 04015 9. In UK £11-24 (incl. p&p) from Elisabeth Kübler-Ross Foundation (see Organisations below).

• Kupfermann, Jeannette, **When the Crying's Done**, Robson Books. Her experience of widowhood; moving and courageous.

• Lake, Dr Tony, **Living With Grief**, Sheldon Press, 1984. Sensitively written.

• Lamm, Maurice, **The Jewish Way in Death and Mourning**, Jonathan David Publishers (NY), 1989.

• Leary, Timothy and Metzner, Ralph and Alpert, Richard, **The Psychedelic Experience – A manual based on the Tibetan Book of the Dead**, Citadel, 1990, 157 pp, $7-95, ISBN 0 8065 0552 4.

• Lee, Dr Elizabeth, **A Good Death - A guide for patients and carers facing terminal illness at home**, Rosendale Press, 1995, 190 pp, £8-99, ISBN 1 872803 16 4.

• ✪✪✪ LeShan, Lawrence, **Cancer as a Turning Point – A handbook for people with cancer, their families, and health professionals**, Gateway Books (The Hollies, Wellow, Bath BA2 8QJ), 1996, 256 pp, £8-95, ISBN 1 85860 046 4. Highly recommended.

• Levine, Stephen, **A Gradual Awakening**, Gateway Books (The Hollies, Wellow, Bath BA2 8QJ), 1979, 192 pp, £6-95, ISBN 0 946551 90 1.

• Levine, Stephen, **Guided Meditations, Exploration, Healings**, Gateway Books (see above), 1992, £8-95.

• Levine, Stephen, **Meetings at the Edge**, Gateway Books (see above), 1982, 264 pp, £7-95, ISBN 0-946551 88 X.

• Levine, Stephen, **Healing into Life & Death**, Gateway Books, 1990, 304 pp, £8-95, ISBN 0 946551 48 0. Contains a number of useful meditations.

• NDC✪✪✪ Levine, Stephen, **Who Dies? – An investigation of conscious living and conscious dying**, Gateway Books, 1986, 336 pp, £8-95, ISBN 0 946551 45 6.

• Lewis, C. S., **A Grief Observed**, Faber & Faber, 1966 (reprinted 1985), £4-99.

• Litten, Julian, **The English Way of Death – The common funeral since 1450**, Robert Hale, 1991, 254 pp, £25, ISBN 0 7090 4350 3.

• Lorimer, David, **Whole in One – The Near-Death Experience and the ethic of interconnectedness**, Arkana (Penguin), 1990, 340 pp, £8-99, ISBN 0140.192581.

• Maclanan, Maggie, and Kelley, Patricia, **Final Gifts**, Hodder and Stoughton, £9-99, ISBN 0 340 57471 X. 'The subtleties of communicating with the dying.'

• Manning, Doug, **Don't Take My Grief Away – What to do when you lose a loved one**, Harper & Row, 1984.

• Marie Curie Cancer Care, **Partners in Caring**, booklet, £7 from Marie Curie (see Organisations below). Aimed at people caring for a relative at home.

• Mathias, Beverley and Spiers, Desmond, **A Handbook on Death and Bereavement – Helping Children Understand**, National Resource Centre for

Children with Reading Difficulties, 1992, ISBN 0 948664 10 X. (Out of print in 1996. New edition planned for 1997.)

• Melonie, Bryan and Ingpen, Robert, **Beginnings and Endings, With Lifetimes in Between**, Bantam Books (USA), 1983, £4-95, ISBN 1 850288 038 X. For children 8 to 11.

• Messenger, Daly, **Ceremonies for Today**, Armadale (Brian Zouch Publications, Victoria), 1979. Examples of Australian life-centred funerals.

• Morgan, Ernest, **Dealing Creatively with Death**, Barclay House, 1990, 167 pp, $11-95, ISBN 0 935016 79 1.

• Morse, Melvyn, **Closer to the Light – Learning from the Near-Death Experiences of children**, Ivy Books (Ballantine, New York), 1990, 237 pp, ISBN 0 8041 0832 3.

• Mullin, Glenn H., **Death and Dying – The Tibetan tradition**, Arkana (Penguin), 1986, 251 pp, £7-99, ISBN 0140 190139.

• Nearing, Helen, **Loving and Leaving the Good Life**, Chelsea Green Publishing Company (Post Mills, Vermont, USA), 1992, 197 pp, $19-95, ISBN 0 930031 54 7; £10 hardback in UK (p&p extra) from Kathleen Jannaway, 47 Highlands, Leatherhead, Surrey KT22 8NQ. The life and dying of Scott Nearing.

• Neuberger, Julia, **Caring for Dying People of Different Faiths**, Austen Cornish, 59 pp, £5-50, ISBN 1 870065 00 X.

• Owens, Dr R. G. and Naylor, F., GP, **Living While Dying – What to do and what to say when you are, or someone close to you is dying**, Thorsons, 1989, 112 pp, £4-99, ISBN 0 7225 1620 7.

• Putter, Ann Marie, **The Memorial Rituals Book for Healing and Hope**, Baywood Publishing Co Inc (Amityville, New York, USA), 1997, 88 pp, ISBN 0 89503 143 4.

• Riemer, Jack (ed), **Jewish Reflections on Death and Mourning**, Shocken Books (New York), 1976.

• Ring, Kenneth, **Heading Toward Omega – In search of the meaning of the Near-Death Experience**, Quill, 1985, 348 pp, $8-95, ISBN 0 688 06268 7.

• ✪✪✪ Rinpoche, Sogyal, **The Tibetan Book of Living and Dying**, Rider/Random House, 1992, 427 pp, hardback, £16-99, ISBN 0 7126 5437 2. Spiritual help for the dying, adapted for the Westerner. It gives the background of the teachings, rather than being a prayer book to use. (See also Rigpa in Organisations, below.)

• Rose, Gillian, **Love's Work**, Chatto & Windus, 1995, 136 pp, hardback £9-99, ISBN 0 7011 6304 6. Courageous and passionate memoirs of a philosopher facing cancer.

• St Christopher's Hospice, **Someone Special Has Died**, St Christopher's Hospice (see Bookshops below), 8 pp. An illustrated booklet for children.

• St Christopher's Hospice, **Your Parent Has Died**, St Christopher's Hospice (see Bookshops below), 1991.

• Sanders, Dr Catherine, **Surviving Grief and Learning to Live Again**, John Wiley and Sons Inc (New York), 1992, 238 pp, £11-99, ISBN 0 471 53471 4.

• Schiff, Harriet Sarnoff, **The Bereaved Parent**, Souvenir Press, 1979 (& 1992), 146 pp, £6-99, ISBN 0 285 64891 8.

• Smale, David A., **Davies' Law of Burial, Cremation and Exhumation** (sixth edition), Shaw and Sons, 1993.

• Smith Cheryl K. and Docker, Chris G. and Hofsess, John and Dunn, Dr. Bruce, **Beyond Final Exit – New research in self-deliverance for the terminally ill**, The Right to Die Society of Canada (PO Box 39018, Victoria, British Columbia, V8V 4X8, Canada), 1995, 116 pp, ISBN 1 896533 04 3.

• Society for Companion Animal Studies (SCAS), **Death of an Animal Friend**, SCAS (1a Hinton Road, Milngavie, Glasgow G62 7DN, tel 0141 956 5950), 1993, 31 pp, £2-50, ISBN 0 9515453 2 9.

• Spottiswoode, Jane, **Undertaken with Love**, Robert Hale, 1991, 175 pp, £12-95 hardback, £5-95 paperback, ISBN 0 7090 4979 X. About a funeral without an undertaker.

• ✪✪✪ Staudacher, Carol, **Beyond Grief – A guide to recovering from the death of a loved one**, Condor (Souvenir Press), 1988, 244 pp, £8-95, ISBN 0 285 65069 6.

• Stickney, Doris, **Waterbugs and Butterflies**, Mowbrays, 1987, booklet, £12-50 (Pack of ten), ISBN 0 264 67233 X. Explaining death to children under 5.

• Stillbirth and Neo-Natal Death Society (SANDS), **The Loss of Your Baby**, booklet for bereaved parents, available from SANDS (see Organisations below).

• Stuart, Alexander and Totterdel, Ann, **5$^{1}/_{2}$ x 3 – The short life and death of Joe Buffalo Stuart**, Vintage, 1991, 306 pp, £5-99, ISBN 0 09 988330 9.

• NDC✪✪✪ Taylor, Allegra, **Acquainted with the Night – A year on the frontier of death**, Fontana (HarperCollins), 1989, 187 pp, £3-99, ISBN 0 00 637249 X.

• Thorpe, Graham, **Enabling More Dying People to Remain at Home**, a paper in the British Medical Journal, October 9th 1993.

• Todd, Jacquelyne, **Living with Lymphoedema – Your guide to treatment**, available from Marie Curie Trading, Unit 1, Enterprise House, Cheyney Manor Industrial Estate, Swindon SN2 2YZ, £5-45 incl. p&p.

• Wallbank, Susan, **Facing Grief – Bereavement and the young adult**, available from CRUSE (see under Organisations below), £7-99 incl. p&p.

• ✪✪✪ Walter, Dr Tony, **Funerals – And how to improve them**, Hodder & Stoughton, 1990, 307 pp, £9-99, ISBN 0 340 53125 8.

• Waugh, Evelyn, **The Loved One**, Penguin, 1951, 127 pp, £3-99, ISBN 0 14 018249 7. A satire on the funeral industry in the United States.

• Wells, Rosemary, **Helping Children Cope with Grief – Facing a death in the family**, Sheldon Press, 1988, £2-95.

• Wertheimer, Alison, **A Special Scar**, Routledge, 1991, ISBN 0 41501 763 7. Experiences of people bereaved through suicide, excellent for both the bereaved and professionals.

• Which? Books, **Guide to Giving and Inheriting**, Which? Ltd. (tel 0800 252 100), £9-99 incl. p&p.

• Which? Books, **Making Your Will – A practical guide to making your own will (England and Wales)**, Which? Ltd (tel 0800 252 100),1992, 28 pp plus forms, £9-99 incl. p&p, ISBN 0 340 56631 0.

• Which? Books, **What To Do When Someone Dies**, Which? Ltd. (tel 0800 252 100),1994. This edition makes mistakes on the law and is not recommended.
• Which? Books, **Wills and Probate**, Which? Ltd. (tel 0800 252 100),1991, 224 pp, £10-99 incl. p&p, ISBN 0 340 56632 9.
• White, John, **A Practical Guide to Death and Dying**, Quest, 1988, 196 pp, $7-50, ISBN 0 8356 0633 3. Available in UK from Airlift Book Company, 8, The Arena, Mollison Avenue, Enfield, Middlesex EN3 7NJ (tel 0181 804 0400; fax 0181 804 0044).
• Wilber, Ken, **Grace and Grit**, Shambhala, 1992. About the death of his wife from cancer.
• Wilkins, Robert, **The Fireside Book of Death**, Robert Hale, 1990, 256 pp, £14-95, ISBN 0 7090 4144 6. (Out of print.)
• Williams, Pam, **Knowing About Caring for the Dying**, available from author (c/o The University of Sheffield, School of Nursing and Midwifery, Barnsley District General Hospital, Gawber Road, Barnsley S75 2EP). How nurses' training is now and how it could be improved.
• ✪✪✪ Willson, Jane Wynne, **Funerals Without God – A practical guide to non-religious funerals**, British Humanist Association (see under Organisations below), 1989, 67 pp, £5 incl. p&p, ISBN 0 901825 14 X.
• Worden, William, **Grief Counselling and Grief Therapy**, Tavistock (Routledge), 1989, £7-99, ISBN 0 415 02923 6.
• Young, Michael and Cullen, Lesley, **A Good Death – Conversations with East Londoners**, Routledge, 1996, 249 pp, ISBN 0 415 13797 7.
• Zaleski, Carol, **Otherworld Journeys – Accounts of Near-Death Experience in medieval and modern times**, OUP (New York), 1987, 274 pp, $8-95, ISBN 0 19 505665 5.

BOOKSHOPS: The Natural Death Centre book service, 20 Heber Road, London NW2 6AA (tel 0181 208 2853; fax 0181 452 6434) sells (or will pass on your order for) only the highly recommended books above which are marked 'NDC✪✪✪'. Please add 20% for postage and packing (50% foreign airmail) and make any cheque payable to 'ISI'. Further copies of this present Handbook are also obtainable from the Centre for £11 incl. p&p. If urgent, phone your order through for these books, giving your Access, Visa or Mastercard number. Please add the extra 4% which the bank charges for this credit card service. Otherwise, probably one of the best bookshops in London for books on dying is **Watkins**, 21 Cecil Court, London WC2N 4EZ (tel 0171 836 2182); sometimes good for American imports is **Compendium Bookshop**, 234 Camden High St, London NW1 8QS (tel 0171 484 8944), or **Airlift** distributors (tel 0171 607 5792 for mail order). **St Christopher's Hospice** have a book service too: 51-59 Lawrie Park Road, London SE26 6DZ (tel 0181 778 9252). Outside London, **Meditec**, St John's Court, Brewery Hill, Grantham, Lincolnshire NG31 6DW (tel 01476 590505) has a large catalogue of mail order books on death and dying. The Natural Death Centre can help with fuller details on publishers' addresses, etc, for some of the books on this booklist, if required.

Tapes and videos

• **Ananda Network Cassette Library**, c/o Ray Wills, 5 Grayswood Point, Norley Vale, Roehampton, London SW15 4BT (tel 0181 789 6170). The Ananda Network has a library of cassettes and videotapes which they will loan for free, with talks on living, dying, death and rebirth, mainly from a **Buddhist perspective**.

• **Boerstler, Richard**, **Letting Go: A Holistic and Meditative Approach to Death and Dying**, Associates in Thanatology, 115 Blue Rock Road, South Yarmouth, MA 02664, USA. Half hour video ($29 incl. p&p) about this simple method. Make sure it is playable on your UK machine. See also book version, above.

• **British Holistic Medical Association** (see Organisations below) – tapes at £9-95 incl. p&p include: **Imagery for Relaxation**, **Coping with Persistent Pain**, **Coping with Stress**, **Introducing Meditation** and **The Breath of Life** (relaxation).

• **Buddhist Death Ritual for Dharmachari Ajita**, on Super VHS, available also on Betacam SP, from Survyaprabha, LBAC (tel 0171 607 9480).

• **Collick, Elizabeth**, **Through Grief**, tape available from CRUSE (see under Organisations below), £5-50 incl. p&p. Also available as a book (see above). Offers sensible maxims.

• **Gold, E. J.**, tapes ($15)– **Bardo Dreams**, **The Lazy Man's Guide to Death and Dying** and **How I Raised Myself from the Dead in 49 Days or Less** – also Gold's books in the UK from Donald Suckling, 2 Boyswell House, Scholes, Wigan WN1 3QG (tel 01942 43551).

• **Jones, Ken**, **Caring as a Spiritual Practice**, £27 video from Meridian Trust (tel 0171 289 5443). Promoting the sharing of common generosity of spirit.

• **Kübler-Ross, Elisabeth**, **Life, Death & Life After Death** (audiotape £6), **Aids, Life and Love** (a video conversation), and other such tapes and videos, all from The Elisabeth Kübler-Ross Foundation (see Organisations below).

• **Levine, Stephen** tapes are available from Gateway Books (see Levine's books, above, for address) who will send a free catalogue on request. His tapes (and his schedule of workshops) are also available from Warm Rock Tapes, PO Box 108, Chamisal, NM 87521, USA. Send two international reply coupons for details.

• Long, Barry, **Seeing Through Death**, audiotape from Barry Long Audio, BCM Box 876, London WC1N 3XX (tel 01736 756742). (Previously published as **May I speak to you of Death?**)

• **Mental Health Media Council**, 380 Harrow Road, London W9 2HU (tel 0171 286 2346) puts out a catalogue (price £3-50) of films and videos available for sale or hire in the UK on the subjects of **Death and Bereavement**, many of them aimed at professionals, some about euthanasia, others on Near-Death Experiences, etc.

• **Relaxation for Living**, 168/170 Oatlands Drive, Weybridge, Surrey KT13 9ET (tel 01932 858355). Tapes, classes on relaxation, 85p article on easing grief, large SAE for info.

• **Roach, Steve**: his **Structures from Silence** music (and a 60 minute piece on the album World's Edge) recreates the sounds he heard during his Near-Death Experience (tel USA 00 1 602 760 0004; fax 00 1 602 760 0551; UK distributor Laurence Aston at TM records, tel 01734 312 580; fax 01734 312 582). Also Gilles Bédard in Quebec (tel 00 1 514 279 2413; fax 00 1 514 279 3033) is working with Roach to produce a Soundquest to Omega album of NDE music.
• **Tibetan Book of the Dead** reading at a cremation in Ladakh – Fields of the Senses video, part 3 of Tibet: A Buddhist Trilogy by Thread Cross Films, Bath.
• **Yeshe, Lama**, **Death and the Transference of Consciousness**, a video about the Tibetan view of death and life. £32 from Meridian Trust (tel 0171 289 5443).

Useful organisations and individuals

• **AB Wildlife Trust Fund**, 7, Knox Road, Harrogate, North Yorkshire HG1 3EF (tel 01423 530900). Advises dying and bereaved people on funerals and burials in any land, anywhere in the country. The Trust was set up by John Bradfield, a social worker, conservationist and author of 'Green Burial - The DIY Guide to Law and Practice'. This summarises the authoritative research undertaken for the Trust and the third edition may be available in 1997. This is the only charity in the country able to give sound advice on emotional needs, the full extent of choices, all aspects of the law, environmental health and using burials to promote wildlife. 'Funds are desperately needed to provide the free advice service, train volunteers from all parts of the country and to buy land, so more burials can be arranged in nature reserves in the Harrogate area. Obtaining advice by telephone may continue to be difficult, unless the Trust is supported with donations and grants.' Send five second class stamps for details which include writing a simple will and the basics of law.
• **Age Concern**, Astral House, 1268 London Road, London SW16 4ER (tel 0181 679 8000). Their postal will-writing Service, run by a solicitor, can draw up a simple will for £50, based on a self-completion questionnaire. A factsheet (No. 27) on arranging a funeral is available free of charge. Please send an SAE.
• **Alder Centre**, Royal Liverpool Children's NHS Trust, Alder Hey, Eaton Road, Liverpool L12 2AP (tel 0151 228 4811; see Child Death Helpline for freephone helpline). For all those affected by a child's death. Counselling, groups, befriending (see also The Compassionate Friends).
• **Alzheimer's Disease Society**, Gordon House, 10 Greencoat Place, London SW1P 1PH (tel 0171 306 0606; fax 0171 306 0808). Information on aids, services and resources.
• **Ananda Network**. This is a fine initiative: the Network's volunteers offer companionship to the dying or bereaved of any religion or none. (See Buddhist Hospice Trust below for address and tel.)
• **Asian Family Counselling Service**, 74, The Avenue, Ealing, London W13 (tel 0181 997 5749).
• **Association of Burial Authorities**, 139 Kensington High Street, London W8 6SU (tel 0171 937 0052; fax 0171 937 1393).

• **Association for Children with Life-threatening Conditions and their families** (ACT), 65 St. Michael's Hill, Bristol BS2 8DZ (tel 0117 922 1556; fax 0117 930 4707). Advice and information.

• **Association for Death Education and Counselling**, 638 Prospect Avenue, Hartford, CT 06105-4250, USA (tel 001 860 232 4825). Conferences and courses.

• **Association of Crossroads Care Attendant Schemes**, 10 Regents Place, Rugby, Warwickshire CV21 2PN (tel 01788 573653). Trained carers who take over from the regular carer completely in looking after a disabled person at home, so as to give the carer a break.

• **BACUP** (British Association of Cancer United Patients), 3 Bath Place, Rivington St, London EC2A 3JR. A national charity providing information and counselling for people with cancer, their families and friends. For information on any aspect of cancer call BACUP's Cancer Information Service, staffed by specialist nurses (tel 0171 613 2121 or 0800 181199 Monday to Thursday 10am to 7pm; Friday 10am to 5.30pm) or write to the address above. Face-to-face counselling is available in London (tel 0171 696 6000) and Glasgow (tel 0141 553 1553) Monday to Friday 9.30 am to 5pm. A minicom textphone is available. All BACUP's services are provided free of charge and in confidence. Donations are very welcome.

• **The Befriending Network**, 11 St Bernards Road, Oxford OX2 6EH (tel Oxford 01865 316200; fax 01235 768867; or London 0181 208 2853). Volunteers who can visit those with critical illnesses, for two to three hours per week.

• **Benefits Agency**: for how to claim benefits, etc, phone your local office, under Social Security or Benefits Agency in your local phone book, or phone their Public Enquiry Office (tel 0171 712 2171). Potentially relevant leaflets to ask for include 'Help when someone Dies' (FB29), 'National Insurance for widows' (CA 09), 'Rates of war pensions and allowances' (MPL 154), 'War widows and other dependants' (MPL 152), 'What to do after a death in England and Wales' (D49), 'What to do after a death in Scotland' (D49 S) and 'Widow's benefits' (NP 45).

• **Bristol Cancer Help Centre**, Grove House, Cornwallis Grove, Clifton, Bristol BS8 4PG (tel 0117 980 9500). Holistic treatment and publications. Grief, loss, death and dying workshops, and phone-in service.

• **British Association for Counselling**, 1 Regent Place, Rugby, Warwickshire CV21 2PJ (tel 01788 578328; office 01788 550899). Has information on organisations, counsellors and therapists nationwide that you can pay to see – although some are free.

• **British Holistic Medical Association**, Rowland Thomas House, Royal Shrewsbury Hospital South, Shrewsbury, Shropshire SY3 8XF (tel 01743 261155). Self-help breathing, relaxation, meditation and diet books and tapes (see Tapes and Videos, above) and an informative newsletter.

• **British Humanist Association**, 47 Theobald's Road, London WC1X 8SP (tel 0171 430 0908). Can provide officiant (normally charging £50-£60) for non-religious funeral. Ceremonies Helpline directs callers to their local organiser (0990 168122). See also Jane Wynne Willson under books, above.

• **British Medical Association**, BMA House, Tavistock Square, London WC1H 9JP (tel 0171 387 4499; fax 0171 383 6400). The governing body for the British medical profession.

• **British Organ Donor Society** (BODY), Balsham, Cambridge CB1 6DL (tel 01223 893636). Information and emotional support for recipients and families of organ donors, and general enquiries.

• **The Buddhist Hospice Trust**, 5, Grayswood Point, Norley Vale, Roehampton, London SW15 4BT (tel c/o Ray Wills 0181 789 6170). A particularly friendly organisation. 'It was established in 1986 to explore Buddhist approaches to dying, death and bereavement. It is nonsectarian and welcomes both Buddhists and non-Buddhists alike. Its purpose is to bring together, in a creative way, the teachings of the Buddha and the philosophy of modern hospice care.' In fact it confesses that it is at this stage just a network of people, 'a hospice of the heart', rather than a building. Has a biannual magazine Raft (£5 subs.), publishes pamphlets and holds meetings. Volunteers in its Ananda Network are prepared to sit with and befriend the terminally ill. See also Tapes and Videos, above.

• **CALL Centre** (Cancer Aid and Listening Line), Swan Buildings, 20 Swan St, Manchester M4 5JW (tel 0161 835 2586; national helpline manned Mon-Thur noon-3pm; emergencies will be dealt with at any time). Emotional support and practical advice for cancer patients and families.

• **CancerLink**, 11-21 Northdown Street, London N1 9BN (tel 0171 833 2818; Freephone cancer information helpline 0800 132905 (textphone: use voice announcer). Freephone Asian cancer information helpline in Hindi, Bengali and English 0800 590415, Freephone MAC helpline for young people affected by cancer 0800 591028; fax 0171 833 4963; e-mail: <cancerlink@canlink. demon.co.uk>. A central information and publishing resource for cancer patients and their families. One of its aims is to organise local self-help groups. Useful pamphlets on everything from sexuality to complementary alternative treatments and caring for the dying at home.

• **CancerLink** in Scotland, 9 Castle Terrace, Edinburgh EH1 2DP (tel 0131 228 5567; fax 0131 228 8956; e-mail:<cancerlink@cislink.demon.co.uk>). Other details as above.

• **Care for the Carers Council**, Railway Lane, Lewes, East Sussex BN7 2AQ (tel 01273 486625; information 01273 486641). Advice, information and support, primarily for the East Sussex area.

• **Carers National Association**, Ruth Pitter House, 20-25 Glasshouse Yard, London EC1A 4JS (tel 0171 490 8818; fax 0171 490 8824). Advice for carers and former carers. Local support groups.

• **The Center for Attitudinal Healing**, 33 Buchanan Drive, Sausalito, California 94965, USA (tel 00 1 415 331 6161; fax 00 1 415 331 4545; e-mail:<HOME123@AOL.COM>). Works with children and children facing serious illnesses, and with children whose parents have cancer, etc. Their video 'Under the Sun' (which emphasises that health is inner peace and that the present instant is the only time there is) may be available on loan from the Buddhist Hospice Trust (see above).

• **Chai-Lifeline, Jewish Cancer Support and Health Centre**, Norwood House, Harmony Way, off Victoria Road, Hendon, London NW4 2BZ (tel 0181 202 4567). Provides support groups, visitors and complementary therapies.

• **Child Bereavement Trust**, Harleyford Estate, Henley Road, Marlow, Bucks SL7 2DX (tel 01628 48801).

• **Child Death Helpline**, c/o Bereavement Services Department, Great Ormond Street Hospital, London. (Freephone helpline 0800 282986 staffed every night 7 to 10pm. and Wednesday mornings 10am to 1pm; administration 0171 813 8551 or 0151 252 5391.) Run jointly by Great Ormond Street Hospital and The Alder Centre, Liverpool. Trained volunteers, virtually all of whom are bereaved parents themselves, offer free telephone counselling to anyone affected by the death of a child (of any age).

• **The Cinnamon Trust**, Foundry House, Foundry Square, Hayle, Cornwall TR27 4HH (tel 01736 757900). Care for pets belonging to the elderly and terminally ill.

• **Citizens Advice Bureau**, free, impartial, confidential advice about death, bereavement, financial and all other matters. See your local phone book or contact the HQ, Myddelton House, 115-123 Pentonville Rd, London N1 9LZ (tel 0171 833 2181; fax 0171 833 4371) for details of your nearest branch.

• **The Compassionate Friends**, 53 North Street, Bristol BS3 1EN (helpline tel 0117 953 9639; admin tel 0117 966 5202). Befriending bereaved adults. Also a very fine newsletter and a postal lending library for books.

• **The Cot Death Helpline**, (tel 0171 235 1721) 24-hour manned helpline, which can also arrange 'befriending' for those who have suffered sudden infant death.

• **Counsel and Care, advice and help for older people**, Twyman House, 16 Bonny St, London NW1 9PG (tel 0171 485 1566, 10.30am - 4pm). Provides advice on finding and paying for residential and nursing care; publishes free factsheets on welfare issues. Undertakes research. Organises conferences and training events.

• **Court of Protection**, The Public Trust Office, Protection Division, Stewart House, 24 Kingsway, London WC2B 6JX (tel 0171 269 7300). If you need to apply to manage the financial affairs of someone who has become mentally incapacitated.

• **Cremation Society of Great Britain**, 2nd Floor, Brecon House, 16/16a Albion Place, Maidstone, Kent ME14 5DZ (tel 01622 688292). Can tell you the nearest crematorium. Publishes a free booklet on 'What You Should Know About Cremation', and a directory of crematoria (£18).

• **CRUSE**, Cruse House, 126 Sheen Road, Richmond, Surrey TW9 1UR (tel 0181 940 4818). Counsellor available on 0181 332 7227 weekdays 9.30am to 5pm. For all those who have suffered a bereavement: socials and advice, counselling and excellent publications.

• **Death and Immortality Course**, c/o Paul Badham, University of Wales, Lampeter, Ceredigion, Wales SA48 7ED (tel 01570 422351).

• **DeathNET**, the American Internet site with news of the progress of the euthanasia movement – at the location <http://www.islandnet.com/~deathnet/>).
• **Death Studies Journal**, Taylor and Francis Ltd, 4 John St, London WC1N 2ET, subs. £39.
• **Disability Information Trust**, Mary Marlborough Centre, Nuffield Ortho-paedic Centre, Headington, Oxford OX3 7LD (tel 01865 227592). Books on a range of aids.
• **Disabled Living Foundation**, 380-384 Harrow Road, London W9 2HU (tel 0171 289 6111). Advice on incontinence, equipment and aids.
• **Disablement Income Group**, Unit 5, Archway Business Centre, 19-23 Wedmore Street, London N19 4RZ (tel 0171 263 3981). Working to improve the financial circumstances of disabled people.
• **Disaster Action**, PO Box 6784, London N5 2PY (tel 0171 704 6446). Self-help group for those bereaved following a major disaster such as plane crash.
• **Elisabeth Kübler-Ross Foundation**, Panther House, 38 Mount Pleasant, London WC1H 0AP. (In the USA the Foundation's phone number is 001 703 396 3441.) Can supply a list of books by Elizabeth Kübler-Ross (see above).
• **The Family Welfare Association**, 501-505 Kingsland Road, Dalston, London E8 4AU (tel 0171 249 6636). Gives grants to individuals and families.
• **Federation of British Cremation Authorities**, 41 Salisbury Road, Carshalton, Surrey SM5 3HA (tel 0181 669 4521).
• **Federation of Independent Advice Centres**, 13 Stockwell Road, London SW9 9AU (tel 0171 274 1839). Contact to find a local advice agency for any aspect of social welfare law..
• **The Foundation for the Study of Infant Deaths**, 14 Halkin Street, London SW1X 7DP, London SW1X 8QB (tel 0171 235 0965; 24-hour staffed helpline for families and professionals 0171 235 1721). Information, fund-raising for cot deaths research, befriending service, local groups.
• **Funeral and Memorial Societies of America** maintain a site on the Internet with information on American alternatives to costly funerals. The location is <http://vbiweb.champlain.edu/famsa>.
• **The Funeral Ombudsman**, 31 Southampton Row, London WC1B 5HJ (tel 0171 430 1112; fax 0171 430 1012). For complaints about Co-op and non-NAFD funeral directors.
• **Funeral Service Journal**, PO Box IW73, Leeds LS16 9XW (tel 0113 284 1177; fax 0113 284 2152; e-mail:<106324.107@compuserve.com>). Founded 1886. The best of the funeral journals.
• **Garden of Remembrance** on the Internet, where obituaries can be placed permanently and without charge: The World Wide Cemetery at <http://www.cemetery.org/>. Its snail mail address is PO Box 723, Station F, Toronto, Canada N4Y 1TO. There are many other Gardens of Remembrance online, but some charge and some offer only temporary postings.
• **Helen House – A Hospice for Children**, 37 Leopold Street, Oxford OX4 1QT (tel 01865 728251). There are other children's hospices in Yorkshire, Lanca-shire, Shropshire, Norfolk, Birmingham, Manchester, Leicester, Barnstaple,

Kinross and Cambridge, with more planned.

• **Hospice Arts**, Dr David Frampton, Chelmsford Hospice, 212 New London Road, Chelmsford CM2 9AE (tel 01245 358130 or c/o 0171 377 8484). Helps hospices to run art projects.

• **The Hospice Information Service**, at St Christopher's Hospice, 51-59 Lawrie Park Road, Sydenham, London SE26 6DZ (tel 0181 778 9252; fax 0181 776 9345). Information about local hospices.

• **Ian Rennie Hospice at Home**, 93 Western Road, Tring, Herts HP23 4BN (tel 01442 890222). Trained nurses provide free full nursing breaks for those caring for the terminally ill in the Buckinghamshire area.

• **Institute of Burial and Cremation Administration**, One The Terrace, City of London Cemetery, Manor Park, London E12 5DO (tel & fax 0181 989 9496). Publishes the excellent Charter for the Bereaved (the full 72 page reference copy costs £25).

• **The Internet** holds a vast amount of information on death and dying, including most of the Natural Death Centre's books. Many libraries can now help you access the Internet. The most comprehensive index of all this Internet material – Death, Dying and Grief Resources – is to be found at <http://www.cyberspace.com/~webster/death.html>. Death-related subjects covered include: grief, ageing, euthanasia, suicide, children, Gardens of Remembrance, religions and ethnic groups, hospices, pet loss, survivors, Near-Death Experiences, funerals, death in literature and the arts, cemeteries, self-help groups, newsgroups and list services.

• **Jewish Bereavement Counselling Service**, PO Box 6748, London N3 3BX (tel 0181 349 0839 answerphone).

• **John Bell and Croyden**, 50 Wigmore St, London W1 (tel 0171 935 5555 ext 212). Chemist for specialist medical requirements, everything from a sheepskin rug to a walking frame.

• **Kübler-Ross Foundation**, see Elizabeth Kübler-Ross, above.

• **Law Centres** can provide free advice about wills etc for those who are hard-up. See the Helplines page in the front of your local Thomson Phone Directory or phone 0171 387 8570 to find your nearest one.

• **Lesbian and Gay Bereavement Project**, Vaughan M. Williams Centre, Colindale Hospital, London NW9 5GJ (tel 0181 455 8894 helpline, 0181 200 0511, office hours). Counselling, support and information on subjects including wills and funerals.

• **London Association of Bereavement Services**, 356 Holloway Road, London N7 6PN (tel 0171 700 8134; fax 0171 700 8146). Supporting and linking London bereavement services.

• **London Lighthouse**, 111-117 Lancaster Road, London W11 1QT (tel 0171 792 1200). 'A centre for people facing the challenge of AIDS.' They have facilities for people who have died from HIV/AIDS.

• **Lymphoedema Support Network**, Appeal Office, The Royal Marsden Hospital, Fulham Road, London SW6 6JJ (tel Sally Harrison on 01258 473191 or Christine Elliot-Bell on 0171 727 6973).

• **Macmillan nurses**, c/o Cancer Relief Macmillan Fund, 15-19 Britten St, London SW3 3TZ (tel 0171 351 7811). The Fund's nurses can help with emotional support, pain and symptom control. It provides financial assistance for some cancer patients and financially supports or helps funding of organisations caring for patients with cancer.

• **Malik, Yvonne**, Sweet Briar, Wray, Near Lancaster LA2 8QN (tel 015242 21767). Accepts commissions for decorated coffins, for meditative glass pictures and for Celebration Box memorials.

• **Marie Curie Cancer Care**, 28 Belgrave Square, London SW1X 8QG (tel 0171 235 3325) Phone for information about this organisation's hospice centres, and advice about the availability of night nurses, who are free, but normally obtained through your health authority's community nursing manager.

• **Medline**, for all the information your doctor may have neither the time nor the inclination to impart. Abstracts of almost every major medical article are accessible free on the Internet at the location <http://www.healthgate.com/HealthGate/MEDLINE/Search-advanced.shtml>.

• **Memorials by Artists**, Snape Priory, Saxmundham, Suffolk, IP17 1SA (tel 01728 688 934). Nationwide service to put people in touch with designer-carvers who make individual memorials. £5 booklet, incl. p&p, second edition, contains articles, advice and 38 photographs.

• **Miscarriage Association**, Clayton Hospital, Northgate, Wakefield WF1 3JF (tel 01924 200799). Support and information.

• **Motor Neurone Disease Association**, PO Box 246, Northampton NN1 2PR (tel 01604 250505 or 01604 22269). Advice, information, equipment loan. Regional advisers and local groups. Financial help.

• **Mortality journal**, School of Cultural and Community Studies, University of Sussex, Falmer, Brighton BN1 9QN. Co-edited by Revd. Dr Peter Jupp, director of the National Funerals College.

• **National Funerals College**, Braddan House, High Street, Duddington, Stamford, Lincolnshire PE9 3QE (tel 01780 444269). The College issues the Dead Citizens Charter.

• **National Association of Bereavement Services**, 20 Norton Folgate, London E1 6DB (tel 0171 247 1080 referrals; 0171 247 0617 admin).

• **National Association of Funeral Directors**, 618 Warwick Road, Solihull, West Midlands B91 1AA (tel 0121 711 1343). Its members' Code of Practice is available free. If complaining about a funeral director, you are supposed to write first to the funeral director for satisfaction, though there is nothing to prevent you going direct to the Association or to the trading standards department (see local council's phone number) or to a small claims court. The association's magazine is called 'The Funeral Director'.

• **National Association of Memorial Masons**, Crown Buildings, High Street, Aylesbury, Buckinghamshire HP20 1SL (tel 01296 434 750). Code of Practice and Ethics for members. It issues a list of members, highlighting those who will do individually crafted memorials.

• **National Federation of Spiritual Healers**, Old Manor Farm Studio, Church

Street, Sunbury-on-Thames TW16 6RG (tel 01932 783164).
• **National Association of Widows**, 54-57 Allison Street, Digbeth, Birmingham B5 5TH (tel 0121 643 8348). Information sheet, plus local branch socials. A young widows' contact list is also available
• **Natural Death Centre**, 20 Heber Road, London NW2 6AA (tel 0181 208 2853; fax 0181 452 6434; e-mail: <rhino@dial.pipex.com>). The Centre edited this present book. Please send any updates to this address. Further copies of this book are available from the Centre for £12-95 incl. p&p. Many of the Centre's publications are accessible free on the Internet via the death and dying section at <http://www.newciv.org/GIB/>.
• **Office of Fair Trading**, Field House, 15-25 Breams Buildings, London EC4A 1PR (tel 0171 242 2858; fax 0171 269 8543).
• **Open University 'Death and Dying' course**, c/o The Course Manager, Dept of Health and Social Welfare, Walton Hall, Milton Keynes MK7 6AA (tel 01908 653743; fax 01908 654124).
• **Pagan Hospice and Funeral Trust** in the UK, BM Box 3337, London WC1N 3XX. It is now called the Voyager Trust.
• **People's Dispensary for Sick Animals (PDSA)**, Whitechapel Way, Priorslee, Telford, Shropshire TF2 9DQ (tel 0800 591248). They have a will-making advice pack and provide a re-homing service for the pets of the deceased (if they leave the PDSA money).
• **Pet Loss Support Service**, a helpline offering aid to grieving pet owners. Callers are linked to a befriender. This is an 0891 high-charging number (tel 0891 615285).
• **Pets As Therapy (Incorporating P. A. T. Dogs)**, c/o Lesley Scott-Ordish, Rocky Bank, 4 New Road, Ditton, Maidstone, Kent ME20 6AD (tel 01732 848499 or 01732 872222). Arranges dogs to visit the sick and the elderly.
• **PRISMA**, Fruits of Life Project, c/o Jozef van der Put, Postbus 10346, 5000 JH Tilburgh, Netherlands (tel 0031 13 5441440; fax 0031 13 5440605). Helping those who are dying to develop life stories and to resolve unfinished business.
• **Probate Registry**, Personal Applications Dept, 2nd Floor, Principal Registry, Family Division, Somerset House, Strand, London WC2R 1LP (tel 0171 936 6983 answerphone or 0171 936 6939). Or see your local phone book under 'Probate' for your nearest office.
• **Rainbow Trust**, Rainbow House, 47 Eastwick Drive, Great Bookham, Surrey KT23 3PU (tel 01372 453309). Help and respite haven for terminally ill children and their families.
• **React**, St Luke's House, 270 Sandycombe Road, Kew, Richmond, Surrey TW9 3NP (0181 940 2575; fax 0181 940 8188). Money and equipment for children with reduced life expectancy. Applications via doctor or a professional worker.
• **Red Cross Medical Loans Service**: see local phone book. Branches can supply medical equipment for short term loan – wheelchairs, commodes, etc. Or contact British Red Cross, 9 Grosvenor Crescent, London SW1X 7EJ (tel 0171 235 5454).

• **Rigpa**, 330 Caledonian Road, London N1 1BB (tel 0171 700 0185). Tibetan Buddhist centre founded by Sogyal Rinpoche. Runs courses on death and dying (see also Sogyal Rinpoche's book, above). Also a support group for people with life-threatening conditions. And seminars entitled 'Spiritual Care for the Living and Dying' designed for professional and trained volunteer care givers.

• **Samaritans**, 10 The Grove, Slough, Berks SL1 1QP (tel 0345 90 90 90). Or see local phone book. For those in despair or suicidal.

• **Self-help groups**: Lists are maintained by CancerLink (above), the College of Health (tel 0345 678 4444), the Patients Association (tel 0181 981 56767), Contact A Family (tel 0171 383 3555) and In Touch (tel 0161 905 2440). See also the Internet entry above.

• **Shadow of Suicide** (SOS), 53 North Street, Bristol BS3 1EN (tel 0117 953 9639). Support for parents (and possibly grandparents and siblings) where a child (of any age, including adult) has died by suicide.

• **Caroline Sherwood**, 10 Edward Street, Bath BA2 4DU (tel 01225 338707) offers counselling and teaching by phone or mail for people wanting help with fear of death, bereavement and associated issues. Also week-long retreats for women by the sea.

• **Social Security**, see Benefits Agency.

• **Society of Allied and Independent Funeral Directors (SAIF)**, Crowndale House, 1 Ferdinand Place, London NW1 8EE (tel 0171 267 6777; fax 0171 267 1147). Coordinating body for the smaller independent firms.

• **Spiritual healing** (see also National Federation of):
John Avery, 31 Wakefield Gardens, London SE19 2NR (tel 0181 653 3982), who 'works more and more with the terminally ill'.
Rosy Creasy, 165 Lower Richmond Road, Putney, London SW15 1LY (tel 0181 788 6214). 'I use colour, sound and visualisation to help people to love themselves.'
Philippa Pullar, 7 St Mary's Grove, London SW13 OJA (tel 0181 789 0243). Author of 'Spiritual and Lay Healing', she draws comfort from her own Near-Death Experience.
Inga Marie Solders, Roslagsgatan 19B, S-11355 Stockholm, Sweden (tel 00 468 612 5809), believes she can help the soul to pass over the river of death.

• **The Starlight Foundation**, 8A Bloomsbury Square, London WC1A 2LP (tel 0171 430 1642). Attempts to grant the wishes of chronically and terminally ill children.

• **The Stillbirth and Neonatal Death Society (SANDS)**, 28 Portland Place, London W1N 4DE (tel 0171 436 5881). Befriending, local groups, information and publications.

• **Support After Murder or Manslaughter (SAMM)**, Cranmer House, 39 Brixton Road, London SW9 6DZ (tel 0171 735 3838; fax 0171 735 3900). Support groups around the UK for those affected by murder or manslaughter.

• **Terrence Higgins Trust** , 52-54 Grays Inn Road, London WC1X 8JU (admin tel 0171 831 0330; helpline 12 noon to 10pm daily tel 0171 242 1010). A registered charity to inform, advise and help on AIDS and HIV infection.

• **Twins and Multiple Births Association – Bereavement Support Group**, PO Box 30, Little Sutton, South Wirral L66 1TH (tel 0151 348 0020).

• **Unitarian Churches**, Matthew Smith, Information Officer, Essex Hall, 1-6 Essex St, Strand, London WC2R 3HY (tel 0171 240 2384). Unitarian ministers conduct flexible funerals – reflecting the life and beliefs of the deceased – without dogma.

• **Victim Support**, National Office, Cranmer House, 39 Brixton Road, London SW9 6DZ (tel 0171 735 9166). Trained volunteers in local schemes help victims of crime.

• **Voluntary Euthanasia Society**, 13 Prince of Wales Terrace, London W8 5PG (tel 0171 937 7770). The Society pioneered the Living Will (advance directive) in the UK and is pressing for wider choice at the end of life.

• **Voluntary Euthanasia Society of Scotland**, 17 Hart Street, Edinburgh EH1 3RN (tel 0131 556 4404; fax 0131 557 4403; e-mail:<didmsnj@easynet.co.uk>; web site: <http://www.netlink.co.uk/users/vess/>). Christopher Grant Docker there is very knowledgeable about the varieties of Living Will texts worldwide.

• **The Voyager Trust,** previously the Pagan Hospice and Funeral Trust, BM Box 3337, London WC1N 3XX.

• **War Widows Association of Great Britain**, Mrs I. Bloor, 'Bryn Hyfryd', 1 Coach Lane, Stanton-in-Peak, Near Matlock DE4 2NA. Advice for all war widows. Can supply a local contact.

• **Welfare State International**, Engineers of the Imagination, The Celebratory Arts Company, The Ellers, Ulverston, Cumbria LA12 0AA (tel 01229 581127; fax 01229 581232; e-mail: <104047.2252@compuserve.com>). Publishers of 'The Dead Good Funerals Book' by Sue Gill and John Fox. Run short residential courses in the Lake District on alternative funerals; coffin painting; offer consultancies for imaginative memorial services, lanterns, urns, etc.

• **Yad b'Yad** (Hebrew for 'Hand in Hand'). The contact person is Louise Heilbron (tel 0181 444 7134). A Jewish child bereavement project.

Index

This forms on this page can be cut out or photocopied

Friends of The Natural Death Centre

Please help the Natural Death Centre to stay in existence. If you can afford it:
(1) Please become a Friend of the Natural Death Centre by filling in the standing order below to the Centre's parent body for £20 per annum and returning it to the Natural Death Centre, 20 Heber Road, London NW2 6AA (NOT to your bank).
(2) Please also consider leaving the Centre some money in your Will, to help those who come after you who are dying at home (if you already have a will, simply fill in the codicil form below, and leave it with your will or send it to the person looking after your will – without stapling it or attaching it to your will in any way. Your signature will need witnessing by two people).

STANDING ORDER

Date.....................................

To (Name and Address of your bank:) (CAPS)...
....

Please pay to the credit of the Institute for Social Inventions Account Number 38843803 at NATIONAL WESTMINSTER BANK PLC 60-13-34, Maida Vale, Elgin Avenue Branch, 298 Elgin Avenue, London W9 1JT
on the..................day of...[month & year]
the sum of............................pounds............................pence,
and the same sum on the same day **ANNUALLY** until cancelled by me and debit my Account Number...accordingly.
My name and Address (CAPS)
....
....Tel No..
Signature...

■ ■

CODICIL TO WILL

This is the first codicil to the will dated..................of me (name:)...............................
....................of (address:)...
I give £.................. to the Fourth World Educational and Research Association Trust, 20 Heber Road, London NW2 (tel 0181 208 2853) Registered Charity Number 283040 for the benefit of their project The Natural Death Centre. I declare that the receipt of the charity's treasurer or other person professing to be the duly authorised officer shall be a full and sufficient discharge to my executors.
Date:...................................   My signature:...................................
Signed by (your name:)...................................
in our presence and then by us in the presence of the signatory:
Signature of first witness:........................   Signature of second witness:......................
Name:..   Name:...
Address:..   Address:...
....
Occupation:...   Occupation:..